# Modern
# JavaScript
## DEVELOP AND DESIGN

## Larry Ullman

Peachpit
Press

**Modern JavaScript: Develop and Design**

Larry Ullman

Peachpit Press
1249 Eighth Street
Berkeley, CA 94710
510/524-2178
510/524-2221 (fax)

Find us on the Web at: www.peachpit.com
To report errors, please send a note to: errata@peachpit.com
Peachpit Press is a division of Pearson Education.
Copyright © 2012 by Larry Ullman

Acquisitions Editor: Rebecca Gulick
Copy Editor: Patricia Pane
Technical Reviewer: Jacob Seidelin
Compositor: Danielle Foster
Production Editor: Katerina Malone
Proofreader: Liz Welch
Indexer: Valerie Haynes-Perry
Cover Design: Peachpit Press

13-digit ISBN: 978-0-321-81252-0
10-digit ISBN:    0-321-81252-2

9 8 7 6 5 4 3 2

Printed and bound in the United States of America

*This book is dedicated to Doug and Christina,*
*and to their family and friends,*
*for the extraordinary, life-changing gift.*

# SO MANY, MANY THANKS TO...

Rebecca, Nancy, and Nancy, for working very hard to make this project happen and for their supreme flexibility. And, of course, for continuing to work with me time and again.

Patricia, for her diligent editing and attention to detail.

Jacob, for providing a top-notch technical review, and for not being afraid to say "Not what I would do...."

Danielle, for magically converting a handful of random materials into something that looks remarkably like an actual book.

Liz, for the sharp proofreading eye. Never too late to catch a mistake!

The indexer, Valerie, who makes it easy for readers to find what they need without wading through all of my exposition.

Mimi, for the snazzy interior and cover design work. I love the tool motif!

All the readers over the years who requested that I write this book and provided detailed thoughts as to what they would and would not want this book to be. I hope it's what you were looking for!

Jonas Jacek (`http://jonas.me/`) for permission to use his HTML5 template.

Sara, for entertaining the kids so that I can get some work done, even if I'd rather not.

Sam and Zoe, for being the kid epitome of awesomeness.

Jessica, for doing everything you do and everything you can.

# CONTENTS

# INTRODUCTION

JavaScript is one of the most widely used programming languages today, found on almost every Web page (certainly all the new ones). Over the past ten years, between economic changes and expansions in how JavaScript is used, more and more Web developers and designers are expected to know this language. These facts make it all the more ironic that so few people respect JavaScript as the true programming language that it is. Furthermore, many books still present JavaScript in a legacy manner, as a technology to be used piecemeal to implement gimmicks and distractions. This book was written to address these problems, presenting JavaScript in a way that you can easily understand, actually master, and appropriately utilize as a productive asset in today's dynamic Web sites.

## WHO THIS BOOK IS FOR

This book was written primarily with two types of readers in mind:

- Those who don't know JavaScript at all (and perhaps have never done any programming)
- Those who may have played with JavaScript some, but don't have a solid understanding of why one does what one does in the language.

You may be a Web developer who has written code in other languages but merely dabbled with JavaScript. Or, you may be a Web designer, with a graphical focus but an increasing need to learn JavaScript. Whatever the case, if you have a sincere interest in understanding modern JavaScript and knowing how to use it, well, then this book is for you.

## WHAT YOU WILL LEARN

By reading this book, and trying the many examples, you will come to comprehend what JavaScript is and how to reliably program with it, regardless of the task. The book's content is organized in three sections.

### PART 1: GETTING STARTED
The first part of the book starts with JavaScript's history and its role in today's Web. You'll also learn the fundamental terms and concepts, particularly when it comes to using JavaScript with HTML in a Web page. The last chapter in Part 1 thoroughly covers the types of tools you'll need to develop, design, debug, and test JavaScript code.

## PART 2: JAVASCRIPT FUNDAMENTALS

The bulk of the book is in this second part, which teaches the core components of the language. These fundamentals include the kinds of data you'll work with, operators and control structures, defining your own functions, handling events, and Ajax. Two chapters focus on the browser and HTML forms.

## PART 3: NEXT STEPS

All books have their limits, and this book purposefully stops short of trying to cover everything, or attempting to turn you into a true JavaScript "ninja." But in the third part of the book, you will be introduced to what your next logical steps should be in your development as a JavaScript programmer. One chapter is on frameworks, another is on advanced JavaScript concepts, and a third walks through a real-world integration of JavaScript and PHP for a practical Web application.

## THE CORRESPONDING WEB SITE

My Web site can be found at www.LarryUllman.com. To find the materials specific to this book, click on *Books By Topic* at the top of the page, and then select *JavaScript* > *Modern JavaScript: Develop and Design*. On the first page that comes up you will find all of the code used in the book. There are also links to errata (errors found) and more information that pertains directly to this book.

The whole site is actually a WordPress blog and you'll find lots of other useful information there, in various categories. The unique tag for this book is *jsdd*, meaning that www.larryullman.com/tag/jsdd/ will list everything on the site that might be useful and significant to you. While you're at the site, I recommend that you also sign up for my free newsletter, through which I share useful resources, answer questions, and occasionally give away free books.

The book has a corresponding support forum at www.LarryUllman.com/forums/. You are encouraged to ask questions there when you need help. You can also follow up on the "Review and Pursue" sections through the forums.

## LET'S GET STARTED

With a quick introduction behind you (and kudos for giving it a read), let's get on with the show. In very first chapter, you'll learn quite a bit about JavaScript as a language and the changing role it has had in the history of Web development. There's no programming to be done there, but you'll get a sense of both the big picture and the current landscape, which are important in going forward.

## WELCOME TO JAVASCRIPT

A great thing about programming with JavaScript is that most, if not all, of the tools you'll need are completely free. That's particularly reassuring, as you'll want a lot of the following items in order to develop using JavaScript in a productive and reliable way. Chapter 3, Tools of the Trade, goes into the following categories in much more detail.

### BROWSERS

Presumably, you already have at least one Web browser, but you'll want several. All the key modern browsers are free and should be used: Chrome, Firefox, Safari, Opera, and even Internet Explorer.

### TEXT EDITOR

To write JavaScript code, you can use almost any text editor, although some are clearly better than others. The quick recommendations are Notepad++ on Windows and BBEdit or TextMate on Mac OS X.

### IDE

If you prefer an all-in-one tool to a text editor, select an Integrated Development Environment (IDE). The free Aptana Studio is wonderful and runs on most platforms; fine commercial alternatives exist, too.

### DEBUGGER

Debugging is a big facet of all programming, and better debugging tools means less stress and a faster development time. Firebug is the clear champion here, although many browsers now have sufficiently good debugging tools built in.

### WEB SERVER

Examples in two chapters require a PHP-enabled Web server, plus a MySQL database. If you don't have a live Web site with these already, you can download and install the free XAMPP for Windows or MAMP for Mac OS X.

# 1

# (RE-)INTRODUCING JAVASCRIPT

JavaScript today is one misunderstood programming language. From what JavaScript can do, to what it can't, to what JavaScript isn't (*JavaScript is not Java*), there's a lot of confusion about this technology that's at the heart of today's Web. As you can't effectively use any technology without comprehending its essence, this first chapter in the book provides an overview of modern JavaScript.

Most of the chapter discusses what JavaScript is and how it came to be in its current state. Next, you'll find some basic information as to JavaScript versions and browser support. The chapter concludes with the approach you ought to have when programming JavaScript, which is also the perspective being taught by this book.

# WHAT IS **JAVASCRIPT**?

JavaScript is, technically speaking, an object-oriented, weakly typed, scripting language. One could toss more jargon into this definition, but those are the most critical aspects of the language. Let's look at them in detail.

First, JavaScript is an *object-oriented* programming language, as opposed to a procedural one. This distinction has several implications. First and most important among these is that almost all of the variables you'll work with are, in fact, objects. An object is a special variable type that can have its own subvariables, called *properties*, and functions, called *methods*. Together, an object's properties and methods are called its *members*.

For example, here is a string in JavaScript, a string being any number of quoted characters:

```
var name = 'Larry Ullman';
```

That string variable, name, is actually an object of type String. Because it's a JavaScript String object, name automatically has a *property* called length, which reflects the number of characters in the string. For this particular string, length has a value of 12, which includes the space. Similarly, name automatically has several defined methods, like substring() and toUpperCase(). (With an object's members, the parentheses distinguish properties from methods.)

With object-oriented programming, you'll use *object notation* extensively to refer to an object's members: someObject.someProperty or someObject.someMethod(). This means that, using the name example, name.length has a value of 12, and to capitalize the string, you could code

```
name = name.toUpperCase(); // Now 'LARRY ULLMAN'
```

Conversely, in procedural PHP code, you would write

```
$name = 'Larry Ullman';
$name = strtoupper($name); // Now 'LARRY ULLMAN'
```

And

```
$length = strlen($name); // 12
```

As you can see, to apply a function to a variable in procedural code, the variable is passed to the function as an argument. In object-oriented code, the variable's own function (i.e., its *method*) is called by the object itself.

The object (or dot) notation can also be *chained*, allowing you to access nested properties and methods:

```
someObject.someProperty.someMethod()
```

The fact that JavaScript is an object-oriented language is quite significant and has many ramifications as to how the language can be used. In fact, as you'll eventually see, even functions and arrays in JavaScript are objects! JavaScript is a different kind of OOP language, though, in that you don't define classes and then create objects as instances of those classes, as you do in most object-oriented languages. As you'll learn in time, this is because JavaScript is *protoype-based*, not class-based. This somewhat uncommon type of object-oriented language changes how you perform OOP in JavaScript, especially in more advanced-level programming.

> **NOTE:** It's conventional in OOP to use camel-case for variable and function names: someObject and someMethod(), not some_object and some_method().

The second part of the JavaScript definition says that JavaScript is a *weakly typed* language, meaning that variables and data can be easily converted from one type to another. For example, in JavaScript, you can create a number and then convert it to a string:

```
var cost = 2;
cost += ' dollars'; // cost is now a string: "2 dollars"
```

In a *strongly typed* language, the creation of a new variable, such as cost, would also require indicating its strict type. Here is how the variable declaration and assignment would be done in ActionScript, a language otherwise very similar to JavaScript:

```
var cost:int = 2; // cost must be an integer!
```

Moreover, in a strongly typed language, attempts to convert a number to a string (as in the JavaScript code) would generate an error.

Some programmers appreciate the flexibility that weakly typed languages offer; other programmers consider weak typing to allow for sloppy coding. To be fair, bugs *can* occur because of implicit type conversion. (JavaScript is also called *dynamically typed*, because conversions can happen automatically, as in the above code.) But if you're aware of type conversions as you program, the potential for bugs will be mitigated and you can take full advantage of the language's flexibility.

Third, to say that JavaScript is a *scripting* language means that JavaScript code is run through a program that actually executes the code. By comparison, the instructions dictated by a language such as C must first be compiled and then the compiled application itself is executed. In this book, almost all of the JavaScript will be executed within a Web browser, where the JavaScript "executable" is the Web browser's JavaScript engine (and different browsers use different JavaScript engines).

## JAVASCRIPT'S HISTORY

JavaScript began life in 1995, originally under the names Mocha, then LiveScript. Version 1.0 of JavaScript, using that new name, was released in 1996, by Netscape. If you're old enough, you'll have heard of Netscape, as Netscape Navigator was one of the first Web browsers, in time losing all of its market share, primarily to Internet Explorer. Eventually, Netscape created and spun off as Mozilla, creators of the Firefox Web browser (www.mozilla.com) and one of the key participants in JavaScript's continued development.

JavaScript is an implementation of *ECMAScript* (pronounced ECK-MA-Script), a standardized international scripting language that most people have never heard of (ECMA is short for European Computer Manufacturers Association). ActionScript, mentioned a page or so ago, is also an ECMAScript derivation, and has many similarities to JavaScript. JavaScript's syntax was influenced by the Java programming language, but the two languages are neither related nor that similar otherwise.

Although JavaScript even today is primarily used within the Web browser, JavaScript can also be embedded into PDFs, used to create desktop widgets, and can even be the basis of dynamic server-side functionality.

But these details are just basic facts. In order to know modern JavaScript, you should also be aware of JavaScript's seedy past.

**NOTE:** Microsoft named its implementation of JavaScript JScript because JavaScript is a trademarked name.

## A SOMETIMES UGLY HISTORY

When I first began doing Web development, in 1999, JavaScript was moderately useful at best and quite annoying at worst. To the greater detriment of the Web, JavaScript was used to create alerts (shudder), pop-up windows (ugh), and playing audio files (please don't). Less annoying but common applications of JavaScript included image rollovers and browser status-bar manipulations. At the time, common attempts to add significant dynamic functionality required HTML frames, thus mandating extra work to make the page still seem coherent. In the 1990s, the best possible use, or perhaps the only good use, of JavaScript was for improving and validating HTML forms. In short, JavaScript was treated as a "toy" language, and the application of it warranted little respect.

Added to the poor use of JavaScript were two key factors regarding the state of the Web a decade-plus ago. First, broadband Internet access was just becoming regularly available to home users (in the largest Internet market at the time: the United States). Without high-speed Internet access, prudent developers kept their Web-page sizes small, and they limited use of JavaScript and media as much as possible. Back then, the idea of transmitting 14 KB of data—the size of a common JavaScript framework today—to the end user, just to be able to add some flash (pun intended), or a bit of functionality, to a site was impractical.

Second, although browser support for JavaScript is not remotely consistent today, in the late 1990s, the browser differences were huge. At the time, the two primary browsers were Internet Explorer and Netscape Navigator, with the popular Internet Service Provider (ISP) America Online (AOL) using its own custom browser. With such browser differences, writing reliable cross-browser JavaScript was a significant hurdle.

Fortunately, many things have changed.

## THE SECOND COMING OF AJAX

One of the most significant developments in the history of JavaScript is the rise of *Ajax*. First described in 2005, Ajax is really just a label given to functionality that browsers were capable of for some time previously. The term Ajax either does or does not mean *Asynchronous JavaScript and XML*; the person who originally coined the term, Jesse James Garrett, now says Ajax is not an acronym. Regardless, the premise behind Ajax is this: While the user is doing stuff within the browser,

**FIGURE 1.1** A simple HTML form, which could be part of a registration process (left).

**FIGURE 1.2** Problems with the form data should be reflected to the end user, giving him or her the opportunity to correct the mistakes and resubmit the form (right).

events are triggered (e.g., by clicking on a link, using a form, mousing over an element, or whatever). These events can be handled by JavaScript *asynchronously*, meaning that JavaScript can do its thing in the background without forcing the user to wait for JavaScript to respond to the event. The "thing" that JavaScript will do in Ajax is make a request of a server-side resource. When Ajax was first defined as a term, the results of that request were returned to the JavaScript using the XML (eXtensible Markup Language) format.

I say that Ajax is a significant development, but its benefits were lost on many for quite some time. And, to be fair, it's hard for a book to convey how useful Ajax is. To best understand how the invention of Ajax affects Web functionality, let's look at an example.

Say you have a registration form on your Web site, where a user enters a username, email address, password, and so forth (**Figure 1.1**). After the user completes the form, he or she clicks the submit button to send the form data to the server. At that point, the server-side script would validate the form data. If the data was okay, the user would be registered. If there were errors, the form would have to be displayed again, with the errors shown but data retained (**Figure 1.2**). This process would be repeated until the point at which the form is completed properly, the user is registered (Step Y, **Figure 1.3**), and the user is redirected to the next logical HTML page (Step Z).

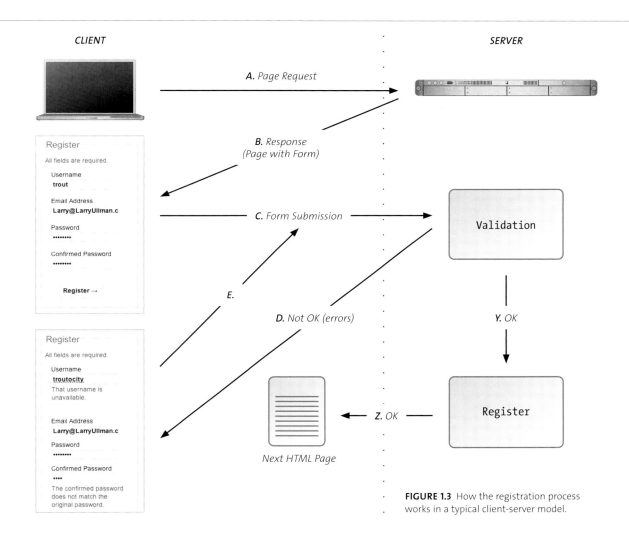

CLIENT

SERVER

*A. Page Request*

*B. Response (Page with Form)*

Register

All fields are required.

Username
**trout**

Email Address
**Larry@LarryUllman.c**

Password
••••••••

Confirmed Password
••••••••

**Register →**

*C. Form Submission*

Validation

*E.*

*D. Not OK (errors)*

*Y. OK*

Register

All fields are required.

Username
**troutocity**
That username is unavailable.

Email Address
**Larry@LarryUllman.c**

Password
••••••••

Confirmed Password
••••

The confirmed password does not match the original password.

Next HTML Page

*Z. OK*

Register

**FIGURE 1.3** How the registration process works in a typical client-server model.

This is a perfectly fine, workable system. Moreover, this is still the approach that would be used should the user's Web browser not support Ajax for any reason. But with modern JavaScript, this system and the user experience can be greatly enhanced. As it stands, each form submission requires a complete download and redrawing of the entire HTML page. If there's just one problem with the form data, all of the HTML code, images, and so forth, must be resent to the browser (aside from whatever content was cached) and redrawn. The time required to do all this—send the form data to the server, process it on the server, resend the complete page back to the user, and redraw the page in the browser—isn't dramatic, but will be apparent to the end user.

A better solution is to perform client-side form validation using JavaScript. With JavaScript running in the browser, you can easily confirm that a form is completed and immediately report upon problems, without any server requests at all (**Figure 1.4**). (Note that, as shown in Figure 1.4, as a server security measure, server-side validation would still be in place, but that validation would only catch a form error if the user had JavaScript disabled.)

For a long time, basic form validation was one of the better uses of JavaScript. But with just client-side JavaScript, there is a limit as to what kind of validation can be performed, really only checking a form's completeness. When it comes to more complex validation, such as confirming that a username is available (Figure 1.2), a server-side request is still required (because the username data is stored in a database on the server). This is one just one situation where Ajax really shines!

**NOTE:** Because JavaScript can be disabled in the browser, server-side form validation must always still be used.

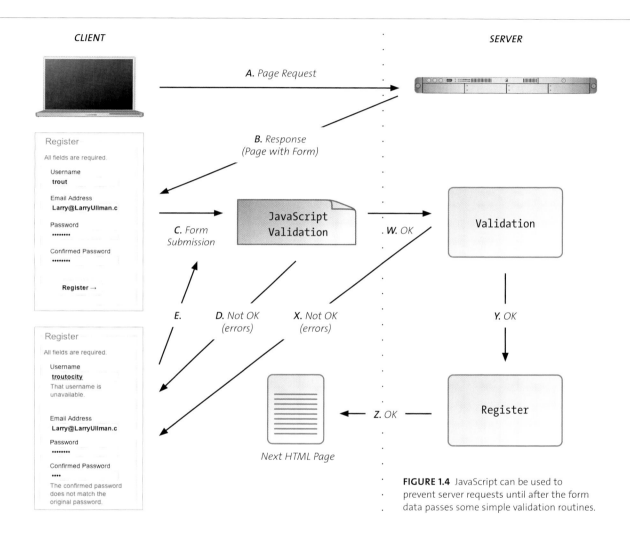

CLIENT

SERVER

**A.** *Page Request*

**B.** *Response*
*(Page with Form)*

Register

All fields are required.

Username
**trout**

Email Address
**Larry@LarryUllman.c**

Password
••••••••

Confirmed Password
••••••••

**Register →**

**C.** *Form Submission*

JavaScript Validation

**W.** *OK*

Validation

**E.**

**D.** *Not OK (errors)*

**X.** *Not OK (errors)*

**Y.** *OK*

Register

All fields are required.

Username
**troutocity**
That username is unavailable.

Email Address
**Larry@LarryUllman.c**

Password
••••••••

Confirmed Password
••••

The confirmed password does not match the original password.

Next HTML Page

**Z.** *OK*

Register

**FIGURE 1.4** JavaScript can be used to prevent server requests until after the form data passes some simple validation routines.

Ajax allows client-side JavaScript to make server-side requests in a way that's not obvious to the user. Continuing with this form-validation example, when the user clicks the submit button, the JavaScript could pause the submission of the form and send the form data to a server-side script. That script would perform all of the validation and return data that indicates a simple status or a list of errors. If errors were returned, the JavaScript would parse the errors and update the page, indicating any and all errors accordingly, and add highlighting to further emphasize the problems. If the returned status indicated that no errors occurred, the JavaScript would do whatever to move the user along in the process (**Figure 1.5**). Now, in looking at the process outlined in the figure, it may seem that applying Ajax just makes everything way more complicated. And, well, it *is* more complicated. But the key benefits gained by incorporating Ajax are:

- As much work as possible is being done within the Web browser
- As little data (e.g., HTML, CSS, media, and so forth) is being transmitted by the server as possible

The end result for the user is a more efficient and responsive process.

In the years since the idea of Ajax was first formalized, its usage and acceptance has greatly expanded without too many changes in the underlying technology. One primary difference between the original idea of Ajax and today's Ajax is that the transmitted data won't necessarily be in XML format. The data could also be JSON (JavaScript Object Notation) or just plain text. Secondarily, how one performs an Ajax request has become more consistent among the browsers.

**NOTE:** Chapter 11, Ajax, covers Ajax in all its glory.

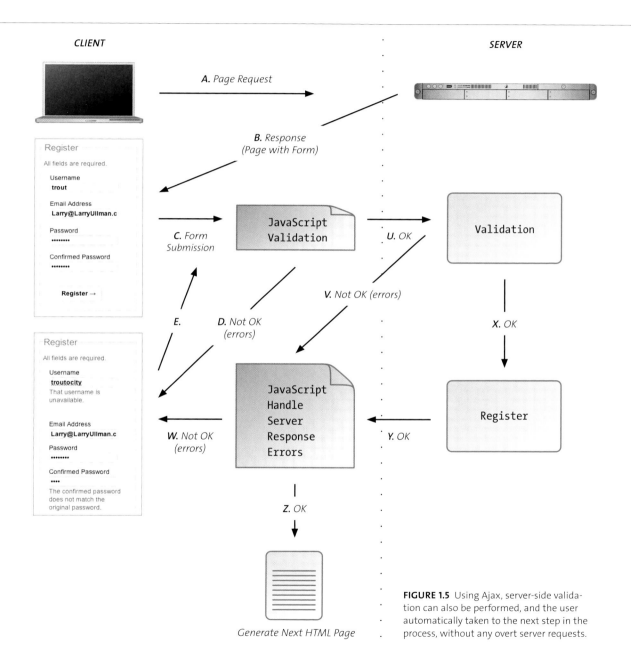

CLIENT

SERVER

**A.** *Page Request*

**B.** *Response (Page with Form)*

Register

All fields are required.

Username
**trout**

Email Address
**Larry@LarryUllman.c**

Password
••••••••

Confirmed Password
••••••••

**Register →**

**C.** *Form Submission*

JavaScript Validation

**U.** *OK*

Validation

**V.** *Not OK (errors)*

**E.**

**D.** *Not OK (errors)*

**X.** *OK*

Register

All fields are required.

Username
**troutocity**
That username is unavailable.

Email Address
**Larry@LarryUllman.c**

Password
••••••••

Confirmed Password
••••

The confirmed password does not match the original password.

**W.** *Not OK (errors)*

JavaScript Handle Server Response Errors

**Y.** *OK*

Register

**Z.** *OK*

*Generate Next HTML Page*

**FIGURE 1.5** Using Ajax, server-side validation can also be performed, and the user automatically taken to the next step in the process, without any overt server requests.

## BROWSER IMPROVEMENTS

JavaScript has been historically difficult to learn for three reasons. For one, JavaScript is a language unlike many others, in terms of where and how it's used and in terms of its prototyped object nature, as already discussed (e.g., it's an OOP language that doesn't let you define your own classes). Second, because JavaScript is primarily used in a Web browser, it's a language that historically fell under the purview of Web *designers*, not *programmers*. And third, creating reliable, cross-browser JavaScript was extremely tedious. Just to do a simple thing using JavaScript, you'd have to write the code one way for one group of browsers and another way for other browsers. Changes in subsequent versions of the same browser required further considerations. Attempting to create code that was 100 percent reliable on all browsers was a huge hurdle, resulting in "solutions" like:

```
if (navigator.appName == "Netscape") { // It's Netscape!
    if (parseInt(navigator.appVersion) >= 4) { // At least version 4!
    } else { // It's an earlier version. Bah!
    }
} else { // Let's assume it's IE?
}
```

Those are just conditionals that attempt to identify the browser type and version. Code within each clause would do the actual work, using JavaScript particular to the browser and version identified. Considering that common browsers today include Internet Explorer, Mozilla Firefox, Apple Safari, and Google Chrome, and that many different versions of each browser can be found on different computers (at the time of this writing, 6 through 9 for IE, 3 through 6 for Firefox, and so forth), the mere notion of programming for a specific browser and version is implausible. (And that list doesn't take into account the myriad number of mobile and gaming devices.)

**TIP:** When it comes to Web development in general and JavaScript in particular, the golden rule is: Initially develop using a good browser, such as Firefox, then later test on Internet Explorer to make your clients happy.

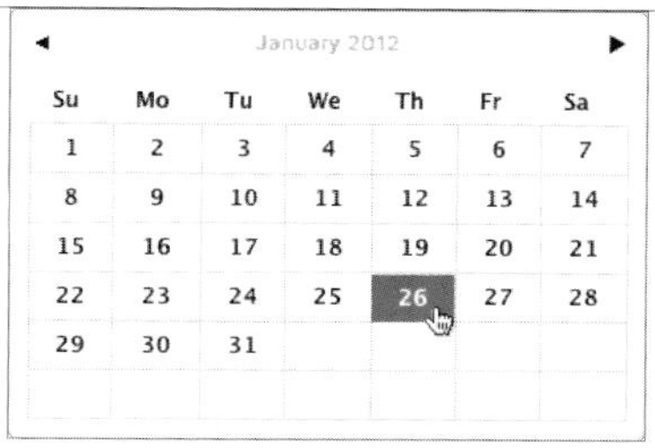

**FIGURE 1.6** A date-picking calendar widget, created by the YUI framework.

Ironically, despite this increasingly wide range of options, in terms of functionality, browsers today can be lumped into two broad categories: Microsoft's Internet Explorer and everything else. As any Web developer with even the slightest amount of experience will tell you, designing HTML and CSS, or programming JavaScript for Internet Explorer (IE) is a bother (I'm being polite here). Fortunately, over time Microsoft has improved how nicely IE plays with others, and, or perhaps because, fewer and fewer people are using Internet Explorer. The other category of browsers—"everything else"—primarily means Firefox, Chrome, and Safari as I write this, although Opera is worth mentioning despite its low market share. Generally speaking, these browsers all adhere to the standards much more closely than IE, and, well, are just better (let's be honest about that). The end result is that developing Web applications in such a way as to guarantee a reasonable level of uniform user experience has become significantly easier. More importantly, though, a new approach is being used to write code that reliably works on any browser. You'll learn about that near the chapter's end.

## THE RISE OF FRAMEWORKS

The third major development in the history of JavaScript is the creation of *frameworks*. A framework is just a library of code whose purpose is to expedite development. In any programming language there are oodles of tasks and processes that get repeated. Rather than just re-create the appropriate code each time, it's better, in the long run, to write a framework that will easily and quickly replicate that code for you. JavaScript libraries have been around for years, but they were historically smaller in scope and usage. Today's frameworks are powerful, yet flexible. JavaScript frameworks can create user interface widgets such as date-picking calendars (**Figure 1.6**), simplify form validation and Ajax integration, and enhance common Web elements, such as paginating and sorting tables of data.

More importantly, a framework can create code that's browser-agnostic, meaning it will work successfully regardless of the browser in use (assuming the browser still has JavaScript enabled, that is). For example, MooTools (`http://mootools.net/`) is "compatible and fully tested with" Safari 3+, Internet Explorer 6+, Firefox 2+, Opera 9+, and Chrome 4+. For many developers, the cross-browser reliability alone is reason enough to use a framework.

Choosing a framework is a personal decision and one that can be complex (I go into the topic in Chapter 13, Frameworks). The first JavaScript framework I used was script.aculo.us (`http://script.aculo.us`), and then I moved on to YUI, the Yahoo! User Interface (`http://developer.yahoo.com/yui/`). For the past couple of years, though, I've adored jQuery (`http://jquery.com`), as have many others. In this book, I primarily discuss and demonstrate jQuery and YUI, but other JavaScript frameworks that are highly regarded include MooTools, script.aculo.us, and:

- ExtJS (`http://www.sencha.com/`)

- The Dojo Toolkit (`http://dojotoolkit.org/`)

- Prototype (`http://www.prototypejs.org/`)

All that being said, there are several reasonable arguments against the use of frameworks. First, frameworks require extra learning while still requiring complete comfort with the language itself (e.g., you'll need to learn JavaScript, and then learn jQuery or whatever). Second, trying to use a framework for very advanced or custom purposes can be hard at best or nearly impossible at worst, depending upon your skill level. Finally, frameworks almost always mean worse performance when compared with writing your own code. With JavaScript in particular, tapping into a framework means that the browser has to download much more code than it would if just JavaScript alone were to be used.

In the 15 years since JavaScript was created, the adoption of Ajax, improvements in browsers, and creation of frameworks have greatly expanded the usefulness and usability of this language. However, the interesting thing is that relatively little about the language itself has changed in that time. In describing the sometimes ugly history of the language, one could say that history is really the story of people at first not using a technology well, and later learning how to make the most of JavaScript's potential.

# JAVASCRIPT ISN'T...

Now that you have an understanding of what JavaScript *is* (hopefully), let's take a minute to talk about what JavaScript *isn't*. This could also be called the "Myth Busters" section of the chapter!

First, *JavaScript is not Java*. This is a common point of confusion and reasonably so (they both start with "Java," after all). But, no, JavaScript is not Java. In fact, JavaScript is unrelated to Java, is a different type of object-oriented language, is a scripting language (Java is compiled), and is used for very different purposes. If you're going to learn JavaScript, the first thing you must do is stop calling it "Java."

Second, JavaScript is not just for mouseovers, alerts, and pop-up windows. *JavaScript*, in the Web browser, *is for improving the user experience*.

Third, JavaScript is not just a client-side technology anymore, although that's still its primary purpose and use. Over the past couple of years, server-side JavaScript has been developed, in many forms.

Fourth, JavaScript is not hard to learn, provided you have the right resource that is! (Ahem.) This book treats JavaScript as a true programming language—which it is, providing you with the context and structured approach to help you truly learn, and appreciate, JavaScript.

Fifth, JavaScript is not hard to debug. OK, compared to other languages, debugging JavaScript isn't quite as easy, but given the right tools—see Chapter 3, Tools of the Trade—you can debug JavaScript efficiently.

Finally, JavaScript is not a security measure. Because JavaScript is easy for users to disable or manipulate, you should never rely on JavaScript for security purposes.

# HOW **JAVASCRIPT COMPARES** TO...

I never really appreciated the lessons of English grammar until I started studying foreign languages: Sometimes you just need something to compare and contrast to in order to grasp an idea. In the next couple of pages, I'll explain how JavaScript compares to other common technologies with which you may be familiar, in the hopes that you can then more fully understand the language you're about to master.

## HTML AND CSS

HyperText Markup Language (HTML) is the technology used to create Web pages. (As an aside, if you don't already know that, you'll want to learn HTML before going any further with this book.) HTML is like JavaScript in that both are primarily destined for Web browsers, but the comparisons stop there. HTML is a way to present content to users; JavaScript is a way to make that content dynamic.

Cascading Style Sheets (CSS) are also intended for Web browsers, but focus on the visuals. CSS could be described as somewhat dynamic in that CSS rules can apply differently from one browser to the next, but this is not the same level of dynamism as JavaScript can offer. CSS, like JavaScript, makes use of the Document Object Model (DOM), which is a representation of the HTML found in a page. In fact, the jQuery framework uses CSS-like selectors for its own DOM manipulations.

You may have heard of the MVC (Model, View, Controller) design pattern, which is an approach to software development that separates the data (called the Model) from the visuals (the View) from the actions (the Controller). In those terms, it may help to think of HTML as the Model—the data with which you're dealing, CSS as the View—the presentation, and JavaScript as the Controller—the agent of change and activity.

## PHP

PHP is the most popular language used to create dynamic Web sites (and is one of my favorite languages). PHP, like JavaScript, is a *scripting* language, which means two things:

- Code responds to events

- Scripts are run through an executable

By comparison, C and C++, among other languages, can be used to write standalone applications. Such applications can even take actions on their own, regardless of events.

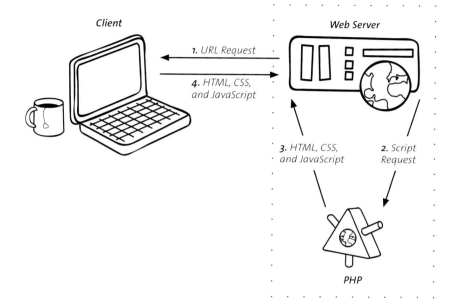

**Client**

1. *URL Request*

4. *HTML, CSS,
and JavaScript*

**Web Server**

3. *HTML, CSS,
and JavaScript*

2. *Script
Request*

*PHP*

**FIGURE 1.7** PHP can dynamically generate HTML, CSS, and
JavaScript on the Web server,
which is then sent to the
browser.

The biggest difference between PHP and JavaScript is that JavaScript primarily
runs in a Web browser (aka, a client) and PHP only runs on a server. Whereas the
Web *browser* includes the JavaScript engine for executing JavaScript code, the Web
*server* application, such as Apache, includes the PHP module for executing PHP code.
Whereas JavaScript reacts to user and browser-based events, PHP reacts to server-
based events, such as the request of a particular page or the submission of a form.

There is a little overlap as to what the languages can do (e.g., they can both work
with cookies, generate images, and redirect the Web browser, but the overlaps don't
go much further). PHP can be used to dynamically generate JavaScript, though, just
as PHP can be used to create HTML or CSS on the fly (**Figure 1.7**). PHP can also
be written taking either a procedural or an object-oriented approach, whereas
JavaScript is only an object-oriented language. But both languages are weakly typed.

All that being said, if you already know PHP, JavaScript should be comparatively
easy to learn. As Web programmers are now repeatedly expected to know how to
do both client-side and server-side programming, it's appropriate to learn both. In
this book, PHP will be used for any server-side needs, such as in the Ajax examples,
but you do not need to be a PHP master to follow along with those examples.

### FLASH

I include Flash in the list of technologies to compare and contrast to JavaScript because Flash is often an alternative to JavaScript for adding dynamic behavior to Web pages. Modern Web sites, which respond better to user interaction, communicate with servers, and more, are really *Web applications*, and are often called *Rich Internet Applications* (RIAs). RIAs are primarily created using either JavaScript or Flash. Flash is a proprietary technology managed by Adobe that can be created in a couple of different ways (Flash itself is not a programming language).

Although Flash can be used for many of the same purposes as JavaScript, how Flash works in the Web browser—it requires a Flash Player plugin—is a key difference. Whereas JavaScript can interact with the HTML page via the DOM, Flash content is really separate from the HTML page itself (although JavaScript can be used to communicate between Flash and the Web browser). Also, Flash has complications when it comes to mobile devices, accessibility, and other nontraditional Web experiences. All that being said, there's an argument to be made that the most advanced RIAs—such as games, presentation of lots of data using charts and graphs, and so forth—can be more quickly and reliably created in Flash. But, again, not everyone can run Flash...

**NOTE:** While I was writing this book, Adobe started signaling a change in its attitude toward Flash, meaning this ubiquitous technology's future is now surprisingly uncertain.

### ACTIONSCRIPT

ActionScript is the programming language of Flash and Flex (Flex is a framework for creating Flash content). ActionScript is extremely similar to JavaScript, as both are derived from the same parent: ECMAScript. But while both languages are object-oriented, ActionScript is strongly typed and is not prototype-based (i.e., you can define classes in ActionScript). Still, if you know ActionScript, it will be easy to pick up JavaScript, and vice versa.

# WHY **JAVASCRIPT** IS
# A **GOOD THING**

If you're reading this book, you presumably have an interest in learning JavaScript, but I'd be remiss if I didn't also present my thoughts as to why JavaScript is a *Good Thing*. The most important and obvious reason is that JavaScript is useful. A large swath of the dynamic functionality that's normal in today's Web sites is accomplished using JavaScript. In fact, much of this functionality is so expected by users, that not using JavaScript would be a noticeable omission. Moreover JavaScript...

- Can improve a site's performance (e.g., thanks to Ajax)

- Can be used to fix browser deficiencies, such as support for newer CSS features

- Can be used in mobile devices (depending upon the device)

- Is entirely reliable, when done right

- Pushes some of the processing onto the client and off of the server, easing the server's load

One of the great things about JavaScript is that the language itself is counter-intuitively responsible for undermining its own reputation. Or more simply put: you can use JavaScript without really knowing it. While it's true that using JavaScript *well* requires sound knowledge, using it *some* is quite easy. Moreover, because JavaScript runs in the Web browser, anyone's JavaScript code is readily viewable: When you encounter a feature or an effect on a page that you like, you can just copy the HTML, JavaScript, and CSS for your own purposes (I'm setting aside the moral and legal issues here). By comparison, Java and C++ code are not easy to use piecemeal: You really have to know these languages to do much in them. Secondarily, compiled applications make seeing the underlying code anywhere from hard to impossible.

Finally, JavaScript is a Good Thing because someone else has almost certainly already figured out how to accomplish what you're trying to do. This is true for all established languages, of course, but with JavaScript, perhaps because the code will always be public anyway, smart programmers are inclined to share. Often, smart programmers create a public library or framework out of the snazzy code, too.

# JAVASCRIPT VERSIONS AND BROWSER SUPPORT

As already stated, the core of JavaScript comes from ECMAScript, which is currently in version 5 as of 2009. The most current version of JavaScript, based upon ECMAScript 5, is JavaScript 1.8.5, which came out in July of 2010. When programming in JavaScript, however, these facts are less critical than *what's possible in what browsers*. Most modern browsers support ECMAScript 3 and parts of ECMAScript 5 (no version 4 of ECMAScript was ever officially released).

"Modern browsers" is a phrase you'll see a lot in this book and elsewhere. Roughly speaking, modern browsers support core JavaScript, DOM manipulation, the XmlHttpRequest object (used to make Ajax requests), and basic CSS. In sum, modern browsers are capable of making the most of today's dynamic Web technologies. This broad definition includes most versions of Firefox, Chrome, Opera, and Safari, and versions of Internet Explorer after IE6 (IE6 has been the Web developer's arch nemesis for years).

Note that the loose definition of "modern browsers" isn't based solely upon JavaScript, but also upon other advances, such as the ability to perform DOM manipulation. JavaScript is frequently used to manipulate the DOM, but the DOM is defined and managed by the W3C (World Wide Web Consortium, www.w3.org). Different browsers also support the DOM in different ways, which means that when creating dynamic Web sites, one has to factor in not only variations in JavaScript support, but also DOM support and CSS support (and HTML5 support, should you choose).

As of August 1, 2011, Google decided to start supporting a more modest list of modern browsers (supporting for Web applications; the Google search engine is usable in any browser, of course). Google's criteria is simply the most current release of Chrome, Firefox, IE, and Safari, plus the preceding release of each. On the one hand, this approach does exclude a decent percentage of Web users and some browsers that would otherwise be deemed "modern." On the other hand, the approach acknowledges that changes come with new versions of browsers, and that there's a good reason to drop older versions, just as users ought to be constantly upgrading their browsers, too.

**TIP:** If you want, you can keep an eye on ECMAScript 5 compatibility, using sites such as http://kangax.github.com/es5-compat-table/.

Yahoo!, in conjunction with the Yahoo! User Interface (YUI) JavaScript framework (http://yuilibrary.com), developed its own Graded Browser Support system (http://yuilibrary.com/yui/docs/tutorials/gbs/). Rather than identify what browsers are officially supported, the list identifies the browsers one ought to test a site on. Yahoo!'s list, as of July 2011, includes Internet Explorer versions 6 through 9, Firefox versions 3 through 5, the latest stable version of Chrome, and Safari 5.

But what do any of these lists mean for you as a JavaScript programmer? Knowing what different versions of different browsers can do is good for your own edification, but will not be the basis of your JavaScript programming. A decade ago, when there weren't that many browsers, JavaScript code was written specifically checking the browser type and version (as shown in earlier code): Is this Internet Explorer or Netscape Navigator? Is it version 4 or 5 or 5.5? With literally thousands of different browser types and versions available (when you factor in mobile devices), it's impossible to target specific browsers and versions. Furthermore, for any number of reasons, browsers will wrongfully identify themselves. And even if you can overcome those two hurdles, the code will be outdated with the next release of a new browser, a new browser version, or a new device with its own internal browser.

Instead, in today's modern JavaScript, code is written not for the browser but for the browser's *capabilities*. It's a subtle but significant difference, and part of the basis for proper modern JavaScript programming. In this book, you'll learn many techniques for programming to what's possible, rather than what browser is running.

Still, after developing the code, you should still test the site on a range of browsers, like those in Yahoo!'s or Google's lists. When working on a project for a client, you and the client will need to come up with your own list of supported browsers (this is something that ought to be stipulated in the contract, too). Keep in mind that a properly designed site should still fully function in a nonsupported browser; it just won't be able to take advantage of the dynamic functionality added by JavaScript and other modern tools (like CSS3 and HTML5).

**NOTE:** Search engines generally don't recognize the effects of scripting. To make a site's content findable by, and meaningful to, a search engine, it must exist in a nonscripted form.

# JAVASCRIPT
## PROGRAMMING **GOALS**

In starting a new endeavor, whether it's learning JavaScript for the first time or learning better, more modern JavaScript techniques, one ought to have a sense of the goals before starting out. The purpose of a Web site, of course, is for it to be viewable and usable by clients—end users with their Web browsers. If visitors cannot use a site, you have failed in your job as a Web developer. Toward this end, the site's functionality should be possible on all browsers, including those on mobile devices, nonvisual browsers, browsers with JavaScript disabled, and simply old browsers. This is easier to accomplish than you might think thanks to an approach called *progressive enhancement*.

Progressive enhancement is the process of creating basic, reliable functionality, and then enhancing that functionality on browsers that support the enhancement. For example, the standard way to handle a form submission is to send the form data to a server-side resource (see Figure 1.3). JavaScript, as already discussed, can accomplish the same thing using Ajax (as in Figure 1.5). Progressive enhancement says that you should implement the standard approach first, and then intercept that approach when possible. How you implement progressive enhancement will be demonstrated repeatedly throughout this book, starting in the next chapter.

This is not to say that there aren't situations when it's reasonable to exclude users. For example, it's not possible for a site demonstrating the wonders of HTML5 to be properly rendered on an antiquated browser. Or, iOS devices—the iPod, iPad, and iPhone—do not support Flash. If a site must absolutely use Flash, it should do so with the understanding that many people will be excluded. But for the most part, the goal should be to support every browser as much as possible.

Not only should a Web site work regardless of the browser, but it should not attempt to break the browser's normal behavior. For years, JavaScript programmers have attempted to prevent the user from clicking the back button, otherwise using the browser's history, accessing contextual menus, and so forth. *JavaScript*, for the most part, *should improve the user experience*, not radically alter it. There's no justification for attempting to make the browser behave in ways other than what the user is accustomed to. (At the very least, if your site relies upon disabling common browser behavior, you'll eventually run into trouble when a user without JavaScript visits.)

Second, to make code easier to maintain, one should also employ the technique of *unobtrusive JavaScript*. This phrase refers to the separation of JavaScript code from the HTML page, and Chapter 2, JavaScript in Action, starts discussing how this impacts actual code.

Finally, modern JavaScript programming should be appropriate for the current state of the Web as a whole. Think of this like being a model citizen or a good parent: demonstrate the qualities that ought to be emulated. This applies not only to JavaScript, but to HTML and CSS, too. Again, Chapter 2 will establish some parameters toward this end, such as the adoption of *semantic HTML*.

These are the goals of modern JavaScript programming. The goal of this book, then, is to properly implement these goals in real-world code, while simultaneously teaching JavaScript as a language in its own right.

## WRAPPING **UP**

This chapter provides a long-winded introduction to JavaScript, but context is valuable when you begin learning the language. Some of the key thoughts to take away from this chapter are:

- JavaScript is an object-oriented language, albeit a different kind of one.

- JavaScript is weakly typed.

- JavaScript is a subset of ECMAScript.

- Ajax is awesome.

- Frameworks are wonderful, too.

- JavaScript is not a security measure.

- JavaScript is still primarily a client-side technology.

Those are mostly facts, plus a smattering of opinion. Philosophically, as you learn JavaScript, you should also strive to adhere to these principles:

- JavaScript should improve the user experience.

- JavaScript should be used unobtrusively.

- A reliable user experience for all user types can be achieved through progressive enhancement.

- Write code based upon what browsers can do, not what they are.

All of this, and more, will be explained in this book, starting in Chapter 2.

# 2

# JAVASCRIPT
# IN ACTION

JavaScript, like object-oriented programming in general, is something the lay programmer can use without fully understanding it. This quality is both an asset and a liability of the language. Although this book will teach you complete and proper JavaScript in time, this chapter provides a glimpse into real-world JavaScript without all that tedious formal training. To be sure, this is an unorthodox way to begin, but by doing so, the book acknowledges that you may already be mucking about with JavaScript (informally). Further, this early chapter will present a target toward which the next several chapters can aim. All that being said, the chapter also introduces some basics, especially when it comes to Web development and design in general, starting with the impact that the DOCTYPE will have on everything else you do.

# CHOOSING A DOCTYPE

When I first began doing Web development, I had no appreciation of an HTML page's document type declaration, aka DOCTYPE. I believe I was using HTML 3.2 at the time, and only understood that meant pages must begin with:

```
<!DOCTYPE HTML PUBLIC "-//W3C//DTD HTML 3.2 Final//EN">
```

The DOCTYPE is a declaration of the version of HTML in use by the page, with each new version of HTML supporting new features (in the form of HTML elements). For example, HTML 2.0 didn't even support tables and HTML 3.2 had limited support for style sheets. For the past several years, the two most common DOCTYPES have been HTML 4.01 and XHTML 1.0. XHMTL is basically HTML, with tighter adherence to XML syntax (more on this in the next section). Both HTML 4.01 and XHTML 1.0 come in three flavors: Strict, Transitional, and Frameset. Strict is obviously the most restrictive of the three, allowing for the smallest set of elements. The Transitional version is Strict plus deprecated elements and more. The Frameset version is Transitional plus support for frames.

If you're like me, you made a decision between HTML and XHTML, and then probably went with the Transitional option, as it's the most forgiving:

```
<!DOCTYPE html PUBLIC "-//W3C//DTD XHTML 1.0 Transitional//EN"
"http://www.w3.org/TR/xhtml1/DTD/xhtml1-transitional.dtd">
```

Taking things a step further, you may have been in the habit of *validating* your HTML pages, using sites like the W3C Markup Validation Service (http://validator.w3.org/). If so, then you probably knew that such tools perform validation based upon the page's DOCTYPE. For example, if you used a deprecated element or a frame in a Strict document, that would be flagged. The same goes for not adhering to XML syntax in an XHTML document (**Figure 2.1**).

**NOTE:** The DOCTYPE needs to be the absolutely first thing in your Web page, without even a space before it.

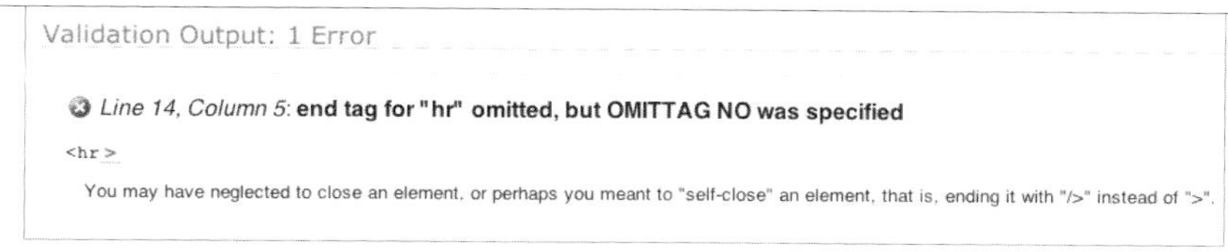

ℹ *Line 14, Column 5:* **end tag for "hr" omitted, but OMITTAG NO was specified**

`<hr >`

  You may have neglected to close an element, or perhaps you meant to "self-close" an element, that is, ending it with "/>" instead of ">".

**FIGURE 2.1** Validation services confirm that a document adheres to its stated standard.

Hopefully you already know all this, but if you don't, or if you don't know anymore than this, that's understandable. The real goal, though, isn't to just create (X)HTML pages that pass the validation routines, but to have the pages look and function correctly in the Web browser. And here's where the DOCTYPE also comes into play: *Web browsers will choose one of two operating modes based upon a document's* DOCTYPE. If a valid DOCTYPE exists, the browser will run in "standards-compliant" mode (often just called "Standards" mode), in which HTML, CSS, and the DOM are all treated as they are intended to work. If a document does not have a DOCTYPE, or if the DOCTYPE is incorrect, the browser will run in "Quirks" mode, in which the browser will treat the HTML, CSS, and DOM in a way consistent with older browsers. For example, when Internet Explorer 8 gets switched into Quirks mode, it will render a page in the same way that Internet Explorer 5.5 did. (IE5.5 is well over a decade old now, so imagine what it means to view your beautiful new Web page using 10-year-old technology.)

## WHAT IS THE DOM?

The DOM, first mentioned in Chapter 1, (Re-)Introducing JavaScript, is short for Document Object Model. The DOM is a way to represent and navigate XML data, which includes HTML and XHTML. With respect to Web browsers, the DOM standard is managed by the World Wide Web Consortium (W3C). The current standard is DOM Level 3, released in 2004. Despite the fact that this standard has been around for years, it's still not consistently implemented across all browsers. To be clear, the DOM is not part of core JavaScript, but JavaScript uses the DOM to interact with the Web browser, a technique often called *DOM manipulation*.

## CONFIRMING THE BROWSER MODE

Some Web browsers readily show what mode they are operating in for the loaded Web page. For example, Firefox's Page Info panel, under the Tools menu, shows this information as its "Render Mode." To view the current mode in Opera, select View > Developer Tools > Page Information. The value is then displayed under "Display Mode." No other browser shows this information as readily, but in Chapter 9, JavaScript and the Browser, you'll see how to access the rendering mode using JavaScript.

And if that's not bad enough, even valid DOCTYPEs will trigger Quirks mode on some browsers, or in situations where invalid elements are encountered in an otherwise-valid document with a valid DOCTYPE. Thus, when it comes to trying to make a Web page that looks and behaves consistently across all browsers, the DOCTYPE plays a significant role. In this book, as in your Web development life, a decision has to be made as to what DOCTYPE should be used. And in this book, the choice is:

```
<!DOCTYPE html>
```

This DOCTYPE has several benefits:

- It's easier to type and you're less likely to make a mistake in entering it.

- There are fewer characters, meaning a, perhaps imperceptibly, smaller file is being sent to, and loaded by, the user's Web browser.

- It's supported by all major browsers.

- It automatically puts the browser into Standards mode.

If you haven't come across this DOCTYPE yet, that's because this is the new DOCTYPE for HTML5. Now, HTML5 isn't an accepted standard yet—it's still being discussed, so how is it safe to use? Let's look at that in detail.

**NOTE:** Not all browsers switch modes in the same way. For example, Opera has, for years, defaulted to Standards mode, and Mozilla has its own "Almost Standards" mode.

# AN **HTML5 PRIMER**

As I write this book with 2012 almost upon us, HTML5 is a curious beast. It's been around in some form or another for a couple of years now, but it wasn't that long ago that the XHTML 2.0 progress was halted, which made HTML5 the de facto next standard for Web development. Still, HTML5 hasn't been formally standardized and released, which means that the final implementation of HTML5, whenever that comes out, will undoubtedly be different than the HTML5 being discussed today. Normally, with something as ubiquitous and varied as a Web browser, one would be wise to steer clear of such a novelty. But there are ways you can have the best of both worlds: use some HTML5 features, without wrecking the user experience. Let's first look at a generic HTML5 template, and then learn about the best new HTML5 form elements.

> **TIP:** HTML5 is not just an individual standard, but rather a name given to the HTML standard plus a collection of other new features.

## AN HTML5 TEMPLATE

This next code block shows the HTML5 template that I'll use as the basis of all the HTML scripts in this book. Take a look at it, and then I'll explain its particulars in detail.

```
<!doctype html>
<html lang="en">
<head>
    <meta charset="utf-8">
    <title>HTML5 Template</title>
    <!--[if lt IE 9]>
    <script src="http://html5shiv.googlecode.com/svn/trunk/
    ↪ html5.js"></script>
    <![endif]-->
</head>
<body>
    <!-- template.html -->
</body>
</html>
```

To start on line 1, as already stated, the simple HTML5 DOCTYPE will put the browser in Standards mode, which is the first desired goal. Next, you have your html element, with head and body elements within that. Oddly, HTML5 does not require the head element, but it creeps me out not to use it. HTML5 does still need a title tag, whether or not you use head. You should also be in the habit of indicating the encoding (i.e., the character set in use). As you can see, that meta tag has been simplified, too (line 4). If you're unfamiliar with character sets and encoding, you should research the topic, but *utf-8* is the normal value used here, as UTF8 encoding supports every character in every language. Also, as you can see, I've added the lang attribute to the opening html tag (line 2), although it's not required, either.

**NOTE:** The encoding must be indicated early in the document, so always place it after the opening head tag and before the title element.

That's the basic syntax of an HTML5 document. In the next section of the chapter, I'll highlight the main reason I'm using HTML5 for this book: the bevy of new and very useful form elements. But quickly, two more things about the HTML5 template. First, if you're going to use an external style sheet, as many examples in this book will, the correct syntax is:

```
<link rel="stylesheet" href="css/styles.css">
```

You may notice that the link element in HTML5 doesn't use the type attribute as it's just assumed that this type will be *text/css* when the rel attribute has a value of *stylesheet*.

Second, HTML5 defines many new semantic elements, such as article, footer, header, nav, and section. The creation of these tags was determined by mining the Web for the most common ID and class elements found. For example, in HTML4, many designers used a div with an ID of *header* for representing the top section of the page; then CSS would style and position the div accordingly. In HTML5, you'd just create a header element, and style it. Most older browsers, which cannot handle HTML5, won't have a problem when they encounter these new HTML tags and can still apply styling correctly. Unfortunately, Internet Explorer versions prior to 9 are not capable of styling unknown elements, meaning that any user running IE8 or earlier won't see the properly formatted document. The solution is a clever piece of JavaScript called the "HTML5 shiv," created by a series of very smart people. The code works by having JavaScript generate elements of the new types, which has the effect of making Internet Explorer recognize, and therefore style them, appropriately. The HTML5 shiv library has been open sourced and is now hosted on Google Code. To incorporate it, use this code:

```
<!--[if lt IE 9]>
<script src="http://html5shiv.googlecode.com/svn/trunk/html5.js">
  </script>
<![endif]-->
```

This block begins and ends with *conditional comments*, only supported in Internet Explorer. The specific conditional checks to see if the current browser version is less than (*lt*) IE9. If so, then the `script` tag will be added to the page automatically. Because these are conditional comments, only meaningful to IE, other browsers will not attempt to load this script.

You may have noticed that this `script` tag, like the `link` tag, also does not use a type attribute, as *text/javascript* is assumed.

In Chapter 3, Tools of the Trade, I'll list some HTML validators, but I'll also note here that you can validate HTML5 at `http://html5.validator.nu/` or using the standard W3C validator. At the time of this writing, both are considered experimental, but then again, HTML5 is borderline experimental, too!

> **NOTE:** Very few of the book's examples will use the newer elements that warrant the inclusion of the HTML5 shiv, but I will use this template consistently, including the shiv, regardless.

**FIGURE 2.2** The new HTML5 number input type.

**FIGURE 2.3** HTML5 form elements are self-validating, like the URL typed here.

**FIGURE 2.4** The new HTML5 search input type.

## HTML5 FORM ELEMENTS

There are two reasons I've decided to use HTML5 in this book despite the fact that HTML5 hasn't been finalized. One reason is that HTML5 is clearly the future of Web development. Another is that HTML5 offers new form elements that make for a better user experience. In particular, I'm thinking of these new types of inputs:

- email
- number
- range

- search
- tel
- url

These elements are for the user to enter email addresses, a number using a "spinbox" (**Figure 2.2**), a number using a slider, search terms, a telephone number, or a URL. For browsers that support these elements, built-in client-side validation will ensure that only valid data is entered. For example, a url input will only allow the user to enter a URL (when that input type is supported, **Figure 2.3**). A couple of these input types have ancillary benefits. For example, when an email input is given focus on a mobile device such as the iPhone, a keyboard for entering email addresses is proffered to the user. As another example, the search input type will be styled like the Mac's standard search box, with rounded corners (**Figure 2.4**, although it does not automatically include the *Search...* text).

The reason it's safe to use these new elements is that for browsers that do not support them, the user will be presented with a standard text input instead. Furthermore, browsers also render unknown elements inline by default, so using these new input types shouldn't even throw off your layout!

HTML5 forms have also defined a few new input attributes worth considering. The first is autofocus, which marks the element that should have the browser's focus when the form is loaded:

```
<input type="text" name="username" autofocus>
```

**NOTE:** At the time of this writing, of all the browsers, Opera does the best job of supporting these new input types.

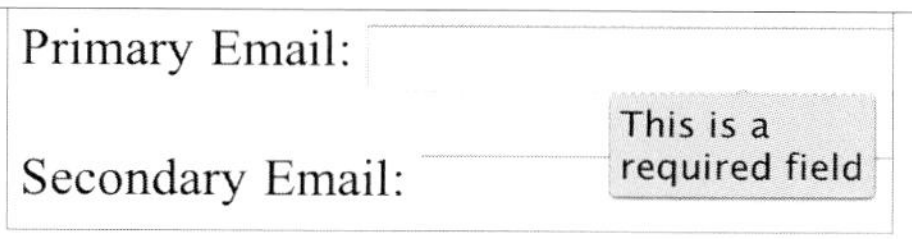

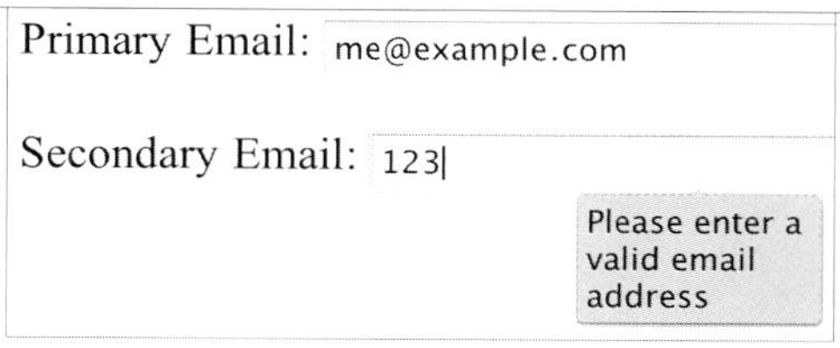

Primary Email: [                    ]
                          This is a
Secondary Email: [        required field]

Primary Email: [me@example.com]

Secondary Email: [123|]
                       Please enter a
                       valid email
                       address

The second is `placeholder`, which sets the text the input should initially have (Figure 2.4):

```
<input type="search" placeholder="Search...">
```

HTML5 also introduces the `required` attribute, which is tied to HTML5's automatic form validation. When the `required` attribute is present, the user must supply data for that element that will pass the associated validation. For example, if an email address is required, then the user must enter a syntactically valid email address there. When an element is not required, no data need be submitted; but if data is provided, it must still pass muster (**Figures 2.5** and **2.6**):

```
Primary Email: <input type="email" name="email1" required>
Secondary Email: <input type="email" name="email2">
```

To restrict the amount of text submitted for a text element, use the `maxlength` attribute. This attribute has been around for years, but is now more binding (different browsers will respond to too much text in different ways), and can even be applied to textareas:

```
<textarea name="comments" rows="8" cols="40" maxlength="300">
  </textarea>
```

Finally, to disable automatic form validation, add the `novalidate` attribute to the opening `form` tag:

```
<form action="somepage.php" method="get" novalidate>
```

As a warning in advance, some of the examples, especially in the earlier chapters, use JavaScript to perform validation. If you're testing those examples with a browser that supports HTML5, you'll need to add the `novalidate` attribute to the form or else the browser will never let invalid data get to the JavaScript.

Now that you've got a sense of what it means to use HTML5, let's get back to the JavaScript!

**FIGURE 2.5** Validation applies to an element whether or not the element is required (see Figure 2.6).

**FIGURE 2.6** When nonrequired elements do have values, the values must pass the associated validation.

## HTML5 VS. XHTML

XHTML required strict XML syntax, which is one of the reasons I always preferred it over HTML (forcing strict behavior cuts down on mistakes). The stricter XHTML has several rules that don't apply to HTML. In particular:

- Elements without closing tags, such as img, input, and br, need to be closed with a slash in the opening tag, as in:

```
<img src="file.png" alt="img" />
```

- Attributes need to be quoted, as in the above.
- Attributes always need values, as in:

```
<option value="yes" selected="selected">Yes</option>
```

HTML5, though, like earlier versions of HTML, does not require strict XML syntax. This has many implications, including the fact that none of the above rules apply. The two XHTML code snippets above could be valid HTML5 like so:

```
<img src=file.png alt=img>
```

```
<option value=yes selected>Yes</option>
```

Personally, I'm willing to drop the closing slash and the attribute values (when appropriate), as the syntax is cleaner without affecting the meaning. However, I still recommend quoting attributes. For one, doing so makes the attribute values stand out. Second, there are instances when you *must* quote the attribute value, such as if the value has a space in it:

```
<img src="file.png" alt="My Vacation">
```

Finally, because some attributes may need to be quoted, it will be more consistent—and more consistent is always better—if all attributes are routinely quoted.

**TIP:** HTML5 also creates a new pattern attribute, which ties the element's validation to a regular expression.

# ADDING **JAVASCRIPT** TO **HTML**

This chapter demonstrates some real-world JavaScript, admittedly using ideas that you'll more formally learn in Part 2: JavaScript Fundamentals. Some basics need to be introduced here, though, including how to add JavaScript code to an HTML page, something I suspect you already know how to do.

To embed JavaScript within an HTML page, use the `script` element:

```
<script></script>
```

In earlier versions of HTML, the tag's type attribute was required, and should have a value of *text/javascript*. That's no longer the case in HTML5. If you're using an older version of HTML, then do use `type`.

The JavaScript code is then placed between the opening and closing `script` tags. When the browser loads the Web page, it will execute the code found there.

Alternatively, the JavaScript code can be stored in an external file that will be included by the HTML page using the `script` element's `src` attribute:

```
<script src="path/to/file.js"></script>
```

The *path/to* part needs to be accurate, but the path can be *relative* to the HTML page or *absolute* (see the following sidebar).

It's still common for small pieces of JavaScript to be written directly within the HTML page, not in a separate file. But as your JavaScript code gets more complicated, or as it's repeated on multiple pages of a Web site, it makes more sense to use external files, where the JavaScript code is easier to maintain. When you use an external JavaScript file, that file can just begin with the JavaScript code, without the `script` tags (because those are HTML tags). Conventionally, external JavaScript files use the `.js` file extension.

A side benefit of using an external JavaScript file is that it can be cached by the user's Web browser. This means that if multiple pages on a site use the same external JavaScript file, the browser will only need to download that file once.

There are five more things you should know about using `script`. First, as with most HTML elements, you can use multiple instances of `script` within a single HTML page. In fact, you commonly will.

Second, each use of `script` can present inline JavaScript code *or* incorporate an external JavaScript file *but not both*. If a single HTML page needs to do both, you'll have to use two instances of `script`.

Third, if you're using strict XHTML, you'll need to wrap all of the JavaScript code within CDATA tags, which leads to some awkward and ugly syntax:

```
<script>//<![CDATA[
// Actual JavaScript code!
//]]></script>
```

## RELATIVE VS. ABSOLUTE PATHS

A common point of confusion, especially among beginning Web developers, is the proper way to reference other files and folders. There are two options: use an *absolute* path or a *relative* path. An absolute path begins at a fixed and consistent point, such as the root of the Web site. In HTML, absolute paths always begin with either `http://domain/` or just `/` (replace *domain* with your actual domain, such as *www.example.com*). Therefore, the absolute path to the index file in the Web root directory would be `http://domain/index.html` or just `/index.html`. An absolute path to `file.js`, found in the root directory's js folder, would be `http://domain/js/file.js` or just `/js/file.js`. The benefit of using an absolute path is that it will always be correct, regardless of where you use it: An absolute reference works and is the same for `index.html` in the main directory and for `somepage.html` in a subdirectory.

A relative path is always relative to the HTML page making the reference and will not begin with either `http://` or `/`. To begin a relative path, you can start with a file name. For example, `another.html` is a relative reference to the file `another.html`, found in the same directory as the current file. To create a relative path to a file found within a subdirectory, start with the subdirectory's name, followed by the name of the file (or by other subdirectories as needed): `js/file.js`. Some people prefer to begin relative paths with a single period and a slash, the combination of which represents the current directory. Thus, `./another.html` is the same as `another.html`, and `./js/file.js` equates to `js/file.js`. To move up to a parent directory, use two periods together. For example, if `page.html`, in a subdirectory, needs to include `file.js`, in the main directory's js folder, the correct relative path would be `../js/file.js`: up a directory and then into the js directory.

Relative paths can be harder to get right, but they continue to remain accurate even when files and even entire sites are moved (so long as the files retain the same relative relationship).

The technical reason for this is complicated, but it has to do with how data within `script` is parsed in XHTML. The `<![CDATA[]]>` wrapper prevents certain entities from causing problems. However, because `[CDATA[]]` is a parsing indicator and not JavaScript, both the opening `<![CDATA[` and the closing `]]>` tags must be prefaced, on the same line, with the JavaScript comment combination (`//`). You only have to do this if you're using XHTML and have JavaScript written within the `script` tags; this isn't required (or recommended) for HTML, including HTML5, or when the JavaScript code is in an external file. I'm just mentioning this, as you might see it when looking at other people's code.

Fourth, it's common to place `script` elements within the HTML head, but that's not required. In fact, many current developers advocate placing `script` elements near the end of the HTML whenever possible. Yahoo!, for example, recommends putting `script` tags just before the closing body tag. The argument for doing so is that it improves how quickly the page *seems* to load in the browser. This is because when the browser encounters a `script` tag, it will immediately start downloading that script (assuming the script is not already cached). The browser will not be able to continue downloading the HTML, and therefore display it, until the script(s) have downloaded.

Finally, try not to use too many external scripts in the same HTML page. Doing so will also hurt performance.

## KEY DEVELOPMENT APPROACHES

Before looking at some code, there are three development approaches that should be discussed in detail. Which approaches you take—and you can simultaneously take more than one—impacts the code you write and, more importantly, the end user's experience.

### GRACEFUL DEGRADATION

The converse of the `script` element, used to add JavaScript to any HTML page, is the `noscript` element. It's used by a page to provide an alternative message or alternate content when the browser does not support JavaScript:

```
<noscript>Your browser does not support JavaScript!</noscript>
```

Anything placed within the tags will be shown to the user should JavaScript not be enabled. This includes text and/or HTML.

Statistics vary, but generally speaking, somewhere around 1–3 percent of all clients accessing Web sites are not capable of executing any JavaScript for one reason or another. This includes people who:

- Have purposefully disabled JavaScript in the Web browser

- Are running NoScript (`http://noscript.net`), a Firefox extension that implements a white-list approach for allowing JavaScript to run on pages in a given site

- Are using screen readers (i.e., assistive devices for the vision impaired)

- Are using mobile or gaming device browsers

- Are connecting via console software that doesn't support JavaScript (such as the command-line `wget` or `curl`)

- Aren't actually people, but are really a bot, such as a search engine

That's a really small percentage of the overall market, but it's up to you to decide how to best handle these situations. There are three approaches:

1. Pretend non-JavaScript clients don't exist.

2. Apply *graceful degradation.*

3. Apply *progressive enhancement.*

I'm not here to tell you how to do your job, but the first option isn't a good one, especially with the increased usage of mobile and gaming devices, let alone whatever new technologies are coming down the pipeline. And yet, a surprising number of developers don't recognize that some users cannot execute JavaScript. With such sites, the end result may be a broken page, without any explanation as to what's wrong. There are certainly valid reasons why a Web site would require JavaScript, but non-JavaScript clients need to be informed of that requirement. Not preparing for that possibility is bad for the end user and it reflects poorly on the Web developer (and/or company whose site it is).

**FIGURE 2.7** Progressive enhancement applies dynamic layers on top of base functionality.

For years, the second option was the most common response, and is still seen occasionally. *Graceful degradation* is a tactic where you design a site to be fully functioning as you want it to be, and then provide an alternative interface, or just a message indicating the need for JavaScript, to devices that can't use the site as you had designed it. Sound familiar? Yes, this is in effect what the noscript tag does. Graceful degradation is a big improvement over merely ignoring the problem. The main difference is that graceful degradation does let the user know that a problem exists and what the solution should be (i.e., come back with JavaScript enabled).

Still, there is a better approach, called *progressive enhancement.*

## PROGRESSIVE ENHANCEMENT

Progressive enhancement is a term first coined in 2003 but whose adoption still continues to this day. Progressive enhancement takes the opposite stance as graceful degradation: Whereas graceful degradation begins with the desired functionality and offers alternative content if the full functionality isn't supported, progressive enhancement starts with a baseline of minimum functionality and then improves upon that—enhances the user's experience—by adding "rich" features only if the client supports them (**Figure 2.7**). Not only does progressive enhancement ensure that all clients will be able to use your site, I personally find it easier to develop using this approach.

Progressive enhancement involves not just JavaScript but also CSS. There are entire books dedicated to the subject of progressive enhancement (such as *Designing with Progressive Enhancement*, New Riders, 2010), and I cannot spend too many pages on the subject here, but the process you need to understand is simpler than you might think.

To start, you should use standards-compliant, well-structured, clean, semantic HTML. *Semantic HTML* uses HTML tags to clearly indicate the *intent or meaning* of content, not how the content should be presented. For example, you should stop using the i tag to italicize text, and use em, for emphasis, instead. It may seem like a fine distinction, but with em tags, there's no absolute browser sense of what emphasis means in terms of styling. Speaking of styling, with semantic HTML, all of the presentation gets moved into CSS, where it belongs. In situations where there are no tags that indicate the meaning of a page component, classes are used for that purpose. In fact, commonly used semantic classes such as *footer*, *header*, and *nav* were inspirations for new elements in HTML5.

Once you've created a nice semantic HTML page, you should validate it, to be certain that it's problem free and unlikely to send browsers into Quirks mode. You should also test that the HTML and base CSS alone renders properly in the browsers you're targeting. Once you've done all that, you can enhance the experience for the clients that are capable of handling more modern features. As an example of this, let's turn back to the registration form example discussed in Chapter 1.

The baseline functionality for that form, as well as for all forms, is that when the form is submitted, the form data is sent to a server-side script. The server-side script performs the validation and then reacts accordingly. For a registration form, this means either there were no errors and the user is registered in the database, or there were errors, and those are reported to the user, so that the user may correct the mistakes and resubmit the form (see Figure 1.3). The next step in the progressive enhancement process, after creating the semantic HTML page that contains the form, would be to create the server-side script that handles the form. This completes the baseline functionality, and involves no JavaScript (or high-end CSS). It's in this regard that I think this approach is easier: because you first confirm that the simple process is working, before trying the more complicated approach (e.g., Ajax, which is a bit harder to debug).

The final steps are to apply CSS and JavaScript to add layers of more advanced features and design, but only when the browser supports it. The focus in this book is just on the JavaScript, of course. To determine whether or not a browser supports a feature, the modern JavaScript programmer makes use of *object detection*, as already mentioned in Chapter 1. This approach creates reliable cross-browser JavaScript, regardless of the browser type or version. And, object detection is brilliantly simple: Check to see if the browser can support feature *X*, and if so, then use feature *X*. You'll see a specific implementation of this in just a couple of pages.

Through this process, applicable browsers will be progressively enhanced and no one will be left out. This is definitely a "have your cake and eat it too" solution!

## UNOBTRUSIVE JAVASCRIPT

Before getting into some actual code (about time, right?), there's one more concept to introduce: *unobtrusive JavaScript*. Back in the day, JavaScript was often liberally interspersed within HTML. For example, a function might be called when a link is clicked:

```
<a href="javascript:createWindow();">A Link</a>
```

Or, a different function would be called when a form is submitted:

```
<form action="somepage.php" method="post"
→   onsubmit="return validateForm();">
```

Both code examples would still work today, but this practice is frowned upon, and rightfully so. For starters, embedding JavaScript within an HTML page makes the whole page of code harder to read and much more difficult to maintain. Having to browse through lines and lines of HTML to edit inline JavaScript is too impractical. Secondarily, inline JavaScript violates the principle of progressive enhancement in three ways:

- HTML with inline JavaScript is clearly more than just semantic.

- It assumes that the client is capable of handling JavaScript.

- One can't apply the reliable technique of object detection with embedded JavaScript.

The rule for modern JavaScript, therefore, is simple: Put all JavaScript between script tags or in an external file.

> **NOTE:** Avoid using dummy links (links to # or JavaScript function calls) in HTML, as those will fail on browsers without JavaScript capability.

# COBBLING TOGETHER SOME CODE

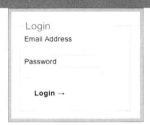

**FIGURE 2.8** The login form, with a modicum of CSS styling.

With some of the fundamentals covered, let's go ahead and start dabbling with JavaScript. I don't expect you to know JavaScript already, of course—that's the purpose of this book—but this next example demonstrates how accessible JavaScript is and provides a sense of context for Part 2's material (i.e., the formal training).

## DEVELOPING BASE FUNCTIONALITY

As a simple but practical example, let's create a login form that is then validated using JavaScript. In later chapters you will learn how to apply Ajax to this form, but adding Ajax here would be a bit too complicated for this early point in the book.

To start, create the HTML form. The form will have three elements: an email address, a password, and a submit button. Below is the most critical HTML, stored in a file named login.html (**Figure 2.8**).

```
<form action="login.php" method="post" id="loginForm">
    <fieldset>
        <legend>Login</legend>
        <div><label for="email">Email Address</label>
            <input type="email" name="email"
            id="email" required></div>

        <div><label for="password">Password</label>
            <input type="password" name="password"
            id="password" required></div>

        <div><label for="submit"></label><input type="submit"
            value="Login &rarr;" id="submit"></div>
    </fieldset>
</form>
<script src="js/login.js"></script>
```

**TIP:** You can download all of the book's code from the corresponding Web site at www.LarryUllman.com.

For simplicity's sake, there's nothing else on the page except for the form. The page also uses a basic CSS file to add some styling; you can download that from the book's corresponding Web site (the CSS file will be in the ch02 folder of the complete downloadable scripts).

The form as written will be submitted to login.php. That script would:

- Validate the submitted email address

- Validate that submitted password

- Confirm that the submitted values match those previously stored in a database

- If a match was made, send a cookie or start a session to track the user

- Redirect the user to a welcoming page

In a later chapter, you'll see all this in action, should you not know how to implement that yourself in PHP and MySQL already. This is the baseline functionality, which will work in all browsers regardless of the browser's JavaScript settings and capabilities. If the client can load an HTML page, this system will be fine. The next step is to progressively enhance it.

## ADDING THE JAVASCRIPT LAYER

In this particular case, progressive enhancement means that JavaScript will be used to validate the form data in the client, only allowing the form to be submitted to the server should the data pass (as in the registration example shown in Figure 1.4).

To start, note that the only thing different about this form from one that wouldn't be tied to JavaScript is that each element has both a name attribute and an id attribute. The name value will be used when the form data is submitted to the server-side PHP script. The id value will be used by the JavaScript. Logically, these two values are the same for each element. Each element on the page, form or otherwise, must also have a unique id value.

The progressively enhanced page also makes use of an external JavaScript file, named login.js. It should be included by the HTML page just before the closing body tag:

```
<script src="js/login.js"></script>
```

Now, here's where things get a little bit complicated, at least for this point in the book. To understand what JavaScript code should go in the file, you must have basic knowledge of event handling.

## HANDLING EVENTS

As mentioned in Chapter 1, JavaScript is an event-driven language, meaning that it only does something after an event has occurred. Examples of events include:

- The loading of a Web page
- Clicking upon an element, like a button or link
- Entering text within a form element
- Moving the cursor over an element (i.e., a *mouseover*)
- Moving the cursor off an element (i.e., a *mouseout*)

In order to have JavaScript validate an HTML form, you must determine what event will trigger the validation code. The events most commonly used for form validation are:

- The form's submission
- Clicking of the submit button (which also triggers a form-submission event)
- Changing the value of a form element
- When a form element loses focus (triggered whether or not the value changed)

Chapter 8, Event Handling, goes into the discussion of events in greater detail. For now, let's just validate the form upon submission. To do that, an *event listener* must be added to the form. An event listener says that when *this event* happens on *this object*, *this function* should be called. Each object, whether it's the entire browser window or a specific element in the page (form element or not), has certain events that it can trigger. The function to be called will normally be a function you define yourself. This combination—object, event type, and function—leads to any number of possibilities.

To watch for the submission event on the form, let's start by grabbing a reference to the form itself. A simple and reliable way of doing that is to use the getElement-ById() method of the document object. The document object refers to the entire HTML content: from the opening html tag to the head and body elements and so on. The document object has a getElementById() method, which takes an ID name as an argument and returns a reference to the corresponding element. That returned value can be assigned to a variable for later use:

```
var loginForm = document.getElementById('loginForm');
```

At this point, so long as there is one element (to be clear, of any type) that has an id value of *loginForm*, the loginForm variable will be a reference to that element. Chapter 9 goes into DOM manipulation in much more detail, but the getElementById() method is so important and yet easy to use, that it's worth introducing here in Chapter 2.

Now that there's a reference to the form, an event listener can be added to it using the code:

```
element.onevent = function;
```

For example:

```
loginForm.onsubmit = validateForm;
```

The sidebar explains this syntax in more technical detail, but this line just says that when the loginForm element experiences a submission event, the validate-Form() function should be called. Note that the function's name is used on the right side of the assignment, without quotation marks around it or parentheses at its end. Neither of these is correct:

```
loginForm.onsubmit = 'validateForm'; // NO!
loginForm.onsubmit = validateForm(); // NO!
```

In theory, the next step would be to define the validateForm() function, which performs the actual form validation. Unfortunately, one more step is required first. I'll explain…

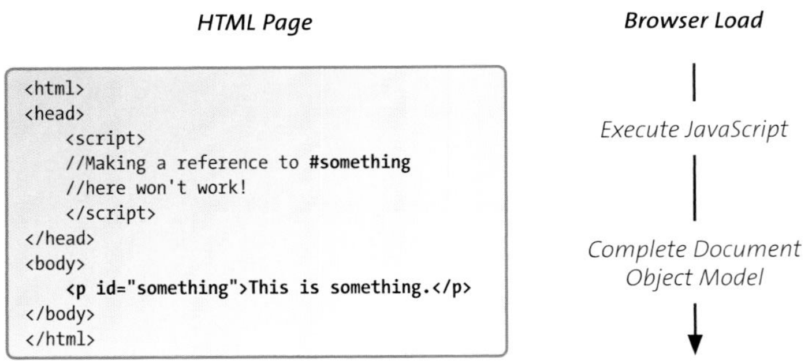

FIGURE 2.9 How a browser
loads an HTML document and
creates the DOM.

*HTML Page*

*Browser Load*

```
<html>
<head>
    <script>
    //Making a reference to #something
    //here won't work!
    </script>
</head>
<body>
    <p id="something">This is something.</p>
</body>
</html>
```

*Execute JavaScript*

*Complete Document
Object Model*

When a client requests a document from a server, the client will receive the document's data in order. For an HTML page, this literally means that the browser first receives the DOCTYPE, then the opening html tag, then the head tag, then the head's content, then the body and the body's content, and so on, until the end of the document. When the browser encounters references to other materials that must be downloaded—CSS files, images and other media, JavaScript, Flash, and so forth, the browser will need to download those, too. In terms of DOM manipulation, this process is important, as the browser cannot present a representation of the DOM until it has a full sense of the HTML page (**Figure 2.9**). In terms of JavaScript, this means that you cannot safely use document.getElementById() until the page's HTML has been loaded by the browser.

The most reliable way to know that it's safe to reference a DOM element is to confirm that the browser has completely loaded the entire page. This, of course, is an event, which means that an event listener can be set to watch for this occurrence:

```
window.onload = init;
```

**TIP:** The reason Web sites seem to load faster when JavaScript is placed near the end of the document is that the browser must pause the rendering of the HTML while it waits for the JavaScript to load.

**NOTE:** I'm simplifying how the browser downloads and loads a Web page to convey the key points. If you're really curious, the gritty details can be found by searching online.

## OBJECT EVENT PROPERTIES

As mentioned in Chapter 1, an object is a special variable type that has predefined *attributes* (i.e., its own internal variables) and *methods* (aka functions). The object notation, or dot, syntax is used to access an object's attributes and methods. The code `loginForm.onsubmit = validateForm` is simply assigning the `validateForm()` function to the `loginForm` object's `onsubmit` property. This may seem strange, but it's the same idea as assigning a numeric value to a variable:

```
var num = 2;
```

In the event listener case, though, the variable is an attribute of an object and the value being assigned is a function: slightly more complicated, but the same principle.

The `loginForm` object has an `onsubmit` property because `loginForm` represents a form element and form elements trigger submission events. This code would not work with, say, a link, because links do not have an `onsubmit` property (links do have `onclick`, though). When referencing an object's event-based properties, use all lowercase: `onsubmit`, not `onSubmit`.

As for the assignment itself, a function needs to be associated with this event; thus the function's *name* is provided on the right side of the assignment. You would not place the function's name in quotation marks, as that would be a string value, not a function. Nor would you use `functionName()`, with the parentheses, as that would be an actual function call.

This code says that the `init()` function should be called when the window object triggers a load event. That `init()` function can then add the event listener to the form, because at that point it's safe to make DOM references:

```
function init() {
    var loginForm = document.getElementById('loginForm');
    loginForm.onsubmit = validateForm;
}
```

Chapter 7, Creating Functions, covers everything you need to know about defining your own functions, but the fundamentals are really simple. First, use the keyword *function*, followed by the function's name and parentheses. (It's common to call a function like this *init*, short for *initialize*, as the function is used to initialize some necessary JavaScript and browser behavior.) The function's actual code—the stuff that will happen when the function is called—goes between curly brackets.

As an added protection, let's add *object detection* here so that the form's event listener will only be added if the browser supports the document.getElement-ById() method:

```
function init() {
    if (document && document.getElementById) {
        var loginForm = document.getElementById('loginForm');
        loginForm.onsubmit = validateForm;
    }
}
```

At this point in time, there are two event listeners. The first is listening for the *load* event of the window, which is an event that will only naturally occur once per page. When that event is triggered, the init() function is called. The second listener is awaiting the submission of the form, which could happen any number of times, including never. For each occurrence of that event, the validateForm() function is called. Defining that function is the final step of this progressive enhancement.

**NOTE:** In reality, browsers have supported the document object and the getElementById() method for more than a decade now, so this particular use of object detection is not really necessary.

### PERFORMING THE VALIDATION

The validateForm() function should validate the form data and return a Boolean value indicating the data's validity. If the function returns true, the form's submission will be allowed to continue onto the server-side script. If the function returns false, the form's submission to the server-side script will be prevented.

The shell of the function looks like this:

```
function validateForm() {
}
```

Now it's time to perform the basic validation, which goes within that shell. For the email address and password, the validation should check that *some value* is present (it's possible to confirm that an email address is of a valid format, but that requires a ton of code). For text inputs, simple validation can be achieved by checking the *length* of its value (i.e., was anything entered). To start, grab a reference to each input, again using getElementById():

```
var email = document.getElementById('email');
var password = document.getElementById('password');
```

> **TIP:** Remember that if the Web page uses HTML5 and the browser supports HTML5, automatic client-side validation will apply, too (as shown in earlier figures).

At this point, each variable is a reference to the corresponding form element. To find that element's current value, refer to the variable's value property: email.value and password.value. Because both are textual elements, the value property of each will have a string value, even if it's an empty string. All strings in JavaScript have a length property, which stores the number of characters in that string. Thus, email.value.length is the number of characters entered into the email input. This, then, can be used to create a simple conditional:

```
if ( (email.value.length > 0) && (password.value.length > 0) ) {
    return true;
} else {
    return false;
}
```

> **NOTE:** Checking the length of an element's value works for text inputs; other form element types are validated in different ways.

FIGURE 2.10 The JavaScript alert, as it appears in Safari.

And there is a simple validation routine. Unless something is entered into both form elements, the form's submission will be prevented from going to the server-side script. However, besides just preventing the submission of the form, the user ought to be made aware of the problem. There are more professional ways of doing so, but for now, an alert box can suffice (**Figures 2.10** and **2.11**):

```
if ( (email.value.length > 0) && (password.value.length > 0) ) {
    return true;
} else {
    alert('Please complete the form!');
    return false;
}
```

**NOTE:** Client-side validation is a convenience to the end user; server-side validation is always still required.

And there you have a simple, progressively enhanced, unobtrusive use of Java-Script that validates an HTML form, prior to sending it to the server. The code block below shows all of this code put together, with some comments documenting the key pieces. There are three top-level (i.e., not nested) components to the script:

- The definition of the validateForm() function

- The definition of the init() function

- The registration of the init() function as the window.onload event handler

**NOTE:** Because the login.php server-side script hasn't been written yet, you will see a server error when the form does pass the validation and the browser tries to access that nonexistent file.

## INVOKING STRICT MODE

JavaScript's own strict mode, which is different than the browser's strict mode already discussed, is a way to enforce more stringent JavaScript behavior in the code you write. Strict mode was added in ECMAScript 5, and is invoked by placing this string within your JavaScript:

```
'use strict';
```

That line can be used once at the top of each script, but is more reliably used as the first line within each function, as you'll see in this book.

When strict mode is invoked, JavaScript code will be executed in slightly different ways than in non-strict mode. Generally speaking, strict mode will:

- Cause errors to be generated by potentially problematic code
- Improve security and performance
- Warn you about using code that will be removed in future standards of the language

In short, strict mode forces you to write better code, which is a very, very good thing.

If you want to see the details of the changes enforced by strict mode, you can find those online, although most of them will not mean much to you at this point in your learning.

Although, for very technical reasons, it doesn't matter in what order these three components are written, I've chosen to code them in that order so that:

- The validateForm() function is defined before it is referenced within the init() function.
- The init() function is defined before it is assigned to the window.onload property.

Again, this isn't required, but it makes logical sense to structure the code in this way. Each function also begins with:

```
'use strict';
```

The reason for this line is explained in the sidebar "Invoking Strict Mode."

```
// login.js
// Function called when the form is submitted.
// Function validates the form data and returns a Boolean value.
function validateForm() {
    'use strict';
    // Get references to the form elements:
    var email = document.getElementById('email');
    var password = document.getElementById('password');
    // Validate!
    if ( (email.value.length > 0) && (password.value.length > 0) ) {
        return true;
    } else {
        alert('Please complete the form!');
        return false;
    }
} // End of validateForm() function.
// Function called when the window has been loaded.
// Function needs to add an event listener to the form.
function init() {
    'use strict';
    // Confirm that document.getElementById() can be used:
    if (document && document.getElementById) {
        var loginForm = document.getElementById('loginForm');
        loginForm.onsubmit = validateForm;
    }
} // End of init() function.
// Assign an event listener to the window's load event:
window.onload = init;
```

# STEAL THIS JAVASCRIPT

As I say in this chapter's introduction, the fact that you can use JavaScript without really knowing it is both a blessing and a curse. If you've attempted JavaScript on a project while only barely knowing what you're doing, don't be embarrassed: Lots of programmers have done it, even me. Hopefully, you were able to accomplish what you set out to do. But more than likely, the JavaScript you used wasn't optimal or reliable, which is why you've turned to this book to master the language.

Toward that end, one recommendation I would make to aid in your learning is that you regularly get in the habit of looking at other JavaScript you find online. I don't just mean in tutorials and documentation, but also in the sites you visit, because JavaScript in the browser is, without limitation, viewable. Just like most content loaded in the Web browser, such as images, there's no way to prevent users from seeing the raw JavaScript source code being used on a page.

So get in the habit of viewing other people's JavaScript, not to steal it (but "View This JavaScript" isn't nearly as flashy a section heading), but for your own edification. You'll certainly come across code that's way beyond your comprehension, code that's outdated, and code that's conflicting in approach with what this book advocates. But by examining what others are doing, you'll get a great sense of the scope, abilities, and history of this vital programming language. When you do come across something that's confusing or contradictory, make a note of it and see if you don't find the answer, or a better solution, over the course of this book.

**TIP:** For any JavaScript help, turn to the book's supporting forum at www.LarryUllman.com/forums/.

**NOTE:** You shouldn't actually steal JavaScript code from other sites not just for moral reasons, but because the code could have security flaws or dependencies that would undermine your site.

# WRAPPING **UP**

Whereas Chapter 1 provides a big picture introduction to the JavaScript language as a whole, Chapter 2 is a gentle introduction to JavaScript code and implementation. In it, you read about:

- DOCTYPE and the browser modes

- HTML5, its new form elements, and the new form attributes

- Embedding JavaScript within HTML, using the `script` element

Along the way you also saw the HTML5 template to be used as the basis for all HTML pages in this book.

The bulk of the chapter used real-world code to walk through a specific example: validating a login form upon submission. You learned the absolute basics about event handling, creating your own functions, and referencing page elements via `document.getElementById()`. You can refer back to this example if you get confused by some of these foundational elements as you continue to learn new things in subsequent chapters.

Going forward, I also recommend that you:

- Be careful about file paths in your HTML code (i.e., absolute vs. relative)

- Remember to add the `novalidate` attribute to opening `form` tags so that the JavaScript code can do its thing in browsers that would otherwise perform HTML5 validation

- Keep the approaches of *unobtrusive JavaScript*, *progressive enhancement*, and *object detection* in mind

- Consider looking at the JavaScript code in use on the Web sites you visit

If you don't already know the easy ways you can view a site's JavaScript in your Web browser, then continue to the next chapter where I explain how, while also introducing many other key JavaScript development tools.

# 3

# **TOOLS** OF THE **TRADE**

The goal for the first part of this book is to provide a context for the rest of the book, especially Part 2: JavaScript Fundamentals. As you saw in the first two chapters, this context includes an overview of what JavaScript is, a bit of its history, some programming approaches, and a quick introduction to how you'll use JavaScript within HTML. This chapter discusses the last piece of the introductory puzzle: the software you'll use to write, execute, and debug JavaScript. Along the way you'll also find plenty of online resources with which you should familiarize yourself.

# THE GREAT **DEBATE**:
# **TEXT EDITOR** OR **IDE**?

**FIGURE 3.1** A JavaScript file, with its correct syntax nicely formatted.

```
3    // Function called when the form is submitted.
4    // Function validates the form data and returns a Boolean value.
5    function validateForm() {
6        'use strict';
7
8        // Get references to the form elements:
9        var email = document.getElementById('email');
10       var password = document.getElementById('password');
11
12       // Validate!
13       if ( (email.value.length > 0) && (password.value.length > 0) ) {
14           return true;
15       } else {
16           alert('Please complete the form!');
17           return false;
18       }
19
20   } // End of validateForm() function.
```

The first piece of software you'll need is something to actually program JavaScript in. When making this decision, you'll need to choose between a *text editor* or an *Integrated Development Environment* (IDE). I'll say up front that my historical preference when it comes to programming is to use a plain text editor, but that doesn't mean a text editor is best for you. But to start, let's look at some key features of text editors and IDEs: what they mean and why they're useful.

## COMMON FEATURES

Obviously, the first quality an application must have is that it's available for the operating system you're using. But I'll add that if you regularly work on multiple computers that have different operating systems—say, a Mac at home but Windows at work, you should select an application that runs on multiple operating systems. By doing so, you can have a familiar programming environment regardless of where you're sitting.

On a similar note, you should choose an application that directly supports the language or technology with which you're working, JavaScript in this case. Most programming applications support multiple languages, but you want it to specifically support JavaScript (or whatever else you're looking for at the time). This may seem obvious, but there are many benefits of true language support, beginning with *syntax highlighting*. When an application supports a programming language, the application is aware of keywords and structures found in the language, and will format the code accordingly (**Figure 3.1**). Not only does syntax highlighting

```
 9    var email = Document.getElementById('email');
10    var password = document.getElementById('password');
```

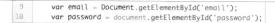

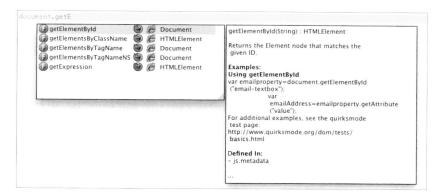

make code easier to read, but it tends to minimize errors, as syntax highlighting is implicitly a syntax validator: invalid keywords and syntax will not be formatted properly (**Figure 3.2**).

Higher-end support for a language includes *code intelligence*, a broad category of features that will literally do some of the work for you. For example, if the software performs simple balancing of quotation marks, parentheses, brackets, and braces, when you create, say, an opening parenthesis, the application will create the closing one immediately. Not only does this automatic insertion save you a keystroke, but it makes it less likely that you will fail to properly balance such characters, a common cause of syntax errors. As another example, software used for Web development will normally create the closing HTML tag when you enter an opening tag.

Another type of code intelligence is *code completion*, where the application offers up specific suggestions of variables or functions that you can select (**Figure 3.3**).

With a suggestion selected, pressing Enter/Return or Tab inserts that item into your code. Code completion is based upon both the language or technology in use and the actual code you've written, meaning the variables you've created will be present in the list of options. Even higher-end code intelligence includes *refactoring*: you change, for example, the name of a variable, function, or file, and the application will automatically update all references to that item.

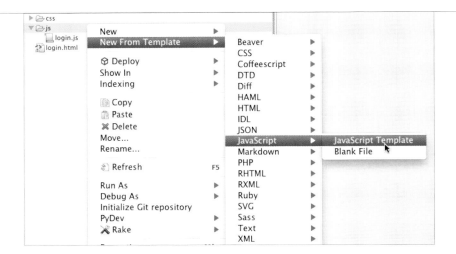

**FIGURE 3.4** Aptana Studio allows you to create new files directly within existing projects.

Another way that a text editor or IDE can "support" a language or technology is by being able to execute code within the application itself. Although this can be nice, many applications choose to run JavaScript and HTML by invoking external browsers, as how the page looks and works in the browser is the goal.

You'll appreciate it if the software you choose has a good way of managing files and projects. With some applications, creating a new document is done the same way as you would when using, say, Microsoft Word (you walk through some variation on File > New, navigate to where the file should be saved on the computer, and then provide a name for the file). With other programs, you can create new files entirely within the application itself, immediately adding it to the current project (**Figure 3.4**). This may seem like a minor distinction, but it's the little things that add up to big differences. Some applications can recognize different projects, letting you readily access any file in that project. Some software also support *workspaces*, which is a destination for a group of projects (you might have one workspace for client projects and another for personal ones). Next, if the output is destined for the Web, having built-in FTP capability is great, saving you that trip to the separate FTP application. And if you're using *version control software*, such as Git (http://git-scm.com/) or Subversion (http://subversion.apache.org/), see if your particular version control package is supported, too.

**NOTE:** Code intelligence is probably the biggest difference between IDEs, which normally do have it, and text editors, which normally don't.

FIGURE 3.5 A network monitor—this one in Safari—shows network activity, including Ajax requests.

Next up is *debugging*. No matter how smart, thorough, or careful you are, program in any language and you'll spend a good amount of time debugging. If an application has a built-in debugger (which would be language-specific), you can execute code in either standard or debugging mode. In debugging mode, you can set breakpoints to stop the code's execution at certain spots. By doing so, you can perhaps see the logic that is, or is not, being followed, and examine the values of variables and crucial points. You'll see examples of this in action during the discussion of Firebug, toward the end of the chapter. More sophisticated debuggers allow you to change the values of variables on the fly to see what happens, or to otherwise execute new bits of code in the hope that doing so will illuminate the problem.

Some applications have built-in support for *unit testing*, which is a programming approach in which you write tests to verify that specific bits of code are working as they should. Then you run your code against those tests. As you modify the code, continue to run the tests to confirm that nothing has broken as a result of the latest changes. Taken further, Test Driven Development (TDD) *begins* with the unit tests and then writes code that passes those tests.

Another handy debugging feature is a *network monitor*: a tool that displays the network requests being made, including the data being sent and the response received (**Figure 3.5**). When working with something like Ajax, having a network monitor is a great asset.

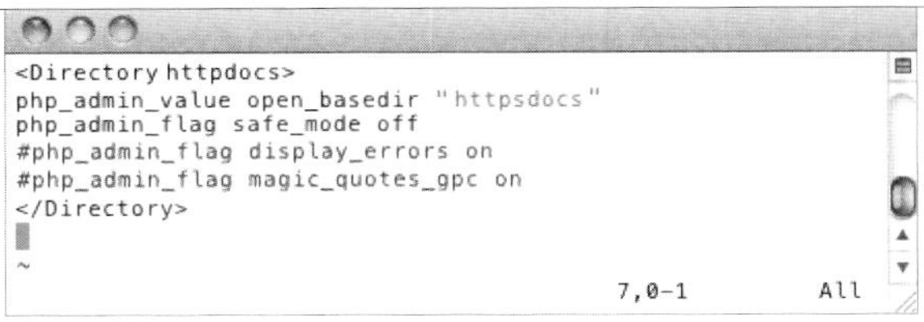

FIGURE 3.6 The nongraphical vi editor, being used to edit a text file on a remote server.

```
<Directory httpdocs>
php_admin_value open_basedir "httpsdocs"
php_admin_flag safe_mode off
#php_admin_flag display_errors on
#php_admin_flag magic_quotes_gpc on
</Directory>

~
                              7,0-1          All
```

Finally, I'll add that with Web development in particular, selecting an application that can render HTML and CSS (i.e., What You See Is What You Get, WYSIWYG, functionality) is beneficial, as is a DOM viewer and manipulator. With any application, regardless of the language you're using it for, a good help system, manual, and other documentation is a must. I also like my software to have top-notch search and replace features, including support for regular expressions (but you have to know regular expressions in order for that to be useful).

**NOTE:** Chapter 12, Error Management, introduces unit testing.

## COMPARING THE TWO

With a sense of what features matter the most, let's look at the primary differences between text editors and IDEs. After that, I'll highlight a handful of specific applications in both categories. First, though, I should say that the decision between a text editor or an IDE, let alone a specific application within each group, is a surprisingly personal thing, with virtual online wars being waged over the virtues of application *X* versus application *Y*. My intent isn't to advocate for one application type, let alone a specific program, but to present a guidebook to help you in making your decision.

Text editors, also called *plain text editors*, are simpler than IDEs, and are often much cheaper. A cheap commercial text editor may only run you around $20 or $40, with an expensive text editor nearing $100. Conversely, a cheap commercial IDE probably starts around $70, with expensive ones costing several hundred.

Text editors require fewer hardware resources to run—disk space, memory, and processor activity, meaning they are better choices if you have an older computer. In fact, the most basic text editors such as **vi** and **emacs** have no graphical interface at all and can be used to edit text when connected to a remote server (e.g., using SSH, **Figure 3.6**).

The focus in a text editor is the text itself. The benefit of this approach, and the reason why I generally prefer text editors, is that it means you can master a single application and then use it for many different technologies and languages.

Just because text editors tend to be simpler than IDEs does not mean they are simple. The best text editors have a slew of features built in, are easily extended (to add features or support for other languages), and can execute code without leaving the application. While text editors are easy to begin using, you should plan on spending some time reading the application's documentation in order to learn how to make the most of the software.

When it comes to features, though, a text editor should provide syntax highlighting, but often won't do much in terms of code intelligence. File management can vary: For example, TextMate supports version control but not FTP, and TextMate allows you to open a folder of files at once, but has no formal sense of projects. Built-in debugging is more rare with text editors, but some do have the ability to execute the code you write from the application, either internally or via a connection to an external executable.

And then there are the IDEs. IDEs are going to have all of the bells and whistles, which is great once you've mastered the program, but this is a hurdle to overcome when you're first starting. If you need code intelligence, project management, top-of-the-line debugging, and more, you'll want to find a good IDE. If you do so, plan on doing more research to select the right IDE for you, and after that, spend some time reading the application's documentation, or watching online screencasts, to learn how best to use it. Frankly, even properly installing and configuring an IDE can be a challenge (for some IDEs).

With IDEs, you'll also probably need a bigger budget and a more robust computer, as an IDE requires more disk space, memory, and a faster processor than a text editor requires. But if you want code completion, you'll probably need an IDE. Built-in debugging? An IDE. Built-in executable? An IDE. WYSIWYG editor? You guessed it: an IDE. And, to be fair, the same IDE can often support multiple technologies.

When it comes to choosing between a text editor and an IDE, you obviously need to decide what's right for you, based upon:

- The hardware you're using
- The other languages and technologies you regularly work with
- What features you need
- How much time you're willing to spend to get going
- Your budget

In many ways, this decision is also about short-term vs. long-term goals and benefits. You can select, download, install, start, and begin using a text editor in a fraction of the time it will take you to do all that with an IDE. But once you're comfortable with the IDE, you'll probably be able to write and debug the same code in less time than it would take you with a text editor.

Instead of choosing between the two, you may want to consider selecting one of each. Clearly, there are merits to both application types; by mastering a text editor and an IDE, you can then decide which to use for any particular task or project.

## A HANDFUL OF TEXT EDITORS

If you think that a text editor may suit you, the following applications are worth your consideration:

**TIP:** Most commercial applications have a free trial available.

- **Komodo Edit** (www.activestate.com/komodo-edit): runs on Windows, Mac OS X, and Linux; free.
- **UltraEdit** (www.ultraedit.com): Windows, Mac OS X, and Linux; $60.
- **Notepad++** (http://notepad-plus-plus.org/): Windows; free.
- **EditPlus** (www.editplus.com): Windows, $35.
- **TextMate** (http://macromates.com): Mac OS X; approximately $57.
- **TextWrangler** (www.barebones.com): Mac OS X; free.

- **BBEdit** (`www.barebones.com`): Mac OS X; $100.

- **Emacs** (`www.gnu.org/software/emacs/emacs.html`): most operating systems; free.

- **Vim** (`www.vim.org`): most operating systems; free.

> **NOTE:** All prices are in U.S. dollars and accurate at the time of this writing.

I will say that I don't regularly use Windows and certainly not for development purposes, so I can't provide an educated recommendation as to a good Windows text editor. That being said, those listed here are the ones I see most frequently recommended, and this book's technical editor loves Notepad++. For Mac OS X, I've used the ones listed here and can wholeheartedly recommend them all.

## A COUPLE OF IDES

If you think an IDE is more appropriate for you, there are again several to choose from. In all likelihood, though, you're not going to find an IDE dedicated to just JavaScript, but rather an IDE oriented toward another language, that also supports JavaScript. To start, here are two commercial and one open source IDE:

- **Adobe Dreamweaver** (`www.adobe.com/go/dreamweaver/`): Windows and Mac OS X; $400.

  Dreamweaver (often represented as *DW*) is a Web development application, not a programming IDE. This means it does WYSIWYG rendering of HTML and CSS, and recognizes JavaScript. DW has even been extended to support PHP, allowing you to write both client-side and server-side code in one application.

- **Komodo IDE** (`www.activestate.com/komodo-ide`): Windows, Mac OS X, and Linux; $295.

  ActiveState makes both the free Komodo Edit and the commercial Komodo IDE. The IDE has code intelligence, FTP support, an integrated debugger, version control, and more. Komodo IDE can also be used for PHP, Ruby, Python, Perl, and other languages. Komodo IDE recognizes many common JavaScript frameworks, and has a network monitoring tool.

- **Aptana Studio** (`www.aptana.com`): Windows, Mac OS X, and Linux; free.

   Aptana Studio is an excellent, free IDE, based upon Eclipse (more on Eclipse in a moment, but this means you can install Aptana Studio as a standalone application or as a plug-in for the Eclipse you're already using). Aptana Studio features code intelligence, FTP support, an integrated debugger, version control, and more. Aptana Studio can also be used for PHP, Ruby, and Python.

For what it's worth, many Web developers are already using Dreamweaver, which makes it a reasonable choice, although it's not much of a programmer's application. I've heard great things about Komodo IDE, but haven't used it personally. Aptana Studio is my IDE of choice for JavaScript development (it's good and the fact that it's free fits in nicely with my frugality).

Finally, I'll mention three pillars of the IDE community. The first two are both long-standing, open source projects, but they can be less approachable for beginners. The third company has a handful of commercial applications for you to choose from.

**Eclipse** (`www.eclipse.org`) is such a powerful IDE that many other IDEs are just technology-specific implementations of it, including Aptana Studio and Adobe Flash Builder. Eclipse runs on Windows, Mac OS X, and Linux, and is free.

**NetBeans** (`www.netbeans.com`) is a common alternative to Eclipse, runs on Windows, Mac OS X, and Linux, and is also free. NetBeans is primarily a Java IDE (not JavaScript), but supports other languages, too.

The company JetBrains (`www.jetbrains.com`) makes a series of excellent IDEs, starting with **IntelliJ IDEA** (their Java IDE). Their Web development IDE, **WebStorm**, starts at $70 for a personal license. Their **PhpStorm** application adds PHP support to WebStorm, and starts at $100. The JetBrains applications run on Windows, Mac OS X, and Linux, and have a range of features depending upon the exact model you choose.

# THE **BROWSER**: YOUR **FRIEND**, YOUR **ENEMY**

To use the Web, you need a Web browser. To develop Web sites, you need as many Web browsers as you can get your hands on. If everyone accessing a Web site was only using the same version of the same browser with the same screen resolution and roughly the same connection speed, being a Web developer would be so much easier. As you know, none of those criteria applies in reality, particularly with the ability for people to now load a Web site on their mobile phone, electronic reader (e.g., Kindle, Nook), other portable devices, and gaming machines (e.g., Xbox, PlayStation, Wii). It has become a challenge to test a site on even a small subset of the potential clients. But unless you're developing a site exclusively to be accessed via mobile devices, your first testing tool is still the desktop Web browser. In this section, I'll briefly introduce the most common browsers (as I write this today; something new and significant may come out tomorrow).

Keep in mind that I'm really focusing here on *the browser as a development tool*, not which browser you should regularly use. In fact, there's an argument to be made for distinguishing between your default personal browser and your development browser. For example, I normally surf using Safari, then Chrome, but develop in Firefox and Opera (Internet Explorer is for final testing). I find this arrangement works well for me because Safari does not have all the development tools I want, but after loading Firefox up with all the add-ons I need, the browser becomes painfully slow for regular use.

As a point of reference, the most current stats (October 2011, at the time of this writing) for browser usage, grouped by browser (i.e., all versions together), are:

- Internet Explorer, 34.2%
- Firefox, 26.2%
- Chrome, 22.2%
- Safari, 6.4%
- Opera, 2.4%
- Mobile and other browsers, 8.6%

Let's take a quick look at the main five browsers, in alphabetical order. For each, I'll present some perspective for that browser, and what extensions you'll want to consider installing in order to make it a better development tool. When it comes to the browser as debugging and development software, having a wide range of possible extensions makes all the difference.

FIGURE 3.7 The Web Developer extension.

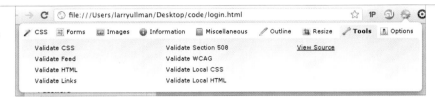

## GOOGLE CHROME

Google's Chrome (www.google.com/chrome) is one of the newest browsers around, and with the weight of Google behind it, has quickly risen to a third-place market share (by the time you read this, it might be in second place). One great aspect of Chrome is that the application automatically updates itself, so barring specific interference, Chrome users are always running the most current version of the browser. Extensions you ought to consider include:

- *Web Developer*, a slew of useful tools for HTML, CSS, JavaScript, and more (**Figure 3.7**)

- *Pendule*, another collection of excellent Web development tools

- *Firebug Lite*, a stripped-down version of the excellent Firebug utility

- *JavaScript Tester*, a simple way to test JavaScript on the page

- *Speed Tracer*, for checking the page's performance (created by Google)

- *Validity*, an interface for validating HTML

**NOTE:** Firebug Lite does not include many of the features that make Firebug so great, such as JavaScript debugging, JavaScript profiling, and a network monitor.

## MOZILLA FIREFOX

Firefox (www.mozilla.org) is a descendant of one of the original browsers, Netscape Navigator. Firefox has long been considered the best browser for Web developers; in fact, Web developers probably represent a good portion of Firefox's market share. The reason Firefox makes such an excellent developer tool is that it was one of the first browsers to be extensible, and therefore has a wonderful library of available extensions:

- *Firebug*, the original, best Web developer extension, to be covered in detail shortly

- *Web Developer*, a slew of useful tools for HTML, CSS, JavaScript, and more

- *YSlow!*, for checking the page's performance (created by Yahoo!)

- *Greasemonkey*, an interface for executing additional JavaScript code if it were part of the page (e.g., to change the page's behavior)

- *Total Validator*, for validating the HTML of a page, validating its accessibility, and testing for broken links and spelling errors

- *View Source Chart*, a quick, visual way to view a page's HTML source (**Figure 3.8**)

- *Console2*, a better JavaScript console

- *JS View*, a quick-access menu to view the JavaScript source code of the page, including that in external files (**Figure 3.9**)

**FIGURE 3.8** How View Source Chart visually represents the HTML source code.

**FIGURE 3.9** JS View provides direct access to a page's JavaScript code and style sheets.

## MICROSOFT INTERNET EXPLORER

And then, there's Microsoft Internet Explorer (`www.microsoft.com/ie`). What can I say about IE? It's certainly the most used browser. Still. The fact is that, as a Web developer, you should not be using IE. Not to be one of "those people," but even if the day comes when IE is the best browser around—and that day won't come—you still shouldn't use IE as payback for how difficult IE has made life for the Web developer. On the other hand, maybe having to create sites that work on both good browsers *and* IE has kept Web developers in business. But still...

With that diatribe out of the way, I'll repeat quite frankly that you shouldn't be using Internet Explorer as a development browser: it just doesn't have the muscle of the others. For example, while there are a couple of extensions that you can add to IE—I'd specifically recommend the IE Developer Toolbar (also created by Microsoft) and the Web Accessibility Toolbar—the possibilities just don't measure up to what's available for Firefox and Chrome. Don't get me wrong, the Developer Toolbar added in more recent versions of IE is good, and comparable to Safari's Web Inspector, but that's about the extent of debugging tools for IE.

The best advice I can give you regarding browsers is this: Get your site working perfectly using another browser, and then start testing it in IE. Because lots of regular people are using IE. Still.

**TIP:** The IE Developer Tools in IE9 and later allow you to run pages while emulating earlier versions of IE, too.

## OPERA

Opera (`www.opera.com`), released by Opera software, is one of the oldest browsers around, but has been routinely overlooked. In part, this was because it used to be a commercial application, and few people saw the need to pay for a tool when free alternatives were available. But from a user's perspective, Opera has often been at the forefront of supporting emerging technologies, meaning that Opera users (both of them!) often get a better Web experience.

**FIGURE 3.10** Opera's Dragonfly development tool, built into the browser itself.

Opera supports a few good extensions, but recommend you just start with Dragonfly (**Figure 3.10**), their own Web development tool, built into the browser. Just of few of Dragonfly's features include:

- A DOM inspector

- High-end JavaScript navigation and debugging

- A network monitor

- An error console

You should download Opera and check it out for yourself!

**TIP:** Opera is frequently used on many mobile devices.

## APPLE SAFARI

For years, Safari (`www.apple.com/safari`) was a browser only used by Mac people, and not necessarily the browser of choice for all Mac users, either. Although Safari is available on Windows, I can't imagine that many Windows people are inclined to use it, either out of preference or habit. But Safari has become an extremely important browser over the past couple of years. How? By being the default browser on the iPhone, iPod Touch, and iPad, making it the browser being used on the most popular mobile devices today.

For years, Safari wasn't very good as a developer's browser (one of the few things that Safari and IE have in common), but things have improved some. More current versions of Safari include a collection of a developer tools, similar to IE's Developer Toolbar and Opera's Dragonfly. To access Safari's developer tools, you

**FIGURE 3.11** Check the box at the bottom of the panel to enable the Develop menu.

**FIGURE 3.12** Safari's Web Inspector provides a nice interface for viewing all the page's resources, including cookies and local storage.

must check the "Show Develop menu in menu bar" option on the Advanced Preferences pane (**Figure 3.11**).

**TIP:** The Develop menu also provides the option to disable JavaScript, so you can experience your page as some of your users might.

On older versions of Safari, you can only enable this menu by executing the following command within the Terminal application:

```
defaults write com.apple.Safari IncludeDebugMenu 1
```

The Develop menu includes several options, such as the ability to profile the page's JavaScript code, but the most important option is Show Web Inspector. Like Opera's Dragonfly, Safari's Web Inspector provides:

- A DOM inspector

- The ability to view the particulars of every page resource (**Figure 3.12**)

- A network monitor

- A JavaScript debugger

- A console interface

- Tools to profile the page's performance and JavaScript

## TESTING ON MULTIPLE BROWSERS

The focus in the past couple of pages was how to use browsers as development tools. At some point in the development process, though, you'll need to start testing your masterpiece on various browsers in order to see how good the page looks and how well it behaves. This is a challenge. If you have one computer, you can only have a single version of each browser installed, which will prevent you from testing a site on, say, both Firefox 6 and Firefox 8 or Safari 5 and Safari 4. But this is a solvable problem, especially if you're able to throw some money at it.

You ought to do two things before attempting to test your site in a bevy of browsers: Have the site fully functioning and looking as it should on the browsers you do have on your computer. Identify, with your client when applicable, exactly which browsers and versions you need to test against.

As you get more comfortable with JavaScript and the other areas of Web development, you'll learn what JavaScript, HTML, and CSS works reliably across all browsers and what code does not. And remember that if you're adhering to the concept of *object detection*, browser-specific complications will be less common.

Once you've established basic, reliable functionality and appearance, and identified target browsers, you can begin testing your work against those targets. To just test the look of an HTML page, there are tools such as the free Browsershots (`http://browsershots.org/`) and the commercial Adobe BrowserLab (`http://browserlab.adobe.com/`), among others. These services provide snapshots of how your page rendered in a long list of browsers. This is great, but when you're working with JavaScript, you need to know how it *runs*, not just looks.

> **TIP:** When also using Dreamweaver, Adobe BrowserLab supports testing of various JavaScript states in multiple browsers.

One option is to purchase multiple computers, running different operating systems and different versions of the various Web browsers. Unless you're part of a large organization with the finances and physical space to accommodate multiple computers, this is impractical.

A second option is to use virtualization software on your computer, thereby creating multiple virtual machines, running different operating systems and browser versions. This is not an unreasonable solution, but requires a powerful primary computer (the one running the virtualization software), with lots of RAM and hard drive space.

There are other options that require no installation on your computer and no maintenance of multiple operating systems. First, there's Spoon (www.spoon.net), which is application-emulation software that represents most of the key browsers. At the time of this writing, Spoon is free. Unfortunately, Spoon doesn't run on a Mac (again, at the time of this writing), and Microsoft forced Spoon to stop providing emulated versions of Internet Explorer. That being said, there are software packages available for just testing a page on a range of IE versions (e.g., IETest, www.my-debugbar.com), and the latest versions of IE can do that tool, thanks to the IE Developer Toolbar.  These, though, only run on Windows, still leaving Mac users out in the cold.

In order to be able to perform live testing of your site in multiple browsers, without installing and maintaining multiple operating systems, you can turn to one of several online services, such as:

- CrossBrowserTesting (www.crossbrowsertesting.com)

- BrowserCam (www.browsercam.com)

- Sauce Labs (www.saucelabs.com)

- Browsera (www.browsera.com)

- browserling (www.browserling.com)

- Mogotest (www.mogotest.com)

- Cloud Testing (www.cloudtesting.com)

These are all commercial services, with a range of prices based upon usage. Some of these sites provide virtualization capability, letting you directly interact with your Web page using the browser of choice. Others don't actually provide you with a virtual browser to use, but, like the snapshot services, automatically run your page and, instead of just returning screen shots, also report any JavaScript errors encountered. A couple of these services also offer up mobile virtualization, in order to see how a site looks and functions in various smart phones and such.

Manufacturers of most devices or device operating systems also provide emulators for you to use to test your software or Web site, often at no cost (although you may need to be enrolled in some sort of developer program).

## TESTING JAVASCRIPT

With a sense of the browser landscape, it's time to talk about how you can directly test JavaScript code. You can certainly create an HTML page and embed JavaScript within it using the `script` element (as explained in the previous chapter), but sometimes it's nice to be able to simply execute a bit of JavaScript without making a big production of it. In fact, this is exactly the approach that several of the following chapters will take to demonstrate new ideas.

Without creating an HTML page, there are other ways you can execute JavaScript code:

- Using your IDE or text editor's capabilities

- Using a browser's tools or extensions

- Using third-party sites

How you go about the first method—executing JavaScript within an IDE or text editor—depends entirely upon the application you're using. To figure out how to do that, just check out the software's corresponding documentation (assuming it's not obvious). Here I'll explain how to use a third-party site, and the end of the chapter will cover executing JavaScript using Firebug in Firefox.

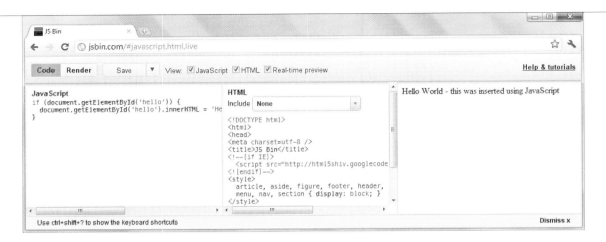

**FIGURE 3.13** JS Bin is an amazing Web-based service for practicing JavaScript.

A wonderful tool, by the brilliant Remy Sharp, is JS Bin (www.jsbin.com). JS Bin provides up to three panes: one for the JavaScript, one for the HTML, and one for the rendered result (**Figure 3.13**). You ought to look at the help and tutorials pages, because this is a wonderful, useful tool, but here's a quick start guide:

**NOTE:** JS Bin is frequently updated with new features, so some of the particulars I explain here may change in time.

1. Load www.jsbin.com in any modern browser.

2. Use the View check boxes to dictate which panes you want visible.

3. Use the vertical dividers to resize the panes as needed.

4. Manipulate the HTML, if needed, for the code to be tested.

   You'll note that the default HTML is an HTML5 document, similar to the template outlined in Chapter 2, JavaScript in Action.

5. If you're using a framework, select it from the HTML pane's Include menu (**Figure 3.14**).

   You can include many different frameworks in the test, including multiple frameworks (such as both jQuery and jQuery UI). How great is that?

**Keyboard Shortcuts**

| Shortcut | Action |
|---|---|
| ctrl + → | Focus HTML panel |
| ctrl + ← | Focus JavaScript panel |
| ctrl + 1 | Source tab |
| ctrl + 2 | Rendered preview tab |
| ctrl + / | Toggle comment on single line |
| ctrl + alt + . | Close current HTML element |
| esc | Code complete (JavaScript only) |
| ctrl + s | Save current Bin |
| ctrl + shift + s | Clone current Bin |
| tab | Indents selected lines |
| shift + tab | Unindents selected lines |

**FIGURE 3.14** JS Bin supports inclusion of all the common frameworks.

**FIGURE 3.15** JS Bin's keyboard shortcuts.

6. Enter your JavaScript in the JavaScript panel.

   Depending upon the specific code, the results may be reflected in real time as you type!

   If there are problems, you'll see those listed in a red block at the bottom of the JavaScript panel.

7. Press the Escape key to invoke code completion!

   Type "d" and press Escape, and JS Bin will automatically complete the code as *document*. Again, how great is that?

8. Press Control + Shift + ? to bring up a list of keyboard shortcuts (**Figure 3.15**).

   There aren't that many shortcuts, but they're useful. Press Escape to close the keyboard shortcuts window.

9. Select an option from the Save menu to save the work you've done.

   For example, you can download the complete HTML and JavaScript to your computer, you can save it as a custom JS Bin template, or just click Save to create a URL specific to the work you've just done.

An alternative to JS Bin is jsFiddle (www.jsfiddle.net). The intent is the same, but jsFiddle has a more complex interface, letting you also work with CSS, among other features.

# ERRORS AND DEBUGGING

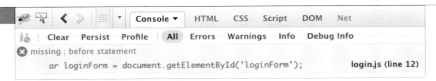

**FIGURE 3.16** A syntactical error shown in Firebug's Console panel.

Tragically, debugging is a skill only really learned through practice, but the good news is that you'll get lots of practice! To be completely honest, JavaScript can be a challenge to debug, more so than other languages in my experience, largely due to those pesky browsers. But there are definitely tricks to be learned, the most important of which are presented in this chapter, along with some of the basics of error types and causes.

In Chapter 12, you'll learn how to handle the errors that do arise in a graceful manner.

## ERROR TYPES

Three general types of errors may occur:

- Syntactical

- Run-time

- Logical

Syntactical errors are caused by improper syntax and prevent JavaScript from running at all. For example, failing to balance all quotation marks, parentheses, and curly brackets will have this effect. Syntactical errors can be minimized by using a text editor or IDE that provides syntax highlighting and character balancing. The good news about syntactical errors is that they're generally easy to find and fix. Just be certain to watch your browser's error console (**Figure 3.16**) so you're made aware of syntactical errors when they occur. The bad news about syntactical errors is that the error message won't necessarily accurately represent the problem. For example, Figure 3.16 says there's a "missing ; before statement," but the actual problem is that the keyword var was entered as just *ar*.

**NOTE:** If your JavaScript code doesn't seem to execute at all, it could be because of a syntactical error.

Run-time errors are those that occur while the JavaScript code is being executed. Examples include referencing objects or functions that don't exist. Again, the browser's error console will report such problems. Many browser-specific issues (e.g., varied support for specific features) qualify as run-time errors.

Logical errors aren't true errors in the sense that the browser or IDE will report a problem, but occur when the result of some code isn't what you expect it to be. In a word, logical errors are *bugs*, commonly caused by the code doing exactly what you told it to, meaning that the source of the mistake can be found between the keyboard and your chair! Fortunately, applying some best practices—covered in this book—will help to prevent logical errors. When they do occur, and they inevitably will, applying the debugging techniques outlined in a couple of pages should help you squash the bug.

## COMMON ERROR CAUSES

The causes of many common errors won't mean much to you yet, as you haven't been formally taught most of the language (acknowledging that you've probably played with JavaScript some). Still, there are a few things you should know to watch out for:

- **Variable names**

  Variable names in JavaScript are case-sensitive, meaning that `myVar` and `myvar` are two different things. Find a consistent naming scheme (to be discussed in the next chapter) and stick to it!

- **Function names**

  Function names are also case-sensitive, whether you're the one who has defined the function or not (i.e., the function is predefined for you).

> **NOTE:** JavaScript is a case-sensitive language!

- **Object names**

  Object names are, yes, also case-sensitive. When using, say, the `Math` object in Chapter 4, Simple Variable Types, you must write `Math`, not *math* or *MATH*.

- **An imbalance of quotation marks, parentheses, angle brackets, or curly braces**

  As I just stated, an imbalance of quotation marks, parentheses, angle brackets, or curly braces all lead to syntactical errors. Having a good text editor or IDE can go a long way toward ensuring there's a closing character for each opening one.

- **Mistakenly using = instead of ==**

  In the next chapter, you'll formally learn that a single equals sign (=) is the *assignment* operator, and in Chapter 5, Using Control Structures, you'll see that a double equals sign (==) is the *equality* operator. The first assigns a value to a variable; the second tests if two values are equal. Using a single equals sign when you should use two leads to logical errors.

- **Referencing objects that don't yet exist**

  Explained in Chapter 2, this can happen if JavaScript attempts to access DOM elements before the DOM has been fully loaded (among other reasons).

- **Treating an object of one type as if it were another type**

  This will mean more in time, but you'll sometimes get errors—both runtime and logical—if you treat, for example, a non-string as a string or a non-number as a number.

- **Using a reserved word**

  There are a couple dozen reserved words in JavaScript: `var`, `function`, and so forth. You cannot use one of those reserved words as the name of your variable or function. That being said, I've never been inclined to include the list of reserved words in a book: many resources online will do that for you and the list is too long to memorize regardless. But if you use descriptive names for the variables and functions you create, you're unlikely to conflict with a reserved word, which are more generic by design.

## DEBUGGING TECHNIQUES

With an understanding of the fundamental error types and common causes, let's look at some debugging techniques.

- **Get a good text editor or IDE.**

  Not to belabor the point, but choosing and mastering a good text editor or IDE will make your JavaScript life much, much easier. That's its raison d'etre, after all!

- **Get a good development browser.**

  This topic was also discussed earlier in the chapter: choose a good browser with the right extensions (when applicable) and learn how to make the most of it.

- **Keep the browser's console open at all times.**

  For better or for worse, browsers don't make a big fuss when things go wrong, meaning there can be problems you're unaware of. By keeping the browser's error console visible, you'll see the problems that occur.

- **Use a JavaScript validator.**

  Just as there are HTML validation services, there are JavaScript validation services. One such site is JSLint (www.jslint.com), created by Douglas Crockford, a JavaScript master. JSLint is a "code quality tool" that identifies both problematic and potentially problematic code.

  A more pleasant alternative is JSHint (www.jshint.com), derived from JSLint. The argument against using JSLint is that it's rather conservative and strict, advocating for doing things pretty much how Crockford thinks you should. JSHint serves the same purpose, but can be customized to be flexible as to what is or is not considered to be a code quality issue.

- **Use rubber duck debugging!**

  Rubber duck debugging is a great technique with a lovely name. It works like this: Get a rubber duck, set it on your desk, and explain to the duck what your code is doing. Will people think you are crazy? Perhaps. But this is highly effective. Often, the experience of attempting to explain—out loud—what code should be doing is enough to make you realize why it is or is not working properly.

- **Write JavaScript in external files.**

  Not only will it be easier to work with the JavaScript code when using external files (because you won't have to hunt through HTML), the JavaScript debugger will be more likely to provide a correct line number.

- **Save the file and refresh the browser!**

  If you fail to save your JavaScript file after making changes, or if you fail to reload the browser you're running the JavaScript in, then the browser will not reflect the latest changes, and you'll spend an eternity attempting to fix the problem.

- **Try a different browser.**

  Some JavaScript errors you'll encounter will be browser-specific. Until you really get comfortable with how the different browsers behave on a JavaScript level, get in the habit of running JavaScript code in multiple browsers. Isolating the specific browsers that are experiencing the problem can help you more quickly determine the underlying cause.

  Conversely, if you see the same problem regardless of the browser, then you know the problem must be in the code itself.

- **Take a break!**

  I've solved many harrowing problems not by doing anything on the computer but by stepping away from it. Take a walk. Eat an apple. When all else fails, do something other than continuing to actively debug the problem. Often, the few minutes it takes to clear your head will allow you to come back to the problem with fresh eyes and a new approach.

In terms of coding, there are a couple of techniques you can use that shouldn't be too advanced to introduce here. A simple, beginner's way of debugging is to use `alert()` to notify you of a script's progress, the value of variables, and so forth. When you don't know what's going on in your code, adding an onslaught of alerts can really help (**Figure 3.17**):

**FIGURE 3.17** Alert boxes are a simple and overt way to provide debugging information.

**FIGURE 3.18** Writing messages to the console is another way of providing debugging data.

```
alert('Now in the XXX function!');
alert('myVar is ' + myVar);
```

On the other hand, alerts are unseemly and you can tire of having to always close them. A better alternative is to write those same messages to the JavaScript console. To do that, call the `log()` method of the console object, providing it with the message to be written (**Figure 3.18**):

```
console.log('Now in the XXX function!');
console.log('myVar is ' + myVar);
```

Because the console log is nonintrusive, you can use it generously, such as to indicate each step in the logical process. For example, each step in the code could be marked by outputting a number:

```
// Start!
console.log(1);
// Some code.
console.log(2);
```

Alternatively, you can just invoke `console.trace()`. This function, used without providing any additional information, sends a message to the console indicating the current function being executed (called a stack trace). For example, the following code would print the string *init* within the console when this function is called:

```
function init() {
    console.trace();
}
```

Finally, when using JavaScript in a networked manner, such as performing Ajax requests, using a browser or IDE with a network monitoring tool will be a great asset, letting you confirm:

- What requests are being made

- The data included in the requests

- The data included in the response.

You'll also want to validate the received data when you're having problems. For example, if the returned data is meant to be XML or JSON (you'll learn about both in Chapter 11, Ajax), validating that the data is syntactically correct XML or JSON is a good step to take. More on this in Chapter 11.

### USING FIREBUG

Firebug has long been the savior of the Web developer. It's free, has a ton of features, and continues to be well supported. I want to provide a brief introduction to using Firebug here, focusing solely on its JavaScript-related tools, but I recommend that you seek some online videos that visually represent this same information, as well as go into more details about Firebug.

Note that Firebug was originally developed for the Firefox Web browser. The Firebug Lite extension is now available for other browsers, but the full Firebug on Firefox is still the best. Although the Web developer tools now shipping with Safari (i.e., the Web Inspector), Opera (Dragonfly), and Internet Explorer (Developer Toolbar) are worthwhile, Firebug is the gold standard in this area and I'd be remiss not to give Firebug the preferential treatment it has earned.

**FIGURE 3.19** Click these circles to control Firebug's presence.

**FIGURE 3.20** Use the Firebug Console panel to execute single or multiple lines of JavaScript.

To open Firebug, you must have a browser window open, although not necessarily with a Web page loaded in it. In the upper-right corner of the Firebug interface are three circles (**Figure 3.19**). Clicking the first (an inverted chevron) minimizes Firebug but keeps it active. Clicking the second (a standard chevron) opens Firebug in a separate window. Clicking the third (an X), closes Firebug, thereby also making it inactive.

Within a blank Web page, you can use Firebug's Console tab to execute any random bits of JavaScript. You can enter single lines of JavaScript code at the prompt at the bottom of the window, and the output will be displayed in the console. To test larger blocks of JavaScript, click the Command Editor icon in the lower-right corner (another chevron). Then you can insert larger blocks of code and execute it by clicking Run (**Figure 3.20**).

> **TIP:** The single-line console prompt supports code completion.

To apply Firebug to a Web page, load the page in your browser, and then bring up Firebug. If there are any errors in the page, or any `console.log()` output, you'll see that information in Firebug's Console panel. You can also enter JavaScript into the console to test aspects of the page, such as support for particular objects or the values of page variables.

Within the console, the `inspect()` function provides all of the information about a given variable:

```
inspect(someVar);
```

And you can enter `clear()`, to clear the console's contents.

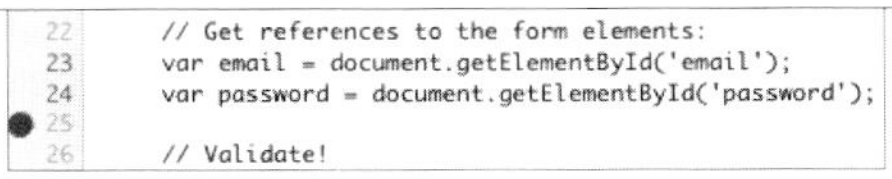

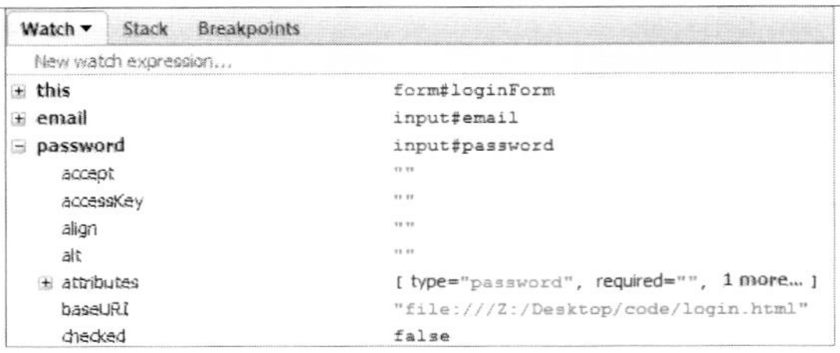

```
22    // Get references to the form elements:
23    var email = document.getElementById('email');
24    var password = document.getElementById('password');
25
26    // Validate!
```

| Watch ▼  Stack  Breakpoints | |
|---|---|
| New watch expression... | |
| ⊞ this | form#loginForm |
| ⊞ email | input#email |
| ⊟ password | input#password |
| accept | " " |
| accessKey | " " |
| align | " " |
| alt | " " |
| ⊞ attributes | [ type="password", required="",  1 more... ] |
| baseURI | "file:///Z:/Desktop/code/login.html" |
| checked | false |

**FIGURE 3.21** A breakpoint has been set on the JavaScript code.

**FIGURE 3.22** Use the Watch tab to see the variables that exist at the break, and their values.

For debugging purposes, the Script panel is a real time-saver. First, you can select what JavaScript code to view in the Script panel, whether it's an external file or inline. This is useful, but using Watch and Breakpoint capabilities is where the advanced debugging techniques come into play.

A *breakpoint* is a command to have the code stop executing at a certain point. One of the hardest things about debugging JavaScript is that so much happens, and so quickly, that it's difficult to know what's causing a problem, what's happening to various variables, what the logic flow is, and so forth. Breakpoints give you a way to pause the script's execution so that you can take a look around.

For example, if you load the login form from Chapter 2, you'll see that login. js can be shown in Firebug's Script panel. If there's a problem with, say, the form validation, you can set a breakpoint inside of the validateForm() function to take a peek at that point in the process. To set a breakpoint in Firebug, just click on the line number beside the script, and a red circle will appear (**Figure 3.21**). Note that the breakpoint takes effect *before that line is executed*. In other words, if you set a breakpoint on line 25, line 24 will be the last executed line of code before the pause.

When Firebug encounters a breakpoint, you can turn your attention to the Watch tab in the right-side pane. By default, the Watch tab lists the variables that exist and their values at the moment of the break. This is a huge debugging asset. For complicated variable types (e.g., objects), clicking the arrow beside the variable name reveals the properties and methods of that object (**Figure 3.22**).

At the top of the Script panel, there are five buttons where you can decide what to do next, after encountering a breakpoint (from left to right):

- Rerun
- Continue
- Step Into
- Step Over
- Step Out

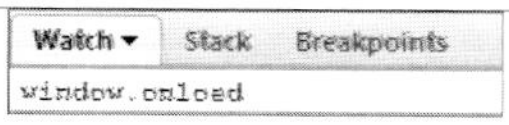

| Watch ▼ | Stack | Breakpoints |
|---------|-------|-------------|
| window.onload | | |

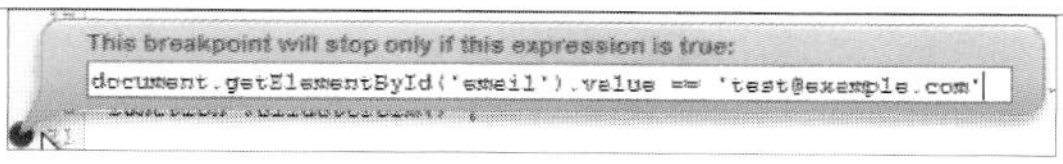

This breakpoint will stop only if this expression is true:
document.getElementById('email').value == 'test@example.com'

**FIGURE 3.23** This new watch expression does not reference a specific breakpoint.

**FIGURE 3.24** This watch expression is for an existing breakpoint.

The meanings of these can be a bit confusing for those new to Firebug, so I'll just put them in simplest terms. Rerun restarts the execution of the code. Continue will continue the script's execution until its end or another breakpoint is encountered. Step Into, Step Over, and Step out all dictate whether the debugger will go into, over (i.e., not into), or out of the definition of the next function call. When you feel ready to learn more, see the Firebug Wiki (http://getfirebug.com/wiki/index.php/Script_Panel) or search online.

Getting back to the breakpoints, another way of setting breakpoints is to click the icon in Firebug's upper-left corner, which looks like a pause button with a small play button on it. This enables Firebug's "Break On Next" setting, which means that Firebug will break on the next executed line. (There's a similar icon on the Console panel for breaking on the next line that causes an error.)

Finally, you can set *conditional breakpoints*, which are *watch expressions*. For example, click *New watch expression* in the Watch pane, then enter *window.onload* in the text field (**Figure 3.23**). This establishes a breakpoint when the window.onload event is triggered (you'll need to reload the page to see this watch expression be triggered). You can also create a watch expression by right-clicking (or Control+Clicking) on a breakpoint icon (the red circle to the left of a line number). In the resulting pop-up, enter the condition that must be met for this breakpoint to take effect (**Figure 3.24**). Watch expressions are most commonly used to set breakpoints based upon the value of a variable.

I don't want to overwhelm you with debugging JavaScript using Firebug when you don't formally know the language in the first place, so that's enough about Firebug for now. My recommendation is to get in the habit of using it, and slowly build up familiarity with its multitude of features. There are oodles of tutorials and screencasts online for how to use it, and you'll see some more recommendations toward that end a time or two in this book.

## ONLINE **RESOURCES**

Unlike PHP (www.php.net), Ruby (www.ruby-lang.org), and other languages, there's no one, go-to Web site for JavaScript. You'll find plenty of references interspersed throughout the book, but I want to mention a number of good, general sites here as well.

To start, most of the companies that make Web browsers also have pretty good documentation on JavaScript and Web development in general:

- Opera (http://dev.opera.com)

- Mozilla (https://developer.mozilla.org/en/JavaScript)

- Chrome (http://code.google.com/doctype/)

Microsoft and Apple have their own documentation on Web development, but tend to be more specific to their browsers. Many of the sites specific to a JavaScript framework have other good information on general JavaScript. These will be discussed in Chapter 13, Frameworks.

Beyond those sites, there are many *people* whose work you ought to follow, or at least be aware of, as they are among the founding fathers of JavaScript and/or visionaries when it comes to modern JavaScript:

- Brendon Eich (http://brendaneich.com)

- Douglas Crockford (http://crockford.com)

- John Resig (http://ejohn.org)

- Dean Edwards (http://dean.edwards.name)

- Paul Irish (http://paulirish.com)

- Alex Sexton (http:// alexsexton.com)

- Remy Sharp (http://remysharp.com)

- Christian Heilmann (http://christianheilmann.com)

- Thomas Fuchs (http://mir.aculo.us)

These are all more brilliant minds than mine, so I should warn you that much of what you might read by, or see from, people such as these could be over your head when you're first starting. But much of how JavaScript came to be, and how it's being used today, is greatly influenced by these and others.

You should also bookmark the JavaScript sites mentioned earlier in this chapter for executing and debugging JavaScript code: JS Bin, jsFiddle, JSLint, and JSHint. And in the previous chapter, I referenced the W3C's validator service (http://validator.w3.org/).

You can find the pages associated with this book at my Web site, www.LarryUllman.com. If you have any questions or problems, you can use the book's corresponding forum, at www.LarryUllman.com/forums/.

## WRAPPING **UP**

This final chapter in the first part of the book completes the introduction to Java-Script by covering the software you'll use to create, test, and debug JavaScript code. For starters, this means the text editor or IDE you use: many specific features and recommended titles were detailed. Next, you'll need lots and lots of browsers to test your code, as it'll certainly be executed by an even larger array of browsers and devices in the real world. I strongly recommend that you pick a couple of browsers that you're most comfortable with, and install some good extensions or plug-ins, as doing so will make the development process less taxing.

In this chapter you also learned several different ways you can practice using JavaScript code without creating formal scripts and HTML pages. These options range from the Web-based JS Bin to just using the browser's console interface. And, of course, there's Firebug. And although it's hard to learn debugging techniques when you don't know how to actually program, you did see the types of errors that will occur, the common causes, and what steps you might take to help find and fix the errors that arise. The most important debugging step, especially when you're most frustrated, is to stop, step away from the computer, and take a break. Maybe you should take a quick break now, because in the next chapter, you'll start formally programming in JavaScript!

# 4

# SIMPLE **VARIABLE** **TYPES**

All programming comes down to taking *some action* with *some data*. In this chapter, the focus is on the data side of the equation, represented by variables. Even if you've never done any programming, you're probably familiar with the concept of a variable: a temporary storage container. This chapter starts with the basics of variables in JavaScript, and then covers number, string, and Boolean variables. Along the way you'll find plenty of real-world code, representing some of the actions you will take with these simple variable types.

# BASICS OF VARIABLES

I think it's easiest to grasp variables by starting with so-called "simple" variables, also called "primitive" variable types. By *simple*, I mean variables that only store a single piece of information at a time. For example, a numeric variable stores just a single number; a string, just a sequence of zero or more quoted characters. Simple variables will be the focus in this chapter, with more advanced alternatives—such as arrays and objects—coming in Chapter 6, Complex Variable Types.

To be completely accurate, it's the *values* in JavaScript that are typed, not the variables. Further, many values in JavaScript can be represented as either a *literal* or an *object*. But I don't want to overwhelm you with technical details already, especially if they won't impact your actual programming. Instead, let's focus on this line of code:

```
var myVar = 'easy peasy';
```

**TIP:** Remember that you can practice much of the JavaScript in this chapter using your browser's console window.

That's a standard and fundamental line of JavaScript programming, declaring a variable named myVar, and assigning to it the string *easy peasy*. The next few pages will look at the four components of this one line in detail:

- var, used to declare a variable
- the variable's name
- =, the assignment operator
- the variable's value

## DECLARING VARIABLES

To declare a variable is to formally announce its existence. In many languages, such as C and ActionScript, you must declare a variable prior to referencing it. JavaScript does not *require* you to declare variables, you can just immediately begin referencing them, as in:

```
quantity = 14;
```

(The semicolon is used to terminate a statement. It's not required, but you should always use it.)

Now, to clarify, you don't *have to* declare variables in JavaScript, but *you actually should.* To do that, use the var keyword:

```
var fullName;
```

   or

```
var fullName = 'Larry Ullman';
```

The distinction between using var and not using var has to do with the variable's *scope*, a topic that will mean more once you begin defining your own functions (see Chapter 7, Creating Functions). Undeclared variables—those referenced for the first time without using var—will have *global* scope by default, and global variables are frowned upon (see the sidebar for more).

Also understand that whether or not you assign a value to the variable when it's declared has no impact on its scope. Both lines above used to declare the fullName variable result in a variable with the same scope.

As discussed in Chapter 1, (Re-)Introducing JavaScript, JavaScript is a *weakly typed language*, meaning that variables are not strictly confined to one type or another. Neither of the above uses of fullName decree that the variable is a string. With either of those lines of code, this next line will not cause a syntax error:

```
fullName = 2;
```

That line would most likely cause a logical or run-time error, as other code would expect that fullName is a string, but the larger point is that a JavaScript variable isn't typed but has a type based upon its value. If fullName stores a quoted sequence of zero or more characters, then fullName is said to be a string; if fullName stores 2, then it's said to be a number.

Note that each variable is only declared once, but you can use var to declare multiple variables at the same time:

```
var firstName, lastName;
```

You can even declare multiple variables at the same time while simultaneously assigning values:

```
var firstName = 'Larry', lastName = 'Ullman';
```

## GLOBAL **VARIABLES**

All variables have a *scope*, which is the realm in which they exist. As you'll see in Chapter 7, variables declared within a function have *function-level* scope: They only exist within that function. Other languages, but not JavaScript (currently), have *block-level* scope, where a variable can be declared and only exist between a pair of curly braces. Variables declared outside of any function, or referenced without any use of var, have *global* scope. There are a few reasons to avoid using global variables.

First, as a general rule of programming, applications should only do the bare minimum of what's required. If a variable does not absolutely need to be global, it shouldn't be. Second, global variables can have an adverse effect on performance, because the application will have to constantly maintain that variable's existence, even when the variable is not being used. By comparison, function variables will only exist during that function's execution (i.e., when the function is called). Third, global variables can cause run-time and logical errors should they conflict with other global variables. This can happen if your code has a variable with the same name as a poorly designed library you might also be including in the same page.

All this being said, understand that for the next few chapters, you will occasionally be using global variables in your code. This is because variables declared outside of any function, even when using the var keyword, will also have global scope, and you won't have user-defined functions yet. Still, while it's best not to use global variables, using them is not a terrible, horrible thing, and it's much better to *knowingly* create a global variable than to *accidentally* do so.

You'll rarely see this done in the book, as I will want to better focus on each variable declaration, but lines like that one are common in real-world JavaScript code.

As a final note on the var keyword, you should always declare your variables as soon as possible in your code, within the scope in which they are needed. Variables declared outside of any functions should be declared at the top of the code; variables declared within a function definition should be declared as the first thing within that function's code. The technical reason for this is because of something called "hoisting," but declaring variables as soon as possible is also standard practice in languages without hoisting issues.

## VARIABLE NAMES

In order to create a variable, you must give it a name, also called an *identifier*. The rules for names in JavaScript are:

- The name must start with a letter, the underscore, or a dollar sign.
- The rest of the name can contain any combination of letters, underscores, and numbers (along with some other, less common characters).
- You cannot use spaces, punctuation, or any other characters.
- You cannot use a reserved JavaScript word.
- Names are case-sensitive.

This last rule is an important one, and can be a frequent cause of problems. The best way to minimize problems is to use a consistent naming scheme. With an object-oriented language like JavaScript, it's conventional to use "camel-case" syntax, where words within a name are broken up by a capital letter:

- fullName
- streetAddress
- monthlyPayment

In procedural programming languages, the underscore is often used to break up words. In procedural PHP, for example, I would write $full_name and $street_address. In JavaScript, camel-case is conventional, but the most important criterion is that you choose a style and stick with it.

As a final note, you should not use an existing variable's name for your variable. For example, when JavaScript runs in the browser, the browser will provide some variables, such as document and window. Both of these are quite important, and you wouldn't want to override them by creating your own variables with those names. You don't need to memorize a list of browser-provided variables, however; just try to be unique and descriptive with your variable names (e.g., theDocument and theWindow would work fine).

## ASSIGNING VALUES

As you probably already know or guessed from what you've seen in this book or online, a single equals sign is the assignment operator, used to assign a value on the right to the variable on the left. Here is the declaration of, and assignment to, a numeric variable:

```
var rate;
rate = 5.25;
```

This can be condensed into a single line:

```
var rate = 5.25;
```

That one line not only declares a variable, but *initializes* it: provides an initial value. You do not have to initialize variables when you declare them, but sometimes it will make sense to.

## SIMPLE VALUE TYPES

JavaScript recognizes several "simple" types of values that can be assigned to variables, starting with numbers, strings, and Booleans. A number is exactly what you'd expect: any quantity of digits with or without a single decimal point. Numeric values are never quoted and may contain digits, a single decimal point, a plus or minus, and possibly the letter "e" (for exponential notation). Numeric values do not contain commas, as would be used to indicate thousands.

A string is any sequence of zero or more quoted characters. You can use single or double quotation marks, but you must use the same type to end the string as you used to begin it:

- 'This is a string.'

- "This is also a string."

If you need to include a single or double quotation mark within the string, you can either use the other mark type to delineate the string or *escape* the potentially problematic character by prefacing it with a backslash:

- "I've got an idea."

- 'Chapter 4, "Simple Variable Types"'

- 'I\'ve got an idea.'

- "Chapter 4, \"Simple Variable Types\""

What will not work is:

- 'I've got an idea.'

- "Chapter 4, "Simple Variable Types""

Note that a string does not need to have any characters in it: Both '' and "" are valid strings, called *empty* strings.

JavaScript also has Boolean values: `true` and `false`. As JavaScript is a case-sensitive language, you must use *true* and *false*, not *True* or *TRUE* or *False* or *FALSE*.

Two more simple, yet special, values are `null` and `undefined`. Again, these are case-sensitive words. The difference between them is subtle. `null` is a defined non-value and is best used to represent the consequence of an action that has no result. For example, the result of a working Ajax call could be `null`, which is to say that no data was returned.

Conversely, `undefined` is no set value, which is normally the result of inaction. For example, when a variable is declared without being assigned a value, its value will be undefined (**Figure 4.1**):

```
var unset; // Currently undefined.
```

Similarly, if a function does not actively return a value, then the returned value is undefined (you'll see this in Chapter 7).

Both `null` and `undefined` are not only different from each other, but different from `false`, which is a known and established negative value. As you'll see in Chapter 5, Using Control Structures, when used as the basis of a condition, both `null` and `undefined` are treated as FALSE, as are the number 0 and the empty string. Still, there are differences among them.

> **TIP:** As a reminder, the combination of two slashes together (//) creates a comment in JavaScript.

**FIGURE 4.1** Because this variable has not yet been assigned a value, its value is undefined.

# WORKING WITH NUMBERS

Unlike a lot of languages, JavaScript only has a single number type, used to represent any numerical value, from integers to doubles (i.e., decimals or real numbers) to exponent notation. You can rest assured in knowing that numbers in JavaScript can safely represent values up to around 9 quadrillion!

Let's look at everything you need to know about numbers in JavaScript, from the arithmetic operators to formatting numbers, to using the Math object for more sophisticated purposes.

## ARITHMETIC OPERATORS

You've already been introduced to one operator: a single equals sign, which is the assignment operator. JavaScript supports the standard arithmetic operators, too (**Table 4.1**).

**TABLE 4.1** Arithmetic Operators

| SYMBOL | MEANING |
| --- | --- |
| + | Addition |
| - | Subtraction |
| * | Multiplication |
| / | Division |
| % | Remainder |

The modulus operator, in case you're not familiar with it, returns the remainder of a division. For example:

```
var remainder = 7 % 2; // 1;
```

One has to be careful when applying the modulus operator to negative numbers, as the remainder itself will also be negative:

```
var remainder = -7 % 2; // -1
```

These arithmetic operators can be combined with the assignment operator to both perform a calculation and assign the result in one step:

```
var cost = 50; // Dollars
cost *= 0.7373; // Converted to euros
```

You'll frequently come across the increment and decrement operators: ++ and --. The increment operator adds one to the value of the variable; the decrement operator subtracts one:

```
var num = 1;
num++; // 2
num--; // 1
```

These two operators can be used in both *prefix* and *postfix* manners (i.e., before the variable or after it):

```
var num = 1;
num++; // num now equals 2.
++num; // num is now 3.
--num; // num is now 2.
```

A difference between the postfix and prefix versions is a matter of *operator precedence*. The rules of operator precedence dictate the order operations are executed in a multi-operation line. For example, basic math teaches that multiplication and division have a higher precedence than addition and subtraction. Thus:

```
var num = 3 * 2 + 1; // 7, not 9
```

**Table 4.2** lists the order of precedence in JavaScript, from highest to lowest, including some operators not yet introduced (I've also omitted a couple of operators that won't be discussed in this book). There's also an issue of *associativity* that I've omitted, as that would be just one more thing you'd have to memorize. In fact, instead of trying to memorize that table, I recommend you use parentheses to force, or just clarify, precedence, without relying upon mastery of these rules. For example:

```
var num = (3 * 2) + 1; // Still 7.
```

That syntax, while two characters longer than the earlier version, has the same net effect but is easier to read and undeniably clear in intent.

Some of the operators in Table 4.2 are *unary*, meaning they apply to only one operand (such as ++ and --); others are binary, applying to two operands (such as addition). In Chapter 5, you'll learn how to use the one *trinary* operator, which has three operands.

```
                        Console ▼
      Clear  Persist  Profile   All
>>> 2 * 'cat';
NaN
>>> 1/0
Infinity
```

**FIGURE 4.2** The result of invalid mathematical operations will be the special values NaN and Infinity.

**TABLE 4.2** Operator Precedence

| PRECEDENCE | OPERATOR | NOTE |
|---|---|---|
| 1 | . [] | member operators |
| 1 | new | creates new objects |
| 2 | () | function call |
| 3 | ++ -- | increment and decrement |
| 4 | ! | logical not |
| 4 | + - | unary positive and negative |
| 4 | typeof void delete | |
| 5 | * / % | multiplication, division, and modulus |
| 6 | + - | addition and subtraction |
| 8 | < <= > >= | comparison |
| 9 | == != === !== | equality |
| 13 | && | logical and |
| 14 | \|\| | logical or |
| 15 | ?: | conditional operator |
| 16 | = += -= *= /= %= <<= >>= >>>= &= ^= \|= | assignment operators |

The last thing to know about performing arithmetic in JavaScript is if the result of the arithmetic is invalid, JavaScript will return one of two special values:

- NaN, short for *Not a Number*

- Infinity

For example, you'll get these results if you attempt to perform arithmetic using strings or when you divide a number by zero, which surprisingly doesn't create an error (**Figure 4.2**). In Chapter 5, you'll learn how to use the isNaN() and isFinite() functions to verify that values are numbers safe to use as such.

## CREATING CALCULATORS

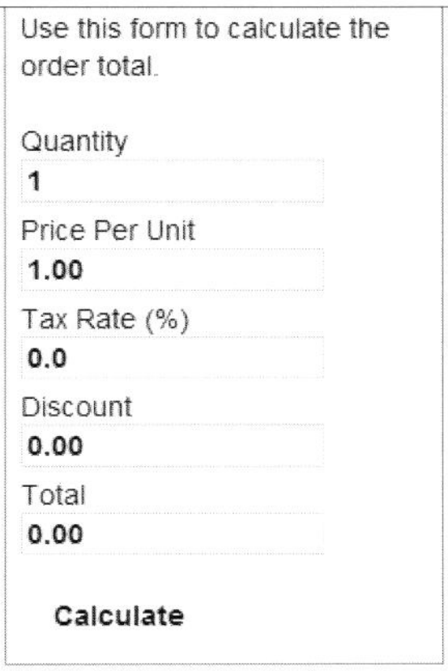

At this point in time, you have enough knowledge to begin using JavaScript to perform real-world mathematical calculations, such as the kinds of things you'd put on a Web site:

- Mortgage and similar loan calculators
- Temperature and other unit conversions
- Interest or investment calculators

For this particular example, let's create an e-commerce tool that will calculate the total of an order, including tax, and minus any discount (**Figure 4.3**). The most relevant HTML is:

```
<div><label for="quantity">Quantity</label><input type="number"
→  name="quantity" id="quantity" value="1" min="1" required></div>

<div><label for="price">Price Per Unit</label><input type="text"
→  name="price" id="price" value="1.00" required></div>

<div><label for="tax">Tax Rate (%)</label><input type="text"
→  name="tax" id="tax" value="0.0" required></div>

<div><label for="discount">Discount</label><input type="text"
→  name="discount" id="discount" value="0.00" required></div>

<div><label for="total">Total</label><input type="text" name="total"
→  id="total" value="0.00"></div>

<div><input type="submit" value="Calculate" id="submit"></div>
```

That would go in a page named shopping.html, which includes the shopping.js JavaScript file, to be written in subsequent steps. You'll notice that the HTML form makes use of the HTML5 number input type for the quantity, with a minimum value. The other types are simply text, as the number type doesn't deal well with decimals. Each input is given a default value, and set as required. Remember that as Chapter 2, JavaScript in Action, explains, browsers that don't support HTML5 will treat unknown types as text elements and ignore the unknown properties. The final text element will be updated with the results of the calculation.

**FIGURE 4.3** A simple calculator.

**To create a calculator:**

1. Create a new JavaScript file in your text editor or IDE, to be named shopping.js.

2. Begin defining the calculate() function:

```
function calculate() {
    'use strict';
```

This function will be called when the user clicks the submit button. It does the actual work.

3. Declare a variable for storing the order total:

```
var total;
```

As mentioned previously, you should generally declare variables as soon as you can, such as the first line of a function definition. Here, a variable named total is declared but not initialized.

4. Get references to the form values:

```
var quantity = document.getElementById('quantity').value;
var price = document.getElementById('price').value;
var tax = document.getElementById('tax').value;
var discount = document.getElementById('discount').value;
```

In these four lines of code, the values of the various form elements are assigned to local variables. Note that in the Chapter 2 example, variables were assigned references to the form elements, and then the element values were later checked. Here, the value is directly assigned to the variable.

At this point in time, one would also perform validation of these values, prior to doing any calculations. But as Chapter 5 more formally covers the knowledge needed to perform validation, I'm skipping this otherwise needed step in this example.

**TIP:** You can download all the book's code at www.LarryUllman.com.

5. Calculate the initial total:

```
total = quantity * price;
```

The total variable is first assigned the value of the quantity times the price, using the multiplication operator.

6. Factor in the tax rate:

```
tax /= 100;
tax++;
total *= tax;
```

There are a couple of ways one can calculate and add in the tax. The first, shown here, is to change the tax rate from a percent (say 5.25%) to a decimal (0.0525). Next, add one to the decimal (1.0525). Finally, multiply this number times the total. You'll see that the division-assignment, incrementation, and multiplication-assignment operators are used here as shorthand. This code could also be written more formally:

```
tax = tax/100;
tax = tax + 1;
total = total * tax;
```

You could also make use of precedence and parentheses to perform all these calculations in one line.

An alternative way to calculate the tax would be to convert it to decimal, multiply that value times the total, and then add that result to the total.

7. Factor in the discount:

```
total -= discount;
```

The discount is just being subtracted from the total.

8. Display the total in the form:

```
document.getElementById('total').value = total;
```

The value attribute can also be used to *assign* a value to a text form input. Using this approach, you can easily reflect data back to the user. In later chapters, you'll learn how to display information on the HTML page using DOM manipulation, rather than setting the values of form inputs.

9. Return false to prevent submission of the form:

```
return false;
```

The function must return a value of false to prevent the form from actually being submitted (to the page named by the form's action attribute).

10. Complete the function:

```
} // End of calculate() function.
```

11. Define the init() function:

```
function init() {
    'use strict';
    var theForm = document.getElementById('theForm');
    theForm.onsubmit = calculate;
} // End of init() function.
```

The init() function will be called when the window triggers a load event (see Step 12). The function needs to add an event listener to the form's submission, so that when the form is submitted, the calculate() function will be called. To do that, the function gets a reference to the form, by calling the document object's getElementById() method, providing it with the unique ID value of the form. Then the variable's onsubmit property is assigned the value *calculate*, as explained in Chapter 2.

12. Add an event listener to the window's load event:

```
window.onload = init;
```

This code was also explained in Chapter 2. It says that when the window has loaded, the init() function should be called.

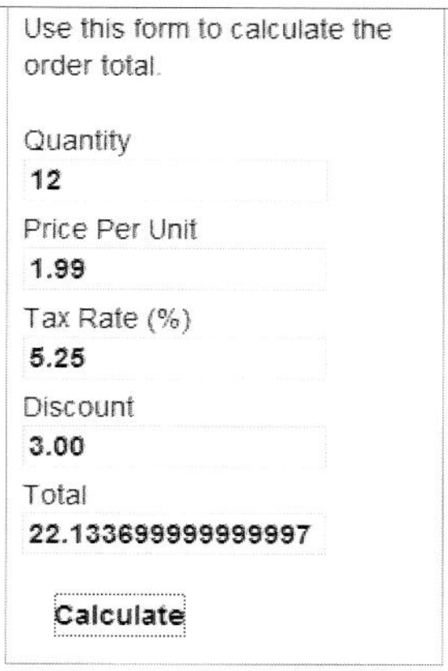

Use this form to calculate the order total.

Quantity
12

Price Per Unit
1.99

Tax Rate (%)
5.25

Discount
3.00

Total
22.133699999999997

Calculate

Use this form to calculate the order total.

Quantity
cat

Price Per Unit
1.99

Tax Rate (%)
5.25

Discount
3.00

Total
NaN

Calculate

**FIGURE 4.4** The result of the total order calculation.

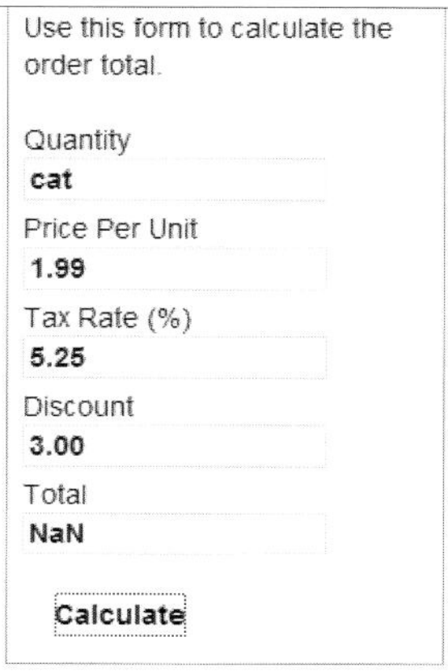

**FIGURE 4.5** Performing arithmetic with invalid values, such as a quantity of *cat*, will result in a total of NaN.

It's a minor point, as you can organize your scripts in rather flexible ways, but this line is last as it references the init() function, defined in Step 12, so that definition should theoretically come before this line. That function references calculate(), so the calculate() function's definition is placed before the init() function definition. You don't have to organize your code this way, but I prefer to.

13. Save the file as shopping.js, in a js directory next to shopping.html, and test in your Web browser (**Figure 4.4**).

Play with the numbers, including invalid values (**Figure 4.5**), and retest the calculator until you're comfortable with how arithmetic works in JavaScript.

## FORMATTING NUMBERS

Although the previous example is perfectly useful, and certainly a good start, there are several ways in which it can be improved. For example, as written, no checks are made to ensure that the user enters values in all the form elements, let alone that those values are numeric (Figure 4.5) or, more precisely, positive numbers. That knowledge will be taught in the next chapter, which discusses conditionals, comparison operators, and so forth. Another problem, which can be addressed here, is that you can't expect someone to pay, say, 22.1336999 (Figure 4.4). To improve the professionalism of the calculator, formatting the calculated total to two decimal points would be best.

A number in JavaScript is not just a number, but is also an object of type Number. As an object, a number has built-in methods, such as toFixed(). This method returns a number with a set number of digits to the right of a decimal point:

```
var num = 4095.3892;
num.toFixed(3); // 4095.389
```

Note that this method only returns the formatted number; it does not change the original value. To do that, you'd need to assign the result back to the variable, thereby replacing its original value:

```
num = num.toFixed(3);
```

If you don't provide an argument to the toFixed() method, it defaults to 0:

```
var num = 4095.3892;
num.toFixed(3); // 4095
```

The method can round up to 20 digits.

Similar to toFixed() is toPrecision(). It takes an argument dictating the total number of significant digits, which may or may not include those after the decimal.

Let's apply this information to the calculator in order to add some better formatting to the total.

**To format a number:**

1. Open shopping.js in your text editor or IDE, if it is not already.

2. After factoring in the discount, but before showing the total amount, format the total to two decimals:

   ```
   total = total.toFixed(2);
   ```

   This one line will take care of formatting the decimal places. Remember that the returned result must be assigned back to the variable in order for it to be represented upon later uses.

   Alternatively, you could just call total.toFixed(2) when assigning the value to the total form element.

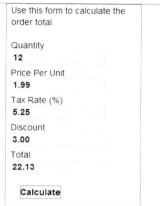

Use this form to calculate the order total.

Quantity
**12**

Price Per Unit
**1.99**

Tax Rate (%)
**5.25**

Discount
**3.00**

Total
**22.13**

Calculate

```
>>> var radius = 20;
undefined
>>> var area = Math.PI * radius * radius;
undefined
>>> area;
1256.6370614359173
```

**FIGURE 4.6** The same input as in Figure 4.4 now generates a more appropriate result.

**FIGURE 4.7** The area of a circle, πr2, is calculated using the Math.PI constant.

3. Save the file, reload the HTML page, and test it in your Web browser (**Figure 4.6**).

An even better way of formatting the number would be to add commands indicating thousands, but that requires more logic than can be understood at this point in the book.

## THE MATH OBJECT

You just saw that numbers in JavaScript can also be treated as objects of type Number, with a couple of built-in methods that can be used to manipulate them. Another way to manipulate numbers in JavaScript involves the Math object. Unlike Number, you do not create a variable of type Math, but use the Math object directly. The Math object is a global object in JavaScript, meaning it's always available for you to use.

The Math object has several predefined *constants*, such as π, which is 3.14... and E, which is 2.71... A constant, unlike a variable, has a fixed value. Conventionally, constants are written in all uppercase letters, as shown. Referencing an object's constant uses the same dot syntax as you would to reference one of its methods: Math.PI, Math.E, and so forth. Therefore, to calculate the area of a circle, you could use (**Figure 4.7**):

```
var radius = 20;
var area = Math.PI * radius * radius;
```

Use this form to calculate the volume of a sphere.

Radius
12

Volume
7238.2295

**Calculate**

The Math object also has several predefined methods, just a few of which are:

- `abs()`, which returns the absolute value of a number
- `ceil()`, which rounds up to the nearest integer
- `floor()`, which rounds down to the nearest integer
- `max()`, which returns the largest of zero or more numbers
- `min()`, which returns the smallest of zero or more numbers
- `pow()`, which returns one number to the power of another number
- `round()`, which returns a number rounded to the nearest integer
- `random()`, which returns a pseudo-random number between 0 (inclusive) and 1 (exclusive)

There are also several trigonometric methods like `sin()` and `cos()`.
Another way of writing the formula for determining the area of a circle is:

```
var radius = 20;
var area = Math.PI * Math.pow(radius, 2);
```

To apply this new information, let's create a new calculator that calculates the volume of a sphere, based upon a user-entered radius. That formula is:

$$\text{volume} = 4/3 * \pi * \text{radius}^3$$

Besides using the $\pi$ constant and the `pow()` method, this next bit of JavaScript will also apply the `abs()` method to ensure that only a positive radius is used for the calculation (**Figure 4.8**). The relevant HTML is:

```
<div><label for="radius">Radius</label><input type="text"
    name="radius" id="radius" required></div>

<div><label for="volume">Volume</label><input type="text"
    name="volume" id="volume"></div>

<div><input type="submit" value="Calculate" id="submit"></div>
```

The HTML page includes the `sphere.js` JavaScript file, to be written in subsequent steps.

**To calculate the volume of a sphere:**

1. Create a new JavaScript file in your text editor or IDE, to be named `sphere.js`.

2. Begin defining the `calculate()` function:

```
function calculate() {
    'use strict';
    var volume;
```

Within the function, a variable named `volume` is declared, but not initialized.

3. Get a reference to the form's radius value:

```
var radius = document.getElementById('radius').value;
```

Again, this code closely replicates that in `shopping.js`, although there's only one form value to retrieve.

4. Make sure that the radius is a positive number:

```
radius = Math.abs(radius);
```

Applying the `abs()` method of the `Math` object to a number guarantees a positive number without having to use a conditional to test for that.

5. Calculate the volume:

```
volume = (4/3) * Math.PI * Math.pow(radius, 3);
```

The volume of a sphere is four-thirds times $\pi$ times the radius to the third power. This one line performs that entire calculation, using the `Math` object twice. The division of four by three is wrapped in parentheses to clarify the formula, although in this case the result would be the same without the parentheses.

6. Format the volume to four decimals:

```
volume = volume.toFixed(4);
```

Remember that the `toFixed()` method is part of `Number`, which means it's called from the `volume` variable, not from the `Math` object.

7. Display the volume:

```
document.getElementById('volume').value = volume;
```

This code is the same as in the previous example, but obviously referencing a different form element.

8. Return false to prevent the form's submission, and complete the function:

```
    return false;
} // End of calculate() function.
```

9. Add an event listener to the form:

```
function init() {
    'use strict';
    document.getElementById('calcForm').onsubmit = calculate;
} // End of init() function.
window.onload = init;
```

This is the same code used in shopping.js. As in that example, when the form is submitted, the calculate() function will be called.

10. Save the file as sphere.js, in a js directory next to sphere.html, and test it in your Web browser.

## WORKING WITH STRINGS

Strings and numbers are two of the most common types used in JavaScript, and both are easy to comprehend and use. You've seen the fundamentals when it comes to numbers—and there's not all that much to it, really, so now it's time to look at strings in more detail.

### CREATING STRINGS

Informally, you've already witnessed how strings are created: just quote anything. As with a number, once you have a string value, you also have predefined methods that can be used to manipulate that value. Unlike numbers, though, strings have a lot more methods, and even a property you'll commonly use: length. The length property stores the number of characters found in the string, including empty spaces:

```
var fullName = 'Larry Ullman';
fullName.length; // 12
```

If you're following this book sequentially, you'll have already seen this in Chapter 2:

```
var email = document.getElementById('email');
if ( (email.value.length > 0) { ...
```

What you're actually seeing here is the beauty of object-oriented programming: A string is a string, with all the functionality that comes with it, regardless of how the string was created. The assignment to the email variable starts with the document object, which is a representation of the page's HTML. That object has a getElementById() method, which returns an HTML element. The specific element returned by that line is a text input, in other words, a text object. This is assigned to email. That object has a value property for finding the text input's value (or for setting its value). Since the value returned by that property is a string, you can then refer to its length property. Thanks to the ability to chain object notation, this could be reduced to one line:

```
if ( (document.getElementById('email').value.length > 0) { ...
```

## DECONSTRUCTING STRINGS

Once you've created a string, you can deconstruct it—break it into pieces—in a number of ways. As a string is just a sequence of length characters, you can reference individual characters using the charAt() method. This method takes an *index* as its first argument, an index being the position of the character in the string. The trick to using indexes is that they begin at 0, not 1 (this is common to indexes of all types across all programming languages). Thus, the first character of string fullName can be retrieved using fullName.charAt(0). And a string's last character will be indexed at length - 1:

```
var fullName = 'Larry Ullman';
fullName.charAt(0); // L
fullName.charAt(11); // n
```

Sometimes you don't want to know what character is at a specific location in the string, but rather if a character is found in the string at all. For this need, use the indexOf() method. This method returns the indexed position where the character is first found:

```
var fullName = 'Larry Ullman';
fullName.indexOf('L'); // 0
fullName.indexOf('a'); // 1
fullName.indexOf(' '); // 5
```

The first argument can be more than a single character, letting you see if entire words are found within the string. In that case, the method returns the indexed position where the word begins in the string:

```
var language = 'JavaScript';
language.indexOf('Script'); // 4
```

The indexOf() method takes an optional second argument, which is a location to begin searching in the string. By default, this is 0:

```
var language = 'JavaScript';
language.indexOf('a'); // 1
language.indexOf('a', 2); // 3
```

However you use indexOf(), if the character or characters—the *needle*—is not found within the string (the *haystack*), the method returns -1. Also, indexOf() performs a case-sensitive search:

```
var language = 'JavaScript';
language.indexOf('script'); // -1
```

Another way to look for needles within a string haystack is to use lastIndexOf(), which goes backward through the string. Its second argument is also optional, and indicates the starting point, but the search again goes backward from that starting point, not forward:

```
var fullName = 'Larry Ullman';
fullName.indexOf('a'); // 1
```

```
fullName.lastIndexOf('a'); // 10
fullName.lastIndexOf('a', 5); // 1
```

To pull a substring out of a string, there's the `slice()` method. Its first argument is the index position to begin at. Its optional second argument is the indexed position where to stop. Without this second argument, the substring will continue until the end of the string:

```
var language = 'JavaScript';
language.slice(4); // Script
language.slice(0,4); // Java
```

A nice trick with `slice()` is that you can provide a negative second argument, which indicates the index at which to stop, counting backward from the end of the string. If you provide a negative starting point, the slice will begin at that indexed position, counting backward from the end of the string:

```
var language = 'JavaScript';
language.slice(0,-6); // Java
language.slice(-6); // Script
```

However you use `slice()`, this method only returns a new string, without affecting the value of the original.

JavaScript also has a `substring()` method, which uses the same arguments as `slice()`, but it has some unexpected behaviors, and it's recommended that you use `slice()` instead.

JavaScript has another string method for retrieving substrings: the aptly named `substr()`. Its first argument is the starting index for the substring, but the second is the number of characters to be included in the substring, not the terminating index. In theory, you can provide negative values for each, thereby changing both the starting and ending positions to be relative to the end of the string, but Internet Explorer doesn't accept negative starting positions.

> **NOTE:** In Chapter 6, you'll learn about the `split()` method, which breaks a string into an array of strings.

Enter your comments below
(100 characters max).

Comments

culpa qui officia
deserunt mollit anim
id est laborum.

Character Count

**446**

Result

adipisicing elit, sed
do eiusmod tempor
incididunt ut labore

**Submit**

**FIGURE 4.9** The HTML form, as it works in Internet Explorer.

To test using slice(), let's create some JavaScript code that limits the amount of data that can be submitted by a textarea. For the time being, a second textarea will show the restricted string; in Chapter 8, Event Handling, you'll learn how to dynamically restrict the amount of text entered in a text area in real time. The relevant HTML for this example is:

```
<div><label for="comments">Comments</label><textarea name="comments"
   id="comments" maxlength="100" required></textarea></div>

<div><label for="count">Character Count</label><input type="number"
   name="count" id="count"></div>

<div><label for="result">Result</label><textarea name="result"
   id="result"></textarea></div>

<div><input type="submit" value="Submit" id="submit"></div>
```

The HTML form has one textarea for the user's input, a text input indicating the number of characters used, and another textarea showing the truncated result. To make the truncated text more professional, it'll be broken on the final space before the character limit (**Figure 4.9**), rather than having the text broken midword. The page, named text.html, includes the text.js JavaScript file, to be written in subsequent steps.

To deconstruct strings:

1. Create a new JavaScript file in your text editor or IDE, to be named text.js.

2. Begin defining the limitText() function:

   ```
   function limitText() {
       'use strict';
       var limitedText;
   ```

   The limitedText variable will be used to store the edited version of the user-supplied text.

3. Retrieve the original text:

   ```
   var originalText = document.getElementById('comments').value;
   ```

   The original text comes from the first textarea in the form and is assigned to originalText here.

4. Find the last space before the one-hundredth character in the original text:

```
var lastSpace = originalText.lastIndexOf(' ', 100);
```

To find the last occurrence of a character in a string, use the `lastIndexOf()` method, applied to the original string. This script is not looking for the absolute last space, though, just the final space before the hundredth character, so 100 is provided as the second argument to `lastIndexOf()`, meaning that the search will begin at the index of 100 and work backward.

5. Trim the text to that spot:

```
limitedText = originalText.slice(0, lastSpace);
```

Next, a substring from `originalText` is assigned to `limitedText`, starting at the beginning of the string—index of 0—and stopping at the previously found space.

6. Show the user the number of characters submitted:

```
document.getElementById('count').value = originalText.length;
```

To indicate that the user submitted too much data, the original character count will be shown in a text input.

7. Display the limited text:

```
document.getElementById('result').value = limitedText;
```

The value of the second textarea is updated with the edited string.

8. Return `false` and complete the function:

```
    return false;
} // End of limitText() function.
```

> **TIP:** It'd be more professional to break the text on a space or comma or the end of a sentence, but that capability is beyond this point in the book.

Enter your comments below
(100 characters max).

Comments

Enter your comments below (100
characters max). Enter your
comments below (100 characters
max). Ente

Character Count

**100**

Result

Enter your comments below (100
characters max). Enter your
comments below (100 characters
max).

**Submit**

**FIGURE 4.10** In Chrome,
which supports the textarea's
maxlength attribute, only 100
characters can be submitted,
but the partial word is still
chopped off.

9. Add an event listener to the form:

```
function init() {
    'use strict';
    document.getElementById('calcForm').onsubmit = limitText;
} // End of init() function.
window.onload = init;
```

This is the same basic code used in the previous example. When the form
is submitted, the limitText() function will be called.

10. Save the file as text.js, in a js directory next to text.html, and test it in
your Web browser (Figure 4.9).

Try using different strings (**Figure 4.10**), and retest, to make sure it's working as it should.

## MANIPULATING STRINGS

The most common way to manipulate a string is to change its value using *concatenation*. Concatenation is like addition for strings, adding more characters onto
existing ones. In fact, the concatenation operator in JavaScript is also the arithmetic
addition operator:

```
var message = 'Hello';
message = message + ', World! ';
```

As with the arithmetic addition, you can combine the plus sign with the assignment operator (=) into a single step:

```
var message = 'Hello';
message += ', World! ';
```

This functionality is duplicated by the concat() method, although it's less commonly used. This method takes one or more strings to be appended to the string:

```
var address = '100 Main Street';
address.concat(' Anytown', ' ST', ' 12345', ' US');
```

Two methods exist to simply change the case of the string's characters: toLowerCase() and toUpperCase(). You can apply these to a string prior to using one of the previously mentioned methods, in order to fake case-insensitive searches:

```
var language = 'JavaScript';
language.indexOf('script'); // -1, aka not found
language.toLowerCase().indexOf('script'); // 4
```

Added to JavaScript in version 1.8.1 is the trim() method, which removes extra spaces from both ends of a string. It's supported in more current browsers—Chrome, Firefox 3.5 and up, IE9 and above, Safari 5 and up, and Opera 10.5 and above, but isn't available on older ones.

Note that, as with slice() and the other methods already covered, toLowerCase(), toUpperCase(), and trim() do not affect the original string, they only return a modified version of that string. Concatenation, however, does alter the original.

**FIGURE 4.11** The values entered in the first two inputs are concatenated together to create a formatted name.

To test this new information, this next example will take a person's first and last names, and then format them as *Surname, First Name* (**Figure 4.11**). The relevant HTML is:

```
<div><label for="firstName">First Name</label><input type="text"
→  name="firstName" id="firstName" required></div>

<div><label for="lastName">Last Name</label><input type="text"
→  name="lastName" id="lastName" required></div>

<div><label for="result">Formatted Name</label><input type="text"
→  name="result" id="result" required></div>

<div><input type="submit" value="Submit" id="submit"></div>
```

This would go into an HTML page named names.html, which includes the names. js JavaScript file, to be written in subsequent steps. By this point in the chapter, this should be a simple and obvious exercise for you.

**To manipulate strings:**

1. Create a new JavaScript file in your text editor or IDE, to be named names.js.

2. Begin defining the formatNames() function:

   ```
   function formatNames() {
        'use strict';
        var formattedName;
   ```

   The formattedName variable will be used to store the formatted version of the user's name.

3. Retrieve the user's first and last names:

   ```
   var firstName = document.getElementById('firstName').value;
   var lastName = document.getElementById('lastName').value;
   ```

4. Create the formatted name:

   ```
   formattedName = lastName + ', ' + firstName;
   ```

   To create the formatted name, assign to the formattedName variable the lastName plus a comma plus a space, plus the firstName. There are other ways of performing this manipulation, such as:

```
formattedName = lastName;
formattedName += ', ';
formattedName += firstName;
```

That code would probably perform worse, though, than the one-line option.

5. Display the formatted name:

```
document.getElementById('result').value = formattedName;
```

6. Return `false` and complete the function:

```
    return false;
} // End of formatNames() function.
```

7. Add an event listener to the form:

```
function init() {
    'use strict';
    document.getElementById('calcForm').onsubmit = formatNames;
} // End of init() function.
window.onload = init;
```

When the form is submitted, the `formatNames()` function will be called.

8. Save the file as `names.js`, in a `js` directory next to `names.html`, and test it in your Web browser (Figure 4.11).

## ESCAPE SEQUENCES

Another thing to understand about strings in JavaScript is that they have certain meaningful *escape sequences*. You've already seen two examples of this: to use a type of quotation mark (single or double) within a string delimited by that same type, the inserted quotation mark must be prefaced with a backslash:

- 'I\'ve got an idea.'

- "Chapter 4, \"Simple Variable Types\""

Three other meaningful escape sequences are:

- \n, a new line
- \r, a carriage return
- \\, a literal backslash

Note that these work within either single or double quotation marks (unlike, for example, in PHP, where they only apply within double quotation marks).

**TIP:** When a user presses Enter or Return within a textarea, that translates to \n in a corresponding JavaScript string.

## PERFORMING TYPE CONVERSIONS

Because JavaScript is weakly typed, different value types can be used together without causing formal errors. In, say, ActionScript, the following would cause an error:

```
var cost:int = 2;
cost += ' dollars';
```

But in JavaScript, you can do that without the browser complaining. That being said, although you *can* use different types together without causing formal errors, it's quite possible to end up with logical errors, which is to say *bugs*, if you're not careful. One complication stems from the fact that the addition operator in math is the same as the concatenation operator for strings. When you add a string to a number, or add a number to a string, JavaScript will convert the number to a string and then concatenate the two. For example, say the shopping example added a shipping value to the total:

```
var shipping = document.getElementById('shipping').value;
total = quantity * price;
tax /= 100;
tax++;
total *= tax;
total += shipping;
```

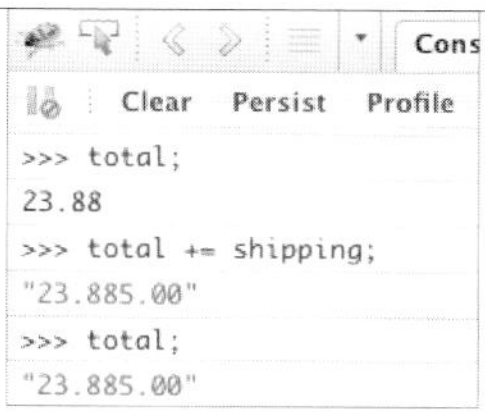

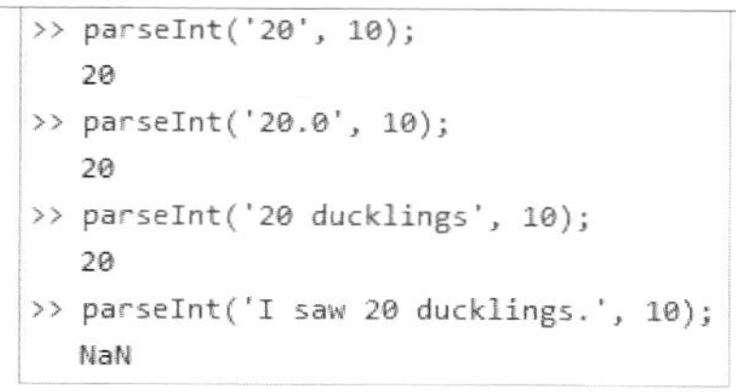

**FIGURE 4.12** Adding the string '5.00' to the total has the impact of concatenation, converting the total number into an unusable string.

**FIGURE 4.13** How the parseInt() function extracts numbers from strings.

By the time JavaScript gets to the final line, total is a number, but shipping is a string, because it comes from a form's text input. That final line won't have the effect of mathematically adding the shipping to the total but rather concatenating the shipping onto the total (**Figure 4.12**).

This issue doesn't apply to other operators, though. For example, subtraction converts a string to a number and then performs the math, as the shopping example already demonstrated.

To perform math using strings, without worrying about creating bugs, you can forcibly convert the string to a number. There are many ways of doing so, starting with parseFloat() and parseInt(). These are "top-level" functions, which is to say they are not associated with any object and can be called directly. The first function always returns a floating-point number (aka, a decimal), and the latter, an integer. Both functions take the value to be converted as its first argument. The parseInt() function takes the *radix* as the second. The radix is the number's base, as in base-8 (aka, octal), base-10 (decimal), and base-16 (hexadecimal). Although the second argument is optional, you should always provide it to be safe, and will normally use a value of 10:

```
total += parseFloat(shipping, 10);
```

To best use these functions, you should have an understanding of how they work. Both functions begin at the start of the string and extract a number until an invalid numeric character is encountered. If no valid number can be pulled from the start of the value, both functions return NaN (**Figure 4.13**):

```
parseInt('20', 10);
parseInt('20.0', 10);
parseInt('20 ducklings', 10);
parseInt('I saw 20 ducklings.', 10);
```

## OBJECTS VS. LITERALS

A point that this chapter has thus far ignored is that values can be represented in two ways: as *objects* or as *literals*. All of the examples in this chapter are literals, such as these:

- 2
- 'JavaScript'
- false

This is the most common way for creating simple variable types, but you can create numbers, strings, and Booleans as formal objects, too:

```
var number = new Number(2);

var fullName = new String('JavaScript');

var flag = new Boolean(false);
```

In that code, the corresponding global function—String, Number, and Boolean—is used to create and return an object of the given type.

Besides being more complicated to write, creating simple types as objects will actually have slightly worse performance and have some unexpected behaviors. And you can continue to use literals as if they were objects, as many of the examples in this chapter have shown, without formally creating the object. In such cases, when needed, JavaScript will convert the literal value to a corresponding object, call the object's method, and then remove the temporary object.

A trickier way to convert a string to a number is to prepend it with a +:

```
total += +shipping;
```

or

```
total += +(shipping);
```

**TIP:** You can also convert a string to a number by multiplying it by 1.

Using this unary operator is the fastest solution, in terms of how quickly JavaScript performs the conversion, but is not as clear in terms of programmer readability as parseInt() and parseFloat().

Converting from a number to a string is far less likely to cause problems, but you can do so by invoking the toString() method:

```
var message = 'Your total is $' + total.toString();
```

The toString() method is supported by most objects and returns a string representation of the object itself.

Earlier in the chapter, I mentioned two other meaningful values in JavaScript: undefined and null. As a gotcha, you should be aware of what happens when an undefined or null value is used as if it were a number. The undefined value translates to NaN when used as a number. When a null value is used as a number, the result is better, although not great: null values are treated as 0 as numbers (**Figure 4.14**). In the next chapter, you'll learn how to verify that a value is numeric prior to attempting to use it as such.

**FIGURE 4.14** How arithmetic is handled if undefined or null is involved.

## REVIEW AND PURSUE

Beginning in Part 2: JavaScript Fundamentals, each chapter of this book ends with a "Review and Pursue" section. In these sections, you'll find questions regarding the material just covered and prompts for ways to expand your knowledge and experience on your own. If you have any problems with these sections, either in answering the questions or pursuing your own endeavors, turn to the book's supporting forum (www.LarryUllman.com/forums/).

### REVIEW

- How do you *declare* a variable?
- What is variable *scope*?
- What are the rules for a variable's name?
- What is the assignment operator?

- What simple types were introduced in this chapter?

- How can you use a single quotation mark within a string? A double quotation mark?

- What does the *= operator do? How about +=? (There are two answers to this last question.) And what about ++?

- What operator can cause bugs when used with a string and a number together?

- What does the toFixed() method do?

- What are some of the differences between Number objects and the Math object?

- What is an empty string?

- What does the charAt() method do? What does indexOf() do? How about lastIndexOf()? What are the arguments to the indexOf() and lastIndexOf() methods? What happens when you use negative numbers for the second argument to either method?

- What function should you use to pull a substring out of a string and how do you use it?

- What are the various ways you can perform concatenation with strings?

- What are escape sequences?

- What are some of the ways you can convert a string to a number?

## PURSUE

- Use a development tool such as Firebug to practice creating and manipulating variables.

- Look up some of JavaScript's reserved words, if you have not already.

- If you're curious, find out what "hoisting" is.

- Create another calculator, such as one that calculates the area of a shape (rectangle, triangle, circle, etc.).

- Look online (e.g., at https://developer.mozilla.org) to research all the Number and Math object properties and methods.

- Look online to learn more about the String object and its methods.

- Create another string manipulation example.

- Update the shopping example to add a shipping cost option, and then rework the JavaScript to properly add the shipping amount to the total.

- Test all of this chapter's code in as many browsers and devices as you can to see the various results.

## WRAPPING **UP**

In this chapter, you started learning the fundamental lessons of real programming in JavaScript, centered around the simple variable types. Those types include numbers, strings, and Booleans. You learned how to declare variables, how to properly name them, and how to assign them simple values.

Next, the chapter looked into the number type in detail, which starts with basic arithmetic. From there, you saw how to use the Number and Math object methods in this object-oriented language to perform such commonplace tasks as formatting numbers and rounding them.

After numbers, similar treatment was given to strings: what they are and how to create them. You also learned that there are several methods defined within the String object that are usable on any string you have. One of the most common manipulations of strings is *concatenation*, accomplished via the plus sign. Attention was also given to using the backslash as an escaping character.

The chapter concluded with a discussion of type conversion between numbers and strings. Implicit conversion can lead to bugs, as demonstrated, so it's best to formally convert values when needed. Along the way you also started creating practical examples, mostly as mathematical calculators.

This knowledge will be expanded in the next chapter, where you will learn about *control structures*. These are primarily conditionals and loops, but Chapter 5 will introduce more operators, too, before Chapter 6 gets into more complicated variable types.

# 5

# USING CONTROL STRUCTURES

Programming is a matter of taking *actions* with *data*. The previous chapter introduced the basics of data— simple variables—and this chapter covers the information you need to know in order to *dynamically* take action. Primarily consisting of conditionals and loops, control structures are a programmatic way to either execute statements only under certain situations or to execute statements repeatedly for a certain number of times. Along the way, you'll learn most of JavaScript's remaining operators. (Chapter 2, JavaScript in Action, snuck in a couple of conditionals and operators, but this chapter teaches the bulk of them in full detail.)

# BASICS OF CONDITIONALS

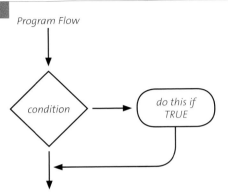

*Program Flow*

**FIGURE 5.1** Conditionals allow you to change the programming flow based upon the particular circumstances of your choosing.

JavaScript has the standard conditionals that exist in most programming languages, which is to be expected as JavaScript's syntax comes from Java and C. The three forms of JavaScript conditionals are the `if`, the `switch`, and the conditional operator. These are all *branching* statements, directing JavaScript to head down different paths based upon the situation (**Figure 5.1**).

To start, let's look at the basics of the `if` conditional, what it means for a conditional to be TRUE, and what operators you'll commonly use to establish conditions. As you read through this chapter, remember that JavaScript is case-sensitive, so it's `if`, not *IF*, or *If*, for example.

## THE IF CONDITIONAL

The `if` conditional is one of the most common and necessary constructs in any programming language. In JavaScript, the conditional uses the syntax:

```
if (condition) {
    // Execute these statements.
}
```

If the condition is TRUE, the statement or statements within the curly braces will be executed. If the condition is FALSE, the statements will be ignored, as if they were never there. The syntax is simple, the complexity comes from establishing the conditions. Technically, JavaScript does allow you to omit the curly braces if there's only one line of code being executed as a result of the condition:

```
if (condition)
    // Execute this statement.
```

However, I would highly recommend that you always include the curly braces. Doing so makes code that is easier to read and less likely to have bugs. Very, very rarely I might omit them, but in those cases, I would put the statement on the same line:

```
if (condition) // Execute this statement.
```

I only do this when I'm willing to compromise clarity for brevity, but, again, I generally recommend using curly braces.

There is an entire war about where the opening curly brace should go: on the same line as the condition or on the following line. Some programmers prefer the symmetry offered by this format:

```
if (condition)
{
    // Execute these statements.
}
```

Which style you use is entirely up to you; there's no right answer just be consistent. For added clarity, you should indent the statements to be executed to visually indicate their subservient position in the code. The indention is normally either four spaces or one tab (again, there are minor skirmishes over spaces versus tabs: pick a style you like and stick with it).

## WHAT IS TRUE?

In order to accurately use any type of control structure, you must fully grasp what constitutes truth in the language. Obviously, the Boolean true is, um, TRUE:

```
if (true) { // Always works!
```

(I'm using the capitalized TRUE and FALSE to indicate truth and falsehood, differentiating those from the Booleans true and false.)

## JAVASCRIPT **COMMENTS**, ONE **LAST TIME**

I haven't formally discussed JavaScript's syntax for comments yet in this book, although there's been the occasional reference and you've certainly seen them several times over. Here, though, is a quick, yet complete, coverage of comments in JavaScript.

One way to create comments is to use two slashes together (//). Anything following those two slashes until the end of the line is a comment. This syntax is used to add documentation either on the line before or on the same line immediately after some code:

```
// Initialize the variable:

var n = 1;

n++; // Add one to n
```

Whenever you use //, understand that they are for single-line comments only. To create multiline comments in JavaScript, use /* to begin the comment and */ to conclude it. This comment format is often used to add more verbose documentation to a file or function:

```
/*

 * somefile.js

 * Created by Larry Ullman.

 * This file does yadda, yadda, yadda.

 */
```

(The use of the additional asterisks on intermediary lines is a convention, but certainly not required.)

The multiline comment can also be used as a debugging tool: just wrap potentially problematic code within these key combinations to render that code inert, without having to delete it from your script. When you do this, be certain not to introduce parse errors, for example, by including an opening curly brace but not a closing one, or vice versa, within the comment:

```
if (condition) {

    /* Start of comment.

} Problem! */
```

As a final note on comments, I generally say that you cannot overdocument your code. Be thorough and accurate in your comments, and be certain to update your comments when you change your code. That being said, since every client will also need to download your comments as it's part of the JavaScript code, there's a good argument for removing comments from the production version of your scripts. Chapter 14, Advanced JavaScript, will explain this concept in more detail.

To understand what is TRUE in JavaScript, one just needs to know what is FALSE: Everything that's not FALSE is TRUE. In JavaScript, the following values are all evaluated as FALSE in a conditional:

- `false`
- `0`
- an empty string (`""` or `''`)
- `NaN` (Not a Number)
- `null`
- `undefined`

Everything else is TRUE. With this in mind, a very simple conditional in JavaScript confirms that a variable has a non-FALSE value:

```
if (myVar) {
```

Behind the scenes, JavaScript converts variables used in a conditional like this to a Boolean object. If the variable has a non-FALSE value, then it will be converted to a Boolean for that conditional.

Four of the values in that list—`false`, `NaN`, `null`, and `undefined`—make sense as FALSE, but both 0 and an empty string can trip you up. Later in this chapter, you'll learn ways to distinguish between values that are *actually* FALSE and those that *just get treated as* FALSE.

## COMPARISON OPERATORS

More sophisticated conditionals require the use of operators. The comparison operators are generally easy to understand and use (**Table 5.1**).

**TABLE 5.1** Comparison Operators

| OPERATOR | MEANING | OPERATOR | MEANING |
|---|---|---|---|
| > | Greater than | == | Equal to |
| < | Less than | != | Not equal to |
| >= | Greater than or equal to | === | Identical to |
| <= | Less than or equal to | !== | Not identical to |

**FIGURE 5.2** Inadvertently using the assignment operator is a common cause of bugs.

**FIGURE 5.3** Reversing a comparison will prevent you from accidentally using the wrong operator.

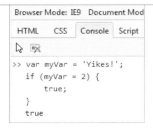

```
Browser Mode: IE9  Document Mod
HTML    CSS    Console   Script

>> var myVar = 'Yikes!';
   if (myVar = 2) {
        true;
   }
   true
```

```
Browser Mode: IE9  Document Mode: IE9 standards
HTML    CSS    Console   Script   Profiler   Netwo

>> var myVar = 'Yikes!';
   if (2 = myVar) {
        true;
   }
❌ "Invalid left-hand side in assignment"
```

For the most part, you shouldn't have a problem with most of these. In fact, Chapter 2 already used a *comparison* operator and a *logical* operator:

```
if ( (email.value.length > 0) && (password.value.length > 0) ) {
```

The `email.value.length > 0` condition will be TRUE if the `email` variable's value property, which is a string, has a `length` (i.e., the number of characters in the string) greater than 0. The entire condition will only be TRUE if both clauses are TRUE, which is how the logical *and* operator works.

Later in the chapter, I'll go through some of the specifics about comparing simple value types–numbers and strings, but first I want to highlight two common causes of problems when using comparison operators. The first is to accidentally use the *assignment* operator when you should be using the *equality* operator. The following conditional will always evaluate to TRUE (**Figure 5.2**):

```
if (myVar = 2) {
```

That code should be:

```
if (myVar == 2) {
```

If you find yourself frequently making this mistake, you can reverse the comparison:

```
if (2 == myVar) {
```

That condition is equivalent to the one just above, but if you accidentally write

```
if (2 = myVar) {
```

you'll see an error (**Figure 5.3**), as the number 2 cannot be assigned a value.

**TIP:** JavaScript validation tools such as JSLint and JSHint will catch misuses of the assignment operator.

The other common problem is more complicated: the difference between two values being *equal* or being *identical*. An equality comparison in JavaScript compares the values, automatically performing type conversion in the process. For example, start with the following:

```
var n = 0;
if (n) {
```

Will that condition be TRUE or FALSE? You might think it'd be TRUE, as n is assigned a value immediately before the conditional. However, the number 0 is evaluated as a FALSE value, and when you use just a variable as the basis of a condition, JavaScript will convert the variable to a Boolean behind the scenes. Thus, that condition is FALSE, as n is *equivalent* to false when used in that way.

In situations where you might be dealing with a FALSE-like value, you can instead perform *identical* comparisons (also referred to as "strict equality"). Three equals signs together constitutes the identical comparison operator. An identical comparison is TRUE if both comparators have the same value *and are of the same type*:

```
if (n === false) { // FALSE!
```

Assuming the same numeric n value, that condition is FALSE, as the value of n is *equal* to false, but not of the same type (n is a Number object; false is a Boolean). The following conditions are all also FALSE:

- `null === undefined`

- `'' === NaN`

- `1 === true`

Conversely, these conditions are all TRUE (note the specific use of both equality and identical comparisons):

- `null == undefined`               - `1 == true`

- `null !== undefined`              - `1 !== true`

(I'm purposefully not making equal and identical comparisons against NaN, as that value behaves a bit differently in this area.)

This can be confusing for the beginning programmer, and a likely cause of bugs, so I'll leave you with one simple rule. You should perform an *identical* comparison when you want to confirm that a variable has a value of undefined, null, or false, not a FALSE-like value (i.e., 0, null, an empty string, and undefined).

To clarify, remember that a variable that's been declared but not assigned a value has an initial value of undefined. Even if the variable has a value of false, 0, an empty string, or even null, the variable will not be *identical* to undefined:

```
if (myVar === undefined) { // No value.
```

or

```
if (myVar !== undefined) { // Has a value.
```

As another example, to distinguish between a FALSE-like value, such as an empty string, 0, null, or undefined, and an actual value of false, again turn to identical comparisons:

```
if (myVar === false) { // Definitely false!
```

or

```
if (myVar !== false) { // Has a non-false value!
```

Later in the chapter, you'll learn about the typeof operator, which is also useful in conditionals like these.

## LOGICAL OPERATORS

Along with the comparison operators, you'll frequently use the three logical operators in your conditionals (**Table** 5.2).

**TABLE 5.2** Logical Operators

| OPERATOR | MEANING |
| --- | --- |
| && | And |
| \|\| | Or |
| ! | Not |

A compound *and* condition will be TRUE only if both subconditions are TRUE:

```
var x = 5;
if ( (0 < x) && (x < 10) ) { // TRUE!
if ( (0 < x) && (x > 10) ) { // FALSE!
if ( (0 > x) && (x < 10) ) { // FALSE!
if ( (0 > x) && (x > 10) ) { // FALSE!
```

A compound *or* condition will be TRUE if at least one of the subconditions is TRUE:

```
var x = 5;
if ( (0 < x) && (x < 10) ) { // TRUE!
if ( (0 < x) && (x > 10) ) { // TRUE!
if ( (0 > x) && (x < 10) ) { // TRUE!
if ( (0 > x) && (x > 10) ) { // FALSE!
```

A negation will be TRUE if the condition being negated is FALSE:

```
var x = 5;
if ( !(0 > x) ) { // TRUE!
if ( !(false) ) { // TRUE!
```

When you start using more operators and creating more complex conditionals, you may want to reconsider JavaScript's list of operator precedence (see Chapter 4, Simple Variable Types). The *and* and *or* operators have lower precedence than most others, aside from the assignment operators, meaning you can generally forgo wrapping subconditions in parentheses when using them. The *not* operator, though, has a higher precedence, above the comparison operators, for example, meaning you should be in the habit of applying the negation to an expression in parentheses, as in the above examples.

Or, you could do what I do in all my code, and just always use parentheses to enforce operator precedence as you need it to be, without having to rely upon your memorization of complicated rules.

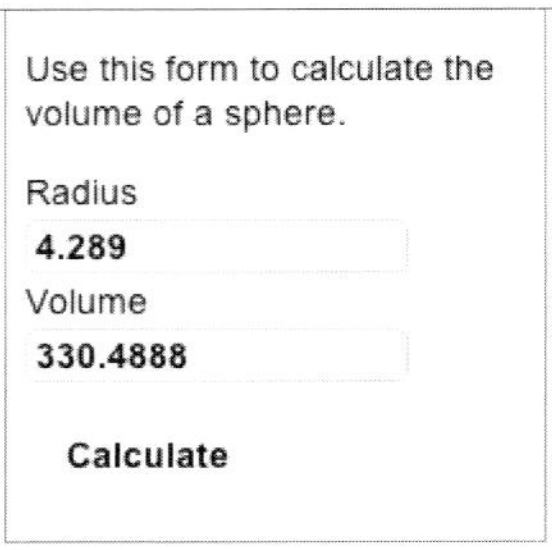

Use this form to calculate the volume of a sphere.

Radius

4.289

Volume

330.4888

Calculate

FIGURE 5.4 The improved version of this calculator now requires a positive radius.

Another factor to be aware of when using the *and* and *or* logical operators is something called *short circuit evaluation*. JavaScript will evaluate such conditionals as efficiently as possible, which is a good thing. This means that if the first condition in an *and* conditional is FALSE, the second condition will not be evaluated, because it's already been determined that the entire condition is FALSE. The converse is true for *or* conditionals: If the first condition is TRUE, the second condition need not be evaluated, because it has already been decided that the entire condition is TRUE.

## PUTTING IT ALL TOGETHER

It's time to put together the information covered thus far to demonstrate a real-world use. This first example will be a simple update of an example from the previous chapter, using a conditional to check for a positive radius value before attempting to calculate the volume of a sphere (**Figure 5.4**). As a reminder, you can download all of the code for this book from www.LarryUllman.com.

**To use a conditional to check for positive values:**

1. Open sphere.js in your text editor or IDE.

2. Change the assignment to the radius variable to read:

    ```
    var radius = document.getElementById('radius');
    ```

    Rather than going straight to the form element's value, this script will now get there in two steps. First, a reference will be made to the element.

3. Replace the use of Math.abs(), line 16 of the original script, with:

    ```
    if (radius && (radius.value > 0)) {
    ```

    The first part of this condition confirms that the radius variable has a TRUE value. So long as the document.getElementById() method was able to find an element in the page that has an id of *radius*, this will be the case. The second part of the condition checks that the radius object's value attribute is greater than 0. This is an improvement over just applying the absolute method to the value, as it more stringently requires that the user entered a positive number.

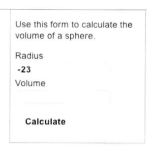

Use this form to calculate the volume of a sphere.

Radius

-23

Volume

Calculate

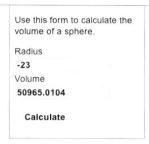

Use this form to calculate the volume of a sphere.

Radius

-23

Volume

50965.0104

Calculate

**FIGURE 5.5** If an invalid radius is provided, nothing happens.

**FIGURE 5.6** The result of the same invalid radius (as Figure 5.5), using the original version of the script.

4. Change the calculation of the volume to:

```
volume = (4/3) * Math.PI * Math.pow(radius.value, 3);
```

Since the radius variable is a reference to the form element, not the form element's value (as in the previous version of the script), the calculation has to be updated accordingly.

5. After displaying the calculated volume, complete the if conditional:

```
} // End of IF.
```

6. Save the file as sphere.js, in a js directory next to sphere.html (from Chapter 4), and test it in your Web browser (**Figure 5.5**).

This script would be improved by indicating an error to the user when a nonpositive number is entered (as in Figure 5.5), but you don't quite know how to do that yet. Still, this version of the script is better than that in Chapter 4, which would have attempted to calculate the volume even when a non-numeric value was provided (**Figure 5.6**).

# MORE **CONDITIONALS**

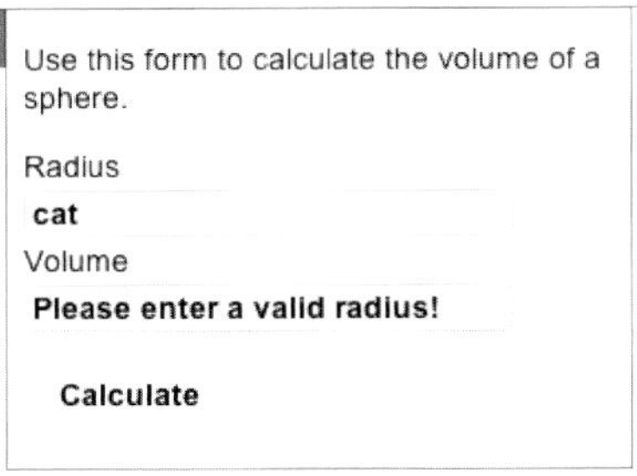

**FIGURE 5.7** Using an else clause, the script now reports problems.

This chapter began with the core principles of conditionals in JavaScript: the basic if conditional, the nature of truth in JavaScript (very philosophical), and the operators you'll often use. Let's now build on that information, covering the other types of conditionals you can create.

## IF-ELSE CONDITIONALS

After the if conditional, the most used is the if-else. That syntax is simply:

```
if (condition) {
    // Execute these statements.
} else {
    // Execute these other statements.
}
```

It's best to think of the else clause as being the default: that which will happen unless a specific criterion is met.

With this in mind, sphere.js could be updated so that a message is displayed when an invalid radius is supplied (**Figure 5.7**):

```
if (radius && (radius.value > 0)) {
    volume = (4/3) * Math.PI * Math.pow(radius.value, 3);
    volume = volume.toFixed(4);
} else {
    volume = 'Please enter a valid radius!';
}
document.getElementById('volume').value = volume;
```

## IF-ELSE IF CONDITIONALS

If you have multiple criteria to consider, there's the `if-else if`:

```
if (condition1) {
    // Execute these statements.
} else if (condition2) {
    // Execute these other statements.
}
```

With `if-else` and `if-else if` conditionals, you can also omit the curly braces if only a single line of code is to be executed, but I highly recommend you never do so. You can have as many `else if` clauses as you need. For performance reasons, I recommend listing the conditions in the order from most likely to be TRUE to least, thereby minimizing how many conditions JavaScript will need to evaluate.

You can also use an `else` clause with `if-else if`, but the `else` clause must always come last, and will again act as the default action:

```
if (gender == 'Female') {
    // It's a Barbie.
} else if (gender == 'Male') {
    // It's a Ken.
} else {
    // Error!
}
```

## NESTING **CONDITIONALS**

Conditionals and other control structures can be *nested* by placing one within another. For example, a registration form would have two inputs for the password: the one used to confirm the value of the other. Validating the password therefore requires:

- That the first password has a value

- That the second password matches the first

This can be succinctly accomplished thanks to an if-else nested within an if-else:

```
if (pass1.length > 0) {

    if (pass1 == pass2) {

        // Good!

    } else {

        // Passwords don't match.

    } // End of inner else.

} else {

    // First password not set.

} // End of primary else.
```

When nesting control structures, I recommend that you:

- Indent subservient code to visually indicate the logical structure

- Completely create one control structure (e.g., one if-else), with all the curly braces and parentheses, and then add the nested control structure

- Use comments to indicate where control structures end

The main thing is that you're very careful when creating nested control structures, as improperly nested control structures are a common cause of parse errors.

## THE SWITCH CONDITIONAL

A third way of writing conditionals is to use `switch`. Its syntax is actually more verbose than any of the other approaches discussed thus far, but it can be a much cleaner, more legible alternative to a long `if-else if-else`:

```
switch (expression) {
    case value1:
        // Execute these statements.
        break;
    case value2:
        // Execute these statements instead.
        break;
    default:
        // No, execute these statements.
        break;
}
```

The expression in parentheses will be compared against the various case values. Often, this expression will just be a variable:

```
switch (sign) {
    case 'Aquarius':
        // Execute these statements.
        break;
    case 'Pisces':
        // Execute these statements instead.
        break;
    /* Etc. */
}
```

Note that, as with any value in JavaScript, strings must be quoted, numbers and Booleans not.

JavaScript will go through the cases in order until an *identity* (not *equality*) match is made. At that point, JavaScript will execute the subsequent statements, stopping when a break is reached. This means that if you fail to use break statements, all of the remaining statements in the switch will be executed.

The default case is optional. If present, the default case is normally listed last, although this isn't required (unlike in most other languages). The default case's statements will be executed only if none of the other cases are a match. You don't have to use a break for the last case, but doing so constitutes parallel structure and consistency that make for good programming.

There are a couple of neat tricks one can pull off when using the switch. The first is the ability to perform *fallthroughs*. A fallthrough is where multiple cases have the same resulting statements, made possible by not using a break for every case:

```
switch (weekday) {
    case 'Monday':
    case 'Wednesday':
    case 'Friday':
        // Execute these statements.
        break;
    case 'Tuesday':
    case 'Thursday':
        // Execute these statements instead.
        break;
    default:
        // The default statements.
        break;
}
```

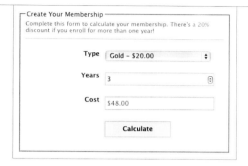

**FIGURE 5.8** The HTML form, with the calculated membership cost.

In that code, if the weekday variable has a value of *Monday*, *Wednesday*, or *Friday*, the first set of statements will be executed. If it has a value of *Tuesday* or *Thursday*, the second set will apply. If weekday has any other value, including but not limited to *Saturday* and *Sunday*, the default statements will be executed.

You can also use more elaborate expressions as the basis of comparison. This next switch replicates the gender conditional created earlier:

```
switch (gender) {
    case 'Female':
        // Barbie!
        break;
    case 'Male':
        // Ken!
        break;
}
```

(To be clear, however, when you only have two cases, you shouldn't be using a switch.)

To use much of this new information, this next example will calculate the total cost of a membership (to whatever site), based upon the membership type and the number of years (**Figure 5.8**). The HTML page will be named membership.html. Its most critical HTML is:

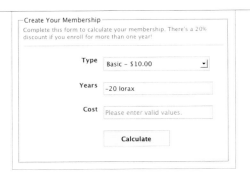

**FIGURE 5.9** If the user does not enter a valid years value, an error message is displayed.

```html
<div><label for="type">Type</label> <select name="type"
→  id="type" required>
    <option value="basic">Basic - $10.00</option>
    <option value="premium">Premium - $15.00</option>
    <option value="gold">Gold - $20.00</option>
    <option value="platinum">Platinum - $25.00</option>
</select></div>
<div><label for="years">Years</label><input type="number"
→  name="years" id="years" min="1" required></div>
<div><label for="cost">Cost</label><input type="text" name="cost"
→  id="cost" disabled></div>
<input type="submit" value="Calculate" id="submit">
```

That would be placed within a form with an id value of *theForm*. The HTML form makes use of the HTML5 number input type for the years, with a minimum value. A select element is used to choose the type of membership being purchased. For now, the final text element will be updated with the results of the calculation (Figure 5.8), or an error message (**Figure 5.9**). It's set as disabled, so that the user cannot change its value.

This page will include the membership.js JavaScript file, to be written in the subsequent steps.

**To create the calculator:**

1. Create a new JavaScript file in your text editor or IDE, to be named membership.js.

2. Begin defining the `calculate()` function:

```
function calculate() {
    'use strict';
    var cost;
```

This function will be called when the form is submitted. Within the function, the cost variable will store the calculated cost of membership.

3. Get a reference to the first two form elements:

```
var type = document.getElementById('type');
var years = document.getElementById('years');
```

4. Convert the year to a number:

```
if (years && years.value) {
    years = parseInt(years.value, 10);
}
```

This conditional confirms that the year variable has a non-FALSE value and that its value property also has a non-FALSE value. This condition will be TRUE so long as there's an HTML element with an id of *years* (because that's how the years variable is first assigned a value) and if that element has a value property whose value is anything other than null, undefined, false, NaN, 0, or an empty string. If this entire condition is TRUE, the value is converted to an integer, as an extra precaution.

Because JavaScript is weakly typed, you can change the years variable from being a reference to a form element to being a number.

5. Validate all the data:

```
if (type && type.value && years && (years > 0) ) {
```

The first two clauses are like those already used on the year form element. The third condition—years—tests that the variable has a TRUE value. It would have a FALSE value if the parsing of years.value couldn't create a number other than 0. The final condition ensures that the number is positive.

**6.** Determine the base cost:

```
switch (type.value) {
    case 'basic':
        cost = 10.00;
        break;
    case 'premium':
        cost = 15.00;
        break;
    case 'gold':
        cost = 20.00;
        break;
    case 'platinum':
        cost = 25.00;
        break;
} // End of switch.
```

Because type.value is based upon a select menu, with multiple possible values, a switch conditional is a great way in JavaScript to make comparisons to those options. Each associated membership type has its own base cost.

**7.** Factor in the number of years:

```
cost *= years;
```

The membership total will be based upon the cost per year times the number of years.

**8.** Factor in the discount:

```
if (years > 1) {
    cost *= .80; // 80%
}
```

The total membership cost is being discounted 20 percent if more than one year is being purchased. A simple if conditional can test for that scenario. To do the math, you can use this code to subtract 20 percent:

```
cost -= (cost * .20);
```

Or you can just multiply the total by .80, to find the remaining 80 percent of the cost, as in the above.

9. Display the total in the form:

```
document.getElementById('cost').value = '$' + cost.toFixed(2);
```

Here the calculated cost is being shown to the end user. To make the total look nicer, it's both rounded to two decimal places and prefaced with a dollar sign.

Understand that JavaScript cost calculations are a convenience to the user. Because JavaScript runs in the client, those calculations could easily be tampered with. Actual e-commerce transactions should always be based upon server-side calculations, which cannot be manipulated in the browser.

10. Show an error if the data wasn't valid:

```
} else { // Show an error:
    document.getElementById('cost').value =
→   'Please enter valid values.';
}
```

If the condition in Step 5 isn't TRUE, then this else clause takes effect (see Figure 5.9).

11. Return false to prevent submission of the form and complete the function:

```
    return false;
} // End of calculate() function.
```

**12.** Add an event listener to the form:

```
function init() {
    'use strict';
    document.getElementById('theForm').onsubmit = calculate;
} // End of init() function.
window.onload = init;
```

This code was explained in Chapter 2 and Chapter 4. The end result is that when the form is submitted, the `calculate()` function will be called.

**13.** Save the file as `membership.js`, in a `js` directory next to `membership.html`, and test it in your Web browser (Figures 5.8 and 5.9).

## CRYPTIC CONDITIONALS

There are a couple of variations on the standard `if-else` conditionals that are worth knowing, although their syntaxes are more cryptic and less obvious. The first alternative is the *conditional operator*, known as the ternary or trinary operator in other languages (it has three components). Its syntax is:

```
(condition) ? return_if_true : return_if_false;
```

The conditional operator returns one of two values depending upon the truth of the condition. Because this operator returns a value, it can be used to assign a value to a variable:

```
var even = ( (n % 2) === 0) ? true : false;
```

That code assigns a Boolean value to the even variable, depending upon whether or not the number n is divisible by 2 without any remainder. That code is equivalent to the longer:

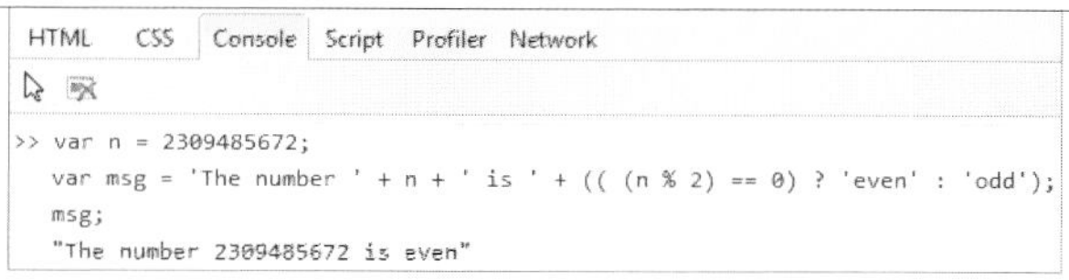

**FIGURE 5.10** Here, the conditional operator is used inline to concatenate one of two different strings onto another string, depending upon a variable's value.

```
var even;
if ( (n % 2) === 0) {
    even = true;
} else {
    even = false;
}
```

Although it is common to use the conditional operator to assign a value to a variable, it can be used in other ways, such as (**Figure 5.10**):

```
alert(((myVar !== undefined) ? 'Has a value' :
    'Does not have a value'));
var msg = 'The number ' + n + ' is ' + (( (n % 2) ==
    0) ? 'even' : 'odd');
```

You should note that when used inline like this, it's best to wrap the entire conditional operator structure within parentheses in order to avoid issues caused by operator precedence.

Another way you can cryptically create a conditional is by taking advantage of how JavaScript evaluates the *and* and *or* logical operators. Take, for example, the following:

```
var x = y || 1;
```

The *and* and *or* operators don't necessarily return a Boolean value, but rather the value of one of the operands. Looking at that line of code, JavaScript will first evaluate the left-hand operand: y. If that variable has a non-FALSE value, its value will be returned. If y has a FALSE value, then 1 will be returned. The end result is that the variable x is assigned the value of the variable y, if it's set, or 1 otherwise. This is equivalent to:

```
var x;
if (y) {
    x = y;
} else {
    x = 1;
}
```

While this is a nice shortcut, if you find the syntax to be confusing, you can stick to the formal conditional structure. Also be aware that:

- With an *or* conditional, the first value will always be returned if it's TRUE (as in the above)

- With an *and* conditional, the first value will always be returned if the first value is FALSE, as the whole condition will therefore be FALSE

This is due to how JavaScript performs short circuit evaluations, as already discussed.

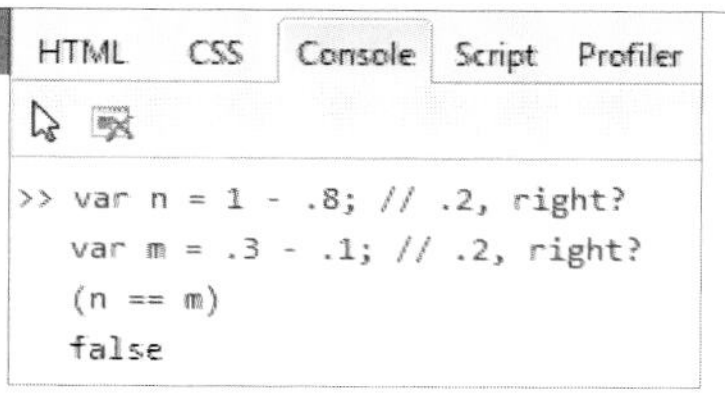

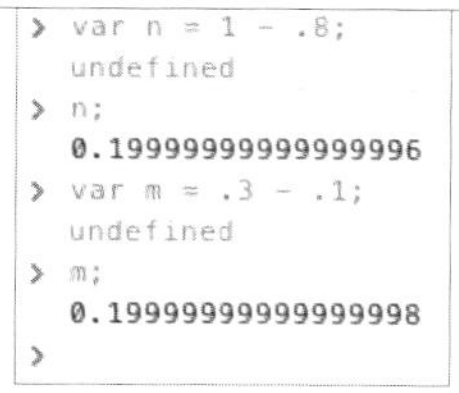

# MORE **COMPLEX CONDITIONS**

**FIGURE 5.11** Arithmetic and numeric equality comparisons in JavaScript do not always work as you might hope.

**FIGURE 5.12** JavaScript, and other languages, represent numbers using approximations.

The heart of any conditional isn't the particular kind in use—if, if-else, the conditional operator, switch, etc.—so much as the particular condition being established. In this section of the chapter, you'll see how best to validate numbers, how conditions can be written using strings, and you'll start learning about validating data by type.

## COMPARING NUMBERS

You would think that making comparisons with numeric values would be straight-forward, and it generally is. There are a couple of technical details to be aware of, however. First, you should know that it's quite difficult for computers to accurately represent numbers. For example, the following does not behave as you would expect (**Figure 5.11**):

```
var n = 1 - .8; // .2, right?
var m = .3 - .1; // .2, right?
if (n == m) { // FALSE!
```

The problem here is that JavaScript cannot cleanly handle the decimals (**Figure 5.12**). This isn't just particular to JavaScript; it's common with most languages, often with integers, too. Fortunately, most code doesn't check the *equality* of two exact values, but rather compares the two to see which is larger or smaller. In fact, with JavaScript, the following condition isn't actually a test if x is greater than or equal to y, but rather that x is not less than y (it's a subtle but meaningful distinction):

```
if (x >= y) {
```

If you need to perform exact equality comparisons of two numbers, there are tricks you can employ to do so reliably. The first is to round the decimals to the digits you need and then make the comparison:

```
var n = 1 - .8;
```

```
n = n.toFixed(1);
var m = .3 - .1;
m = m.toFixed(1);
if (n == m) { // TRUE!
```

This solution works because it drops extraneous decimals and because the toFixed() method converts numbers to strings. The end comparison is between two strings, which is more reliable.

The second option is to use integers for all the math and comparisons, and then convert to a decimal for presentation purposes:

```
var quantity = 5;
var cost = 199; // 1.99, actually.
var total = cost * quantity;
total /= 100;
alert ('The total is ' + total.toFixed(2));
```

Moving on, there's another kind of numeric equality comparison that cannot be done in JavaScript. Mentioned earlier in the chapter, you cannot perform equality or identity comparisons against the value NaN (*Not a Number*), as it's a special kind of value. Oddly, even the following condition will be FALSE:

```
if (NaN === NaN) { // FALSE!
```

Instead, when you need to check if a number is not a number, you can use the isNaN() function:

```
if (isNaN(n)) { // Not a number.
```

This is a "top-level" function, meaning it's not called on any object, as in the above.

You can also validate that a number is a number by invoking the isFinite() function:

```
if (isFinite(n)) { // Usable number.
```

The isFinite() function returns true if the provided number is not NaN or infinite (positive or negative). The function will also attempt to convert the variable to a number, as if you had applied parseInt() or parseFloat().

## COMPARING STRINGS

Next, let's look at how one makes string comparisons in JavaScript. With strings, a simple equality comparison is natural:

```
if (myVar1 == myVar2) {
```

or

```
if (password == 'truthiness') {
```

Such comparisons are *case-sensitive*. To perform a case-insensitive comparison, apply either toLowerCase() or toUpperCase() to both values being compared:

```
if (email.toLowerCase() == storedEmail.toLowerCase()) { // Okay!
```

In Chapter 4, the indexOf() method was introduced as a way to test if one string (i.e., the needle) exists within another (i.e., the haystack):

```
if (comments.indexOf('spam')) { // Contains spam, but…
```

This method returns the value −1 if the needle is *not found*, and the indexed position where it begins if it is found. Taking into account what you've already learned in this chapter, you cannot simply use the above code to test for the presence of the needle in the haystack (hence the "but" in the comment). The indexOf() method would return 0 if *spam* is found at the very beginning of comments, and 0 evaluates to false in this situation. Conversely, if *spam* is not found within comments at all, the method returns −1, which evaluates to true here. Thus, what you'd really want to do is specifically check that the method hasn't returned −1:

```
if (comments.indexOf('spam') != -1) { // Contains spam!
```

Finally, if you need to compare two strings alphabetically to see which comes first, you can use the less than and greater than operators:

```
if ('cat' > 'dog') { // FALSE
if ('cat' < 'catalog') { // TRUE
```

**FIGURE 5.13** The contact form, with two inputs.

**FIGURE 5.14** Error messages are revealed to the user via alert boxes.

**FIGURE 5.13** The contact form, with two inputs.

**FIGURE 5.14** Error messages are revealed to the user via alert boxes.

Again, just apply the case manipulation methods to perform a case-insensitive comparison. One thing to be aware of is that uppercase letters are "less than" lowercase letters:

```
if ('cat' > 'Cat') { // TRUE
```

**TIP:** If you perform a comparison between a string and a number, they'll be compared as numbers.

To use this new information, the next example will perform some validation on a simple contact form (**Figure 5.13**). The relevant HTML, in a page named contact.html, is:

```
<div><label for="email">Email Address</label><input type="email"
→ name="email" id="email" required></div>
```

```
<div><label for="comments">Comments</label><textarea name="comments"
→ id="comments" required></textarea></div>
```

Naturally, this is within a form whose id value is *theForm*.

The HTML form makes use of the HTML5 email input type, plus a text area. The HTML page includes the contact.js JavaScript file, to be written in the subsequent steps. For this example, errors will be shown using alerts (**Figure 5.14**), and the form's submission will only be allowed to go through if no errors occurred. Keep in mind that if your browser supports HTML5, the browser itself will perform the validation, only allowing the JavaScript to be called if the requirements are met.

To avoid that situation, you can switch browsers, not use HTML5, or simply add novalidate to the opening form tag.

**To process a contact form:**

1. Create a new JavaScript file in your text editor or IDE, to be named contact.js.

2. Begin defining the process() function:

```
function process() {
    'use strict';
    var okay = true;
```

The process() function will be called when the form is submitted. The okay variable will be a flag used to indicate whether the form has been completed properly or not. It is initially set to true, as no problem has occurred. When a form element fails its validation, this variable will be set to false.

3. Get a reference to the first two form elements:

```
var email = document.getElementById('email');
var comments = document.getElementById('comments');
```

4. Validate the email address:

```
if (!email || !email.value
|| (email.value.length < 6)
|| (email.value.indexOf('@') == -1)) {
    okay = false;
    alert('Please enter a valid email address!');
}
```

This four-part conditional will be TRUE if *any* of the subconditions are TRUE. The first condition checks if email has a FALSE value, which will be the case if no reference could be made to the form element. The second condition checks if the email variable has a value property, as an added precaution. Next, the third condition confirms that the length of the value is at least six characters, which is the bare minimum for an email address (*a@b.co*). Finally, a condition confirms that @ is found within the value. For a tighter validation, you could confirm that the last instance of @ is found at the same point in the string as the first instance, which is to say that the @ symbol is only being used once.

If any of these conditions is TRUE, the entire conditional is TRUE, in which case the okay variable is set to false and an alert message is shown. More precise validation of an email address requires a complicated regular expression, to be explained in Chapter 10, Working with Forms.

5. Validate the comments:

```
if (!comments || !comments.value
|| (comments.value.indexOf('<') != -1) ) {
    okay = false;
    alert('Please enter your comments, without any HTML!');
}
```

The first two clauses are like those already used on the email form element. The third clause checks for the presence of an opening angle bracket, which would imply the user may have attempted to submit some HTML.

6. Determine the status and complete the function:

```
    return okay;
}
```

Since the okay variable has a Boolean value indicating the status of the form validation, it can be returned directly. If okay is still true, the form's submission will be allowed to go through. If okay has been assigned false, for either reason, the form's submission will be halted.

7. Add an event listener to the form:

```
function init() {
    'use strict';
    document.getElementById('theForm').onsubmit = process;
} // End of init() function.
window.onload = init;
```

This code has been explained many times over by now. When the form is submitted, the process() function will be called.

8. Save the file as contact.js, in a js directory next to contact.html, and test it in your Web browser (Figures 5.13 and 5.14).

## THE TYPEOF OPERATOR

Sometimes, especially in more advanced programming, you don't need to compare a variable's value to another value, but rather determine *what type* of value it is. For example, a number in JavaScript is also an object of type Number and a string is also a String. When you get to working with complex types, being able to confirm what exact type of object you're working with is invaluable, too. In fact, especially in more advanced programming, confirming the type of a variable is often the most reliable approach.

To compare a value's type, you can use the typeof operator:

```
if (typeof myVar == 'number') {
```

The typeof operator returns the object's type as a string. Some of the values typeof could return are listed in **Table 5.3**. The table does omit a couple of types that would not mean much to you at this point.

**TABLE 5.3** typeof Return Values

| TYPE | RETURNS |
| --- | --- |
| Undefined | undefined |
| Null | object |
| Boolean | boolean |
| Number | number |
| String | string |
| Array | object |
| Object | object |

There are a couple of situations where the value returned by typeof can be confusing:

- null returns *object*
- NaN returns *number*
- Array returns *object*

For historical reasons, the null value's type is *object*. In future implementations, it will be *null*. That being said, you don't really need to see if a value is of type *null*, but rather if it is identical to null:

```
if (myVar === null) {
```

In the second situation, NaN, which stands for *Not a Number*, has a type of *number*. Odd as this may seem, it's simply because the NaN value is defined as part of the Number object. In the previous pages, you saw how to test against NaN.

The final example, where an Array object is of type *object*, will be explained in the next chapter.

# BASICS OF LOOPS

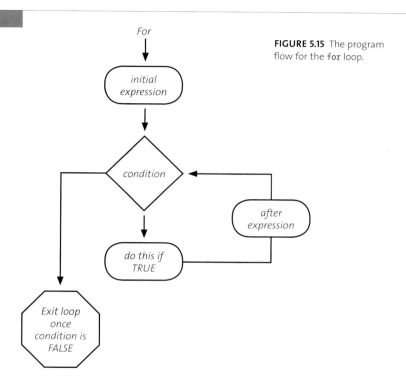

*For*

*initial expression*

*condition*

*after expression*

*do this if TRUE*

*Exit loop once condition is FALSE*

**FIGURE 5.15** The program flow for the for loop.

Along with conditionals, the other major control structure type is the loop. Loops are used to perform an action a repeated number of times. There is also a conditional aspect to loops, though, as every loop uses a condition to determine whether or not to execute the loop's contents. The two primary JavaScript loops are for, which is the more commonly used of the two, and while.

## THE FOR LOOP

The syntax of the for loop can be imposing, especially when you're first learning it:

```
for (initial expression; condition; after expression) {
    // Execute these statements.
}
```

To understand this syntax, one has to comprehend how JavaScript executes the for loop (**Figure 5.15**). The very first time JavaScript encounters the loop, the initial expression will be evaluated (which is to say, executed). This segment of the loop is normally used to define a variable or otherwise establish whatever baseline information will be needed for the loop. This expression will always be executed once (assuming JavaScript gets to that point in the code), and only once.

The second segment is where a condition is established. When the condition is TRUE, the contents of the loop will be executed. When the condition is, or becomes, FALSE, the loop's interaction halts. For some loops, the condition will never be TRUE; for other loops, like when you make a mistake, the condition will always be TRUE, resulting in an infinite loop (which is bad).

The third segment is evaluated *after* the loop's statements are executed. This means that the third expression will be executed the same number of times as the contents of the loop itself.

As a simple example of this, the next for loop iterates ten times:

```
for (var i = 1; i <= 10; i++) {
    // Do something.
}
```

The first time that loop is encountered, the i variable is declared and assigned the value 1. Then the loop checks to see if i is less than or equal to ten. For the ten times that's TRUE, the loop's statements will be executed. After each execution, i is incremented.

Normally, code within the for loop's statements or in the third clause will cause the condition to eventually become FALSE.

The first and last clauses can have more than one expression be evaluated. To do that, separate the expressions with commas while continuing to use semicolons to differentiate between the three parts of the loop structure:

```
for (var i = 1, var j = 0; (i + j) <= 10; i++, j += i) {
    // Do something.
}
```

**FIGURE 5.16** Six random numbers are determined by JavaScript and shown in the text input.

To demonstrate using loops, this next example will output a series of lucky numbers, such as might be used for a lottery (**Figure 5.16**). Rather than using a meaningless form for this purpose, I'm going to introduce a new concept, related to DOM manipulation, otherwise covered in Chapter 9, JavaScript and the Browser.

The HTML page, named random.html, contains this code:

```
<p>Winning Numbers: <span id="output"></span></p>
```

The JavaScript code will get a reference to that span:

```
var output = document.getElementById('output');
```

Using JavaScript, you can dynamically assign text to be placed within an HTML element by assigning a string to that element's textContent or innerText property. The former is the W3C standard and works on most browsers; innerText is for Internet Explorer. To determine which property to use, you can check that one property is not undefined:

```
if (output.textContent !== undefined) {
    output.textContent = 'some string';
} else {
    output.innerText =  'some string';
}
```

The conditional is TRUE if the textContent property is not identical to undefined. In layman's terms, this conditional asks, Does this element have this property? If so, then the string is assigned to that property. Otherwise, the string is assigned to the innerText property. In either case, the end result would be:

```
<p>Winning Numbers: <span id="output">some string</span></p>
```

Note that these properties only allow you to assign text to an element. To assign HTML to an element, you would use innerHTML:

```
output.innerHTML = 'some <a href="page.html">link</a>';
```

This property exists on all modern browsers.

With that new information introduced, the HTML page only needs that paragraph and span, and it will include the random.js JavaScript file, to be written in the subsequent steps. When the page is loaded, the numbers will be generated and shown on the page.

**To generate several random numbers:**

1. Create a new JavaScript file in your text editor or IDE, to be named random.js.

2. Begin defining the showNumbers() function:

   ```
   function showNumbers() {
       'use strict';
       var numbers = '';
   ```

   This function will be called when the page loads. It needs to generate six random numbers and display them on the page. The numbers variable will store the six random numbers as a string. It's given an initial value of an empty string.

3. Begin defining a for loop:

   ```
   for (var i = 0; i < 6; i++) {
   ```

   The first expression creates a variable named i, initially set to 0. The condition then checks that i is less than six. After the loop's body is executed, the post expression increments i. The end result will be six iterations of the loop.

4. Within the loop, add a random number to the string:

   ```
   numbers += parseInt((Math.random() * 100), 10) + ' ';
   ```

   There are a few things happening in this one step, so I'll break it down. To find a random number, invoke the Math.random() method, introduced in Chapter 4. This method returns a random number between 0 (inclusive) and 1 (exclusive). To convert that to a random number up to 100 (exclusive), multiply it by 100. To get just an integer from that, the resulting value is sent through the parseInt() method. This is concatenated onto the numbers variable, along with a single space.

5. Complete the loop:

   ```
   }
   ```

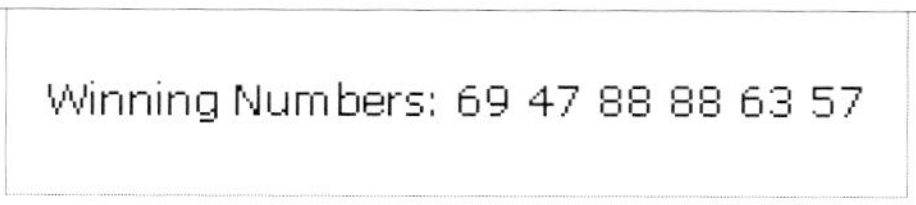

Winning Numbers: 69 47 88 88 63 57

**FIGURE 5.17** Six more random numbers.

6. Display the numbers on the page:

```
var output = document.getElementById('output');
if (output.textContent !== undefined) {
    output.textContent = numbers;
} else {
    output.innerText = numbers;
}
```

This is an application of the code just explained, used to place the value of the numbers variable within the span tags of the HTML page.

If you wanted to be extra neat, you could trim off the final space from numbers before displaying it in the form.

7. Complete the function:

```
} // End of showNumbers() function.
```

8. Add an event listener to the page's load event:

```
window.onload = showNumbers;
```

9. Save the file as random.js, in a js directory next to random.html, and test it in your Web browser (Figure 5. 16).

Reload the page to see new numbers (**Figure 5.17**).

## NESTING **LOOPS**

Just as conditionals can be nested, so can loops. Moreover, you can nest loops within conditionals and conditionals within loops. Whenever you're nesting one control structure within another, be certain to always use curly braces, mind your syntax, and use comments to clearly indicate the structures.

When nesting loops in particular, you'll need to make sure that you use different variables within each loop so that the one loop's variables do not conflict with the other's. For example, an outer loop might use i as a counter, and the inner loop j.

## THE WHILE LOOP

The second primary type of loop in JavaScript is while. Its syntax is much more straightforward:

```
while (condition) {
    // Statements to be executed.
}
```

A counterpart to the while loop is do…while:

```
do {
    // Statements to be executed.
} while (condition);
```

Unlike the while loop, the do…while loop will always be executed at least once, as its condition is not checked until after the first, and every subsequent, execution. Do note that there's a semicolon that terminates the construct, after the condition.

In theory, any time you need a loop you could use either a while or a for. In practice, you'll find that the for loop is best in situations where the number of iterations is knowable in advance and the while loop is best in situations where one doesn't know in advance how many iterations will be required. This distinction will make more sense in time, but the for loop is generally used more often in JavaScript.

## OTHER **STATEMENTS**

Along with the conditionals and loops, there are a couple of useful control statements to be familiar with. You've already seen one: break, used to exit a switch conditional. It can also be used to exit a loop:

```
while (condition) {

    if (some_other_condition) break;

}
```

Once that break statement is executed, the loop stops iterating, even if the loop's condition would have been TRUE on the next iteration.

Note that break terminates the immediate control structure. By that I mean that if you have loop B within loop A, a use of break within loop B closes that loop, returning execution to loop A. You can specify the control structure to exit using a *label*, but that's an esoteric enough concept not to be covered in this book.

The continue keyword leaves the current iteration of the loop but doesn't, in itself, terminate the loop's execution. For a while loop, this means that the condition will be tested again, and whether or not the loop is executed depends upon that condition's truth. The same is true for a do…while loop. For a for loop, this means that the loop's after expression (i.e., the third clause) will be evaluated, and then the condition will be checked.

Another control statement has been used repeatedly throughout this book already: return. When a return statement is executed, the code leaves the current function.

In Chapter 12, Error Management, you'll learn about throw, which is another statement that affects the flow of programming logic. It's used to indicate an error, sending the script progression to the error-handling portion of the code.

# REVIEW AND PURSUE

If you have any problems with these sections, either in answering the questions or pursuing your own endeavors, turn to the book's supporting forum (`www.LarryUllman.com/forums/`).

## REVIEW

- What is the syntax of the `if` conditional? Of `if-else`? Of `if-else if`? Of `if-else if-else`?
- What are other ways you can write conditionals in JavaScript?
- What are some of the operators introduced in this chapter?
- What is the difference between = and ==?
- What is the difference between == and ===?
- How do you perform a case-insensitive comparison of two strings?
- What is the `typeof` operator?
- What is the syntax of the for loop? Of the while loop? Of the do...while loop?
- What are the `textContent`, `innerText`, and `innerHTML` properties and why are they useful?

## PURSUE

- Apply conditionals and the `isNaN()` or `isFinite()` functions to `sphere.js` to ensure that valid numbers are in use.
- Apply the information discussed in this chapter to the examples in Chapter 4.
- Update `membership.js` so that the discount percentage varies based upon the number of years being purchased (e.g., 10 percent for two or three years, 15 percent for four, and 20 percent for five or more).
- Modify `membership.js` to use a paragraph or span, along with `textContent` and `innerText`, rather than a form element to show the calculated cost.

- As suggested in the step sequence, add another condition to `contact.js` that confirms that only one use of @ is present in the email address.

- Use your browser's console interface to practice with variables and conditionals.

- Trim the extra space off of `numbers` in `random.js`, as suggested in those steps.

- Remove the initialization of the `numbers` variable in `random.js` (i.e., remove the assignment of the empty string), and then rerun the script. See what happens and then try to figure out why.

## WRAPPING UP

In this chapter, you've learned quite a lot of information about control structures in JavaScript. The key bits were the conditionals, the loops, the comparison and logical operators, and a slew of ways you can establish conditions. You should remember to pay close attention to uses of =, ==, and ===, and keep in mind that numeric comparisons, including the special NaN value, can be tricky. And always be mindful of your syntax when creating any control structure, let alone complex and nested ones.

Between the knowledge acquired here and in Chapter 4, you should now be familiar with the fundamentals of simple data types and how to dynamically take actions depending upon considerations of your choosing. In short, you have seen what you need to know to do basic JavaScript programming, which includes form validation and then some.

Much of the information covered thus far isn't that different from the syntax, structures, and simple data types you'd see in other programming languages. The content you're about to encounter in the next two chapters will go far toward differentiating JavaScript from other languages, though. Starting, in the next chapter, with objects: the heart of JavaScript.

# 6

# COMPLEX
# VARIABLE TYPES

Chapter 4, Simple Variable Types, introduced the basics of working with variables in JavaScript, including the simplest of types: strings, numbers, and Booleans. The true potential of any language comes through its complex data types. In JavaScript, this primarily means arrays and objects, although I've included the Date type in this chapter, too. While arrays are common to all languages (in one format or another), JavaScript's implementation of objects is significantly different from any other language, and key to understanding JavaScript as a whole.

# GENERATING DATES AND TIMES

**FIGURE 6.1** The creation of a new variable of type Date, representing the current date and time.

The first complex type to be discussed in this chapter is the Date object. Although Date is used quite differently than the array and (generic) object you'll learn about in later pages, Date is more complex than the simple types already discussed, so I've chosen to cover it here. Like all well-designed objects, Date is specific in its intended use, while still being very helpful. The Date object in JavaScript is able to represent any date and time 100 million (yes, 100,000,000) days before or after midnight on January 1, 1970. That's an arbitrary date commonly used by computers as a point of reference, called the *epoch* or *Unix epoch*.

## CREATING DATES

To create a Date object, use this syntax (**Figure 6.1**):

```
var today = new Date();
```

After the first three parts—use of the var keyword, the variable's name, and the assignment operator—this is a different syntax for creating a variable than you've otherwise seen in the book. The new operator is used to create new objects. The specific object type to be created follows the operator. In the above, this is Date. That line creates a new Date object whose value—the date and time it stores—is the current date and time. Understand that when JavaScript is running in the client (e.g., the Web browser), the current date and time are those for the client machine.

There are three ways of creating dates for specific dates and times:

```
var someday = new Date(year, month, day, hour, minute, second,
    milliseconds);
var someday = new Date(milliseconds);
var someday = new Date('date string');
```

FIGURE 6.2 Creating two Date objects, first representing a specific date, but not time, then representing a specific date *and* time.

These three approaches correspond to the three ways dates can be represented:

- As atomic year, month, day, hour, minute, second, and millisecond values

- As a timestamp, which is the number of seconds, or in JavaScript, milliseconds, before or after the epoch

- As a string, such as *July 5, 2012*

Let's look at these options in order.

## USING ATOMIC DATE VALUES

The first way you can create a Date object for a specific date is to provide separate year, month, and day values. The day value is optional and defaults to 1. The time values are optional, too. If provided, those values will be used to set the time on that date, too. The hours start at 0, but use 24-hour time: from 0 to 23. If no time values are provided, the time will be set as 00:00:00 and (0 milliseconds), which is to say midnight.

The year should be set as four digits. The month is one or two digits, but, tragically, start at 0 for January, not 1. I suspect this decision was made because most lists in most programming languages begin counting at 0, but it's frankly a terrible and confusing choice when it comes to identifying months. This decision is made even more egregious when you learn that the day of the month starts at 1. But I digress...

Thus, to create a representation of July 5, 2012, you'd use:

```
var thatDate = new Date(2012, 6, 5); // July is 6, not 7!
```

To create a representation of 1:30 p.m. on that date, you'd use (**Figure 6.2**):

```
var thatDate = new Date(2012, 6, 5, 13, 30); // July is 6, not 7!
```

**FIGURE 6.3** Creating a
Date object by providing a
timestamp.

**FIGURE 6.4** The string
provided must be of a correct
format or else the variable
will be assigned an invalid or
default date.

### USING A TIMESTAMP

The second way to set a specific date and time is to provide a single value to the Date object. This value is a timestamp representing the number of milliseconds since the epoch. As there are 86,400,000 milliseconds in a single day, the value used here will be quite large. For example, to create a Date object representing January 10, 1970—ten days after the epoch, you'd use (**Figure 6.3**):

```
var thatDate = new Date(86400000 * 10);
```

As you'll see over the next pages, rather than calculating your own timestamp and providing it to the Date object, you'll normally use a timestamp calculated in another way (such as by a second Date).

### USING A STRING

The third way to establish a specific date and time is to provide a string to the Date object. The catch is that the string must be formatted appropriately. Examples include:

- *July 5, 2012*

- *Jul 5, 2012*

- *5 July 2012*

- *07/05/2012*

- *07/05/2012 13:30*

- Thu, *05 Jul 2012 13:30:00 GMT-0500*

The caveat with this approach is that if your syntax is incorrect, the result will be an invalid date, or the epoch, depending upon the browser (**Figure 6.4**):

**FIGURE 6.5** Dates occurring before the epoch have negative timestamps (in milliseconds).

The syntax must be in the RFC822/IETF format (that's a more technical statement than I like to make, but check out www.w3.org/Protocols/rfc822/#z28 for details). This syntax generally comes down to *day date time*, with the day and time being optional. If present, the day must be followed by a comma (as in the last example above). And, as you can see, the month can be represented in a number of formats. You can even indicate the time zone, if you want.

## DATE METHODS

Once you've established a Date object that represents a particular date and time, there are oodles of methods you can use for retrieving the date and time, in part or in whole. To start, the getTime() method returns the date and time as the number of milliseconds since the epoch (i.e., as a timestamp):

```
var timestamp = someday.getTime();
```

(Note that in these examples, it's assumed that the someday variable has already been created as a Date object representing a valid date and time.)

As you'll see shortly, the number of milliseconds since the epoch can be used to perform date arithmetic. A negative timestamp means that the date and time is before midnight on January 1, 1970 (**Figure 6.5**):

```
var someday = new Date(1969, 11, 31, 12, 00, 00);
   // Dec 31, 1969 at 12:00:00 PM
```

**Table 6.1** lists many of the methods you can use to retrieve pieces of the represented date and time. There is no method for returning the month name, but you'll see how to do that later in the chapter.

**TABLE 6.1**  Atomic Value Retrieval Date Methods

| METHOD | RETURNS |
| --- | --- |
| getDate() | Day of the month |
| getDay() | Day of the week, with 0 representing Sunday |
| getFullYear() | Year as four digits |
| getHours() | Hours, from 0 to 23 |
| getMilliseconds() | Milliseconds |
| getMinutes() | Minutes |
| getMonth() | Month number, with 0 representing January |
| getSeconds() | Seconds |
| getTime() | Milliseconds from the epoch |

Table 6.2 lists methods that return various strings for different ways the date and time can be represented. To understand these best, the table includes not a description of what each method returns, but an example value.

**TABLE 6.2**  More Date Object Methods

| METHOD | EXAMPLE |
| --- | --- |
| toDateString() | Thu Jul 05 2012 |
| toISOString() | 2012-07-05T17:30:05.000Z |
| toJSON() | 2012-07-05T17:30:05.000Z |
| toLocaleDateString() | July 5, 2012 |
| toLocaleString() | July 5, 2012 1:30:05 PM EDT |
| toLocaleTimeString() | 1:30:05 PM EDT |
| toString() | Sun Aug 05 2012 13:30:05 GMT-0400 (EDT) |
| toTimeString() | 13:30:00 GMT-0400 (EDT) |

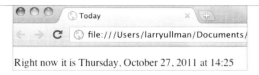

Right now it is Thursday, October 27, 2011 at 14:25

**FIGURE 6.6** The user's current date and time.

You should note that the `toISOString()` and `toJSON()` methods are new in ECMAScript 5, meaning they aren't available in all browsers. You can check for support for these methods before attempting to use them:

```
if (someday.toJSON) { // Safe to use!
} else { // Use another approach.
}
```

It may not be obvious from the example data, but `toISOString()` returns the date and time in the ISO 8601 Extended Format and `toJSON()` returns it in JSON format.

As for the methods with "locale" in the name, those return the stated information—the date and/or time—formatted appropriate for the environment's *locale*. A locale is a combination of language, country, and customs that impact how dates are written, numbers are formatted, and so forth. Most aspects of the user's locale will be established by the computer; others will differ from one browser to another on the same computer.

> **TIP:** When you begin using a new computer and are asked to select your language, country, keyboard, time zone, and so forth, your answers go toward your custom locale.

Let's use all this information to create a page that simply reflects the user's date and time (**Figure 6.6**). The very simple HTML page, named `today.html`, just has an empty paragraph that will be updated by the JavaScript code, using information taught in the previous chapter:

```
<p id="output"></p>
```

That HTML page should include the `today.js` JavaScript file, to be written in the subsequent steps. As a reminder, you can download all the book's code from `www.LarryUllman.com`.

**To show today's date and time:**

1.  Create a new JavaScript file in your text editor or IDE, to be named today.js.

2.  Begin defining the init() function:

    ```
    function init() {
        'use strict';
    ```

    The init() function will be called when the document is loaded. It will do all the work.

3.  Create a new Date object:

    ```
    var today = new Date();
    ```

    As the object is being created without any provided values, the today variable will represent the current date and time for the user.

4.  Create a custom message:

    ```
    var message = 'Right now it is ' + today.toLocaleDateString();
    message += ' at ' + today.getHours() + ':' +
       today.getMinutes();
    ```

    The message variable is a string that reflects the date and time. To fetch the date, the toLocaleDateString() method of the today object is called. To fetch the time, the getHours() and getMinutes() methods are called individually, as the toLocaleTimeString() method also returns the seconds, which I don't want to display.

5.  Get a reference to the paragraph for the output:

    ```
    var output = document.getElementById('output');
    ```

    The paragraph that already exists in the HTML will be used to display the message.

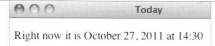

Right now it is October 27, 2011 at 14:30

**FIGURE 6.7** In Safari (here), the day of the week is not shown (compare with Figure 6.6, which is Chrome).

6. Update the appropriate property of the paragraph with the custom message:

```
if (output.textContent !== undefined) {
    output.textContent = message;
} else {
    output.innerText = message;
}
```

This code was explained in Chapter 5, Using Control Structures. On some browsers, the textContent property will exist for HTML elements, and that property can be used to assign plain text to a paragraph. To confirm that this property exists, the condition checks that the property's value does not equal undefined. If it does equal undefined, then the innerText property needs to be used instead. Again, see Chapter 5 for a slightly more thorough discussion.

7. Complete the function:

```
}
```

8. Tell the browser to call the init() function when the window has been loaded:

```
window.onload = init;
```

9. Save the file as today.js, in a js directory next to today.html, and test it in your Web browser (Figure 6.6).

You can reload the script to show the most current time, or view it in another browser to see it how the date might be displayed differently (**Figure 6.7**).

FIGURE 6.8 The standard get*
and to* methods return the
local date and time, even if it
was originally set using UTC.

```
Console ▾    HTML    CSS    Sc
   Clear   Persist   Profile   All   Errors   Warnings
>>> var end = new Date('05 Jul 2012 13:30:00 UTC');
undefined
>>> end;
Date { Thu Jul 05 2012 09:30:00 GMT-0400 (EDT) }
>>> end.toTimeString();
"09:30:00 GMT-0400 (EDT)"
```

## WORKING WITH TIME ZONES

When working with the Date object, one thing to be wary of, especially with times, is the issue of the various time zones that exist in the world. By default, JavaScript represents dates and times using the client's time zone setting. But there are situations where it's best to work with a "neutral" date and time: one that is consistently the same across all clients. For example, if you're running an auction site, you can't just set an auction to end at, say, 8:00 p.m., as my 8:00 p.m. is undoubtedly a different time than yours. The solution is to use a standardized time zone, such as *UTC*, which strangely stands for *Coordinated Universal Time*. UTC represents the same time zone as Greenwich Mean Time (GMT), but UTC is the preferred term to use anymore.

To establish a Date object using UTC, there are a couple of options. The first is to use a UTC-appropriate timestamp. For example, if the details of the hypothetical auction come from a database, and that database stores the information using UTC, the server could provide the UTC timestamp to the JavaScript:

```
// JavaScript code.

var ending = new Date(<?php echo $timestamp; ?>);
```

This approach will work so long as that JavaScript code is being processed by a server-side technology (such as PHP in the above) before being sent to the client.

The second option is to use the string format for creating the date and time, as that format does allow you to identify the time zone, too:

```
var end = new Date('05 Jul 2012 13:30:00 UTC');
```

Now when you fetch the local date and time, it will be adjusted for the user's time zone, from the initial UTC time (**Figure 6.8**):

```
end.toTimeString();
```

Another way of setting a date and time to Coordinated Universal Time is to perform a calculation with the user's time zone offset. You can find that information by calling the getTimeZoneOffset() method (**Figure 6.9**):

```
var now = new Date();
now.getTimezoneOffset();
```

**FIGURE 6.9** The getTimezone Offset() method returns the user's offset, in minutes, from UTC.

The getTimezoneOffset() returns a numeric value that is the number of minutes, plus or minus, that the user's time zone is from UTC.

Just as you can start with a UTC date and time and then retrieve local date and time information (as in Figure 6.8), you can also start with the local date and time and retrieve UTC equivalents. To do that, use getUTC* methods instead of get*: getUTCHours() instead of getHours(), getUTCDate() instead of getDate(), and so forth. For each of the methods listed in Table 6.1, there's a UTC equivalent. To return the entire date as a UTC string, there's toUTCString():

```
var now = new Date();
var london = now.toUTCString();
```

## CHANGING DATES

Moving on, if you need to change the date being represented by a Date object, you can do so using several methods (**Table 6.3**).

**TABLE 6.3** Date Changing Methods

| METHOD | SETS |
| --- | --- |
| setDate() | Day of the month |
| setFullYear() | Year |
| setHours() | Hours |
| setMilliseconds() | Milliseconds |
| setMinutes() | Minutes |
| setMonth() | Month (starting with 0 for January) |
| setSeconds() | Seconds |

Each of these is also available in a UTC-specific version, such as setUTCDate(), setUTCFullYear(), and so forth. The setTime() method can be used to change both the date and the time. It takes a timestamp as its lone argument.

These methods are most useful when combined with date arithmetic.

## DATE ARITHMETIC

The final thing you need to know about using the Date object is how to perform arithmetic. While you wouldn't ever multiply dates and you certainly never divide them (I don't even know what either would mean, although they are possible in JavaScript), being able to add and subtract dates and times is quite useful. For example, you may need to:

- Calculate the interval between two dates and/or times

- Add or subtract days or times from a date

- Time how long a process has taken

This is all easily done when you consider that dates can be represented as a timestamp.

### TIMESTAMP ARITHMETIC

A timestamp just being a number, you can perform any kind of arithmetic with it as you would any other number. For example, to find the date two weeks from now, you can start by getting the current timestamp. One way to do that would be to create a new Date object and invoke its getTime() method:

```
var now = Date();
var ts = now.getTime();
```

This can be cryptically shortened to just:

```
var ts = (new Date()).getTime();
```

The part within parentheses returns a new Date object and then the getTime() method is applied to the returned object. (After this line, the generated Date object is immediately forgotten.)

New in ECMAScript 5 is the now() function, which can be called without creating your own instance of a Date object:

```
var ts = Date.now();
```

That line returns the timestamp that represents the current moment, down to the precise millisecond. This is equivalent to the getTime() method called on a Date object variable, but is instead invoked from the Date object proper. This is the same premise as calling the various methods of the Math object (although, unlike with Date, you never create variables of the Math object type). This new method is well supported by modern browsers, but if you want to use code that's 100 percent reliable for even older browsers, you could use:

```
if (Date.now) {
    var now = Date.now()
} else {
    var now = (new Date()).getTime();
}
```

Returning to the example at hand—fetching the date and time two weeks from now—the goal is to find out how many milliseconds need to be added to the current moment. Two weeks from now is 1000 milliseconds times 60 seconds times 60 minutes times 24 hours times 14 days:

```
var interval = 1000 * 60 * 60 * 24 * 14;
```

```
>>> var now = Date.now() || (new Date()).getTime();
undefined
>>> var interval = 1000 * 60 * 60 * 24 * 14;
undefined
>>> var ts = now + interval;
undefined
>>> var then = new Date(ts);
undefined
>>> then.toString();
"Thu Nov 10 2011 13:57:19 GMT-0500 (EST)"
```

**FIGURE 6.10** Some basic arithmetic and the use of timestamps makes it easy to convert a date from one to another, some time later.

**FIGURE 6.11** Various other ways of changing a date or time by a certain interval.

```
>>> var someday = new Date();
undefined
>>> someday;
Date { Thu Oct 27 2011 15:03:23 GMT-0400 (EDT) }
>>> someday.setDate(someday.getDate() + 7);
1320347003193
>>> someday;
Date { Thu Nov 03 2011 15:03:23 GMT-0400 (EDT) }
>>> someday.setHours(someday.getHours() + 6);
1320368603193
>>> someday;
Date { Thu Nov 03 2011 21:03:23 GMT-0400 (EDT) }
>>> someday.setFullYear(someday.getFullYear() - 1);
1288832603193
>>> someday;
Date { Wed Nov 03 2010 21:03:23 GMT-0400 (EDT) }
```

Now add the two values together:

```
var ts = now + interval;
```

Then, create a new Date object for that value:

```
var then = new Date(ts);
```

To get the resulting date, use one of the appropriate methods (**Figure 6.10**):

```
then.toString();
```

Subtraction, of course, would work much the same way.

USING SETX() AND GETX()

You can also add an interval to a date and time, or subtract an interval from a date and time, via the setDate() method, providing the current date plus the interval as its new value. The generic syntax is:

```
var someday = new Date();
someday.setX(someday.getX() + Y);
```

For example, to add a week (seven days) to the current date, you would use the setDate() and getDate() methods (**Figure 6.11**):

```
var someday = new Date(); // Today!
someday.setDate(someday.getDate() + 7); // One week!
```

To add 6 hours, use setHours() and getHours():

```
someday.setHours(someday.getHours() + 6); // Six hours later!
```

To subtract a year, use setFullYear() and getFullYear():

```
someday.setFullYear(someday.getFullYear() - 1); // Last year!
```

Obviously, if you're changing a date by a single interval—minutes, hours, days, years—using this latest code is the easiest solution. If you're changing a date by a more complicated interval, you can either use the timestamp approach first explained, or use multiple executions of this last bit of code (i.e., first change the days, then the hours).

## CALCULATING INTERVALS

Sometimes, instead of finding the date that's some interval from another date, you may want to find the interval between two dates. To do that, you can actually just subtract the one Date object from the other:

```
var now = new Date();
var then = new Date('07/07/2012 13:30');
var diff = then - now;
```

The resulting value will be in milliseconds and will always be positive, regardless of which Date object is "greater."

> **NOTE:** You cannot directly add two Date objects as the result will be a concatenation of the two date strings, not an addition of the two underlying timestamps.

Returning to the auction example, you could calculate the time remaining for the auction by subtracting the current time from the auction's ending time, and then convert the milliseconds into minutes, hours, and days.

When needed, you can use comparative operators to see which date comes later:

```
if (now > then) { // then is in the past.
```

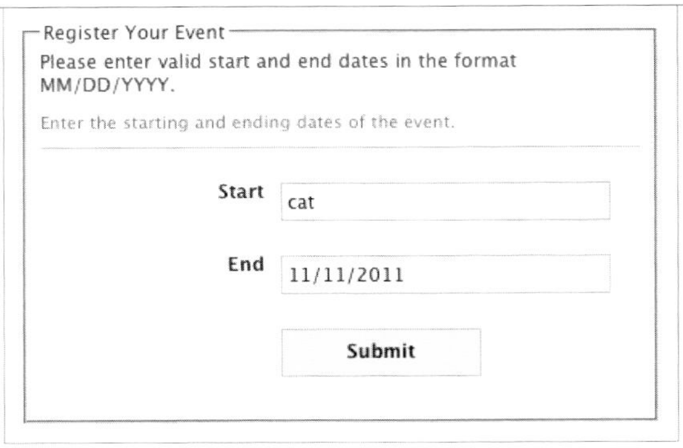

**FIGURE 6.12** After validation, the particulars of the event are reported back to the user.

**FIGURE 6.13** Error messages are revealed to the user, too.

PUTTING IT ALL TOGETHER

Let's use all this information to create a page that lets the user select a starting and ending date for an event. The script will then validate those dates, and calculate how many days they span (**Figure 6.12**). The HTML page, to be named event.html, uses two text inputs for the starting and ending dates. Just above the form is an empty DIV that will be updated by the JavaScript code, providing confirmation (Figure 6.12) or error messages (**Figure 6.13**).

```
<div id="output"></div>

<p>Enter the starting and ending dates of the event.</p>

<div><label for="start">Start</label><input type="text" name="start"
     id="start" placeholder="MM/DD/YYYY" required></div>

<div><label for="end">End</label><input type="text" name="end"
     id="end" placeholder="MM/DD/YYYY" required></div>
```

The HTML page includes the event.js JavaScript file, to be written in the subsequent steps.

**To work with dates:**

1. Create a new JavaScript file in your text editor or IDE, to be named event.js.

2. Begin defining the process() function:

```
function process() {
    'use strict';
```

The process() function will do the work when the form is submitted.

3. Get references to the HTML elements:

```
var start = document.getElementById('start');
var end = document.getElementById('end');
var output = document.getElementById('output');
```

The first two variables reference the two text inputs. The third is a reference to the DIV, where the output will be placed.

At this point, you could also consider validating that the `start` and `end` variables are good, and that both have `value` properties.

4. Declare three variables for the output:

```
var message = '';
var interval = '';
var day = 1000 * 60 * 60 *24;
```

The first two variables are empty strings that will be used for the output: the message to the user. The third variable represents the number of milliseconds in a single day, which will be useful later on in the script, during the calculations.

5. Create two new `Date()` objects:

```
var startDate = new Date(start.value);
var endDate = new Date(end.value);
```

A direct way of creating the `Date` objects is to provide the user-entered dates. This represents the third way of creating `Date` objects for specific dates: using a string.

6. Confirm that the two dates are valid:

```
if ( startDate.getTime() && endDate.getTime() ) {
```

As you saw earlier in the chapter, if you use an invalid string to create a `Date` object, the result will be an invalid date or the epoch (Figure 6.5). But how do you test for that? There are several possible solutions. Here, the `getTime()` method is called on both. It returns a timestamp (i.e., a number), or in the case of an invalid date, the value NaN. That value is evaluated as FALSE in a condition like this. If the created date is assigned the value of the epoch, then getTime() will return 0, as the date will be 0 milliseconds from the epoch. That value will also be evaluated as FALSE.

If either date is not valid, this condition will be FALSE.

7. Make sure the start date comes first:

```
if (startDate < endDate) {
```

A simple use of the comparison operator can quickly confirm that the starting date comes before the ending date.

8. Determine the interval between the two dates:

```
var diff = endDate - startDate;
if (diff <= day) {
    interval = '1 day';
} else {
    interval = Math.round(diff/day) + ' days';
}
```

The first line uses subtraction to calculate the interval between the two dates. The result will be in milliseconds. The code then determines whether this difference is just one day or multiple days, by comparing the difference to the day number already calculated. In either case, a string is assigned to the interval variable. If the difference is more than one day, division is used, and rounded off, to calculate the exact number of days.

Philosophically, I'm treating an event that goes from, say, the first to the third as being a two-day event, but you may consider that to be three days.

9. Generate the message to be displayed:

```
message = 'The event has been scheduled starting on ' +
    startDate.toLocaleDateString();
message += ' and ending on ' + endDate.toLocaleDateString();
message += ', which is a period of ' + interval + '.';
```

The final step (in the good result side of things) is to output a nice message. Here that message is built up, using concatenation, the `interval` variable, and two calls to the `toLocaleDateString()` method.

10. Create the errors as messages:

```
    } else {
        message = 'The start date must come before the
        → end date!';
    }
} else {
    message = 'Please enter valid start and end dates in the
    → format MM/DD/YYYY.';
}
```

These two `else` clauses complete the conditions begun in Steps 6 and 7.

11. Update the page with the custom message:

```
if (output.textContent !== undefined) {
    output.textContent = message;
} else {
    output.innerText = message;
}
```

This is the same code as in the previous example.

12. Complete the function:

```
    return false;
}
```

13. Add an event listener to the form's submission:

```
function init() {
    'use strict';
    document.getElementById('theForm').onsubmit = process;
} // End of init() function.
window.onload = init;
```

**14.** Save the file as event.js, in a js directory next to event.html, and test it in your Web browser.

Try different possible date values to see the results.

As a reminder, if your Web browser supports HTML5, it will do some validation for you, such as not allowing the form to be submitted without you having provided values in both text inputs. To work around this, you can use a nonsupportive browser (gasp!) or add novalidate to the opening form tag.

## WORKING WITH ARRAYS

The defining characteristic of the simple variable types as I'm calling them in this book—numbers, strings, and Booleans—is that they only represent a single value at a time. Conversely, complex data types, even the Date object just covered, can simultaneously store multiple pieces of information. The standard-bearer of complex data types in any programming language is the *array*. An array is simple in theory and a bit more complex in actuality. You can think of an array as just a list of values. For example, an array of people's names is just a list of strings; an array of daily temperatures is a list of numbers. Form data can often be manipulated as an array, as can some data returned by server requests. Over the next several pages you'll learn the fundamentals of creating, using, and manipulating arrays in JavaScript.

### CREATING ARRAYS

As arrays store multiple values, how they are created and accessed differs significantly from the simple variable types. The naming rules for arrays are the same as for other variables, but the similarities largely end there. There are two ways you can create an array. The first is to use the new operator:

```
var myVar = new Array();
```

Similar to how you create a new Date object, that line creates an empty array, as it has no defined values in its list. To establish the array's contents while creating it, add the values, separated by commas, between the parentheses:

```
var myList = new Array(1, 2, 3);
var people = new Array('Fred', 'Daphne', 'Velma', 'Shaggy');
var options = new Array(true, false);
```

As with any value in JavaScript, you should quote strings but not other types.

The second way you can create an array is to use *literal syntax*. Literal syntax, a phrase less advanced than it sounds, is actually something you've been doing thus far. When you create a number, string, or Boolean using the following code, you're using literal syntax:

```
var n = 2;
var lang = 'JavaScript';
var test = true;
```

Those variables can also be created more formally by creating Number, String, and Boolean objects:

```
var n = new Number(2);
var lang = new String('JavaScript');
var true = new Boolean(true);
```

There are minor differences as to the impact on your overall code when you use object syntax (i.e., use new) versus literal syntax, but simple variable types are almost always created literally. With arrays, you can also use literal syntax, with the square brackets being the array notation indicators:

```
var myVar = [];
var myList = [1, 2, 3];
var people = ['Fred', 'Daphne', 'Velma', 'Shaggy'];
```

As with the simple types, it's most common to create arrays using literal syntax. In fact, as you'll see by the end of the chapter, the general preference is to create *any* standard variable type using literal syntax (except for Date, which does not have a literal equivalent).

The above examples are arrays containing the same types of values, but you can mix up the stored types, too:

```
var collection = [1, 'Fred', 'Daphne', 2, false];
```

Because of the nature of arrays in JavaScript, to be explained at the very end of the chapter, mixing types in an array is less common than having the array consist entirely of a single type of value.

Once you've created an array, you can see how many items are in it by checking the array's length property:

```
myVar.length; // 0
myList.length; // 3
people.length; // 4
```

Unlike a string's length property, which reflects the number of characters in the string, there are times when an array's length property does not accurately represent the number of items in the array. To understand why, you must first know how items are stored in an array, and how you access them.

## ACCESSING AN ARRAY ELEMENT

With simple variable types, you can access the variable's value by just using the variable's name, as in:

```
var n = 2;
var four = n + n;
```

With complex variables, storing multiple values, simply using alert() or console .log() reveals all of the values, but won't let you access individual values (**Figure 6.14**):

```
var people = ['Fred', 'Daphne', 'Velma', 'Shaggy'];
console.log(people);
alert(people);
```

As you can see in Figure 6.14, when using alert(), JavaScript converts the array to a string, with each value separated by commas. In the console, the array is displayed using the literal syntax that would create it.

**FIGURE 6.14** Attempting to use just an array variable's name refers to the array's entire contents.

**FIGURE 6.15** Use square brackets to access individual values stored in the array.

To access an individual array item, you once again turn to the square brackets, this time providing the index of the particular item (**Figure 6.15**):

```
alert(people[0]);
```

(Conventionally, the items in an array are called its *elements*, so I'll be using that term in lieu of *items* from here on out.)

To understand indexes, you have to think of arrays not just as a list of values, but as a numbered list. By default, arrays begin indexing at 0, just as a string's characters are indexed beginning at 0.

You can use an array's index to both retrieve an individual element, as in Figure 6.15, or when assigning an item to the array:

```
people[4] = 'Charlie';
```

If there is no element in the array indexed at that position, then a new element will be added to the list. If an element does already exist at that position, its value will be replaced with the new value. Thus:

```
people[0] = 'Mac';
// People now stores 'Mac', 'Daphne', 'Velma', 'Shaggy', 'Charlie'
```

Returning to the topic of an array's length, that property is a misnomer, as it doesn't reflect the number of items in the array but rather one more than the largest index being used:

```
people.length; // 5
people[10] = 'Dennis';
people.length; // 11!
```

FIGURE 6.16 Using an array, you
can easily associate a numeric
month number, starting at 0,
with its name.

```
>>> var months = ['January', 'February', 'March', 'April', 'May', 'June',
'July', 'August', 'September', 'October', 'November', 'December'];
undefined
>>> var now = new Date();
undefined
>>> var thisMonth = months[now.getMonth()];
undefined
>>> thisMonth;
"October"
```

You may wonder what the benefit is of the length property storing that value, rather than the number of elements in the array. One reason is that you cannot add new items to the array using this syntax:

```
people[] = 'Dee'; // Won't work!
```

To add (or change) a value with literal syntax, you must indicate an index. To use an available index, so that you don't overwrite an existing value, provide the array's length as the new element's index:

```
people[people.length] = 'Dee'; // Works!
```

Now that you know how to refer to an individual array element, I can explain how one would quickly find the month name for a given date (mentioned in the first section of this chapter). As stated earlier, the getMonth() method of a Date object returns the month number, indexed beginning at 0. To associate a month name with the getMonth() value, you need to create an array of months, also indexed beginning at 0, which, of course, is the default:

```
var months = ['January', 'February', 'March', 'April', 'May',
   'June', 'July', 'August', 'September', 'October', 'November',
   'December'];
```

With that array defined, you can now do this (**Figure 6.16**):

```
var now = new Date();

var thisMonth = months[now.getMonth()];
```

A new way to find array element values is to use the indexOf() or lastIndexOf() methods, added in ECMAScript 5. Both work like the string counterparts (see Chapter 4), returning the indexed position in the array of the value if it is found. If the value does not exist in the array, both methods return -1:

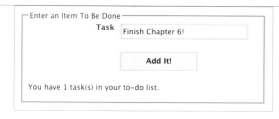

FIGURE 6.17 This application stores a series of tasks the user has to do, presenting a count of them (for added pressure).

```
months.indexOf('February'); // 1
months.indexOf('Smarch'); // -1
```

As with the string uses of these functions, you want to perform a comparison against -1 when using one of these functions as the basis of a conditional:

```
if (months.indexOf('February') != -1) {
```

As with the string versions of these same functions, both take optional second arguments indicating where to begin the search.

PUTTING IT ALL TOGETHER

At this point, let's begin using this array information in some real code. The specific example will be the basis of a "to-do list" management system (**Figure 6.17**). The HTML page, to be named tasks.html, contains an HTML form wherein the user can enter an item to be done. There's a spot underneath the form for indicating the number of items on the list:

```
<form action="#" method="post" id="theForm">
    <fieldset><legend>Enter an Item To Be Done</legend>
        <div><label for="task">Task</label><input type="text"
          name="task" id="task" required></div>
        <input type="submit" value="Add It!" id="submit">
        <div id="output"></div>
    </fieldset>
</form>
```

The page includes the tasks.js JavaScript file, to be written in the subsequent steps.

**To work with arrays:**

1. Create a new JavaScript file in your text editor or IDE, to be named tasks.js.

2. Create a global variable as an array:

```
var tasks = [];
```

Generally speaking, global variables are to be avoided (as first suggested in Chapter 4). However, in this case a global variable is necessary.

The tasks variable is declared here as an empty array. This line of code will be executed the first time the JavaScript is loaded. Within a function that is called whenever the user clicks the submit button, new to-do items will be added to this array. If this variable was declared within that function, then it would cease to exist when the function terminates, and would be declared anew—and empty—with each function call. In other words, global variables have a permanence that function variables do not have.

By declaring this variable here, outside of any function, it will retain its value (until the user refreshes the page or closes the browser).

3. Begin defining the addTask() function:

```
function addTask() {
    'use strict';
```

4. Get references to the HTML elements:

```
var task = document.getElementById('task');
var output = document.getElementById('output');
```

The first variable references the text input where the user enters a task. The second is a reference to the DIV where the output will be placed.

5. Declare a variable for the output:

```
var message = '';
```

The message variable is an empty string that will be used for the output: the message to the user.

6. If a task was entered, add it to the array:

```
if (task.value) {
    tasks[tasks.length] = task;
```

The conditional just confirms that there's a value in the text input. If so, it's added to the array using code already explained.

7. Update the page:

```
message = 'You have ' + tasks.length + ' task(s) in your
➥ to-do list.';
if (output.textContent !== undefined) {
    output.textContent = numbers;
} else {
    output.innerText = numbers;
}
```

The message to be displayed to the end user shows the number of tasks in the list. Because arrays are indexed beginning at 0, the `length` property is the same as the number of elements in the array. This is true so long as the elements are numbered sequentially without "holes," as in this example (see the "Sparsely Populated Arrays" sidebar for more on this subject).

8. Complete the conditional begun in Step 6, and complete the function:

```
    } // End of task.value IF.
    return false;
}
```

As written, if the user doesn't provide a task, nothing happens.

9. Add an event listener to the form's submission:

```
function init() {
    'use strict';
    document.getElementById('theForm').onsubmit = addTask;
```

FIGURE 6.18 Another task has been added.

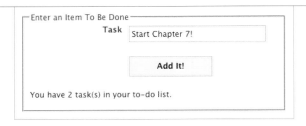

```
} // End of init() function.
window.onload = init;
```

When the user submits the form, the addTask() function will be called.

10. Save the file as tasks.js, in a js directory next to tasks.html, and test it in your Web browser (**Figure 6.18**).

To complete this system, one would add a login system, invoke Ajax to send the tasks to the server to be stored, and add a server-side script to be used when JavaScript is disabled.

### ACCESSING ALL ARRAY ELEMENTS

The previous section demonstrated how to access individual array elements, using the element's index. There is a way to access array elements without knowing the specific indexes: use a loop, which also provides access to every array element. Understanding that arrays begin indexing at 0, and the maximum index is 1 minus the array's length, a for loop can be used to iterate through the array:

```
for (var i = 0; i < myList.length; i++) {
    // Do something with myList[i].
}
```

The first time the loop is encountered, the i variable is set to 0: the first possible indexed position. The condition then checks if i is less than the length property of the array. While that condition is TRUE, the loop's body can do something with myList[i]: myList[0], myList[1], and so forth. Then i is incremented. Once i equals the length of the array, the loop is terminated, as there is no element indexed at myList[length].

For performance reasons, it's best not to compare i against the array's length with each iteration of the loop, as that requires that JavaScript look up the array's length each time. A better version of the same loop assigns the array's length to another variable in the loop's first clause and then uses this new variable for the conditional:

```
for (var i = 0, count = myList.length; i < count; i++) {

    // Do something with myList[i].

}
```

Because an array can be "sparsely populated" (see the sidebar), the for loop may need to have a condition ensuring there is an element indexed at each given position. To do that, you could use:

```
if (myList[i] !== undefined) { // Exists!
```

You can also use the in operator, which returns TRUE if the index exists in the array:

```
if (i in myList) { // Exists!
```

### REMOVING ARRAY ELEMENTS

You can remove an element from an array via the `delete` operator:

```
delete people[0];
```

Again, you use the square brackets and the index to specify the element to be removed. Keeping in mind how the `length` property works with JavaScript's arrays, deleting a specific array element will not change the array's `length` value. In fact, the indexed element will still exist in the array, only it will have a value of `undefined` (i.e., the array will have a "hole" in it).

### ARRAY METHODS

Now that you know how to create an array and access its stored values, it's time to move on to the more powerful ways of working with arrays: using built-in methods.

An alternative way to add an element to an array is to use the `push()` method. It takes one or more arguments as the values to be appended:

```
var primes = [];
primes.push(1); // [1]
primes.push(3, 5, 7); // [1, 3, 5, 7]
```

The `push()` method is common to arrays in many programming languages, and is preferred over the `arrayName[arrayName.length]` syntax.

One thing to be aware of when using `push()` is that if a value being pushed onto an array is itself an array, the new value will be added intact (i.e., creating a multidimensional array; see the following sidebar).

An alternative to `push()` is `unshift()`. It forces new items onto the front of the array, pushing the array's existing elements back as needed:

```
var primes = [3, 5, 7]; // [3, 5, 7]
primes.unshift(1); // [1, 3, 5, 7]
```

The `unshift()` method is slower than `push()` so you should use the latter whenever possible.

## MULTIDIMENSIONAL **ARRAYS**

The values of array elements don't have to be simple; they can also be complex, such as other arrays. When you have an array whose values are other arrays, the result is a multidimensional array:

```
var grid = [[2, 4, 6, 8], [1, 3, 5]];
```

That is a multidimensional array. The primary array has two values, indexed at grid[0] and grid[1], each value also being an array. The primary array's length attribute still represents one more than the largest index in the primary array, not the largest index in any of the arrays. Each subarray has its own length property, too:

```
grid.length; // 2

grid[0].length; // 4

grid[1].length; // 3
```

To reference an element in an inner array, follow the primary array name, plus the appropriate index, followed by the inner array's index:

```
grid[0][0]; // 2, first item in the first subarray

grid[1][2]; // 5, third item in the second subarray
```

You can loop through a multidimensional array by using nested for loops:

```
for (var i = 0, count1 = grid.length; i < count; i++) {

    for (var j = 0, count2 = grid[i].length; j < count2; j++) {

        // Use grid[i][j].

    } // End of inner for loop.

} // End of outer for loop.
```

As shown in that code, do be certain to use different variables and conditions for the inner loop than you use for the outer one.

Another alternative to push() is concat(), which performs concatenation for arrays. It also takes one or more values, but unlike push(), arrays present in the values to be added will be expanded to separate elements and then added:

```
var primes = [];
primes.concat(1, [3, 5, 7]); // [1, 3, 5, 7]
```

In this regard, the concat() method can be used to flatten multidimensional arrays into a one-dimensional array.

Just as you can add elements to an array using multiple methods, there are several methods for removing elements from an array. The first is pop(), which removes the *last* item from the array and returns it:

```
var primes = [1, 3, 5, 7]; // [1, 3, 5, 7]
primes.pop(); // [1, 3, 5]
```

Because this method also returns the element being removed, that value can be assigned to another variable or used in other ways:

```
var primes = [1, 3, 5, 7]; // [1, 3, 5, 7]
var n = primes.pop(); // n == 7; primes == [1, 3, 5];
```

The shift() method removes the first element from the array and returns it. In other words, shift() is the corollary to unshift(), and is similarly slower than pop().

As both pop() and push() are faster than shift() and unshift(), you may wonder why one would ever use the latter two. It all depends on the type of array being used. With push() and pop(), you're working with a *stack*, which is a *Last-In, First-Out* (LIFO) data type. For example, many applications (and dynamic Web pages) have a series of pages, or *views*, that are shown in order. As the user progresses through the application, each new view can be pushed onto the stack of views. To go backward, the top view is popped off the stack.

If you instead use push() and shift(), you're working with a *queue*, which is a *First-In, First-Out* (FIFO) structure.

If you need to cut out elements from the middle of an array, or add new elements there, you can invoke splice(). This method lets you both cut elements out of an array and insert new ones at the same time. Its first argument is the indexed position to begin at. The second argument is the number of elements to remove. The third and subsequent arguments, all of which are optional, are new values to insert.

For example, this code removes the first element:

```
var people = ['Fred', 'Daphne', 'Velma', 'Shaggy'];
people.splice(0,1); // ['Daphne', 'Velma', 'Shaggy']
```

```
>>> var people = ['Fred', 'Daphne', 'Velma', 'Shaggy'];
undefined
>>> people.splice(2, 0, 'Charlie', 'Mac');
[ ]
>>> people;
[ "Fred", "Daphne", "Charlie", "Mac", "Velma", "Shaggy" ]
>>> var people = ['Fred', 'Daphne', 'Velma', 'Shaggy'];
undefined
>>> people.splice(-1, 1);
[ "Shaggy" ]
>>> people;
[ "Fred", "Daphne", "Velma" ]
```

**FIGURE 6.19** The splice() method can be used to manipulate arrays in different ways.

Note that this method returns the element(s) being removed from the array. Moreover, splice() returns the element(s) as an array, regardless of how many elements are spliced from the original:

```
var people = ['Fred', 'Daphne', 'Velma', 'Shaggy'];
var person = people.splice(0,1); // person == ['Fred']
```

This next bit of code does not remove any elements, but adds two new values as the third and fourth items in the array:

```
var people = ['Fred', 'Daphne', 'Velma', 'Shaggy'];
people.splice(2, 0, 'Charlie', 'Mac');
```

If you provide a negative starting point, the alteration will begin counting backward from the end of the array (**Figure 6.19**):

```
var people = ['Fred', 'Daphne', 'Velma', 'Shaggy'];
people.splice(-1, 1);
```

One last array method to be discussed is slice(). The slice() method takes a starting point—an indexed position in the array—and an optional ending point and returns the corresponding element(s):

```
var primes = [1, 3, 5, 7]; // [1, 3, 5, 7]
var twoPrimes = primes.slice(0,2);
// primes == [1, 3, 5, 7]; twoPrimes == [1, 3];
```

The ending point is optional, but is not inclusive (i.e., the element indexed at the ending position is not returned). If the ending point is omitted, the slice continues until the end of the array.

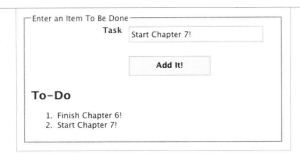

**FIGURE 6.20** The list of tasks is now shown under the form.

Like the string slice() method, the starting point can be a negative number, in which case the starting point counts backward from the end of the array. If a negative ending point is provided, it also counts backward from the end of the array:

```
var primes = [1, 3, 5, 7]; // [1, 3, 5, 7]
var aPrime = primes.slice(-2);  // [5, 7]
var bPrime = primes.slice(-2, -1); // [5]
```

Note that the slice() method never affects the original array and always returns an array, even if it's an array of only one element.

UPDATING THE TO-DO MANAGER

Next, let's update the task management application written earlier in two ways:

- Use push() instead of array notation to add new tasks.

- Use a for loop to display all of the tasks (**Figure 6.20**).

The HTML page does not need to be modified for this purpose, but the tasks.js JavaScript file will be touched up in the subsequent steps.

**To do more with arrays:**

1. Open tasks.js in your text editor or IDE, if it is not already.

2. Change how a new item is added to the array so that the push() method is used:

   ```
   tasks.push(task.value);
   ```

   It's more conventional to use push() than [], so the code is updated accordingly.

**3.** Change the assignment to the message variable to begin:

```
message = '<h2>To-Do</h2><ol>';
```

In this version of the script, the output will contain not the number of tasks but the actual tasks themselves. The best way to display those is as an HTML list of some sort, here, an ordered one. To accomplish that, the message variable will be assigned the appropriate HTML, which will then be added to the page. First, here, the opening ordered list tag is assigned to message, and prefaced with a heading.

**4.** Within a for loop, assign each task to message as a list item:

```
for (var i = 0, count = tasks.length; i < count; i++) {
    message += '<li>' + tasks[i] + '</li>';
}
```

The for loop will be used to access each item in the array. The syntax has already been explained: first, two variables are defined and assigned values. The condition then checks if the i variable is less than count (the number of elements in the array). After completing each loop iteration, the i variable is incremented. Within the loop body, another string is concatenated onto message. The string itself is the specific task—tasks[i]—within the list item tags.

**5.** After the loop, complete the message variable:

```
message += '</ol>';
```

The last step is to close the ordered list element.

**6.** Update the page:

```
output.innerHTML = message;
```

Because message is a string that contains HTML, the innerHTML property of the output element (i.e., the DIV) must be assigned this value (as opposed to using innerText or textContent). The innerHTML property was also introduced in Chapter 5.

**7.** Save the file and test it in your Web browser (**Figure 6.21**).

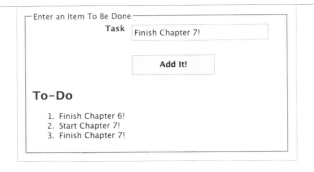

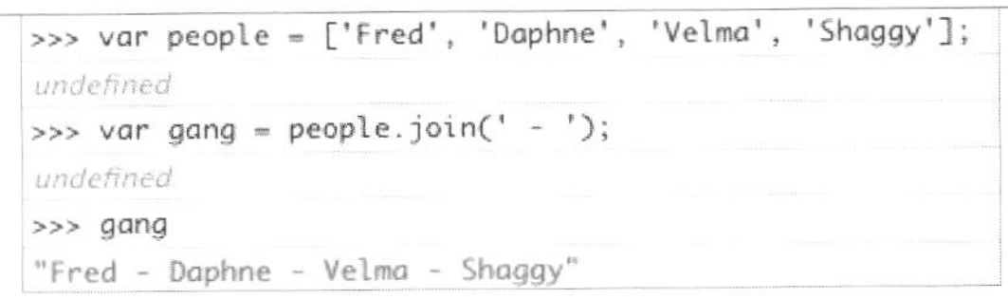

**FIGURE 6.21** And another thing to do!

**FIGURE 6.22** An array of strings is quickly turned into a single string, with a specified glue, using the join() method.

## CONVERTING BETWEEN STRINGS AND ARRAYS

Since JavaScript is a weakly typed language, variables and values are frequently converted from one type to another. For example, in the previous chapter, it was mentioned that variables will be temporarily converted into Booleans in situations such as:

```
if (someVar) {
```

Generally speaking, any conversion that you would do intentionally, or JavaScript would do as a by-product, is from a simple type to another simple type. There are exceptions, of course. A common conversion you'll make in your own code is between a string and an array. To convert an array to a string, call the join() method on the array, providing the character or characters to use as the "glue" between the array pieces in the new string (**Figure 6.22**):

```
var people = ['Fred', 'Daphne', 'Velma', 'Shaggy'];
var gang = people.join(' - ');
```

The default separator is the comma, but you can use any string as the glue, even HTML. The most recent tasks.js code could have its entire for loop, plus the line before and after, replaced with:

```
message += '<ol><li>';
message += tasks.join('<li><li>');
message += '</li></ol>';
```

The end result would be the same.

As a matter of fact, performing a lot of concatenation in JavaScript code is terribly inefficient, as JavaScript creates a new string (and discards the old one) with each concatenation. For performance reasons, many developers prefer to build up an array of strings and then join the array pieces together to create the final string.

To convert a string to an array, invoke the split() method on the string, providing the character or characters used to break up the string into its pieces:

```
var gang = 'Fred,Daphne,Velma,Shaggy';
var people = gang.split(',');
```

## WORKING WITH OBJECTS

As stated several times over by this point in the book, JavaScript is an object-oriented programming language, which means that the object is the fundamental type used in the language. Chapter 1 talks about how JavaScript differs from other object-oriented (OO) languages in that you don't define classes and then create objects using those class definitions. Instead, in JavaScript objects are derived from *prototypes*: model objects. If you've never done any object-oriented programming before, all of this may not mean much to you, but the impact on your day-to-day programming is that you can more easily begin using objects in JavaScript, as you're about to see. (On the other hand, creating your own custom objects is trickier, and there are some limitations on the highest end of OOP in JavaScript.)

An object is made up of both *properties* (also called *attributes*) and *methods* (i.e., functions). If you're reading this book sequentially, then you've already used various object properties and methods many times over. In the next several pages, you'll learn how to create your own objects with your own custom properties. In Chapter 7, Creating Functions, you'll see how to add method definitions to custom objects.

### CREATING OBJECTS

Just as with any variable type in JavaScript, there are two ways of creating objects: using the new operator or literal syntax. Here is the first:

```
var myObj = new Object();
```

That creates a new, empty object. Literal syntax for object creation uses the curly braces:

```
var myObj = {};
```

That line is equivalent to the above in that it creates an empty object. However, literal syntax is generally preferred in JavaScript, and you'll primarily see literal syntax throughout the rest of the book.

To add properties to an object, use the format *property*: *value*, separating each property with a comma, as in:

```
var chapter = {num: 6, title: 'Complex Variable Types'};
```

    or

```
var chapter = new Object(num: 6, title: 'Complex Variable Types');
```

As with any value in JavaScript, strings are quoted, numbers are not. The property names themselves need not be quoted. For the property names, stick to letters (and if absolutely need be, letters and numbers), without spaces or punctuation. Also avoid using any of JavaScript's keywords. And do not place an extra comma after the last property, as that could cause problems in some browsers.

To make it clearer, you can create objects over multiple lines:

```
var chapter = {
    num: 6,
    title: 'Complex Variable Types'
};
```

When creating literal objects, especially over multiple lines, don't forget the semicolon after the closing curly brace, which completes the statement.

The values themselves aren't limited to just simple types; they can even be objects or arrays:

```
var me = {
    name: 'Larry Ullman',
    age: 42,
    car: {
```

```
        make: 'Honda',
        model: 'Fit',
        year: 2008
    },
    favoriteColors: ['Black', 'Blue', 'Gray'],
    tired: true
};
```

As you can see, the object structure is extremely flexible, making it a powerful data type.

## ACCESSING OBJECT PROPERTIES

Once you have created an object, you need to know how to access its properties. You've already seen how arrays use special syntax—specifically, the square brackets—to access individual array elements. There is special syntax to access individual object properties, too: *objName.propertyName*. This, of course, is syntax you've seen many times over by now, called *object notation*:

```
var chapter = {
    num: 6,
    title: 'Complex Variable Types'
};
chapter.num; // 6
```

With an object created, you can change any property using the assignment operator:

```
chapter.title = 'Rather Complex Variable Types';
```

If the named property does not exist in the object, it will be added to it:

```
chapter.startPage = 256;
```

You can confirm that an object has a property in a couple of ways. The first is to just use the syntax *objName.propertyName*:

```
if (chapter.startPage) { // Already exists!
```

This can trip you up with values that get evaluated to `false`, however, such as an empty string or 0.

The second way to test if an object has a property is to use the `in` operator. Its syntax is `'propertyName' in objectName` and it returns `true` if the property is found in the object:

```
if ('startPage' in chapter) { // Already exists!
```

A third option is to use the `typeof` operator, assuming you know what the property's type should be:

```
if (chapter.startPage == 'number') {
```

If you have a more complicated object structure, as in the `me` example, which contains a string, a number, another object, an array, and a Boolean, you can just apply the syntax you already know, whether this means chaining object notation or also using square brackets for an array:

```
me.car.model; // Fit
me.favoriteColors[0]; // Black
```

Another way you can access an object property is to use array notation (i.e., the square brackets), this time quoting the properties as if the object was an array with strings for its indexes instead of numbers. These two lines are equivalent to those just written:

```
my['car']['model'];
my['favoriteColors'][0];
```

You may rightfully wonder why you'd use the array syntax when the object notation already exists. The answer is that there are situations where you *can't* use object notation. For example, say that a string represents the name of a property:

```
var prop = 'title';
```

(Presumably, this string would be assigned its value dynamically, such that the value would not otherwise be known in advance and hardcoded into the page.) Assuming the chapter object exists, you could not use the syntax `chapter.prop`, as that would attempt to look for the prop property of chapter. This code, however, will work:

```
chapter[prop];
```

```
>>> var chapter = {      num: 6,
title: 'Co...      console.log(p + ' = ' +
chapter[p] + '\n'); }
num = 6
title = Complex Data Types
```

**FIGURE 6.23** Object inspectors can be used to show the properties and values of an object.

That code works because array syntax allows you to use expressions instead of literal values to find properties dynamically.

## ACCESSING ALL OBJECT PROPERTIES

Object notational syntax does require that you know what properties exist in the object. To access every object property, you can use a variation on the for loop, called for...in. That syntax is:

```
for (var p in myObj) {
    // Use myObj[p].
}
```

There are a couple of things to be aware of when using a for...in loop. First, the properties will not be returned in any particular order, not even in the order in which they are listed when the object was created. Second, depending upon the object being iterated over, you may end up seeing properties that you did not create. This has to do with JavaScript's *prototypical inheritance*, a more advanced subject (see Chapter 14, Advanced JavaScript). Third, you have to use the array notation to find each object property's value. And, fourth, for...in is a slower construct, that should only be used when no other loop will do.

Using a loop like this, you can create an *object inspector*: a great debugging tool that provides feedback on an object's properties. The code starts off with a simple loop. Within the loop, you may want to display both the property name and its value (**Figure 6.23**):

```
for (var p in myObj) {
    console.log(p + ' = ' + myObj[p] + '\n');
}
```

Within the loop, you can use the typeof operator to distinguish between the object's attributes (i.e., variables) and its methods (functions):

```
if (typeof myObj[p] == 'function') { // Function!
```

## IMMUTABLE AND MUTABLE OBJECTS IN JAVASCRIPT

Pretty much everything in JavaScript either is an object, or can be treated as an object. For example, you can create a string as:

```
var name = 'Larry Ullman';
```

But then still call methods on that variable as it's a string object:

```
name.toLowerCase();
```

The real distinction between the simple types (technically called *primitives*) and the more complex types is that nonprimitive JavaScript types, such as Date, Array, and Object, are *mutable*: their values can be changed. Conversely, when you go to change the value of a simple type, JavaScript—behind the scenes—creates a new variable of that type and destroys the old. As proof of this, think about all the simple type methods you've learned, like toLower-Case() for strings and toFixed() for numbers: these methods don't modify the original value, but return that value in its modified form.

### REMOVING OBJECT PROPERTIES

The only way to actually remove a property from an object is to use the delete operator:

```
delete obj.property;
delete chapter.title;
```

### PUTTING IT ALL TOGETHER

For the final example in this chapter, this next page will present a form through which a user can add new employees (**Figure 6.24**). The HTML page, named employee.html, includes both the form and a DIV for the output:

```
<form action="#" method="post" id="theForm">

    <fieldset><legend>Add an Employee</legend>

        <div><label for="firstName">First Name</label><input
        → type="text" name="firstName" id="firstName"
        → required></div>
```

**FIGURE 6.24** After the user submits the form, JavaScript creates a new employee object that stores the form data.

```
    <div><label for="lastName">Last Name</label>
        <input type="text" name="lastName" id="lastName"
        required></div>
    <div><label for="department">Department</label>
        <select name="department" id="department">
            <option value="Accounting">Accounting</option>
            <option value="Administration">Administration</option>
            <option value="Human Resources">Human Resources</option>
            <option value="Marketing">Marketing</option>
        </select></div>
        <input type="submit" value="Submit" id="submit">
    </fieldset>
    <div id="output"></div>
</form>
```

The page includes the employee.js JavaScript file, to be written in the subsequent steps.

**To work with objects:**

1. Create a new JavaScript file in your text editor or IDE, to be named employee.js.

2. Begin defining the process() function:

```
function process() {
    'use strict';
```

When the user submits the form, the process() function will be called.

3. Get references to the HTML elements:

```
var firstName = document.getElementById('firstName').value;
var lastName = document.getElementById('lastName').value;
var department = document.getElementById('department').value;
```

The form has three elements whose values must be retrieved. To simplify this example, the JavaScript directly grabs the form values. You could alternatively get form element references and then validate the values.

4. Get a reference for the output:

```
var output = document.getElementById('output');
```

5. Create a new object, representing the employee:

```
var employee = {
    firstName: firstName,
    lastName: lastName,
    department: department,
    hireDate: new Date()
}; // Don't forget the semicolon!
```

The employee object has four properties: firstName, lastName, department, and hireDate. The values for the first three come directly from the form. The value for the last one will be a new Date object. The hireDate property is set to the current date, but you could get this value from a form element instead.

6. Create the output as HTML:

```
var message = '<h2>Employee Added</h2>Name: ' +
    employee.lastName + ', ' + employee.firstName + '<br>';
message += 'Department: ' + employee.department + '<br>';
message += 'Hire Date: ' + employee.hireDate.toDateString();
```

The message to be displayed to the end user shows the details of the employee object. The message string also contains some HTML.

FIGURE 6.25 Another hire!

7. Display the output:

```
output.innerHTML = message;
```

8. Complete the function:

```
        return false;

}
```

9. Add an event listener to the form's submission:

```
function init() {

    'use strict';

    document.getElementById('theForm').onsubmit = process;

} // End of init() function.

window.onload = init;
```

10. Save the file as employee.js, in a js directory next to employee.html, and test in your Web browser (**Figure 6.25**).

# ARRAYS VERSUS OBJECTS

The final thing to be discussed in this important chapter on complex data types is how arrays and objects compare. You might have gathered, especially over the past several pages, that arrays and objects have a lot in common. In fact, arrays in JavaScript are rather unique compared with other languages, in that *arrays are just a specific type of object*. This may not surprise you as, in JavaScript, Booleans are objects, numbers are objects, strings are objects, and dates are objects. In fact, as Chapter 7 explains, in JavaScript, even functions are objects! But the fact that all of these types in JavaScript are objects does not mean they are all the same or should be treated equally. The logical question, then, is what object type you should use and when.

Clearly, if you're only representing a single value—a Boolean, a number, or a string—you should stick to the simple types. Even though you can create such values as formal objects, you should stick with literal syntax for them:

```
var test = new Boolean(true); // Unnecessary!
var test = true; // Much better!
```

Secondarily, if you need to represent a date and time, then the Date object is the solution, not a generic object.

The more common question beginning JavaScript programmers have is: When should you use an array and when should you use an object? Because arrays in JavaScript are objects, they don't perform quite as well as arrays in other languages. Arrays are best when any of the following conditions apply:

- The order of the stored values is important.

- The values can be numerically indexed.

- You may need to quickly know how many values are being stored.

For all other situations, you should use objects.

Expanding on these three thoughts, first, keep in mind that *an object is an unordered collection of properties*. You simply cannot sort an object's values in a meaningful way. Thus, if that's a need, use an array.

Second, although you can use strings as the indexes for arrays, JavaScript arrays are really not intended to be used in a such a way. In situations where values should be paired with meaningful labels, you should be using an object instead.

Third, an array differs from an object in that it has a `length` attribute, which represents one more than the highest index in the array. As you've already seen, this property can be used to find out how many values the array is storing, assuming the array does not have "holes." There is no equivalent for objects.

Think of objects as representing a lot of different information about one thing (e.g., an employee or a book chapter or whatever). Think of arrays as representing the same information about a lot of things (e.g., a list of grades, a list of names, and so forth).

## REVIEW AND PURSUE

If you have any problems with these sections, either in answering the questions or pursuing your own endeavors, turn to the book's supporting forum (`www.LarryUllman.com/forums/`).

### REVIEW

- How do you create a new `Date` object? How do you create a `Date` object representing other than the current date and time (there are multiple answers)?

- What are some of the `Date` methods that exist for fetching part of the represented date and time or entire strings for that date and time?

- What is a *timestamp* and what is the *epoch*?

- What is a *locale*?

- What is *UTC*? Why is it useful?

- How can you change what specific date and time is represented by a variable?

- How can you calculate the interval between two dates?

- What is an array? How do you create an array? How do you access an individual array element?

- What does an array's `length` property represent?

- How do you add new values to an array? (There are multiple correct answers.)

- How can you confirm that an array element exists?

- What is a multidimensional array? How do you refer to specific elements in a multidimensional array?

- What does the splice() method do? How do you use it?

- How do you turn an array into a string? How do you turn a string into an array?

- How do you create a variable of type *object* (with properties)?

- How do you reference an object's properties? (This should be really easy for you by now.)

- What control structure is used to access every one of an object's properties?

## PURSUE

- Implement the auction deadline example: choose a specific ending date and time, then show the amount of time left in an auction.

- Update event.js to confirm that the starting date is in the future.

- Update the original tasks.js so that the output also shows a random task.

- Update tasks.js so that the task just added is cleared from the text input after the task has been added to the array.

- If you're the very curious and eager type, search online for more information on the new array and object features added in ECMAScript 5.

- Update tasks.js so that it uses join() to create the final message, instead of concatenating together multiple strings.

- If you're feeling particularly confident, combine the techniques demonstrated in tasks.js and employee.js so that an array of employee objects is created.

# WRAPPING **UP**

This chapter starts off in casual way: merely presenting the complex data types, a corollary to the simple types already covered. But this chapter really breaks open the door on what JavaScript is as a programming language. As you know now, JavaScript is about *objects* (specifically *prototypical objects*). Whether you're working with dates, arrays, or generic objects, at the core, they are all just objects.

The chapter begins with a fairly exhaustive coverage of the Date object. It's a snap to use, but you may have to regularly look up which method you need or what precise syntax is correct. The middle of the chapter walks through arrays, which are objects with their own syntax and several unique methods. Arrays are a great way to represent lists of data. The chapter ends with a discussion of generic objects. Despite being so integral to programming in JavaScript, objects are easy to use, even for those new to object-oriented programming.

In the next chapter, you'll learn all the details you need to know about creating functions in JavaScript, something you've been doing to a basic degree already. As already mentioned, and as you'll see, functions in JavaScript are also objects, which has a huge impact on how they can be used in your code.

# 7

# CREATING
# **FUNCTIONS**

In the past couple of chapters, you've used several functions built into JavaScript, but now it's time to start writing your own. Out of necessity, Chapter 2, JavaScript in Action, explained how to write a most basic function, but in this chapter you'll learn all the particulars of user-defined functions. Not only are user-defined functions necessary in JavaScript for event handling, but, as in any language, being able to create your own functions constitutes a huge step toward creating modular and easily reusable code. The chapter begins with the fundamentals, and slowly works its way into the more advanced concepts.

# THE **FUNDAMENTALS**

This chapter starts by walking through the basics of functions in JavaScript. Not only will the next few pages be stuff you need to know, but it's the most approachable material when it comes to functions, too. In fact, if you've worked with any other programming language, most of the fundamentals will be old hat to you.

## DEFINING YOUR OWN FUNCTIONS

As you've already seen by now (many times over in this book, and probably in code elsewhere), the basic syntax for creating your own function is:

```
function functionName() {
    // Function body.
}
```

The function's name has to adhere to the same naming rules as variables: use letters, numbers, and the underscore (if needed), but the name cannot start with a number. The name cannot also be the same as a reserved JavaScript word. The function name should be descriptive, and is conventionally a verb, as functions take actions: previous examples in the book include addTask(), calculate(), process(), and init(), short for *initialize*. As with everything in JavaScript, function names are case-sensitive.

Unlike with control structures, in which the curly braces are sometimes optional (but, at least for me, almost always recommended), the curly braces that encapsulate the function's body are always required, as are the parentheses. Within the parentheses, you identify the function's *parameters*: placeholders for values to be passed to the function when it's called. The chapter will return to this subject shortly.

Within the body of the function, you'll place the code to be executed when the function is called. Some functions may only contain a single line of code; others will have dozens, including complex control structures. Conventionally, the function's body is indented (four spaces or a tab) from the function keyword, to visually indicate the subservient nature of that code.

If you're following this book sequentially, none of the scripts thus far have had the JavaScript code calling a user-defined function, as every example has only used functions as event handlers. So, once you've defined a function, you can call it in this manner:

```
functionName();
```

With this function, which is defined independent of any object, you only use the function name to call it, just like JavaScript's `parseInt()` function, among others. Later in the chapter, you'll learn how to define a function as part of an object (thereby creating a *method*), in which case invoking the function uses the syntax `objectName.functionName()`, as you've seen many times over by now. As in the function's definition, the parentheses are required in the function's call.

```
>>> function oops() { } oooops();
⊗ ReferenceError: oooops is not defined
    oooops();
```

**FIGURE 7.1** If you misspell or miscapitalize a function's name, or if JavaScript doesn't have access to the function's definition, an error will result.

Conventionally, one defines a function prior to invoking it, although that's not technically required, as functions in JavaScript, like variables, are *hoisted*. This means that JavaScript first looks for function definitions prior to executing any code.

If the JavaScript code cannot find a corresponding function definition, you'll see an error (**Figure 7.1**).

## PASSING VALUES TO FUNCTIONS

Functions defined using the code just explained (and the code frequently used in the book prior to this point) take no arguments: the functions work without any values being passed to them. Many functions require more information, though, which is where function parameters come into play. For example, JavaScript's `parseInt()` function takes a string and a radix as its two arguments, with the first value passed being parsed by the function:

```
var someString = '20 cats';
var n = parseInt(someString, 10); // n == 20
```

To have your function take arguments, place one or more variable names within the function definition's parentheses:

```
function functionName(someVar) {
    // Function body.
}
```

If a function is meant to take multiple arguments, each gets separated by a comma:

```
function functionName(someVar, someOtherVar) {
    // Function body.
}
```

```
function functionName(someVar, someOtherVar) {
    // Function body.
}
functionName(x, y);
functionName('Larry', 'Ullman');
```

Note that you don't use the var keyword in front of these variable names, but the names themselves must adhere to the same rules as any other variable you create in JavaScript.

**NOTE:** To be precise, the variables in a function's definition are technically called *parameters*. The values passed to a function when it's called are *arguments*.

To call a function that takes arguments, provide values within the parentheses of the function call. Each value can be represented by a variable or a literal value:

```
functionName(aVar);
functionName(aVar, true);
doSomethingWithChapter({num: 7, title: 'Creating Functions'});
```

When you place complex objects within a function call, be mindful of the syntax so as not to create an error. It may be more foolproof in such cases to create the array or object first, and then use it in the function call.

To be absolutely clear, the names of the variables used in a function call need not be the same as the names of the variables in the function's definition. The reason why will be explained in time.

A direct association gets made between the values listed in the function call and the variables in the function definition (**Figure 7.2**). You cannot change the order in which the values are passed to the variables.

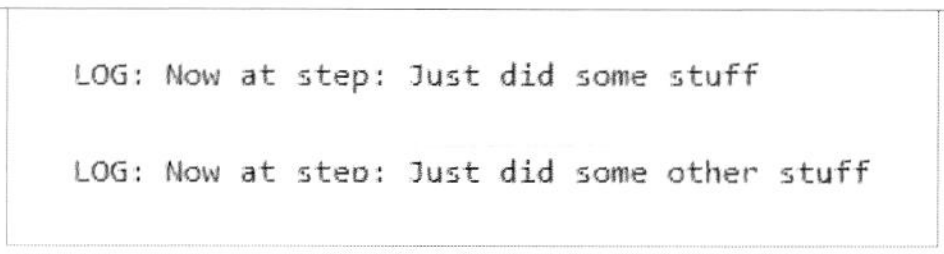

```
LOG: Now at step: Just did some stuff

LOG: Now at step: Just did some other stuff
```

FIGURE 7.3 Repeated calls to the same function with different argument values will output different results.

Once the function has been called and values have been passed to the function's parameters, you can use those parameter variables like any other variable in the function. For example, the following function defines a simple routine for indicating the progress of a script, which can be used as a debugging tool (**Figure 7.3**):

```
function reportStatus(message) {
    console.log('Now at step: ' + message + '\n');
}
```

It would be used in this manner:

```
// Do some stuff.
reportStatus('Just did some stuff');
// Do some other stuff:
reportStatus('Just did some other stuff');
```

Or if you wanted to create an object inspector (another debugging tool), that might be defined like so:

```
function displayObject(obj) {
    for (var p in obj) {
        console.log(p + ' = ' + obj[p] + '\n');
    }
}
```

That code merely wraps functionality explained in Chapter 6, Complex Variable Types, in a function that takes one argument: the object to be inspected. And this is what defining your own functions is about: encapsulating code you repeatedly use, and providing, as arguments, the data the code requires.

## VALIDATING FUNCTION PARAMETERS

Since parameters are common to most functions, there are several factors you ought to be aware of; let's delve into this subject in more detail.

### FUNCTIONS DO NOT CHECK TYPES

One thing to know is that there is no type checking involved with function parameters. This shouldn't surprise you, as JavaScript is weakly typed, with no type declaration for any variable, let alone parameters. This means that although you might have written a function to expect two numbers, it could be sent two strings without error:

```
function add(x, y) {
    x + y;
}
```

If that function is called using the following code, it will perform mathematical addition:

```
add(2, 2);
```

But if that same function is called using one or more strings, it will perform concatenation:

```
add('Hello, ', 'World!');
```

The solution is to add your own type checking, as needed. For example:

```
function add(x, y) {
    if ( (typeof x == 'number') && (typeof y == 'number') ) {
        x + y;
    }
}
```

That's the basic idea; later on you'll learn how to have functions return values, which is an important addition to completing a function like this (the function as written does nothing with the result of the arithmetic). In Chapter 12, Error Management, you'll learn how to have functions *throw errors* when they're not used properly.

## ACCEPTING ANY NUMBER OF ARGUMENTS

Functions automatically have access to a variable called `arguments`. This is an array-like object that reflects every value passed to the function when the function is called. This is not a true array (e.g., you can't add items to it within the function), but it does have a `length` property, like normal arrays. This means that you can use `arguments.length` as the basis of a quick test to see that a function was called with the proper number of arguments:

```
function functionName(someVar, anotherVar, yetAnotherVar) {

    if (arguments.length == 3) { // Good to go!

    } else { // Missing something!

    }

}
```

You can also use a `for` loop within the function to loop through every received argument:

```
for (var i = 0, count = arguments.length; i < count; i++) {

    // Do something with arguments[i].

}
```

The `arguments` variable is used all over the place in JavaScript's built-in methods, such as the `concat()` method, which can take any number of values to be concatenated together:

```
myArray.concat(1);
```

```
myArray.concat(2, 3, 4);
```

There is one more way to pass a variable number of values to a function, and that's to only pass one argument, but of type object:

```
function showText(argObject) {

    // Use argObject.

}
```

To call this function, you would create an object that gets passed to the function when it's called:

```
showText({text: 'Hello, World!', bold: true, size: 12});
```

Another benefit of using objects as a single argument is that objects are passed to functions *by reference*, a subject to be discussed in just a couple of pages.

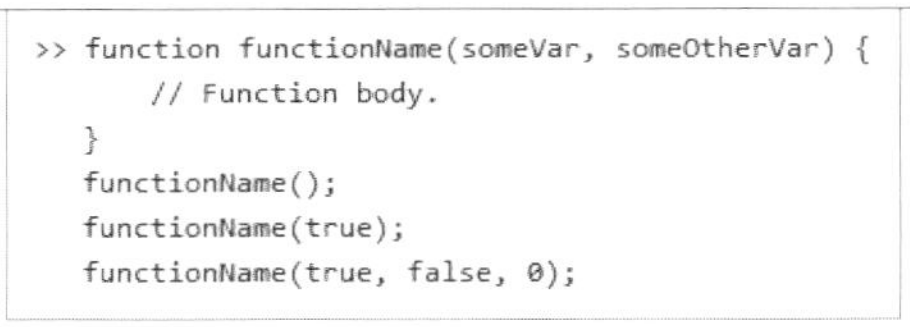

```
>> function functionName(someVar, someOtherVar) {
       // Function body.
   }
   functionName();
   functionName(true);
   functionName(true, false, 0);
```

```
>> function functionName(someVar) {
       console.log(someVar + '\n');
   }
   functionName(true);
   functionName();
LOG: true

LOG: undefined
```

**FIGURE 7.4** No JavaScript errors occur when a function is called with the wrong number of arguments.

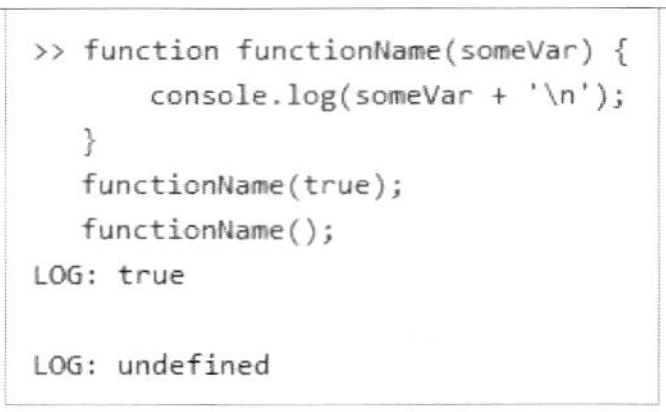

**FIGURE 7.5** This test function just shows the values received by its lone parameter.

## FUNCTIONS DO NOT CHECK THE NUMBER OF PARAMETERS

In most programming languages I've worked with, failing to provide the correct number of arguments when a function is called results in an error. In JavaScript, that is not the case, which is surprising to many learning the language. The following code will not show errors, although presumably the function will not be able to work properly (**Figure 7.4**):

```
function functionName(someVar, someOtherVar) {

    // Function body.

}
functionName();

functionName(true);

functionName(true, false, 0);
```

Proper type checking (just discussed) and variable validation (covered next) will catch misuses of the function, but you can also write functions to purposefully take a variable number of arguments, as discussed in the sidebar on the previous page.

## PARAMETERS CANNOT HAVE DEFAULT VALUES

Moving on, unlike in many languages, function parameters in JavaScript cannot be set with a default value (which has the secondary effect of making them optional). If a function has an parameter that is not passed a value when the function is called, that parameter will have a value of undefined (**Figure 7.5**):

```
function functionName(someVar) {

    console.log(someVar + '\n');

}
functionName(true); // someVar is true

functionName(); // someVar is undefined
```

Using this information, you can test that a value was received in a function parameter by confirming that the parameter variable isn't undefined:

```
function functionName(someVar) {

    if (typeof someVar == 'undefined') { // Not set!

    } else { // Good to go!

    }

}
```

To create default value-like functionality, add a default value assignment within the function:

```
function functionName(someVar) {

    if (typeof someVar == 'undefined') {

        someVar = 'default value';

    }

}
```

Because you cannot skip over parameters when calling a function, if you want to, say, provide a value for the third parameter but not the second, use undefined as the second argument's value:

```
function functionName(a, b, c) {

}
functionName(true, undefined, false);
```

That being said, it'd make the most sense when defining your functions that the parameters are listed in order of most obligatory to least.

**FIGURE 7.6** Simple variables used for function argument values will not be changed inside the function.

```
>> function willNotChange(x) {
       console.log('In the function, x = ' + x + '\n');
       x = 2;
       console.log('After the assignment, x = ' + x + '\n');
   }
   var y = 1;
   console.log('Outside of the function, y = ' + y + '\n');
   willNotChange(y);
   console.log('Outside of the function, y = ' + y + '\n');
LOG: Outside of the function, y = 1

LOG: In the function, x = 1

LOG: After the assignment, x = 2

LOG: Outside of the function, y = 1
```

## HOW VALUES ARE PASSED

A more complicated subject, but one you have to understand, is exactly how values are passed to functions. There are two possibilities: by *value* or by *reference*. In JavaScript, simple values—numbers, strings, and Booleans—are passed by value. Passing by value means that the actual variable (in the function call) is not passed to the function, but rather the variable's value is. Consequently, changes to the simple value within the function have no impact on the variable outside of the function (**Figure 7.6**):

```
function willNotChange(x) {
    console.log('In the function, x = ' + x + '\n');
    x = 2;
    console.log('After the assignment, x = ' + x + '\n');
}
var y = 1;
console.log('Outside of the function, y = ' + y + '\n');
willNotChange(y);
console.log('Outside of the function, y = ' + y + '\n');
```

```
>> function willChange(x) {
      console.log('In the function, x.num = ' + x.num + '\n');
      x.num = 2;
      console.log('After the assignment, x.num = ' + x.num + '\n');
   }
   var y = {num: 1}; // y.num == 1
   console.log('Outside of the function, y.num = ' + y.num + '\n');
   willChange(y);
   console.log('Outside of the function, y.num = ' + y.num + '\n');
LOG: Outside of the function, y.num = 1

LOG: In the function, x.num = 1

LOG: After the assignment, x.num = 2

LOG: Outside of the function, y.num = 2
```

**FIGURE 7.7** When an object is passed to a function, if its properties are changed within the function, those changes alter the object outside of the function.

This behavior—simple values being passed by value—shouldn't trip you up. What can cause problems is that *objects and arrays are passed by reference*. This means that the function does not receive the complex values, but rather references to the original variables. If you change that variable within the function, the variable outside of the function will also be changed, because the function's parameter will refer to the exact same variable, even if the argument has a different name (**Figure 7.7**):

```
function willChange(x) {
    console.log('In the function, x.num = ' + x.num + '\n');
    x.num = 2;
    console.log('After the assignment, x.num = ' + x.num + '\n');
}
var y = {num: 1}; // y.num == 1
console.log('Outside of the function, y.num = ' + y.num + '\n');
willChange(y);
console.log('Outside of the function, y.num = ' + y.num + '\n');
```

The benefit of this behavior is that complex data types can be a vessel for getting complex data back out of a function.

As an example of the information covered thus far, let's take some of the code used in the last chapter and make a function out of it. In Chapter 6, there are many situations where an HTML element's text is updated with new text, using this code:

```
if (output.textContent !== undefined) {
    output.textContent = numbers;
} else {
    output.innerText = numbers;
}
```

As that's frequently replicated code, it makes a good candidate for being converted into a function (see the "Function Design Theory" sidebar later in the chapter for more). The function needs to take two arguments: the id value of the destination element and the message itself.

Although this code was used multiple times in Chapter 6, let's just update today.js. The HTML page itself will not need to be modified, though.

**To create and call your own function:**

1. Open today.js in your text editor or IDE.

2. Begin defining a new function:

   ```
   // This function is used to update the text of an HTML element.
   // The function takes two arguments: the element's ID and the
   text message.
   function setText(elementId, message) {
       'use strict';
   ```

   Since this function will be called by code in the init() function, I would go ahead and define this function before that function (although, as already explained, it doesn't technically matter). When creating your own functions, it's best to include detailed comments before the function's definition indicating what the function does, what arguments the function takes (perhaps including the expected argument types), and so forth.

   This particular function takes two arguments, assigned to the elementId and message variables.

3. Validate the function's parameters:

```
if ( (typeof elementId == 'string')
&& (typeof message == 'string') ) {
```

This function can only work if it receives both values and both are of type String (well, technically, the message could be a number). To validate the parameters, before attempting to actually perform the function code, this two-part conditional checks each parameter's type. If either is not a string, this function will do nothing.

4. Get a reference to the destination HTML element:

```
var output = document.getElementById(elementId);
```

This code is virtually the same as that used elsewhere in the book, but now it uses the elementId parameter as the value provided to document.getElementById(). Note that you need to use the variable name here unquoted. If you were to use 'elementId' instead, the JavaScript would look for an HTML element whose id value is literally *elementId*.

As a next step, the function could validate that output is not null (i.e., that an element with the provided ID exists in the page).

5. Update the element's text:

```
if (output.textContent !== undefined) {
    output.textContent = message;
} else {
    output.innerText = message;
}
```

This is the same code as was first explained in Chapter 5, Using Control Structures.

6. Complete the if conditional begun in Step 3, and the function:

```
    } // End of main IF.
} // End of setText() function.
```

FIGURE 7.8 The end user
would not be aware that this
output was created by a new
user-defined function.

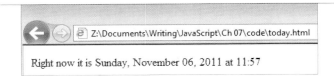

Z:\Documents\Writing\JavaScript\Ch 07\code\today.html

Right now it is Sunday, November 06, 2011 at 11:57

7. Within the `init()` function, replace the creation of the output variable, plus the assignation to its `innerText` or `textContent` property, with a function call:

```
setText('output', message);
```

And that's all there is to using the new function!

8. Save the file and test in your Web browser (**Figure 7.8**).

## RETURNING VALUES FROM FUNCTIONS

Another aspect to a function's definition is what value the function returns. Having a function return a value provides a way for the function to communicate with the code that called it. The function might return a calculated number, a modified string, or a Boolean indicating the success of an operation. In any case, functions return values via the `return` statement:

```
function functionName() {
    // Function body.
    return something;
}
```

The value returned by the function can be a literal value or a variable, and be of any type.

You should know that when a `return` statement is encountered, the function's execution terminates, even if there is more code after the `return` statement:

```
function functionName() {
    // Function body.
    return something;
    // This code will not be executed!
}
```

Hence, only one `return` statement in a function will ever be executed (at most), but this doesn't restrict functions to only having a single `return`. Many functions are written to return a Boolean based upon some criteria:

```
function functionName() {
    if (condition) {
        return true;
    } else {
        return false;
    }
}
```

If a function has no `return` statement, or uses `return` without a value, the function automatically returns the value undefined.

When a function returns a value, you can assign the results of that function call to a variable:

```
var check = functionName(true);
```

You can also use the function call directly within some other code:

```
var msg = 'This ' + functionName() + ' that.';
```

To have a function return multiple values, return an array;

```
function functionName() {
    return [1, 2, 3];
}
var myList = functionName();
```

Or you could have the function return an object:

```
function functionName() {
    return {x: 1, y: 2};
}
var myObj = functionName();
```

```
Winning Numbers: 42 64 9 2 91 32
```

You've already seen the return statement used in this book, but only to return Boolean values. This next example will define two new functions (updating random.js, from Chapter 5, in the process), and make use of setText() just created. The first function will create a shortcut for using the common code document.getElementById(). The second function will return a random number. The end result will be the same as it was in Chapter 5 (**Figure 7.9**), but it will use more modular and portable code.

**To create and call your own function:**

1. Open random.js in your text editor or IDE.

2. At the top of the page, begin defining a new function:

   ```
   function $(id) {
   ```

   Ordinarily, you want function names to be as descriptive as possible. This is an exception, though, in that the sole purpose of the function is to replicate code frequently used elsewhere, specifically document.getElementById(). After defining this function, every use of document.getElementById() in the script can just use $() instead!

   The dollar sign is one of the nonalphanumeric characters that can be used in a function (or variable) name. I specifically chose it here, as this shortcut function is common in the JavaScript community. In fact, the jQuery framework (www.jquery.com) uses this syntax extensively.

3. Complete the $() function:

   ```
   'use strict';
   if (typeof id != 'undefined') {
       return document.getElementById(id);
   }
   } // End of $ function.
   ```

   The function requires that it receive an id value, so that is validated first. Then the function returns the result of calling document.getElementById().

If `document.getElementById()` cannot find an element with the provided `id`, or if no `id` value is provided to the `$()` function, then the function returns `undefined` (implicitly in the latter case).

4. Define the `setText()` function:

```
function setText(elementId, message) {
    'use strict';
    if ( (typeof elementId == 'string')
    && (typeof message == 'string') ) {
        var output = $(elementId);
        if (output.textContent !== undefined) {
            output.textContent = numbers;
        } else {
            output.innerText = numbers;
        }
    } // End of main IF.
} // End of setText() function.
```

This code is the same as explained before, except now it uses the `$()` function to fetch the HTML element reference for the output paragraph.

You could improve this function by having it check if the `$()` function returned an element, prior to trying to update that element.

5. Begin defining a function that returns a random number:

```
function getRandomNumber(max) {
    'use strict';
    var n = Math.random();
```

This function takes one argument, but it will be treated as optional. If provided, the function will return a random integer up to that maximum (not inclusive). If no max value is provided, the function will just return a random decimal between 0 (inclusive) and 1 (exclusive). This is what the `random()` method of the Math object returns.

6. If a max value was received, factor that in:

```
if (typeof max == 'number') {
    n *= max;
    n = Math.floor(n);
}
```

As just explained, if a max argument was provided, and of type Number, it'll be factored into the random number. Because n will be a number between 0 and 1 at this point, multiplying by max will create a random number up to that maximum (e.g., if n equals .7723 and max is 100, the result will be 77.23). Next, the integer is parsed from the number, as the presumption is the decimal won't be needed.

7. Return the number and complete the function:

```
    return n;
} // End of getRandomNumber() function.
```

8. Within the showNumbers() function, call the getRandomNumber() function:

```
numbers += getRandomNumber(100) + ' ';
```

This code goes within the for loop and concatenates each value returned by the function onto the numbers string.

9. Also change the showNumbers() code so that the setText() function is used for the output:

```
setText('output', numbers);
```

10. Save the file and test it in your Web browser (Figure 7.9).

### UNDERSTANDING VARIABLE SCOPE

In Chapter 4, Simple Variable Types, it was said that it's bad to use, or at least to rely upon, *global* variables, but that one couldn't understand global variables, and the broader topic of variable scope, without knowing about user-defined functions. Now that the latter topic has been formally introduced, it's time to return to the issue of variable scope.

## WHAT IS VARIABLE SCOPE?

A variable's scope is simply the realm in which the variable exists and is available. One scope is *global*. Variables defined within a JavaScript file, outside of any function, have global scope. The same goes for a special variable provided by the Web browser (more on that in Chapter 9, JavaScript and the Browser).

When you define a function, that function creates a new level of scope, called *local* scope. A function's parameters—the variables that receive the values passed to the function when it's called—have function-level, or local, scope automatically:

```
function functionName(someVar) {

    // You can use someVar.

}
// You cannot use someVar here.
```

(Each independent function has its own local scope.)

A variable declared within a function also has function-level scope, so long as it was declared using the var keyword:

```
function functionName() {

    var localVar = 'test';

    // You can use localVar.

}
// You cannot use localVar here.
```

Global variables are also available within a function, as they are global (**Figure 7.10**):

```
var globalVar = 'test';
function functionName() {

    // You can use globalVar.

    return globalVar;

}
```

```
>> var globalVar = 'test';
   function functionName() {
       // You can use globalVar.
       return globalVar;
   }
   functionName();
   "test"
```

**FIGURE 7.10** Global variables can be referenced within functions.

```
>> function functionName() {
       var x = 3;
       console.log('In the function, x = ' + x + '\n');
   }
   var x = 2;
   console.log('Before the function, x = ' + x + '\n');
   functionName();
   console.log('After the function, x = ' + x + '\n');
LOG: Before the function, x = 2

LOG: In the function, x = 3

LOG: After the function, x = 2
```

A common and careless mistake made by many beginning JavaScript programmers is to inadvertently create a global variable within a function by failing to use var:

```
function functionName() {
    shouldBeLocalVar = 'test'; // Actually a global variable!
    // You can use shouldBeLocalVar.
}
// You can also use shouldBeLocalVar here!
```

But what happens if there's a global variable and a local variable with the same name? In those cases, the local variable takes precedence, meaning the global variable becomes inaccessible (**Figure 7.11**):

```
function functionName() {
    var x = 3;
    console.log('In the function, x = ' + x + '\n');
}
var x = 2;
console.log('Before the function, x = ' + x + '\n');
functionName();
console.log('After the function, x = ' + x + '\n');
```

```
>> function functionName(someVar) {
       someVar = true;
       console.log('In the function, someVar = ' + someVar + '\n');
   }
   var someVar = false;
   console.log('Before the function, someVar = ' + someVar + '\n');
   functionName(someVar);
   console.log('After the function, someVar = ' + someVar + '\n');
LOG: Before the function, someVar = false

LOG: In the function, someVar = true

LOG: After the function, someVar = false
```

FIGURE 7.12 Even if the variables used in a function call and in the function definition have the same name, they are still two different variables.

## REVISITING FUNCTION PARAMETERS

Earlier in the chapter, it was stated that the variable names used for argument values in the function call need not be the same as those in the function's definition. Let's revisit this idea, taking into account variable scope (**Figure 7.12**):

```
function functionName(someVar) {

    someVar = true;

    console.log('In the function, someVar = ' + someVar + '\n');

}

var someVar = false;

console.log('Before the function, someVar = ' + someVar + '\n');

functionName(someVar);

console.log('After the function, someVar = ' + someVar + '\n');
```

In that code, someVar outside of the function is a global variable, as it is declared outside of any function. The someVar variable that is the function's parameter (in the function definition) is a local variable, as are all function parameter variables. Even though both variables have the same name, and the one is used to provide a value for the other, they are not the same variable—one is global and the other is local. Further, changing the local variable's value does not impact the global variable. This is the case with simple value types. Using complex types for function arguments changes things.

This code was shown earlier:

```
function willChange(x) {
    console.log('In the function, x.num = ' + x.num + '\n');
    x.num = 2;
    console.log('After the assignment, x.num = ' + x.num + '\n');
}
var y = {num: 1}; // y.num == 1
console.log('Outside of the function, y.num = ' + y.num + '\n');
willChange(y);
console.log('Outside of the function, y.num = ' + y.num + '\n');
```

Because the value passed to the function is an object, changes to the object's properties within the function do affect the object outside of the function. This is simply because objects (and arrays) are passed *by reference*, not *value*. The global y and the local x are still two different variables with different scopes, but they both represent the same complex value stored in memory. This would still be true even if both variables were named x:

```
function willChange(x) {
    x.num = 2;
}
var x = {num: 1};
willChange(x);
```

The result of this code is the same as in the previous code, and even though both variables are named x, they are two different variables. But because x outside of the function is an object, its value is passed by reference, and both variables point to the same stored value.

## FUNCTION **DESIGN THEORY**

How you define your own functions is both a syntactical issue and a design one in that there are better and worse uses of custom functions. A proper user-defined function should be easily reusable, and likely to be reused (i.e., if a Web site only ever calls a function once, there's little need for it).

There should also be a "black box" mentality to functions: A programmer shouldn't need to know about the internals of a function in order to use it properly. As an example of this, think of any function built into JavaScript: You probably don't know what the underlying function code does specifically, but you can still make use of it. Toward this end, proper function design suggests that you be extremely cautious when using global variables, as the function should be passed the data it needs to work with.

As a rule of thumb, the more independent a function is, the more useful—and therefore, better—it becomes.

### THE PROBLEM WITH GLOBAL VARIABLES

There are a couple of reasons why global variables are bad. First, the global variables you create can, accidentally or not, conflict with other global variables (such as those provided by the Web browser or by third-party libraries). Such conflicts lead to very pesky bugs that are hard to find and fix. This problem is known as *namespace pollution* or *namespace cluttering*. The fewer the number of global variables, the tidier the environment and the less likely the possibility of conflicts.

Second, as a global variable can also be accessed within any function, it allows for the possibility that any function changes that variable's value, again leading to bugs. This problem is known as a lack of *access control*: access control is a restriction on who or what can use or modify a resource.

Third, there can be a performance hit to using global variables, in that the environment will always need to track the global variables. By comparison, local variables will only exist—be tracked by the environment and require memory to represent them—during a function's execution.

This is not to say that global variables should *never* be used, just that they should only be used deliberately and after the due consideration of the potential problems. A general good rule for programming is: only do what is absolutely required. With that in mind, you should only use a global variable if you absolutely have to.

# FUNCTIONS AS OBJECTS

```
> function getOne() { return 1; }
  undefined
> getOne();
  1
> getOne
  function getOne() { return 1; }
>
```

**FIGURE 7.13** A function variable's value is the function definition.

Functions in JavaScript have a very unique quality in that *functions are also themselves objects*. This makes functions "first-class" citizens in JavaScript: they can be used and manipulated as you would any other value type. This probably sounds rather abstract to you now, but the end result is that you can do things with JavaScript functions that you cannot do with functions in many other languages. Moreover, although the implications are complicated, understanding functions as objects will help you to appreciate some of the things commonly done in JavaScript, including many pieces of code you've already seen.

Looking back at what you already know, say you create a new (and unnecessary) function in JavaScript like so:

```
function getOne() {
    return 1;
}
```

You understand, certainly, that `getOne()` is a function, and that it can be invoked:

```
getOne();
```

However, in JavaScript, a function is an object, specifically of type `Function`. By declaring that function you've also created an object variable, with an identifier of *getOne*, whose value is the function definition (**Figure 7.13**).

Because of this quality, you can test for the presence of a function using code like:

```
if (Date.now) {
```

That code verifies that there is a definition for `now` as part of the `Date` object. This is different than the `Date.now()` function call.

More precisely, you could check that the property is a function:

```
if (typeof Date.now == 'function') {
```

```
> var getTwo = function() { return 2; }
  undefined
> getTwo
  function () { return 2; }
> getTwo();
  2
> typeof getTwo
  "function"
```

FIGURE 7.14 A function definition can be a value assigned to a variable.

Once you understand that a function definition is just another type of value in JavaScript, you might realize that you can do with a function definition what you can do with any value type, such as a number or string, including: assign the function definition to a variable, use it as a value to be passed to another function, or even return a function from another function. I'll explain…

## FUNCTIONS AS VARIABLE VALUES

The syntax used thus far for declaring a function constitutes a JavaScript *statement*. You can also create a function using an *expression*, whereby the creation of the function as a value of a variable is overt:

```
var getTwo = function() {
    return 2;
}
```

This syntax probably seems strange, but the end result is the same: an object of type Function has been created. Because it's a Function object, it can be invoked, unlike other objects (**Figure 7.14**):

```
getTwo();
```

Any value that can be assigned to a variable can also be assigned to an object property, as an object property is just a variable associated with an object. This is code that's been used many times over in this book:

```
window.onload = init;
```

That code assigns to the unload property of the window object the value of the init variable, which is to say the init() function definition.

Note that the code does not invoke the function—it's lacking the invocation parentheses:

```
window.onload = init(); // No!
```

Doing the above would call the `init()` function and assign the value returned by it to the `window.onload` property, which is not the intent.

Taking this further, you can skip the step of naming the function and/or creating a function variable, and just assign a function expression to an object property directly:

```
window.onload = function() {
    // Function body goes here.
}
```

In that code, the function itself is called an *anonymous* function, as it has no name. You'll use anonymous functions frequently in JavaScript.

## FUNCTIONS AS ARGUMENT VALUES

A second way you can use a function as an object is to pass a function definition to another function, as you would any other argument value. This only makes sense, of course, in situations where the function being called expects one of its arguments to be a function. To do this, you can create the function and assign it to a variable, then pass that variable to the other function:

```
var someFunction = function() {
};
someOtherFunction(someFunction);
```

Or, you can also simplify this and write the function definition within the other function's invocation:

```
someOtherFunction(function() {
});
```

When you do this, just be mindful of the syntax so that you don't create a syntactical error. (In both cases, these are also anonymous functions.)

As an example, in Chapter 6, it's said that arrays have a `sort()` method, but that the method is of limited use without knowing how to define your own functions. This is because the built-in `sort()` method can only reliably be used to sort array elements alphabetically. This is fine if you have an array of strings (**Figure 7.15**):

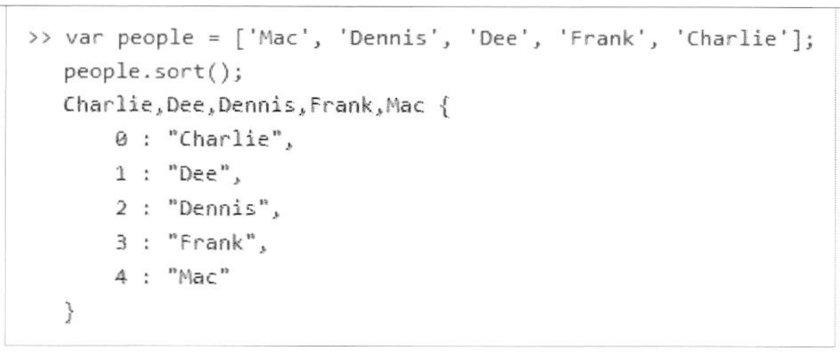

```
>> var people = ['Mac', 'Dennis', 'Dee', 'Frank', 'Charlie'];
   people.sort();
   Charlie,Dee,Dennis,Frank,Mac {
       0 : "Charlie",
       1 : "Dee",
       2 : "Dennis",
       3 : "Frank",
       4 : "Mac"
   }
```

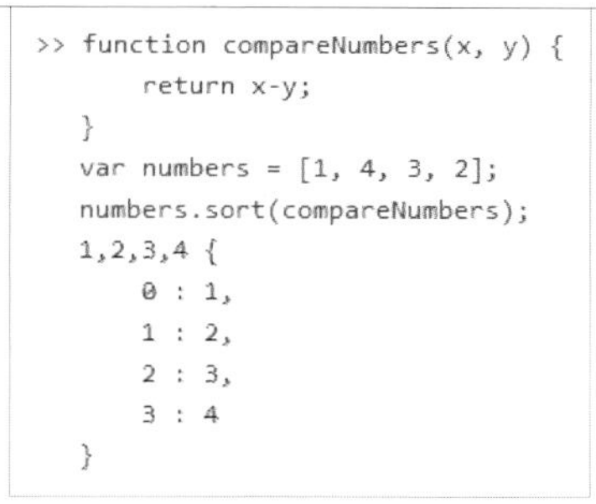

```
>> function compareNumbers(x, y) {
       return x-y;
   }
   var numbers = [1, 4, 3, 2];
   numbers.sort(compareNumbers);
   1,2,3,4 {
       0 : 1,
       1 : 2,
       2 : 3,
       3 : 4
   }
```

```
var people = ['Mac', 'Dennis', 'Dee', 'Frank', 'Charlie'];
people.sort();
```

**FIGURE 7.15** The sort() method will perform a proper, case-sensitive sorting of strings.

In current browsers, sort() will properly sort numbers, but in older browsers, sorting a list of numbers was done alphabetically, too:

```
var numbers = [1, 4, 3, 2];
numbers.sort(); // 4, 1, 3, 2
```

**FIGURE 7.16** To change how array elements are sorted, provide the method with your own function definition.

The solution (again, for the older browsers) was to create a function that will perform the comparison needed, and then to tell the sort() method to use that function instead of its default mechanism. The comparison function needs to take two arguments—the two values being compared—and return:

- A negative value if the first argument comes before the second

- 0, if the two arguments are the same

- A positive value if the second argument comes before the first

Conventionally, the returned values are −1, 0, and 1.

Thus, to sort an array of numbers, the code to use is (**Figure 7.16**):

```
function compareNumbers(x, y) {
    return x-y;
}
var numbers = [1, 4, 3, 2];
numbers.sort(compareNumbers);
```

First, note that the function *identifier* is being used as the argument value to sort(), not a function *call*. Within the function, a little shortcut is being used to determine what value is returned: the second argument is subtracted from the first. If the result of the subtraction is positive, then x must be bigger (e.g., 8-7); if the result is negative, then x must be smaller (e.g., 7-8); if the numbers are the same, 0 will be returned.

As another example, if you wanted to perform a case-insensitive string sort, you can write a function to do that:

```
function caseInsensitiveCompare(x, y) {
    x = x.toLowerCase();
    y = y.toLowerCase();
    if (x > y) {
        return 1;
    } else if (y > x) {
        return -1;
    } else {
        return 0;
    }
}
```

## PUTTING IT TOGETHER

To practice providing functions as arguments to other functions, let's look at some of the new array functions added in ECMAScript 5. Each of these requires a user-defined function in order to work:

- forEach() loops through an array, one element at a time.

- every() tests each array element against a condition and returns a Boolean if every element passes.

- some() tests each array element against a condition and returns a Boolean if at least one element passes.

```
>>> var mix = [1, true, 'test'];
undefined
>>> mix.every(function (value) { return (typeof value == 'string'); });
false
```

**FIGURE 7.17** The every() method returns **false** because not every element in the array is a string.

**FIGURE 7.18** IE9 does not support the every() method.

```
>> var mix = [1, true, 'test'];
   mix.every(function (value) {
       return (typeof value == 'string');
   });
❌ "Object doesn't support property or method 'every'"
```

- map() provides each array element to a function where it will be modified and returned, creating a new array.

- filter() tests each array element against a condition and only returns those that pass, creating a new array in the process.

- reduce() can be used to group an array's elements into a single value.

For example, to confirm that an array contains nothing but strings (e.g., prior to sorting the array), you can use every(). It returns a Boolean value indicating if every element in the array passes the condition set in the user-defined function (**Figure 7.17**):

```
var mix = [1, true, 'test'];
mix.every(function (value) {
    return (typeof value == 'string');
});
```

As a reminder, these are newer functions, and may not be supported by all browsers (**Figure 7.18**). To test for support, and perform the same task regardless, you could use code like this:

```
// Function that returns a Boolean indicating a String:
function testForString(value) {
    return (typeof value == 'string');
}
// Array to be tested:
```

**FIGURE 7.19** A sentence of words is quickly parsed, sorted, and redisplayed by this script.

```
var mix = [1, true, 'test'];
if (mix.every) { // Can use every()!
    var result = mix.every(testForString);
} else { // Must write every() equivalent.
    var result = true; // Assume truth.
    for (var i = 0, count = mix.length; i++) { // Loop through array.
        if (!testForString(mix[i])) { // Is it not a String?
            result = false; // Change result to false.
            break; // Terminate the loop.
        } // IF
    } // FOR
}
```

As another example, this next script will take a list of words from the user, then perform a case-insensitive sort of the words, and output the result (**Figure 7.19**). The relevant HTML, in a page named words.html, is:

```
<div><label for="words">Words</label><input type="text" name="words"
   id="words" required></div>
<input type="submit" value="Sort!" id="submit">
<h2>Sorted Words</h2>
<div id="output"></div>
```

The form uses one text input for the list of words. Just below the submit button is an empty DIV that will be updated by the JavaScript code, providing the sorted output.

The HTML page includes the words.js JavaScript file, to be written in the subsequent steps.

**To sort an array with a user-defined function:**

1. Create a new JavaScript file in your text editor or IDE, to be named words.js.

2. Define the $() function:

```
function $(id) {
    'use strict';
    if (typeof id != 'undefined') {
        return document.getElementById(id);
    }
} // End of $ function.
```

This function, explained earlier, will be used to get references to form elements.

3. Define the setText() function:

```
function setText(elementId, message) {
    'use strict';
    if ( (typeof elementId == 'string')
    && (typeof message == 'string') ) {
        var output = $(elementId);
        if (output.textContent !== undefined) {
            output.textContent = numbers;
        } else {
            output.innerText = numbers;
        }
    } // End of main IF.
} // End of setText() function.
```

This function will also be used by the script.

4. Begin defining the sortWords() function:

```
function sortWords(max) {
    'use strict';
    var words = $('words').value;
```

The sortWords() function does the work when the form is submitted. It starts by getting a reference to the form value.

5. Convert the string to an array:

```
words = words.split(' ');
```

The split() function returns an array of pieces from a string, using the provided argument as the delineator. It was explained in Chapter 6. The result of the operation is assigned back to words, changing that string into an array.

6. Perform a case-insensitive sort of the words:

```
var sorted = words.map(function(value) {
    return value.toLowerCase();
}).sort();
```

That code looks a bit complicated because it has two chained method calls and an anonymous function, but here's what is happening: To the words array, the map() method is applied. The map() method takes a function as its argument, and map() will pass to that function each array element, one at a time. The anonymous function used as the map() argument therefore has to be written to accept a value as an argument. This value can be manipulated and returned: in this case, the value is converted to all lowercase letters. The result of using map() is a new array. To this array, the sort() method is applied. The result of that action is then assigned to the new sorted variable.

You could write this out more overtly as:

```
var changeToLowerCase(value) {
    return value.toLowerCase();
}
var sorted = words.map(changeToLowerCase);

sorted = sorted.sort();
```

You could also combine the code in Steps 5 and 6 to make it more complicated, but a single step.

To save space, this code does not check if the browser supports the map() method. That can be a challenge for you to pursue, using the code already explained as a starting point.

7. Send the output to the page:

```
setText('output', sorted.join(', '));
```

Finally, the HTML page is updated using the setText() function. For the text itself, a function call to join() provides that value. It returns a string using the provided argument as the glue (it was also discussed in the last chapter).

8. Complete the sortWords() function:

```
    return false;
} // End of sortWords() function.
```

9. Add an event listener to the form's submission:

```
function init() {
    'use strict';
    $('theForm').onsubmit = sortWords;
} // End of init() function.
window.onload = init;
```

10. Save the file as words.js, in a js directory next to words.html, and test it in your Web browser.

# THE **FANCIER STUFF**

With the fundamentals in the bag, and an appreciation for functions as objects, let's start looking at some of the fancier things you can do with functions in JavaScript. To be clear, what you'll learn over the remaining few pages aren't just tricks, but rather sophisticated ways to solve sometimes complicated problems.

## CONTEXT AND THIS

In order to be able to fully grasp functions, one has to be aware of *context*, also called *execution context*. For each line of code in a JavaScript file, there is a context in which that line is being executed. For example, the code found between HTML script tags, or in an external JavaScript file, executes within a global context. The code within a function's body operates within a different context, and code within another function's body will have another context. When each function's execution is over, the context returns to what it was previous to that function call. Within each context, different objects exist and different properties will have different values.

A key tool involving context is a special object called this. The this variable gets its value from the execution context. Often this refers to the object on which a function was invoked. For example:

```
var n = 2;
n.toFixed(2); // Returns 2.00
```

Within the toFixed() method, this refers to the n variable, allowing the method's internals to access that variable's value.

When you have a function not associated with an object, the function is actually part of the global object (e.g., window, in the Web browser), meaning that this normally refers to the global object.

Being able to refer to the object invoking the function is a critical component in object-oriented programming. On a level that's easy to understand, the this keyword provides a way for an object to refer to its own properties. For example, as just explained, since a function is an object, a function can be assigned to properties of other objects. What has not been shown yet is that this includes your own custom objects:

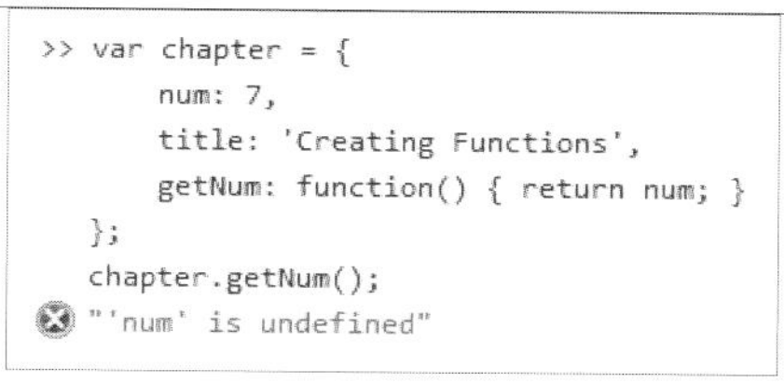

```
>> var chapter = {
      num: 7,
      title: 'Creating Functions',
      getNum: function() { return num; }
   };
   chapter.getNum();
❌ "'num' is undefined"
```

```
>> var chapter = {
      num: 7,
      title: 'Creating Functions',
      getNum: function() { return this.num; }
   };
   chapter.getNum();
   7
```

```
var someObj = {

    someProperty: true,

    someMethod: function() {

        // Function body.

    }

};
```

**FIGURE 7.20** The object method cannot access the object's properties directly.

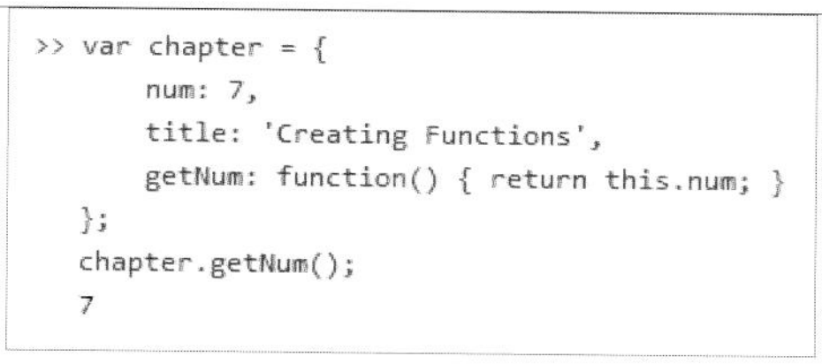

**FIGURE 7.21** By using the special this keyword, an object's method can make use of the object's other properties.

Now you can use someObj.someProperty to get the property value, and use someObj.someMethod() to execute the function defined within the property. Object methods commonly make use of other object properties, but they cannot do so in JavaScript without this (**Figure 7.20**):

```
var chapter = {

    num: 7,

    title: 'Creating Functions',

    getNum: function() { return num; }

};

chapter.getNum();
```

The solution is to use this to refer to the current object (**Figure 7.21**):

```
var chapter = {

    num: 7,

    title: 'Creating Functions',

    getNum: function() { return this.num; }

};

chapter.getNum();
```

The this keyword can also be used to invoke an object method from within another of the object's methods.

To practice with this, let's quickly and slightly modify employee.js from Chapter 6 so that the employee object has a method for returning a formatted version of the employee's name.

**To create an object method:**

1. Open employee.js in your text editor or IDE.

2. Change the creation of the employee object so that it also has a method:

```
var employee = {
    firstName: firstName,
    lastName: lastName,
    department: department,
    getName: function() {
        return this.lastName + ', ' + this.firstName;
    },
    hireDate: new Date()
}; // Don't forget the semicolon!
```

The getName() method is defined within the object. It returns the object's lastName property, followed by a comma and a space, followed by the object's firstName property.

3. Change the assignment to the message variable so that it uses the object's new method:

```
var message = '<h2>Employee Added</h2>Name: ' +
    employee.getName() + '<br>';
```

Once the object has the method defined, it can be invoked using standard object notation.

FIGURE 7.22 Again, the visual result is the same, but the internal workings are getting smarter and smarter!

4. Save the file as employee.js, in a js directory next to employee.html, and test it in your Web browser (**Figure 7.22**).

## ANONYMOUS FUNCTIONS

As mentioned a few pages ago, an interesting and common practice in JavaScript is to create *anonymous functions*. An anonymous function is just a function without a name. They are normally created when a function definition is:

- Assigned to a variable
- Assigned to an object property
- Used as a value being passed in a function call

You've already seen examples of these uses of anonymous functions. Another use of an anonymous function is as an *immediately invoked function*. To do that, you create an anonymous function and wrap it within a function call:

```
(function() {
    // Function body goes here.
})();
```

To understand what's going on with this cryptic syntax, the function code creates an anonymous function. This is wrapped within parentheses—`(function() {...})`, so that the entire construct can be followed by the parentheses needed to invoke the function.

One benefit of an immediately invoked function is that it can be used to separate your variables and other code from the global scope:

```
(function() {
    var someVar;
    // Function body goes here.
})();
```

The function is created and executed, making a local variable in the process. Then the function terminates, leaving no global functions or variables remaining. This may not seem like much on its own right, but you can nest functions in JavaScript, which expands the possibilities.

## NESTED FUNCTIONS

Another thing you can do with JavaScript functions that is rather unique is that you can nest them, which is to say define one within another:

```
function functionName() {
    // Some function body.
    function anotherFunctionName() {
        // This function's body.
    }
}
```

This is possible in JavaScript because objects can have methods, as you know, and functions are just another type of object. Therefore, a function defined within a function is just really a method of the outer function.

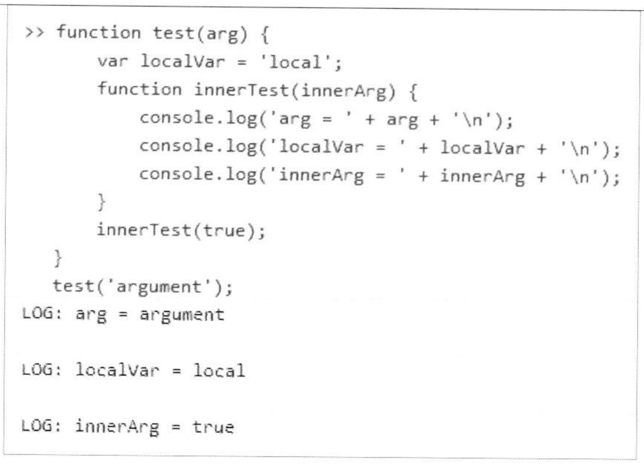

```
>> function test(arg) {
       var localVar = 'local';
       function innerTest(innerArg) {
           console.log('arg = ' + arg + '\n');
           console.log('localVar = ' + localVar + '\n');
           console.log('innerArg = ' + innerArg + '\n');
       }
       innerTest(true);
   }
   test('argument');
LOG: arg = argument

LOG: localVar = local

LOG: innerArg = true
```

FIGURE 7.23 A nested function can access variables found within its parent scope and the global scope.

There are some interesting qualities that come about from this arrangement. For starters, the nested (i.e., inner) function will have its own scope. However, the inner function will also automatically have access to the variables that are local to the parent function, including its arguments (**Figure 7.23**). (Naturally, the inner function also has access to global variables, because those are global.)

```
function test(arg) {
    var localVar = 'local';
    function innerTest(innerArg) {
        console.log('arg = ' + arg + '\n');
        console.log('localVar = ' + localVar + '\n');
        console.log('innerArg = ' + innerArg + '\n');
    }
    innerTest(true);
}
test('argument');
```

Second, the inner function will be "hidden" from the global scope, which means that it cannot be called from outside of the primary, outer function. If the outer function is immediately invoked, the inner function will never be part of the global scope either.

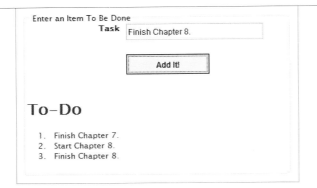

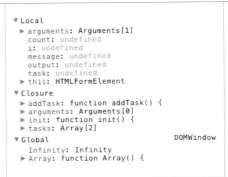

**FIGURE 7.24** The still-working tasks management application!

**FIGURE 7.25** The Web Inspector in Safari no longer lists tasks as one of the global variables.

As a very practical example of this, let's rewrite the tasks application from Chapter 6, without using any global variables or functions. The original script required a global array, but you now have the knowledge to write that same application more purely.

**To create an immediately invoked, anonymous nested function:**

1. Open `tasks.js` in your text editor or IDE.

2. Before the declaration of the `tasks` variable, add:

   ```
   (function(){
   ```

   All of the script's code will get wrapped within an anonymous function definition and call. That begins here.

3. As the very last line of code, add:

   ```
   })();
   ```

   This completes the anonymous function definition and then invokes it.

4. Indent all of the other lines of code to indicate that they constitute the body of the anonymous function.

   This isn't required, but is for the best.

5. Save the file as `tasks.js`, in a `js` directory next to `tasks.html`, and test it in your Web browser (**Figure 7.24**).

6. If your browser's debugging tools lists the global variables, view the results while executing the script (**Figure 7.25**).

You'll notice several things if you look at the variables that exist while the script is running. First, there are a *ton* of global variables, which is one of the reasons not to create any more. Second, the local variables will be those within a specific function, such as addTask(). Third, there will be a new category of variables titled *Closure* (see Figure 7.25), under which you'll find not only the tasks variable but the two named functions. A *closure* is an advanced concept, to be discussed more in Part 3 of the book. In simplest terms, a closure is a function whose definition automatically includes a memorized state of the variables that existed when the function was defined. If that went right over your head, don't worry: closures have been tripping up even seasoned JavaScript programmers for years. Chapter 14, Advanced JavaScript, will return to the topic more deliberately.

## PERFORMING RECURSION

*Recursion* is a concept that's quite simple in theory and rather complex in actuality. Recursion is just the act of a function calling itself, and it's something that's possible in any programming language that allows you to define functions. One of the easiest uses of recursion to grasp is a *factorial* function, where a factorial is the product of all the integers from 1 to the given number:

```
5! = 5 * 4 * 3 * 2 * 1 (120)
```

The following function can be used to calculate and return the factorial of a number:

```
function factorial(n) {
    if (n <= 1) {
        return 1;
    } else {
        return n * factorial(n-1);
    }
}
```

To understand what's happening here, use a specific number and walk through the code. The factorial of 5 is 120: 5 * 4 * 3 * 2 * 1. The first time the function will be called, with 5 provided as the argument value, the `else` clause comes into play. In that case, the function returns n, which is 5, times the value returned by calling the factorial function again, this time providing the value of n-1. In other words:

```
return 5 * factorial(4);
```

The result of that function call will be:

```
return 4 * factorial(3);
```

This makes the returned value of the original function call to be:

```
return 5 * (4 * factorial(3));
```

This process continues until n becomes equal to 1 and 1 is returned:

```
return 5 * (4 * (3 * (2 * (1))));
```

A recursive function is a good solution when the same process needs to be repeated for an unknown number of times. For example, navigating a tree data structure, such as an HTML document, can be done using recursion. Or, as another example, if the tasks application could have subtasks, where each subtask could also have one or more subtasks, recursion would be needed to display the entire list of tasks.

However, there is a limit as to how many times a browser can perform recursion, as recursion is memory intensive (the original function call's `return` statement cannot be executed until every recursive call returns its value). In some situations, simple iteration using a loop can accomplish the same end goal without the larger memory requirement. The factorial function can be written using a loop instead:

```
function factorial(n) {
    for (var product = 1; n > 1; n--) {
        product *= n;
    }
    return product;
}
```

Iteration requires less memory than deep recursion, although loops might otherwise be slower.

# REVIEW AND PURSUE

If you have any problems with these sections, either in answering the questions or pursuing your own endeavors, turn to the book's supporting forum (www.LarryUllman.com/forums/).

## REVIEW

- What is the syntax for defining your own functions? How do you write a function that takes arguments?

- How can you validate the number and types of arguments passed to a function, and why is that necessary?

- How do you establish a default parameter value?

- What does it mean to say that an argument is passed *by value* or *by reference*? Which value types are passed in each way?

- How does a function return a value?

- What is variable scope? What is global scope? What is local scope? Why should you avoid creating global variables?

- What does it mean that functions in JavaScript are "first-class"?

- What is the second (i.e., expression) syntax for defining a function?

- What are some of the new array methods discussed in this chapter? Why were they covered here instead of in the previous chapter (with the other array material)?

- What information and/or values does the this keyword provide to a function or method?

- What is an anonymous function? In what situations are anonymous functions commonly used?

- Why is it possible to nest functions in JavaScript?

- What is recursion and when is it useful? What is an alternative to recursion (in some situations)?

## PURSUE

- Update `today.js` so neither argument can be an empty string.

- Update `today.js` so that `message` can also be a number.

- Update `today.js` so that the `setText()` function validates that the destination element was found.

- Try using the `getRandomNumber()` function in `random.js` with different arguments (i.e., `max` values) to see the result. Be sure to try it with no argument value, too.

- Rewrite `words.js` so it still works even if the browser does not support the `map()` method.

- Search online for some examples using the other new array methods: `forEach()`, `some()`, `filter()`, and so forth.

- Continue reworking `employee.js` so it uses some of the other functions and techniques taught in this chapter, such as the `$()` function.

# WRAPPING **UP**

This chapter walked you through the basics of defining and invoking your own functions in JavaScript. As the first part of the chapter demonstrated, this concept is not that hard to learn, at least on the primary level. Then you learned that functions in JavaScript are actually objects, and that this one fact really changes what can be done with functions. Functions can be assigned to variables, provided to other functions as arguments, and even returned by functions (although you did not see an example of that here).

By the end of the chapter, the information and possibilities got interesting (or messy, depending upon your state of mind). Functions in JavaScript are a really useful *data type*, able to be used anonymously, as an immediately invoked entity, and nested within another function. I even managed to sneak in an example of a *closure* in this chapter: one of the most advanced concepts involving JavaScript functions. While you've learned a goodly amount when it comes to creating and utilizing your own functions, there's more to be had in Part 3 of the book, including more detailed analysis of what, exactly, a closure is and how it works.

But first, there are more fundamentals to learn, beginning with an exhaustive coverage of events in the next chapter. You've already learned a few things about events, starting in Chapter 2 of the book, and now it's time to finish covering the subject.

# 8

# EVENT **HANDLING**

Handling events is one of the fundamental uses of JavaScript. Loading a Web page, moving the cursor, entering text into a textarea, submitting a form: these are all events that occur within the browser to which JavaScript can respond. Out of necessity, Chapter 2, JavaScript in Action, introduced the very basics of event handling, and it also presented two events, used in most of the book's examples thus far. In this chapter, you'll learn everything you need to know to handle the myriad of events in JavaScript.

# THE **PREMISE** OF EVENT HANDLING

Chapter 2 explained that creating an event handler in JavaScript is a matter of associating an *event* and an *object* with a JavaScript *function*. For example:

```
window.onload = init;
```

That one line says that when the *load* event happens with the window, the init() function should be called. Formally speaking, you could say that an *event listener* is created or *registered*, and that the init() function will act as the *event handler* for the load event on the window object.

You've also seen variations on this code multiple times by now:

```
document.getElementById('theForm').onsubmit = process;
```

When the element with an id value of *theForm* triggers a *submit* event, the process() function is called.

Clearly, there are many other events that can occur, and those will be explained in this chapter in detail. There are also alternative ways to create an event listener, which will be covered first. As for the user-defined event handling function, the last chapter covered functions in detail, but there are a few new things to learn when it comes to using functions as event handlers.

As a warning in advance, the vast majority of all the code discussed to this point has been browser neutral, with only a few noted exceptions. When it comes to event handling, one has to start coding more flexibly, as different browsers implement events and event handlers in different ways.

**NOTE:** Events will occur whether they are handled or not.

## **CREATING** EVENT **LISTENERS**

Although only one format has been used in this book to this point, JavaScript supports four different ways of creating event listeners. Over the next few pages, I'll recap the first, and cover the other three, although one of those should no longer be used (I'm including it here as you might see it elsewhere, and sometimes it's best to know why you *shouldn't* do something).

## (DON'T USE) INLINE EVENT HANDLERS

Historically, JavaScript programmers first used *inline* event listeners, accomplished by assigning a JavaScript function to an HTML element property:

```
<form action="#" method="post" onsubmit="validateForm();">
```

or

```
<a href="somepage.html" onclick="doSomething();">Some Link</a>
```

This code was popular because it was easy to write and performed reliably well across all browsers. Although you will still see inline event handling in legacy code, and in some instructional resources, it is to be avoided. One reason is that inline event handling makes a mess of the HTML, interspersing JavaScript here and there. Not only is such code aesthetically harsh, it makes it that much harder for the developer to debug and manage the project. Second, one can't apply the concept of *progressive enhancement* when the JavaScript code is written directly within the HTML. Third, and most importantly, inline event handlers got developers into thinking that JavaScript would always work, often undercutting standard functionality based upon this assumption. For example, this has been a common practice:

```
<a href="#" onclick="doSomething();">Some Link</a>
```

The intention is that the doSomething() function will do what's required when the user clicks the link. That's all fine and good, but without a valid href value, this link would do absolutely nothing for those with JavaScript disabled or unavailable. The end result for those users is that your Web page seems to be broken, having links that don't go anywhere.

I only mention inline event handling as it's still seen, even in reputable places such as Mozilla's own documentation, and it was the standard for years. But inline event handling should be avoided in modern JavaScript.

## TRADITIONAL EVENT HANDLING

The event listening code used in this book since Chapter 2 is normally called the *traditional* approach:

```
window.onload = init;
```

There are two great arguments for using this method: it's easy and it works reliably on every browser released within the last decade or more. For these reasons, it's the route I've chosen to use to this point, and I will actually continue to use the traditional approach for many of the examples in this book. Just remember when assigning event handlers in this way, the property (i.e., *onevent*) must be in all lowercase letters.

Chapter 7, Creating Functions, demonstrated that using the traditional approach for creating an event handler is a perfect time to apply an anonymous function, saving yourself from having to formally declare the function:

```
window.onload = function() {

    // Do whatever.

}
```

I haven't previously mentioned this, but you can remove event handlers when using the traditional approach by assigning null to the proper event property of the object:

```
window.onload = null;
```

As with any object property, you can confirm that an event listener exists by checking the object's property value:

```
if (typeof window.onload == 'function') { // Exists!
```

There are a couple of reasons why you *wouldn't* want to use the traditional approach. First, you can only assign a single event handler this way:

```
document.getElementById('theForm').onsubmit = process;
document.getElementById('theForm').onsubmit = calculate; // Oops!
```

After the second line of code, only the calculate() function will be called when the form is submitted. The original event handler association with the process() function has been replaced. This, then, is the second problem with the traditional route: it's too easy to overwrite an existing event handler.

Both problems can be mitigated by just creating one event-handling function that invokes the two needed functions:

```
document.getElementById('theForm').onsubmit = function() {
    process();
    calculate();
}
```

But this is an ugly kludge, best avoided. Moreover, in a more complicated project, with multiple JavaScript files and libraries, if *any* JavaScript code uses the traditional method, it's possible that it will undo the event registrations that took place in other JavaScript files.

## W3C EVENT HANDLING

Eventually, the W3C (World Wide Web Consortium) came up with its own approach for how event listeners should be created, defined as part of the *DOM Level 2* specification (the DOM specifications define other browser behavior beyond just event handling). This approach is an improvement on both the inline and traditional methods in a couple of ways. First, DOM Level 2 event assignations are done within JavaScript code, not HTML. Second, the DOM Level 2 specification allows you to assign multiple event handlers to the same element.

In the W3C DOM approach, event listeners are created using the addEvent Listener() method. It takes three arguments: the event *type*, the *function* to be called when that event occurs, and a Boolean value indicating the event *phase* to watch for. You'll learn about event phases later in the chapter, but for now, you can always use false for the third argument, or skip it, resulting in a FALSE-like value of undefined (as explained in Chapter 7).

With this in mind, to create an event listener for the window's load event, you would write:

```
window.addEventListener('load', init, false);
```

Note that here it's just *load*, not *onload*: *load* is the event name, *onload* is the corresponding property of the window object. And, as with all function references, use the function's name, without any parentheses (because that would be a function call).

To add multiple event listeners for the same event on the same element, just use multiple addEventListener() calls accordingly:

```
window.addEventListener('load', process, false);
window.addEventListener('load', calculate, false);
```

The corresponding removeEventListener() method removes an event listener (it's aptly named). For the method to work, it needs to be provided with the exact same argument values as the addEventListener() call that's being undone:

```
window.removeEventListener('load', process, false);
```

Assuming the previous two method calls were part of the same script, at this point in time, only the calculate() function will be called when the window triggers a load event.

Understand that you should remove event listeners once they are no longer needed, although many programmers fail to do so. The removeEventListener() method will *not* throw an error if you attempt to remove an event listener that does not exist.

**NOTE:** The inline and traditional event handling are collectively referred to as DOM Level 0, which is to say the approaches existed before there was a standard for event handling.

The W3C DOM Level 2 approach is logical, flexible, and easy enough to apply. It requires a bit more code than the traditional approach, sure, but it's supported in almost every browser. Unfortunately, the one browser that doesn't have addEventListener() is...Internet Explorer, prior to version 9. For older versions of IE, there's another way of creating event listeners.

## IE EVENT HANDLING

Microsoft started off doing things differently in its line of Internet Explorer browsers when it comes to DOM event listeners (and, well, many other things). At first glance, Microsoft's approach won't seem that different than the W3C's, but there are implications to the differences, to be explained in time. To start, instead of addEventListener() and removeEventListener(), IE has attachEvent() and detachEvent(). Both take just two arguments: the event and the function to be called when that event occurs. The IE equivalent of the window.onload event handler is:

```
window.attachEvent('onload', init);
```

Unlike with the W3C DOM version, the "on" is included before the event name again, as in the traditional approach.

Fortunately, IE9 started supporting the W3C DOM methods. Still, developers moving beyond DOM Level 0 event listening need to write event handlers in a way that's cross-platform compatible. That code will be explained next.

## CREATING AN EVENT ASSIGNER

To create reliable event listeners, let's start by looking at how one would write the init() window.onload code in a cross-browser manner:

```
if (window.addEventListener) { // W3C
    window.addEventListener('load', init, false);
} else if (window.attachEvent) { // Older IE
    window.attachEvent('onload', init);
}
```

(To be more precise, each conditional could check that the typeof the corresponding property is a function.)

When adding lots of event listeners to lots of page elements, rewriting this conditional time and again becomes impractical. Therefore, it should be moved into a function whose sole purpose is to add an event in a cross-browser manner. The function will need to take three arguments—the object, the event type, and the function:

```
function addEvent(obj, type, fn) {

}
```

Within the function, replicate the above code, replacing the particulars with the function's arguments:

```
function addEvent(obj, type, fn) {
    if (obj && obj.addEventListener) { // W3C
        obj.addEventListener(type, fn, false);
    } else if (obj && obj.attachEvent) { // Older IE
        obj.attachEvent('on' + type, fn);
    }
}
```

**TIP:** Adding events using addEventListener() and attachEvent() will not overwrite event handlers assigned using the traditional approach.

In that code, I've added checks that the object provided exists (has a non-FALSE value). And, in the attachEvent() method call, the prefix *on* is added to the event's name, to be in keeping with what attachEvent() expects.

You would then call this function using this code, for all browsers:

```
addEvent(window, 'load', init);
```

# CREATING A UTILITY LIBRARY

With this understanding of how to reliably assign event listeners, regardless of the browser in use, it's time to start writing more event-based code. But first, as the addEvent() function will be used by every script throughout the rest of the chapter, it makes sense to define it, along with a couple of functions explained in Chapter 7, in a separate file that can be included by every HTML page. To avoid *polluting the global namespace* with multiple new functions, all of the functions will be defined as part of one global object, simply named *U* (short for *utility*). You'll see how to do this in the next sequence of steps, and how to use this new object in the remaining pages.

As a reminder, you can download all of the necessary code from my Web site at www.LarryUllman.com.

**To create a utilities library:**

1. Create a new JavaScript file in your text editor or IDE, to be named utilities.js.

2. Begin creating a new object named *U*:

   ```
   var U = {
   ```

   The U object will be the lone global variable created by this script.

3. Define the $() method:

   ```
   $: function(id) {
       'use strict';
       if (typeof id == 'string') {
           return document.getElementById(id);
       }
   }, // End of $() function.
   ```

   This function was defined and explained in Chapter 7. The function takes the id value for the element to be retrieved and returns a reference to that element. The only difference here is that the function is defined as a property of the U object. To assign a value to an object's property, use the *property-Name: value* syntax, where *propertyName* is the name of the function and *value* is the function's definition.

4. Define the setText() method:

```
setText: function(id, message) {
    'use strict';
    if ( (typeof id == 'string')
    && (typeof message == 'string') ) {
        var output = this.$(id);
        if (!output) return false;
        if (output.textContent !== undefined) {
            output.textContent = message;
        } else {
            output.innerText = message;
        }
        return true;
    } // End of main IF.
}, // End of setText() function.
```

The setText() function takes two arguments: the id value of the element to be updated and the message itself. Both are validated as strings, and the element is fetched using the internal $() function just defined. To invoke that function, use either this.$() or U.$(). If no corresponding element is found, the function returns false. Otherwise, the function sets the text and returns true.

5. Define the addEvent() method:

```
addEvent: function(obj, type, fn) {
    'use strict';
    if (obj && obj.addEventListener) {
        obj.addEventListener(type, fn, false);
    } else if (obj && obj.attachEvent) {
```

```
        obj.attachEvent('on' + type, fn);
    }
}, // End of addEvent() function.
```

This code has already been explained. Note that it takes an *object* as its first argument, not the id value of the destination element. This is necessary in order to add event listeners to the window or document object.

6. Define the removeEvent() method:

```
removeEvent: function(obj, type, fn) {
    'use strict';
    if (obj && obj.removeEventListener) {
        obj.removeEventListener(type, fn, false);
    } else if (obj && obj.detachEvent) {
        obj.detachEvent('on' + type, fn);
    }
} // End of removeEvent() function.
```

This code just replicates that in addEvent(). Also note that there's no comma after the function's closing curly brace, as this function definition is the last property in the U object.

7. Finish the declaration of U:

```
}; // End of U declaration.
```

Don't forget the semicolon after the closing curly brace, which completes the object declaration statement:

```
var U = { /* functions */ };
```

8. Save the file as utilities.js.

You'll want to place the script, or a copy of it, in the same directory as all the other JavaScript files you write in this chapter.

# EVENT **TYPES**

With a thorough understanding of how one can create event listeners, it's time to go through the range of events that can occur within the Web browser. I've grouped these into four categories:

- Input Device
- Keyboard
- Browser
- Form

Let's look at these groups in order. For each group, I'll highlight the key events, how they're commonly used, and what to be careful about. You won't initially see much in the way of code or images in the next few pages, but there will be full example scripts to demonstrate the new information later on. Note that this chapter, and the book, does not include a complete list of events, but presents those you'll commonly use and therefore need to know.

Be forewarned that not all browsers and devices support all of these event types, let alone some of the specific events. For example, screen readers don't have input devices. This chapter also mentions, but doesn't demonstrate, the touch events, which are only supported in touch-enabled devices.

## INPUT DEVICE EVENTS

Input device events are triggered by mice, trackpads, trackballs, graphic tablets, and the like. Although the keyboard is clearly a device for creating input, too, the input device group is about cursor-driven events.

### INPUT BUTTON EVENTS

The *click* is one of the first events most programmers learn about, but it's not actually as simple as one would think. If you move your cursor over an element and click on it (without moving the cursor while clicking), at least three events take place:

- mousedown
- mouseup
- click

A *click* event is the combination of a *mousedown* and a *mouseup* on the same element. This means that the click event is more exacting than either mousedown or mouseup: if the user clicks on an element, but moves off of it before releasing the button, that will not constitute a click. For this reason, you can have more reliable results by specifically looking for mousedown events instead of click.

Some browsers will only treat a left-button click as a click event. Further, the act of clicking on one element and moving to another is a *drag*, which JavaScript needs to be programmed to handle (prior to HTML5).

There is also the double-click event, *dblclick*, although it is less commonly used. If you do choose to use dblclick, do not also create a click handler on the same element, as that will cause quite a bit of event confusion (as a dblclick will also trigger the click event twice).

And there is the *contextmenu* event, which is triggered when the user attempts to create a contextual menu (e.g., by right-clicking on Windows or Control+clicking on Macs). Sadly, most developers watch for the contextmenu event in order to prevent the user from creating contextual menus, in theory stopping the user from copying an image or some such. This is a topic I'll return to later.

### INPUT MOVEMENT EVENTS

Events can also be triggered by the cursor simply being moved, without any button clicks at all. The three movement-based events are:

- mouseout
- mouseover
- mousemove

*Mouseout* and *mouseover* have been around for years, and are the two most commonly used mouse events, along with click. For example, one of the initial popular uses of JavaScript was to perform image rollovers—changing the image shown when the mouse moves over it, which isn't such a bad thing.

You should only rarely use a *mousemove* event listener, as it can dramatically degrade the performance of the Web page. Once you create a mousemove event listener, the browser will constantly have to watch the cursor's movement, calling the event handler with each incremental change. When you do need to watch the mouse's movement, like if you've created a game, do so within the smallest possible area (i.e., HTML element) you can, and remove the event listener as soon as possible, too.

IE and Opera have the useful *mouseenter* and *mouseleave* events, which are similar to, and arguably better than, *mouseover* and *mouseout*. But those aren't supported in the other major browsers. The hope is that these events, along with other new ones such as *focusin*, *focusout*, and *textinput*, will be part of the next standard: the DOM Level 3 specification.

It has been 1321441165350 seconds since the epoch. (mouseover to update)

It has been 1321441214558 seconds since the epoch. (mouseover to update)

**FIGURE 8.1** When the page is first loaded, some content is shown, along with instructions to the user.

**FIGURE 8.2** Mousing over the text updates its message.

To put this knowledge to the test, this next simple page will update some text when the user mouses over it (**Figures 8.1** and **8.2**). Clearly, doing actual DOM manipulation would be a more practical use of a mouseover, but as DOM manipulation isn't discussed until the next chapter, this example will suffice for now. The HTML page is named epoch.html, and it contains just a paragraph with an id value of *output*:

```
<p id="output"></p>
```

The HMTL page includes the epoch.js JavaScript file, to be written in the subsequent steps, along with utilities.js, already defined. Note that the utilities file must be included first, as epoch.js references its U object.

**To handle a mouseover event:**

1. Create a new JavaScript file in your text editor or IDE, to be named epoch.js.

2. Begin defining the updateDuration() function:

```
function updateDuration() {
    'use strict';
```

This function will be called when the page is first loaded and when the user mouses over some text. In either case, this function performs a calculation and updates some text on the page.

3. Get the current moment:

```
var now = new Date();
```

This line creates a new Date object representing the current moment.

4. Define the message for the output:

```
var message = 'It has been ' + now.getTime();
message += ' seconds since the epoch. (mouseover to update)';
```

The message contains some literal text, invocation of a Date method, and an instruction to the user. Note that newer browsers can just use Date.now() to get the number of seconds since the epoch, without having to create a formal Date object.

## TOUCH DEVICES AND INPUT EVENTS

The advent and rise of touchscreen devices, such as iPods, tablet PCs, and smart phones, has created additional kinks in input event handling. Such devices *do* support click, dblclick, mousedown, mouseup, mouseover, mouseout, and mousemove events, but cannot perform any kind of event that requires both mouse activity and a simultaneous key press (such as a contextual click). There are also new events, and *gestures*, made possible by these devices. For more on this subject, see a resource dedicated to JavaScript development for mobile devices.

5. Update the page and complete the function:

```
U.setText('output', message);
} // End of updateDuration() function.
```

The page is updated by calling the U.setText() function, passing it the id value of the element to be updated and the message itself.

As an added protection, this code could check for the existence of a U object and a U.setText() function before attempting to invoke that function.

6. Within an anonymous function, register an event listener for a mouseover on the paragraph:

```
window.onload = function() {
    'use strict';
    U.addEvent(U.$('output'), 'mouseover', updateDuration);
    updateDuration();
};
```

An event listener cannot be added to any page element until the element has been loaded, so that's best done within a window.onload event handler. The first line of code within the function invokes the U.addEvent() function to create the event listener on the *output* element. The first argument to that function expects an object, so the U.$() function is called as part of the addEvent() function call.

Enter your comments below
(100 characters max).

Comments

I have typed thirty
seven characters.

Character Count

37

**Submit**

**FIGURE 8.3** The input below
the textarea now immediately
reflects the number of characters that have been typed.

Next, to create the initial text, the updateDuration() function is also called directly.

7. Save the file as epoch.js, in a js directory next to epoch.html, and test it in your Web browser.

## KEYBOARD EVENTS

The next batch of events to cover are keyboard events:

- keydown
- keypress
- keyup

These three events parallel mousedown, mouseup, and click, in that a *keypress* requires both a *keydown* and a *keyup*. But just as many browsers will only treat a left-button mouse click as a click event, many browsers also only treat the pressing of a character key as being a keypress event. Other buttons, such as Tab or Shift, may not trigger keypress events. Many browsers do not call event handlers when common OS commands are entered, such as Save (Command+S on Macs; Control+S on Windows). Holding down a key will trigger multiple keydown events.

These events are normally watched for on specific form elements, although you can watch for them on an entire form or the whole document:

```
addEvent(document, 'keypress', handleKeyPress);
```

Later in this chapter, once you learn how to handle events in more advanced ways, you'll see how to check exactly which key, or keys, was used in the event. For now, though, using this new information, the text.html example from Chapter 4, Simple Variable Types, can be updated so that it dynamically counts the number of characters the user has entered, and dynamically limits the total to 100 (**Figure 8.3**). The HTML page is named text.html, which is a slight modification from that in Chapter 4, primarily removing the second textarea used in the original. Here's the relevant HTML:

```
<div><label for="comments">Comments</label><textarea name="comments"
→ id="comments" maxlength="100" required></textarea></div>

<div><label for="count">Character Count</label><input type="text"
→ name="count" id="count" disabled></div>
```

Note that the textarea includes the `maxlength` attribute, which effectively imposes a limit on browsers that do support HTML5. If you want, you can remove that when testing on a browser that recognizes this property on a textarea.

The HTML page also now includes the `utilities.js` file, along with the `text.js` JavaScript file, to be written from scratch in the subsequent steps.

**To handle keyboard events:**

1. Create a new JavaScript file in your text editor or IDE, to be named `text.js`.

2. Begin defining the `limitText()` function:

   ```
   function limitText() {
       'use strict';
   ```

   This function will be called when a keyup event occurs within a specific textarea.

3. Get the textarea's value, and report upon how many characters it contains:

   ```
   var comments = U.$('comments');
   var count = comments.value.length;
   U.$('count').value = count;
   ```

   First, a reference to the textarea is fetched for later use. Then, another variable is assigned the length of that element's value, which is the number of characters in the string. Third, the value of the *count* text input is updated to this number.

4. Cut the textarea's value down to 100 characters:

   ```
   if (count > 100) {
       comments.value = comments.value.slice(0,100);
   }
   ```

   If the number of characters that have been entered is greater than 100, then the form element's value needs to be sliced down to the first 100 characters.

5. Complete the function:

   ```
   } // End of limitText() function.
   ```

FIGURE 8.4 Text over 100 characters long get cut from the textarea.

The function does not need to return `false` (in fact, it shouldn't) as previous examples have. This is because this function is called on keyup events, not form submission events. You'll learn more about what this means near the end of the chapter.

6. Register an event listener within an anonymous function:

```
window.onload = function() {
    'use strict';
    U.addEvent(U.$('comments'), 'keyup', limitText);
};
```

The event listener is added to the *comments* element, on keyup events. If you change the particular handler to watch for the keypress or keydown event, you'll see the reported count will be off by one, because the count won't reflect the keypress that's in progress.

7. Save the file as `text.js`, in a `js` directory next to `text.html`, and test it in your Web browser (**Figure 8.4**).

You may notice that if you modify the value of the textarea without using the keyboard (e.g., use the mouse to drop text in, or use the mouse to select an Edit menu option), the event handler will never be called! You'll see the solution for that shortly.

## BROWSER EVENTS

The events discussed to this point are user-driven, but the browser itself has its own events. You've already seen one: *load*, triggered when an element is loaded. Thus far, event handlers have only watched for load events on the window itself, but you can watch for loading of other resources, too, such as an external CSS file or media (e.g., an image).

There is also the corollary *unload* event, triggered when a resource is being unloaded from the browser. This will happen, for example, when the user attempts to go to another Web page, in which case the current page will be unloaded. Annoying, this event is often used as a way to create a pop-up window, but thankfully one can't use unload to prevent the closing of the window, or its redirection to another page. Most beneficially, unload events can be used in HTML5 as an occasion to save the state of the browser. By doing so, when the user returns to the site, the page's settings can be replicated as they were when the user last left.

Another browser-based event is *resize*, triggered when the user resizes the browser window. Similarly, when the user scrolls within the browser window, a *scroll* event is triggered. This event can be triggered by other elements, too, and is being used today to do things like zoom in and out of a map or other image.

Three more events involve a combination of the browser and the user, tied to commands found under the Edit menu:

- copy
- cut
- paste

These events are both useful and easily misused, and are not reliably supported outside of IE and Firefox. Some developers (or perhaps their clients) attempt to prevent users from "stealing" content from a Web site, whether that content is text or media. To thwart such actions, JavaScript can be invoked to disable this functionality (much like attempting to disable the contextual menu). This provides a false sense of security, though, as simply disabling JavaScript removes the protection and allows users to take what they want. You will not see such an example in this book because:

- As just explained, it's a foolish, unreliable pursuit.
- JavaScript should never be used to break the browser or work against the user's expectations.
- Web pages are, by their very nature, a way to share information. Once a user has loaded a page, that content is literally on his or her computer already. It's silly to think otherwise.

Two other events—*focus* and *blur*—are technically browser ones, but as they are most closely tied to forms, I'll cover them next. If you have multiple browser windows open, a focus event is triggered on a window when it is brought to the front, and blur occurs within a window when it is sent backward.

**FIGURE 8.5** This confirmation prompt can be used to verify a user's intent.

## FORM EVENTS

Form interactions, such as validation, are one of the key uses of JavaScript, so it's no surprise that many of the event handlers you'll create as a JavaScript programmer will be tied to forms and form elements. That being said, there are only a couple of events that are *specific* to forms or form elements.

The first is *reset*, which is triggered when a form is reset (i.e., by clicking a reset HTML button). Personally, I haven't used a reset button in years: users rarely need to formally reset an entire form, and more commonly, users will accidentally click reset when they meant to click submit, thereby having to re-complete the form. But if you do like using a reset button, you could use a reset event to watch for, and prevent, accidental form resetting (**Figure 8.5**):

```
addEvent(document.getElementById('theForm'), 'reset', function() {
    return confirm('Are you sure you want to reset the form?');
});
```

Form elements themselves can trigger *change* events, which occur when an element's value changes. Change events are an excellent trigger for form validation, but keep in mind that when a change event occurs differs from element to element. With checkboxes, radio buttons, and select menus, change events occur when the element's value changes. With text inputs and textareas, change events do not occur until after the element loses focus, assuming its value changed.

Text input and textareas can also trigger *select* events, when the element's textual content is selected. Checkboxes and radio buttons can also trigger click events.

Finally, there are the *focus* and *blur* events. While several browser elements can trigger these, they're mostly used with form elements. The focus event is triggered when an element receives the user's attention. For example, when the user presses the Tab key to navigate to a text input, or uses the mouse to click within it, both actions place the cursor there and give that element focus. The blur event is the opposite, and is triggered when the user's attention has moved elsewhere in the browser (not actual attention, but the cursor or selection is moved).

As a quick example of this, let's add a change event listener to the `text.js` example, so that the character count is updated should the user go in and alter the text without pressing any keys.

**To handle change events:**

1. Open `text.js` in your text editor or IDE, if it is not already.

2. Within the anonymous function that handles the load event, add an event listener to the change event on the textarea:

   ```
   U.addEvent(U.$('comments'), 'change', limitText);
   ```

   This code replicates the existing line in the function (which should remain; you can place this one either before or after it), this time registering an event listener on the change event.

3. Save the file as `text.js`, in a js directory next to `text.html`, and test it in your Web browser.

   Now, changes made to the textarea's value without using a key will be recognized (although you'll need to move the focus out of the textarea in order to trigger the change event).

## EVENT **ACCESSIBILITY**

One thing to be aware of when deciding what events to watch for is *accessibility*. Creating accessible pages was once a matter of ensuring that people with screen readers (for the visually impaired) can still successfully use a Web site. But with the rise of mobile devices and other nonstandard browsers, one has to be even more mindful of what events are *important* and what events are *reliable*. With any browser that does not use an input device, the mouseover and mouseout events are meaningless (which is to say they'll never occur). For example, if you add a mouseover event handler to a link:

```
<a href="somepage.html" id="link">Some Text</a>
// JavaScript:
addEvent(document.getElementById('link'), 'mouseover',
⇒  handleLinkMouseover);
```

That event can only be triggered via a mouse (or other input device that controls a cursor).

This problem is easily mitigated, as browsers controlled only by the keyboard can watch for a focus event, triggered when the keyboard is used to focus on the link. Therefore, a safe way to handle an event for either user environment is to create two event listeners:

```
<a href="somepage.html" id="link">Some Text</a>
// JavaScript:
addEvent(document.getElementById('link'), 'mouseover', doSomething);
addEvent(document.getElementById('link'), 'focus', doSomething);
```

This concept is known as *pairing events*: using the same function to handle comparable events on the same element. The same can be accomplished by applying both a mouseout and a blur event handler, when you need to watch for those kinds of events.

Finally, for improved accessibility, it's best to attach event listeners to the form's submission, not to the clicking of the submit button itself. The end result is the same (i.e., both events have the same intended result), but a button can only be clicked by an input device.

## EVENTS AND PROGRESSIVE ENHANCEMENT

The principle behind the concept of *progressive enhancement*, explained in Chapter 2, is that JavaScript (and CSS) is used to enhance basic functionality, meaning that no user is left behind, regardless of the device she or he is using. *JavaScript should only be required if you're consciously willing to exclude some users.* There are situations where that's reasonable, of course: if a Web page has a game that's written in JavaScript, it's impossible to create a non-JavaScript version. But there are many situations where requiring JavaScript is unnecessary: a form should be submittable (and still validated on the server) with or without JavaScript.

Applying this same thinking to event handling, one has to be careful when adding events to elements that don't already have a default behavior for that event. For example, a form is intended to be submitted; when that occurs, the form's data is sent to the server-side script. Adding a submit event to the form to apply other functionality makes logical sense. Or, a link is intended to be clicked, taking the browser to the linked page. Adding a click event handler to a link in order to apply other functionality again makes sense.

Conversely, there's no default browser reaction when the user mouses over some plain text. If you add an event handler that responds to the user mousing over some text, then you're also leaving non-JavaScript users behind, because nothing will happen for them. Looking back at the first example in this chapter, there is no non-JavaScript equivalent. But in that case, one can't get the date and time on the user's computer without JavaScript anyway, so it's not possible to create a fallback alternative.

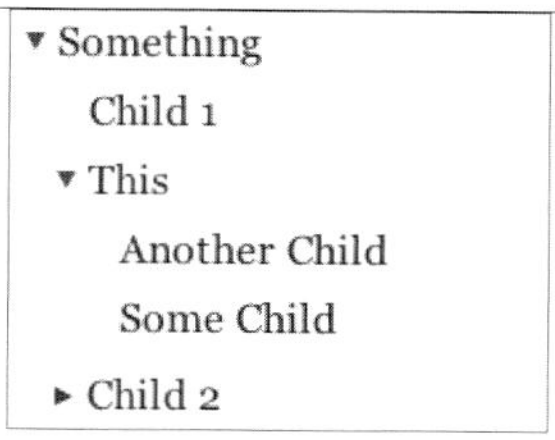

Let's look at another example: the tree structure provides a great way to present a lot of information in a limited amount of space. By clicking on text or images, limbs (or nodes) of the tree can be expanded and collapsed (**Figure 8.6**). There is clearly no JavaScript equivalent for this functionality, but that does not mean users must be left out in the cold. One option is to present the tree in a fully expanded, non-JavaScript format and then use JavaScript to make it dynamic. If you'd rather not muddle up the page with too much information, you could instead present a link to a separate page where the user could see the complete data structure.

As a final note, if you need to provide functionality that is only possible with JavaScript, the recommendation is to use HTML buttons:

```
<input type="button" name="someButton" value="Click Me!">
```

The button, by definition in the W3C specification, is intended to support scripting, and have no default behavior in itself. To use a button in a progressively enhanced manner, one would have JavaScript dynamically add the button to the page (using the DOM manipulation methods discussed in the next chapter). By doing so, only those users with JavaScript enabled will be presented with a button through which more JavaScript functionality is added.

As you'll learn shortly, when there is a default browser action for any event, that action will still take place, but only after the event handler is called. In a few pages, you'll learn how to prevent the default action using JavaScript.

**FIGURE 8.6** The dynamic tree structure allows the user to navigate through a complex, nested amount of data.

# ADVANCED **EVENT HANDLING**

With the basics of event handling covered, it's time to look at the more advanced aspects of this important concept. Unlike with functions, where the advanced ideas can get pretty complex, what you'll learn over the next several pages isn't that complicated, except for the amount of browser disparity. These remaining ideas, though, will make it possible to write event handlers that are more flexible and sophisticated.

## REFERENCING THE EVENT

When an event-handling function is designed for a single event on a single element, it can easily be written to work specifically for that situation. When event handlers might be used by the same event on multiple elements—clicking *any* link, perhaps, or by multiple events on the same element—either mousing over or focusing on an image, then the event handler must be written to allow for flexibility. To do that, having access to the event itself becomes quite useful. How you access the event depends upon the browser in use.

On any browser that supports the addEventListener() method, event handlers will automatically receive a single argument, which represents the event that occurred. You can write your handlers to accept this argument:

```
function someEventHandler(e) {

    // Use e.

}
```

Often the argument is abbreviated as just e or evt, short for *event*.

For Internet Explorer 8 and earlier, which have attachEvent() for registering listeners, the most recent event is represented by the event property of the window object:

```
function someEventHandler() {

    // Use window.event.

}
```

To reliably reference the event regardless of the browser, JavaScript programmers use code like this:

```
function someEventHandler(e) {
    if (typeof e == 'undefined') e = window.event;
    // Use e.
}
```

(Although I almost always recommend using curly braces with conditionals, this example is a rare exception.)

You'll also see it written this way:

```
e = e || window.event;
```

or

```
if (!e) e = window.event;
```

Note that this works whether you establish the event handler using the DOM approach or the traditional approach. It also works even with anonymous functions:

```
someElement.onclick = function(e) {
    if (!e) e = window.event;
}
```

The only caveat is that if you were to use inline event handlers, *which you shouldn't*, you would need to pass the event to the function overtly:

```
<a href="somepage.html" onclick="doSomething(event);">Some Link</a>
```

But, of course, you should not be using inline event handlers. (Did I mention that yet?)

## EVENT PROPERTIES

One benefit of having access to the event itself is that the event object, whether it derives from a value passed to the function or comes from the window object, provides useful information through its various properties. Unfortunately, what properties exist depends again upon the browser in use.

The first property to be aware of is the event's target or srcElement property; the latter is for IE versions 8 and earlier:

```
var target = e.target || e.srcElement;
```

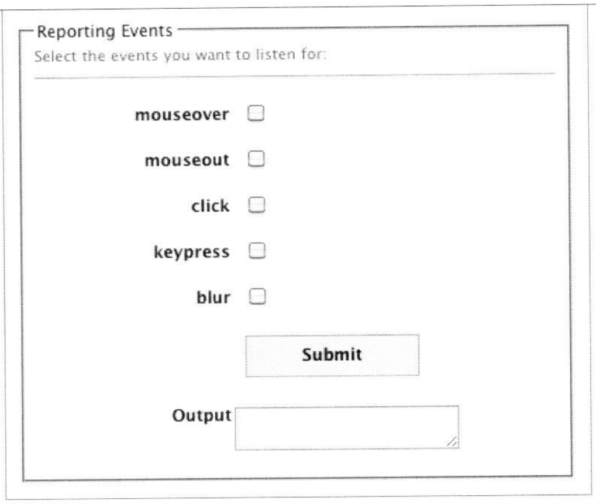

Output

```
DIV: click
LABEL: click
BODY: keypress
BODY: keypress
LABEL: click
INPUT: click
```

**FIGURE 8.7** The form lets the user choose which events to report upon.

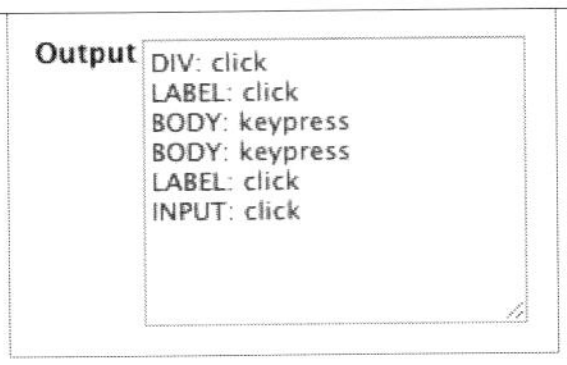

**FIGURE 8.8** The textarea reflects what events occurred on what elements, based upon the user's selections.

Reporting Events

Select the events you want to listen for:

mouseover ☐

mouseout ☐

click ☐

keypress ☐

blur ☐

Submit

Output

Both `target` and `srcElement` point to the HTML element that triggered the event.

Another useful event property is `type`, which fortunately *does* exist across all browsers. This property stores the type of event that just occurred.

In order to learn a bit more about events, the next example is going to be a learning tool, and a good demonstration of more advanced programming at the same time. The HTML page is named `events.html`. It includes the `utilities.js` file and the `events.js` JavaScript file, to be written in the subsequent steps. The HTML page contains a form with several checkboxes, a submit button, and a text-area where some output will be written (**Figure 8.7**). The form allows the user to dynamically determine what events should be handled, and will then report those events when they do occur (**Figure 8.8**).

**To report on events:**

1.  Create a new JavaScript file in your text editor or IDE, to be named `events.js`.

2.  Begin defining the `reportEvent()` function:

    ```
    function reportEvent(e) {
        'use strict';
    ```

    This function will be called when selected events occur, depending upon which of the checkboxes the user has checked. Because it will make reference to the event object, the function is set to accept one argument.

3. Get a reference to the event and the event's target:

```
if (typeof e == 'undefined') e = window.event;
var target = e.target || e.srcElement;
```

This code has already been explained and is a browser-safe way to get references to both the event itself and to the target of the event (i.e., the HTML element).

4. Update the output for this new event, and complete the function:

```
    var msg = target.nodeName + ': ' + e.type + '\n';
    U.$('output').value += msg;
} // End of reportEvent() function.
```

For each event, another string is concatenated onto the output textarea's value. The string itself is the target's nodeName value and the event type, followed by a newline character. The nodeName is the HTML element, in all capital letters (see Figure 8.8).

5. Begin defining the setHandlers() function:

```
function setHandlers(e) {
    'use strict';
    var events = ['mouseover', 'mouseout', 'click',
    → 'keypress', 'blur'];
```

This function will be called whenever the form is submitted. Its purpose is to dynamically set the event listeners based upon which checkboxes were selected. This function will not make use of the event object, so it takes no arguments.

Within the function, an array of strings is created, corresponding to the five events that the example is designed to work with. Later on, you can change the checkboxes in the HTML and change this array to alter the list of events to watch for.

6. Loop through the events array:

```
for (var i = 0, count = events.length; i < count; i++) {
    var checkbox = U.$(events[i]);
```

For each item in the events array, an event listener must be either added or removed. The for loop goes through the array (see Chapter 6 for its syntax). Then, within the loop, a reference is made to the corresponding checkbox. For example, the first time the loop is entered, i is 0, making events[i] have a value of the string *mouseover*. Then the checkbox variable is assigned a reference to the HTML element with an id value of *mouseover*.

7. Add or remove the event listener:

```
if (checkbox.checked) {
    U.addEvent(document, events[i], reportEvent);
} else {
    U.removeEvent(document, events[i], reportEvent);
}
```

If the checkbox is checked, then the user wants an event listener for that event. In that case, the addEvent() method is called, passing it the document object, the name of the event (from the array), and a reference to the reportEvent() function. Because the event listener is added to the entire document, any element within the document can trigger the event. Since the document is a child of the window, window events will not be handled by this script.

If the checkbox is not checked, the removeEvent() method is called, in case an event handler was previously created for that event. As explained earlier, it will not cause errors attempting to remove a listener that does not exist.

8. Complete the for loop and the function:

```
    } // End of FOR loop.
    U.$('output').value = '';
    return false;
} // End of setHandlers() function.
```

The function also clears out the textarea so that the previous events will be erased. The function then returns false to prevent the form's submission.

If you wanted, you could add an alert() or some other mechanism to inform the user that the event handlers have been updated.

## REVISITING **THIS**

In Chapter 7, the special this variable was introduced, which normally represents the object on which a method was called (or the window object, if the function call was not made directly on an object). When it comes to event handling, the this variable *may* represent the HTML element that triggered the event. That will be the case when you use the traditional approach to create an event handler, or use addEventListener(). Unfortunately, on IE8 and earlier, this within an event handler becomes a reference to the global window, making it useless in those cases.

There is a way to make this a useful reference to the object that triggered the event, but that code is rather complicated, well beyond what you would be expected to know at this juncture.

9. Register an event listener within an anonymous function:

```
window.onload = function() {
    'use strict';
    U.$('theForm').onsubmit = setHandlers;
};
```

This line creates an event listener for submission events on the form. The traditional approach is used here, for reasons to be explained shortly.

10. Save the file as events.js, in a js directory next to events.html, and test it in your Web browser.

11. Practice with different events to see the results.

You'll notice that events based upon mouse movement occur quickly, on multiple elements. You might also find that it can be hard to trigger some events on specific elements, such as clicking just the form (instead of a specific form element). You can also trigger keypress events, even without having an input within which to type.

```
>> var charCode = 97;
>> String.fromCharCode(charCode);
   "a"
>> charCode = 65;
   65
>> String.fromCharCode(charCode);
   "A"
```

**FIGURE 8.9** The `fromCharCode()` method of the `String` object returns the character associated with a provided Unicode.

## FINDING THE KEY PRESSED

When a keyboard-based event is triggered, one can determine the specific key pressed through the event object. Unfortunately, the subject is a bit complicated and, of course, differs among the browsers.

The first thing to consider is the difference between a *key* and a *character*. The key is the physical key on the keyboard, but most keys can be used to create more than one character: the A key can create either *A* or *a*, depending upon whether the Shift key is pressed at the same time. Both the key and the character can be represented by Unicode values, and those values will be the same or different, depending upon whether the Shift key is also pressed (for example, the *key code* for both *A* and *a* is 65, the character code for *A* is 65, but the *character code* for *a* is 97). You can find tables correlating characters to Unicode values by searching online. Within the event object, the keyCode and which properties generally represent these two values. However…

Internet Explorer does *not* support the which property; JavaScript running in that browser must use keyCode. Making this more complicated, IE actually stores the *character code* in the keyCode property when a keypress event occurs, and the *key code* in keyCode when the keydown and keyup events occur. Other browsers do use which consistently to store the character pressed. Thus, to get the character in a consistent manner, you can use this code:

```
var charCode = e.which || e.keyCode;
```

Or more precisely:

```
var charCode = (typeof e.which == 'number') ? e.which : e.keyCode;
```

Again, this only works reliably on keypress events. (Many browsers, but not IE, will store the character code in the charCode property, too.)

To find the actual character associated with the character code, you can use the String object's fromCharCode() method (**Figure 8.9**):

```
String.fromCharCode(charCode);
```

With some cases, like creating games and other graphical interfaces, the character isn't important, the key is, such as the specific arrow key that was pressed. In these situations, you can reliably use keyCode in all browsers, so long as you are watching for keydown and keyup events.

Three keys have their own special event properties: shiftKey, ctrlKey, and altKey. Each property has a Boolean value indicating whether or not the key in question was pressed (with or without another key). On Macs, which do not have Alt keys, the altKey property's value indicates if the Option key was pressed. Most browsers, including IE, do not trigger keypress events when these keys are pressed by themselves, as these special keys are only meaningful in conjunction with another key.

## PREVENTING DEFAULT EVENT BEHAVIOR

Earlier, I explained that you should try to use JavaScript events that correlate to basic browser behavior: links are clicked, forms are submitted, and so forth. When an event handler exists, an occurrence of the event invokes the corresponding function. After that function runs, the browser will still go ahead and do what it should normally do when that event occurs. In many situations, because the JavaScript is performing the necessary tasks, you don't want the browser's default behavior to occur. For example, when a form is submitted, a submit event handler might perform client-side validation. If any errors are found, the form's actual submission to the server-side script should be prevented, allowing the user the chance to correct the mistakes. Preventing the event's default behavior in situations like this is something that's been done repeatedly throughout this book, accomplished by returning the value false from the event handler:

```
function handleForm() {
    // Do whatever.
    if (errors) {
        return false;
    } else {
        return true;
    }
}
```

Conversely, returning anything other than `false` allows the default event behavior to occur (in that case, the form's submission).

The problem with returning `false` to prevent the default browser behavior is that it only works reliably when the event listener was registered using the traditional approach. For example, say `events.js` added the form submission event handler using the newer approach:

```
U.addEvent(U.$('theForm'), 'submit', setHandlers);
```

With that code, you would see that the form's submission would go through, meaning that the form itself would be reset (upon resubmission) and the event listeners would not be present (they would have been created, but reset upon submission).

For browsers that don't support the `addEventListener()` method, an alternative way of preventing the default event behavior is to invoke the `preventDefault()` method of the event object:

```
e.preventDefault();
```

For Internet Explorer prior to version 9, one should instead set the `returnValue` property of the event object to `false`:

```
e.returnValue = false;
```

Putting together this code, the following code just prevents the default behavior in a cross-browser way:

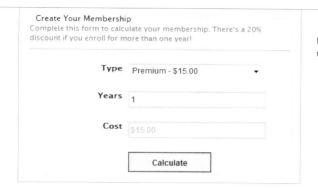

**FIGURE 8.10** The results of the membership cost calculation.

```
if (typeof e == 'undefined') e = window.event;
if (e.preventDefault) {
    e.preventDefault();
} else {
    e.returnValue = false;
}
return false;
```

(The code also returns `false`, as an extra precaution.)

Another benefit to using `preventDefault()` or setting the `returnValue` is that you can do so early in a function, allowing the function code that follows to still execute. Conversely, as soon as a function executes a `return` statement, the function terminates. Secondarily, returning `false` will prevent other event handlers from also being called for that same event. Third, returning `false` terminates the *bubbling phase* of an event (to be discussed shortly).

As an example of this, let's rewrite the `membership.js` example in Chapter 5, Using Control Structures. Originally, the membership cost was only calculated upon submission (**Figure 8.10**). It'd be nice if the cost could also be recalculated when the user changes either of the two factors: the membership type or the number of years. The HTML document only needs to be changed to include the new `utilities.js` file. The original `membership.js` will be updated in the steps below.

**To prevent default behavior:**

1. Open `membership.js` in your text editor or IDE.

2. Change the assignment to the `window.onload` property to:

```
window.onload = function() {
    'use strict';
    U.addEvent(U.$('theForm'), 'submit', calculate);
    U.addEvent(U.$('type'), 'change', calculate);
    U.addEvent(U.$('years'), 'change', calculate);
};
```

   First, I've dropped the formal creation of the `init()` function and just reg-istered the event listeners within an anonymous function (although doing so uses the traditional/DOM Level 0 approach). Second, the `addEvent()` method is used to create the form-submission event listener. And, third, change event listeners are also added to two of the form elements.

3. Change the `calculate()` function so that it takes an event argument:

```
function calculate(e) {
```

   The function needs to take an event argument in order to prevent the default browser behavior.

4. Within the function, get a reference to the event object:

```
if (typeof e == 'undefined') e = window.event;
```

5. Change all uses of `document.getElementById()` to just `U.$()`:

```
var type = U.$('type');
var years = U.$('years');
U.$('cost').value = '$' + cost.toFixed(2);
U.$('cost').value = 'Please enter valid values.';
```

   Since this script now includes the utilities library, it can make use of the `$()` shortcut function.

6. Have an error be reflected only if it's a submission event:

```
if (e.type == 'submit') {
    U.$('cost').value = 'Please enter valid values.';
}
```

With event listeners being added on change events, the user will see an error the first time she or he chooses a membership type without having selected a number of years. That response would be unprofessional, but is easily prevented. This conditional checks the event type, only updating the cost element's value if the type is submitted.

7. Before the `return` line, add:

```
if (e.preventDefault) {
    e.preventDefault();
} else {
    e.returnValue = false;
}
```

Now the form will be properly prevented from being submitted.

8. Save the file as `membership.js`, in a `js` directory next to `membership.html`, and test it in your Web browser.

Although this is an improvement over the previous version of the script, there is now a logical error in it. If this were a live script, there's no way for the user to continue on with the process of purchasing the membership! Fortunately, there are several solutions. One would be to create separate calculate and submit buttons, with the former performing the calculation and the latter allowing the user to proceed. Another option would be to use just one button, but have its value and event listeners change after a successful first use.

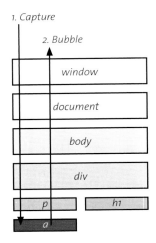

1. Capture

2. Bubble

window

document

body

div

p          h1

a

**FIGURE 8.11** Events go through two phases: capturing to get to the target, and bubbling to leave it.

## EVENT PHASES

A more advanced subject that I've thus far ignored is that events go through two phases: *capturing* and *bubbling*. This concept is best understood by looking at a specific example. Here is a bit of HTML code:

```
<div><h1>This is a Title</h1>
    <p>This is a paragraph.
    <a href="#" id="link">This is a link.</a></p>
</div>
```

Next, let's say that some JavaScript adds a mouseover event to the link:

```
addEvent(U.$('link'), 'mouseover', doSomething);
```

With that code implemented, the link is within the paragraph, which is within the DIV, which is within the HTML body, which is within the document, which is within the window. When the user mouses over the link, the mouseover event will actually go through several steps to get to the target—the link—and back, in two different phases.

The first event phase is the *capturing* phase, which starts with the outermost element and works its way inward. At each step, the browser will look for a corresponding event handler. After the capturing phase has completed, the bubbling phase begins, starting with the innermost element and working out to the outermost one (**Figure 8.11**).

But why is this behavior useful? As a different example, let's say that the event handler is on the DIV, not the link. In that case, the event won't be triggered when you think it might. When the cursor enters the DIV, that's a mouseover. But the DIV contains both a paragraph and a link. As soon as the cursor goes over either of those, the DIV is no longer the active element, meaning it will not be the target of the mouseover (and depending upon the layout, it may be impossible to mouse over the DIV but not the paragraph or link). Thanks to event *bubbling*, the event can still be caught: when the cursor mouses over the paragraph or the link, that event bubbles up, eventually being caught by the DIV's event handler.

## PREVENTING EVENT BUBBLING

One way you can affect the impact of an event is to prevent the browser's default behavior when that event occurs, as already explained. Another impact the event handler can have is to prevent the bubbling of the event. As seen many times in this chapter, doing so requires two different approaches, depending upon whether the browser supports the addEventListener() method or not:

```
if (e.stopPropogation) { // W3C/addEventListener()

    e.stopPropogation();

} else { // Older IE.

    e.cancelBubble = true;

}
```

Having a function return the value false also prevents bubbling, but has other side effects that you may not want. Still, it's not often that you will need to cancel event bubbling.

By default, all event listeners only pay attention to the bubbling phase. In fact, the traditional method of assigning event handlers can *only* be used to listen for events during the bubbling phase. Also, Internet Explorer prior to version 9 cannot be told to watch for events during the capture phase at all (remember that its attachEvent() method does not have an argument to indicate the phase). But to watch for events during the capturing phase on non-IE browsers, use addEventListener(), providing the value true for the third argument:

```
addEventListener(someDiv, 'mouseover', true);
```

> **NOTE:** The focus, blur, change, scroll, and submit events do not have bubble phases.

All that being said, event *capturing* is not commonly used, as it will not work on IE8 and earlier. In browsers that do support capturing, it can be used to intercept an event or prepare the browser for an event that's about to occur on another element. On the other hand, taking advantage of event bubbling is quite useful, and you'll see an example of that in just a few paragraphs.

Returning to an idea mentioned earlier, when taking advantage of event phases, one can use the event's `target` and `srcTarget` properties to pinpoint the target of the event, which can be a different element than has the event handler. Both properties always refer to the element that triggered the event. When defining event handlers, you should consider whether or not the element being watched has child elements, particularly if the event being watched is a mouseover or mouseout. Relatively new is the `relatedTarget` property, available in the event object for mouseover and mouseout events. This property stores the element that the mouse came from (for mouseover) or went to (for mouseout). Microsoft's solution is to create two properties for that same purpose: `fromElement` and `toElement`.

## DELEGATING EVENT HANDLING

With an understanding of event phases, there are now two ways you can apply event handling. The first is what's been used thus far: *binding* event listeners to specific elements. The alternative is to perform event *delegation*. Event delegation is where an event handler is attached to a parent element, catching any events that bubble up from one of its children. Delegation can offer improved performance and streamlined code in situations where multiple elements should have the same event handler.

You've actually already seen one example of delegated event handling: in the `events.js` script, where all event handlers are registered to the document. Another example would be to apply a change event handler to the entire form in `membership.js`, as opposed to doing so to the individual form elements.

# REVIEW AND PURSUE

If you have any problems with these sections, either in answering the questions or pursuing your own endeavors, turn to the book's supporting forum (www.LarryUllman.com/forums/).

## REVIEW

- What four ways of creating event listeners are detailed in this chapter? Which approach should you not use and why? What are the pros and cons of the other three approaches?

- What method works in IE8 for registering event listeners? And in IE9?

- What benefits are gained by creating a utility library, defined within a single global object?

- What three events are triggered when a user clicks on an element? Why can it be better to listen to just the mousedown event, instead of a click?

- What are the three most important keyboard events?

- What is the focus event? What is blur?

- When is a change event triggered?

- Why is it important to pair event listeners and to be mindful of the events being handled?

- How do you reliably access the event that occurred in all browsers?

- What properties are used to see what element triggered an event? What property stores the type of event that occurred?

- How do you determine what key was pressed? Which events do you need to listen for in order to reliably determine the pressed key?

- Why would you want to prevent the default event behavior? How do you do so?

- What are the two phases that events go through and in what order? Which phase is more important?

- How does *event delegation* differ from *event binding*?

## PURSUE

- If you're really curious, and don't mind peeking at code that may be over your head, search online for other variations on an addEvent() custom function.

- Reread Chapter 7's section on global variables, and the section in Chapter 6 on objects, for more thorough explanations as to why creating the U object is a good programming technique.

- Modify epoch.js so that a button element is clicked to update the message.

- Change events.html and events.js to practice with different event types.

- Change events.js so that it notifies the user when the form has been submitted and the event handlers have been registered.

- Learn more about mouse-related event properties by searching online.

- Modify events.js so that it uses addEvent() for the form-submission error handler and then prevents the form's submission using the code also added to membership.js.

- Update membership.js so that it delegates the event handling by registering the change event handler on the entire form.

## WRAPPING **UP**

In this chapter, you greatly expanded your knowledge of events. You learned that there are different ways to create event listeners, and were introduced to the most important events that will occur within the browser. You also saw time and again how the browser in use impacts what values and methods are referenced, but that this hurdle is easily overcome with the right conditionals. Along the way, the importance of maintaining accessibility and implementing progressive enhancement was stressed, with solutions frequently demonstrated.

Two previous examples were updated in this chapter, giving them more of a real-world feel, and a brand-new script, events.js, was written as a tool to help you get a feel for where and how events are triggered in the browser. At the end of the chapter, some of the more advanced concepts were covered, although none were that complicated.

The good news is that, with this knowledge of event handling behind you, the examples in the rest of the book can be that much more realistic, closely emulating what you'll do in your forthcoming Web sites. Next up, Chapter 9, JavaScript and the Browser, looks at the interactions between JavaScript and the browser in more detail, covering such topics as creating secondary windows, working with CSS, and manipulating the DOM.

# 9

# JAVASCRIPT AND THE BROWSER

It may seem strange to have a chapter focused on the browser, as almost every example in the book takes place entirely within a browser. That's what JavaScript is primarily used for after all. But there are plenty of specific things to learn about when it comes to JavaScript and the browser. The most important subject covered in this chapter is *DOM manipulation*, but you'll also pick up quite a few other things, mostly involving the `window` object. I should add that a couple of topics mentioned in this chapter should not be used, or should be used only sparingly. Odd as their inclusion may seem, I still discuss these outdated topics as they were once common, and you may see them in other references. Further, covering them provides an opportunity to explain why you *shouldn't* use them.

# USING DIALOG WINDOWS

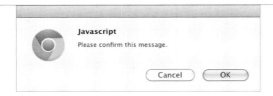

**FIGURE 9.1** A confirmation dialog as presented by Internet Explorer.

**FIGURE 9.2** The same confirmation dialog as presented by Chrome on a Mac.

**FIGURE 9.3** An alert dialog.

This chapter is largely about browser windows, which can be manifested in several forms. The first kind of windows to be discussed in this chapter are *dialogs*: alerts, confirmations, and prompts. These are distinguished from standard browser windows in a couple of ways. First of all, these dialog windows do not contain HTML and CSS, meaning they cannot be styled the way a standard browser window can. Further, different browsers will render them in slightly different ways (**Figure 9.1** and **9.2**).

Second, dialogs are *modal*, meaning that they prevent the user from doing anything else within the browser window until the user addresses the dialog.

For these two reasons, and because good, alternative solutions have arisen, dialogs aren't really used much anymore in today's Web sites. Still, dialogs are easy to use, and a reasonable choice in *limited* situations, so it's worth taking a page or two to go through them.

## ALERTS

An alert is the simplest of the dialog types, just a window with a text message and the ability for the user to click OK to get rid of it (**Figure 9.3**). You create an alert by invoking the aptly named `alert()` function, providing it with the string of text to be displayed:

```
alert('You can click OK now.');
```

I've used `alert()` a time or two in this book to provide feedback, as `alert()` is simple and reliable, especially compared with the DOM manipulation alternatives to be discussed later in this chapter. But `alert()` is truly a shortcut for avoiding better, and more complex, solutions. I'm not saying you should never use `alert()`, but please do so only sparingly.

## CONFIRMATIONS

The confirmation dialog is a wee bit more involved than an alert and is generated via the confirm() function. It, too, takes a string as its lone argument, which will be displayed to the user (Figures 9.1 and 9.2). Unlike with an alert, the user has the choice of two buttons to click: OK or Cancel. Clicking either closes the dialog and returns a Boolean value (true for OK, false for Cancel):

```
var okay = confirm('Please confirm this message.');
if (okay) {
    // User clicked OK, do whatever.
} else {
    // User clicked Cancel, do this instead.
}
```

One potential use of confirmation dialogs is to verify that the user wants to leave the current page. That attempt can be caught by watching for an unload event:

```
window.onunload = function() {
    return confirm('Are you sure you want to leave this page?');
}
```

Not to be redundant, but you must be judicious in your use of confirm(). Code like the above, essentially requiring two steps to leave the page, is appropriate in examples like a content management system (CMS), where work would be lost if the user left the page, but is inappropriate on your average site. If anything, overuse of this technique is more likely to ensure that the user will not return!

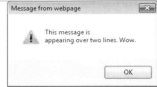

## PROMPTS

The prompt is the most complicated dialog box, and, well, it's not that complicated. The `prompt()` function is used to create a dialog, again taking a string as the message to be displayed to the user. This time, though, the dialog will present the string message, the option to click OK or Cancel, and include an input where the user can type a response (**Figure 9.4**). If the user clicks OK, the response itself will be returned by the function call:

```
var response = prompt('What say you?');
// Do something with response.
```

If the user clicks Cancel, `null` is returned. If the user does not enter any text but clicks OK, an empty string is returned.

The `prompt()` method takes an optional second argument: another string, to be used as the default input value. If provided, that text will be in the input when the dialog is created, although that value can be altered by the user.

```
var response = prompt('What say you?', 'What about...');
```

If the user does not alter the default value, then that value will be returned when the user clicks OK (which is something you would need to watch for).

## CUSTOMIZING DIALOGS

As a security measure, dialogs are not customizable. By enforcing this restriction, browsers prevent malicious hackers from attempting to impersonate another Web site, the computer's operating system, or anything else that looks official.

The only way you can even remotely customize the appearance of a dialog, regardless of the type, is to use the newline character (\n) to make the message appear over multiple lines (**Figure 9.5**):

```
alert('This message is\nappearing over two lines. Wow.');
```

# WORKING WITH THE **WINDOW**

Whereas dialogs are simple, modal windows, best used after very careful consideration, browser windows are capable and vital, able to present a rich user interface with any degree of complexity. JavaScript interacts with the browser window through the `window` object. It's time for this book to stop taking the `window` object for granted, and give it its full due. Over the next several pages, the chapter presents the key properties and methods of the `window` object, explains how to create new windows, and covers common window-related tasks.

## THE GLOBAL WINDOW OBJECT

Because the window is the topmost object when using JavaScript within the Web browser, functions defined outside of any other objects become methods of the global `window` object. Similarly, the `window` object itself is often implied and does not need to be explicitly referenced. For example:

```
function doNothing() {
}
doNothing(); // Calls the function.
window.doNothing(); // Also calls the function.
```

This holds true for variables defined outside of any function:

```
var someVar = true;
someVar; // true
window.someVar; // true
```

There are times where it's conventional to explicitly use the `window` object, and other times where one doesn't. In the above code, it'd be highly unusual to reference your own variables and functions through `window`, and, of course, you should minimize the creation of global variables and functions regardless. See Chapter 7, Creating Functions, for more on global variables and scope.

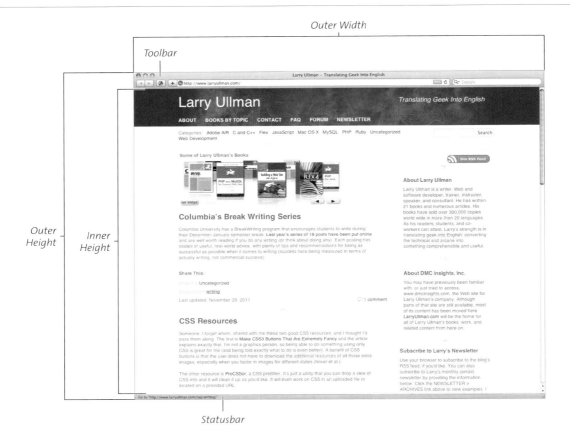

Outer Width

Toolbar

Larry Ullman – Translating Geek Into English

Outer Height

Inner Height

Statusbar

**FIGURE 9.6** The basic elements of a Web browser (the particulars vary from browser to browser; Safari, for example, does not show the menubar as part of the browser window).

Beyond the global variables and functions you create, the `window` object has its own members (properties and functions). In fact, the `alert()`, `confirm()`, and `prompt()` methods belong to `window`, as do the `Math` and `Date` objects, among others. But there are other properties and methods to be familiar with. To understand some of these properties, it helps to know the right terminology for the browser's pieces (**Figure 9.6**).

Three properties of the `window` object reflect whether certain aspects of the browser window are visible or not: `menubar`, `statusbar`, and `toolbar`. You can use the corresponding property to see if the item in question is visible:

```
if (window.menubar.visible) { // Visible!
```

It is technically possible to have JavaScript change the visibility of these bars, but doing so requires the user's permission. And, you really ought not to attempt to change the properties of any active window, as to do so is to impose your will on the user's browser.

A popular concept for a while (about a decade ago) was to change the window's status—the text displayed within the statusbar:

```
window.status = 'Hello. I am your browser.';
```

This ability has been disabled in many browsers since, for security reasons, and many browsers don't show a status bar by default. Moreover, you shouldn't change the status message anyway, as the statusbar is intended to provide the user with useful information.

Speaking of window properties that used to be abused and are largely ignored in modern JavaScript, there's `window.navigator`. This property has multiple sub-properties that store information about the browser itself. This property was often used to perform *browser sniffing*, via `window.navigator.userAgent`. Once again, browser sniffing—writing conditional code based upon the browser type and version in use—shouldn't be done any more, as object detection is a better alternative.

## MANIPULATING THE WINDOW'S SIZE AND POSITION

As with many things in JavaScript, there was a time where it was the "in thing" for a Web page to resize and/or move the user's Web browser. In theory this was done to optimize the user's experience for the design of the page, but I think it was mostly done because it could be. Personally, I'm against a Web page changing the size or location of my Web browser window, but perhaps that's just me.

FIGURE 9.7 How windows
are positioned relative to the
entire screen.

0, 0        200, 100

In any case, to find out where the current window is on the screen, use the
screenX and screenY properties of the window object. These properties reflect the
position of the top-left corner of the browser window relative to the top-left corner
of the user's screen (**Figure 9.7**). This is true for most browsers; IE uses screenLeft
and screenTop, respectively. Except for in Firefox, you cannot change the position
of the window using them, but they can inform you as to whether a move is called
for, when absolutely necessary.

The innerHeight and innerWidth properties reflect the size of the content
within the window, including scroll bars, when present. The outerHeight and
outerWidth properties reflect the size of the entire browser window (see Figure 9.6).
For older versions of IE, which only started supporting these properties in version
9, you need to use document.body.clientHeight and document.body.clientWidth.
You cannot change the size of the window using any of these properties (except in
Firefox), but they can be used as the basis for dynamically changing your layout, if
need be. For example, if a window dimension is particularly small, you could have
JavaScript use smaller images. If a window's width is narrow, perhaps JavaScript
disables a sidebar.

If, for some very, very, very good reason you need to move the browser window, you would call the moveTo() method of the window object. It takes X and Y
pixel values for its arguments, where 0,0 is the top-left corner of the screen (see
Figure 9.7). The following code moves the window to place its top-left corner positioned 100 pixels to the right of the left side of the screen and 200 pixels down
from the top of the screen:

```
window.moveTo(100,200);
```

Whereas `moveTo()` moves the window to a specific location, `moveBy()` moves a window relative to its current location. It, too, takes X and Y values, in terms of the number of pixels to move the window:

```
window.moveBy(25, 50);
```

Positive numbers move the window to the right and down; negative numbers move the window up and to the left. That code moves the window 25 pixels to the right and 50 pixels down from its current location. Note that you will not be allowed to move the window beyond the confines of the screen.

> **TIP:** Remember that you can use your browser's console to practice with random bits of JavaScript, such as moving a window or finding the value of a property.

## SCREEN PROPERTIES

Using JavaScript and the `window.screen` property, you can find out information about the user's physical screen (the one in which the browser is being viewed):

- `window.screen.height` returns the height of the screen in pixels.

- `window.screen.width` returns the width of the screen in pixels.

- `window.screen.availHeight` returns the number of usable pixels, minus any OS features like the Taskbar.

- `window.screen.colorDepth` returns the color depth of the screen (e.g., 16 for 16-bit).

You can use this information to customize the browser window and the user's experience, such as changing the style sheet in use based upon the color support. For example, early versions of the Kindle used 4-bit grayscale for its display, so on such devices, you could have JavaScript use a style sheet that is better tailored to a black-and-white interface. However, more current browsers support such changes using CSS media queries.

## CREATING NEW WINDOWS

Moving on to more valuable information, and better uses of JavaScript, let's look at how you make new windows using the language. Unlike the dialogs already covered, here I'm talking about true browser windows, with HTML, CSS, and all the functionality and behavior of the original browser window. These new windows are also not modal, meaning they allow the user to switch back to the original window as needed. To be fair, fewer and fewer sites are creating separate, new windows, but when done correctly, they can be a positive addition. (The more common way to create window-like behavior these days is to use CSS and JavaScript, to be explained later in the chapter.)

To create a new window, invoke the open() method of the window object, providing it with the URL to open:

```
var popup = window.open('somefile.html');
```

The URL can be either relative or absolute (see Chapter 2, JavaScript in Action, for more on relative versus absolute paths).

By assigning the result of the method invocation to a variable, the script can later reference the other window. In fact, some browsers will have problems if you don't assign the result of a window.open() call to a variable.

Because JavaScript's ability to create new windows was, for years, used to create pop-up advertisements, modern browsers now have built-in pop-up-blocking ability. In those cases, the variable created by the window.open() call will often have a null value:

```
if (popup === null) { // Did not work!
```

Depending upon the particulars of your situation, you may want to, if that conditional is TRUE, redirect the entire browser window to the page that the pop-up was intended to display. You'll see how to do that shortly.

**TIP:** Make sure you do not have window blocking enabled in your browser when you're practicing creating windows!

To close a window created by JavaScript, invoke the close() method of the associated window variable:

```
popup.close();
```

Note that the close() method should only be invoked on windows created using window.open(). JavaScript is restricted when it comes to closing windows that weren't opened by JavaScript, which is appropriate (**Figure 9.8**).

To confirm that a window created by JavaScript has not yet been closed, check its closed property:

```
if ((popup !== null) && !popup.closed) { // Still open.
```

## CUSTOMIZING POP-UPS

The vast majority of the ways you can customize the newly created window comes from the HTML and CSS of the document loaded in the window itself. But there are a few ways you can customize the look and behavior of a pop-up window when it's created.

The open() method takes a second argument, which is a name for the window. You should give the window a meaningful name, but this value isn't that critical (just be certain not to use spaces in the window's name).

The third argument to open(), however, is where you can provide a string of properties that the new window should have (**Table 9.1**). The syntax is *property=value*, with multiple properties separated by commas. Some properties take numeric values, and the others take *yes/no* values (not true/false):

```
var popup = window.open('somepage.html', 'DefinitionsWindows',
    'height=200,width=200,location=no,resizable=yes,scrollbars=yes');
```

As you can see in that syntax, you cannot use any spaces or returns within the property string. Also note that you cannot change these settings after the window is opened.

**TABLE 9.1** New Window Properties

| PROPERTY | NOTES |
| --- | --- |
| height | For the content area; defaults to the height of the parent or recently created window on most browsers; must be at least 100 pixels |
| left | Defaults to about 20 pixels right of the left side of the parent window |
| location | Whether the location bar should be visible |
| menubar | Cannot be hidden on Mac OS X |
| outerHeight | Whole window height; must be at least 100 pixels |
| outerWidth | Whole window width; must be at least 100 pixels |
| resizable | Should always be set to *yes*; may always be resizable on some browsers regardless |
| scrollbars | Should always be set to yes |
| status | Is always shown on some browsers |
| toolbar | Whether or not the toolbar should be visible |
| top | Defaults to about 20 pixels below the top of the parent window |
| width | Content area; defaults to the width of the parent or recently created window on most browsers; must be at least 100 pixels |

Note that if you set any property using the third argument, every other property that takes a yes/no value gets set to *no*, except for `titlebar` and `close` (neither of which is listed in Table 9.1), which default to *yes*. Many of the properties are restricted by one browser or another, and there are a few other properties that lack unified browser support, require special privileges, or just shouldn't be used. You also cannot position windows off of the screen.

Generally speaking, you'll mostly just want to customize the window's size, possibly its location on the screen, and whether or not the toolbar (with the window's address bar) is visible. Remember that you can use values already mentioned, such as those in `window.screen`, to dynamically calculate and set the size and location of the new window.

## CHANGING FOCUS

When you have more than one window open, the focus and blur events, introduced in Chapter 8, Event Handling, come into play. The focus event is triggered on a window when it becomes the active window. The blur event is triggered on a window when another window is made active.

To make a newly created window active, call the `focus()` method on the associated variable:

```
popup.focus();
```

You can check that the window exists prior to doing this:

```
if ((popup !== null) && !popup.closed) {
    popup.focus();
}
```

Of course, you should only focus on another window if it's clear that's what the user would want. This concept, and using windows prudently, are discussed next.

## AN ACCESSIBLE SOLUTION

Now that you know how to create a new window, let's talk about doing so responsibly. Because these secondary windows are being created using JavaScript, there is no accessible alternative. Further, search engines won't see the content in the secondary window when they're opened using JavaScript, which may or may not be a problem for the site in question. Finally, there's the issue of whether the user actually *wants* a new window to be created, which the user may be actively preventing with pop-up-blocking software (built into the browser or otherwise). Taking all of this into account, you should always start by providing access to the secondary window using the standard approach, a link:

```
<a href="definitions.html" id="definitionsLink">
    Keyword definitions can be seen on this page.</a>
```

A pedestrian way to create a new window, rather than having the new page open within the same window, is to add the target attribute to a link, with a value of *_blank*:

```
<a href="definitions.html" id="definitionsLink" target="_blank">
    Keyword definitions can be seen on this page.</a>
```

Or you can use a window name here, as you would in window.open():

```
<a href="definitions.html" id="definitionsLink"
    target="DefinitionsWindow">Keyword definitions can be
    seen on this page.</a>
```

When you set the target attribute to have the document open in another window, you should notify the user of that intent:

```
<a href="definitions.html" id="definitionsLink"
    target="DefinitionsWindow">Keyword definitions can be
    seen on this page.</a> (Will open in a new window.)
```

**TIP:** As a reminder, you can download all of the book's code from www.LarryUllman.com.

**FIGURE 9.9** An extremely basic HTML page, with one link.

**FIGURE 9.10** The custom pop-up window, created by JavaScript.

**FIGURE 9.11** The standard pop-up window, without JavaScript's influence (note the presence of the toolbar).

Now that basic functionality has been established, you can progressively enhance it. Let's do that in the following example. The first page is named popupA.html and it contains just a link with an id value of *link* (**Figure 9.9**). That link goes to popupB.html, with just a paragraph of text. The popupA.html page includes the popup.js JavaScript file, to be written in the subsequent steps. If JavaScript is enabled and pop-ups are not blocked, a smaller, custom pop-up window will be created (**Figure 9.10**). If JavaScript is not enabled, or if the pop-up is blocked, the user will see the same page opened in a full, noncustom window (**Figure 9.11**).

**To create an accessible pop-up:**

1. Create a new JavaScript file in your text editor or IDE, to be named popup.js.

2. Begin defining the createPopup() function:

   ```
   function createPopup() {
       'use strict';
   ```

   This function will be called when the link is clicked.

3. Create the pop-up window:

   ```
   var popup = window.open('popupB.html', 'PopUp',
       'height=100,width=100,top=100,left=100,location=no,
       resizable=yes,scrollbars=yes');
   ```

   The pop-up window will open the page popupB.html, in a window named *PopUp*. Some of the new window's properties are customized, in part to distinguish the pop-up created by the JavaScript (Figure 9.10) from the same document opened by the link click (Figure 9.11).

4. If the window is open, give it focus and return false:

   ```
   if ( (popup !== null) && !popup.closed) {
       popup.focus();
       return false;
   ```

This conditional was already explained and is used to confirm that the window just created is open. If so, then focus is given to that window (in case it doesn't already have focus). Next, the function returns `false`, to prevent the browser's default behavior (in this case, pursuing that link). See Chapter 8 for more on how to prevent default browser behaviors.

5. Complete the conditional begun in Step 4 and the function:

```
    }
} // End of createPopup() function.
```

If the pop-up is not created, the function will not return `false`, which means that the default browser behavior of following the link will be allowed.

6. Within an anonymous function, register an event listener for a click on the link:

```
window.onload = function() {
    'use strict';
    document.getElementById('link').onclick = createPopup;
};
```

I'm specifically using the DOM Level 0 method of creating an event handler, which will work on all browsers. This approach also lets the handling function prevent the default browser behavior by simply returning `false`. Again, see Chapter 8 for a refresher on all this.

Later in the chapter you'll learn how you can write this function to work with any link dynamically.

7. Save the file as popup.js, in a js directory next to popupA.html, and test it in your Web browser.

8. Disable JavaScript in your browser, reload the page, and click the link again.

**TIP:** It's an excellent learning tool to run your pages, and others, with JavaScript disabled in your browser.

## COMMUNICATING BETWEEN WINDOWS

When you have more than one window open as part of the same site, there's some-times a need for the windows to communicate with each other (which is to say, for the JavaScript in one window to interact with the JavaScript in the other). This is actually easier than you might think, once you know how to do it. Let's say window A opens window B, using this line:

```
var windowB = window.open('windowB.html', 'WindowB');
```

Let's say that the JavaScript file included by window B contains this code:

```
var something = 23;
function addToSomething(what) {
    something += what;
}
```

Now, as you also know, any variable or function declared outside of an object or function becomes part of the global window object. This means that in window B, window.something has a value of 23 and window.addToSomething() is a function that takes one argument and adds it to the something variable (technically the function should confirm that what is a number so that addition, not concatenation, takes places, but this is just a demonstration).

You know that in window A, windowB is a reference to the newly opened window. What isn't obvious—but makes sense when you think about it—is that this means you can access the window B's window object through windowB.window. Further, this means you can reference window B's something variable through windowB.window. something and call the addToSomething() function using:

```
// JavaScript in window A:
windowB.window.addToSomething(12);
windowB.window.something; // 35
```

Pretty cool, eh? This is a trivial example, but demonstrates how easy it would be to pass, say, the value entered by a user in a form input in window A to a variable or function in window B:

```
// JavaScript in window A
document.getElementById('theForm').onsubmit = function() {
    var thing = document.getElementById('someElement').value;
    windowB.window.useFormData(thing);
}
```

Working this process from the other side, the opener property of the window object returns a reference to the parent of the current window. Hence, if you place this line in the JavaScript of windowB.html—

```
var windowA = window.opener;
```

—then window B can reference window A's global variables and functions through windowA.window.*propertyName* and windowA.window.*functionName()*.

(The opener property will have a null value if no other window opened the current one.)

Naturally this only works for two windows on the same domain, due to the *same domain policy* (see the sidebar), and the one window has to have created the other in order to have the open window-opener relationship.

## WORKING WITH THE BROWSER'S HISTORY

Another useful property found within the window object is history, which provides access to the current window's viewing history. This object has three useful methods:

- back(), which is the same as if the user clicked the Back button
- forward(), which is the same as if the user clicked the Forward button
- go(), to go to a specific spot in the history

**TIP:** HTML5 adds new methods for manipulating the browser's history.

The go() method takes a number as its lone argument. The number should be relative to the current position in the browser's history, which is indexed at 0. Hence, go(-1) is equivalent to back(), go(1) is equivalent to forward(), and go(-2) is equivalent to invoking back() twice. Hence, a common use of JavaScript is to present a link as part of an instruction for the user to go to the previous page:

```
// JavaScript:
document.getElementById('backLink').onclick = function() {
    window.history.back();
}
<!-- HTML: -->
Please <a href="actualpage.html" id="backLink">go back</a> to
   the previous window and do what needs to be done.
```

There is one less-than-ideal issue with that code: when the user clicks the Back button, the browser will return to the previous page, cached in the browser. When the user clicks a link to go to a page, it may look for and load the cached version, if one exists, or the browser may re-request the page from the server. In this minor regard, this example isn't truly progressively enhanced.

## WORKING WITH FRAMES

Traditional frames have been *deprecated* (meaning you shouldn't use them) in HTML for some time, but the inline frame, or *iframe*, continues to have some usefulness. In particular, iframes are commonly used today to incorporate ads and third-party scripts within the constructs of a whole page.

In terms of JavaScript, the relationship between a primary HTML document and its included iframe is similar to that between one browser window and another that it opens. The iframe page can access the parent document's global variables and methods through the parent object (or more formally, window.parent). If the document is not embedded within an iframe, its window.parent property will match window.self (the latter is a way for a window to recognize itself):

```
if (window.parent != window.self) { // This is a child!
```

In the parent document, the window.frames property is an array representing every frame (and iframe) in the document (and window.length stores the number of frames found). Hence, window.frames[0] is the first frame and window.frames['someName'] references the frame with a name value—not id—of *someName*. Or you can use document.getElementById() to get a reference to the iframe element.

Once you have a reference, you can access that frame's global properties and functions through the contentWindow or contentDocument property, depending upon the browser:

```
var frame = document.getElementById('theFrame');

var frameWindow = frame.contentWindow || frame.contentDocument;

// Access frameWindow.property and frameWindow.function()
```

If you're using HTML5 and using iframes, you should also look into the new attributes added to the specification: the sandbox and srcdoc offer additional security customizations, and the seamless property better integrates the iframe into the rest of the HTML document.

## REDIRECTING THE BROWSER

There are many situations where the browser needs to be redirected to another page. Normally, it's best to redirect the browser using the Web server application (e.g., Apache). For example, if you change the URL of a page, you'd want the Web server to redirect browsers to the new destination, rather than have the browser load the wrong page and then be redirected. Still, there are other occasions when you either cannot use the Web server (e.g., you don't have access to its configuration) or using JavaScript makes more sense anyway.

When you need to redirect the browser using JavaScript, turn to the `window.location` property, which reflects the current page being viewed in the browser. By changing this property's value, you can effectively redirect the browser to another page. There are several variants for doing this, with different implications. The layman's approach is to replace the entire `location` value:

```
window.location = 'http://www.example.com/otherpage.html';
```

To be more precise, you can change the `location.href` property:

```
window.location.href = 'http://www.example.com/otherpage.html';
```

In either case, it's important to know that the net effect of this approach is as if the user had clicked on a link to take the browser to the other page. This means that the previous page—the one with the redirection code—will still appear in the browser's history and can be accessed using the Back button. If there's really no need for the user to view that previous page again, there's another option. Instead of assigning a new `location` or `location.href` value, you can invoke the `location.replace()` method to replace the current location with the new location:

```
window.location.replace('http://www.example.com/otherpage.html');
```

By using `replace()`, the previous page (the one executing the above code) will not appear in the browser's history or be an option via the Back button. If you're redirecting the browser, this behavior may be more in keeping with the intention.

**TIP:** You can redirect the browser to the user's home page by invoking `window.home()`.

The `window.location` property has a couple more properties that are sometimes useful:

- `search` represents the part of the browsers' URL from ? on, as if a value such as search terms had been passed to the page in the URL

- `hash` represents the part of the browser's URL from # on, as if the user had been taken to a specific anchor or ID on the page

For a practical use of `search`, think about how dynamically driven Web sites commonly use standard templates and present different content based upon a value passed along in the URL, such as `http://www.example.com/page.php?id=x`. In that situation, JavaScript can also be used to access the value passed to the page (in the id variable) by referencing `window.location.search`, which would have a value of *?id=x*. You can slice off the question mark, and then break the string into its components:

```
var search = window.location.search;
search = search.slice(1); // Now 'id=x'
search = search.split('='); // An array: ['id', 'x']
// Use search[0] and search[1]
```

If multiple values are passed using this method, they'll be separated by ampersands, as in `http://www.example.com/page.php?s=10&np=7&sort=name`. In that case, `window.location.search` would have a value of *?s=10&np=7&sort=name*, which would then need to have the question mark removed, be split on the ampersands (to access the individual *name=value* pairs), and then each individual value would be split on the equals sign.

For a hash example, URLs can point browsers to specific elements within the Web page using either anchors or just ID values. The URL fragment `page.html#something` could point to either of the following, among other possibilities:

```
<a name="#something">
<h2 id="something">Some Title</h2>
```

Primarily, these hashes have been used to create a link or bookmark to a specific area of a Web page, but they can be used in more advanced ways thanks to JavaScript, as explained next.

## CREATING REPRESENTATIVE URLS

One interesting development in the rise of dynamic JavaScript-driven Web sites is that the browser itself is unprepared in some ways to cope with this new method of dynamic presentation. For example, pages may have JavaScript update or alter what the user sees (using techniques explained over the rest of the chapter). One common approach is to present content within several tabs (**Figure 9.12**).

**FIGURE 9.12** Three tabs are used to show individual blocks of content.

When the user loads a page like that shown in the figure, the first tab will automatically be shown. The user clicks on tab 2 to view that content, which is shown immediately (i.e., without requesting another page), thanks to JavaScript. When an action like this occurs, the page is described as being in a new "state." However, as it stands, the user cannot bookmark that version of the page—tab 2 being viewed—because state changes are not represented by the URL. When the user returns to the URL, he or she has to click on the tab again to get back to the desired state. If that user wants to share the specific tab information (i.e., browser state) with another person, extra instructions are required. By using the `window.location.hash` property, there is a clever fix for this situation, known as *deep linking*.

As just explained, the `window.location.hash` property represents the part of the URL starting with #. Each unique URL represents a unique page and can be individually bookmarked in the browser, including the hash part. Hence, `page.html#something` and `page.html#anything` can be treated as two different bookmarks. JavaScript can use this behavior to create different hashes to represent different states of the page. Going back to the example, `page.html#1` could mean that the first tab of content is to be shown and `page.html#2` means that the second tab of content should be displayed. When the page is loaded, JavaScript can parse the hash and update the page accordingly:

```
var hash = window.location.hash; // Includes the #
var content = hash.charAt(1); // Get the second character
switch (content) {
    case 2:
        // Show tab 2.
        break;
    case 3:
        // Show tab 3.
```

```
        break;
    case 1:
    default:
        // Show tab 1.
        break;
}
```

The actual specifics for how you change the content will be explained later in the chapter.

For this to work, the JavaScript also has to update the URL when the page's state changes. Say the setTab() function is called when the user clicks on a tab and it takes the event as an argument:

```
function setTab(e) {
    if (typeof e == 'undefined') var e = window.event;
}
```

Using the event's target or srcElement property (depending upon the browser; see Chapter 8), the function would know which tab to show. If the function gets that information and stores it in the tab variable, the JavaScript can then dynamically change the URL accordingly:

```
window.location.hash = '#' + tab;
```

And that's all there is to it (in theory). The user can bookmark the page and return to it in the same state as it was when the user left. Even if the user were to refresh the page, the state would remain the same.

The one problem with this system is that the Back and Forward buttons would navigate the various URLs as the browser would navigate any URL in its history. But using those buttons does not force a page load, meaning JavaScript would not be called to update the state when the URL (or, more specifically, the hash part) changes. The solution there is to create a timer that checks for hash (which is to say state) changes. This exact concept will be covered near the end of the chapter. HTML5 mitigates this problem by introducing new state management tools.

## PRINT THIS PAGE

The `window.print()` method invokes the browser's print option, as if the user had selected File > Print (or used the associated keyboard shortcut).

```
// JavaScript:
document.getElementById('printLink').onclick = function() {
    window.print();
}
<!-- HTML: -->
<a href="#" id="printLink">Print this page.</a>
```

Naturally, this isn't possible on many mobile and other nondesktop devices (and, of course, it assumes JavaScript is enabled). You can check for printing support using object detection, confirming that the window object has a `print()` function:

```
if (typeof window.print == 'function') {
```

If that condition is TRUE, instead of hardcoding that link, you can have JavaScript create a button for invoking the `print()` function, which you'll learn how to do momentarily. Then you associate the clicking of that button with the calling of the `print()` function:

```
document.getElementById('printButton').onclick = function() {
    window.print();
}
```

## THE DOCUMENT OBJECT

To wrap up this section of the chapter, let's look at one of the most important window properties: document, which represents the HTML loaded in the window. The document object has several critical methods, such as the ubiquitous `getElementById()`, used to quickly reference elements within the page. The document object also has some methods that should no longer be used, such as `write()` and `writeln()`.

When I first learned JavaScript, document.write() and document.writeln() were used extensively. Both methods write data to the document, the latter writing a line of data, equivalent to adding \n to the end of the data being written. You'll still see either method used in some resources, but there are reasons why you should not use them yourself:

- They won't work in XHTML documents.

- If used after the page has loaded, the data being written can overwrite the existing content.

- Using write() and writeln() can mess up the DOM representation of the page.

- The DOM manipulation methods discussed later in the chapter are far better.

Still, there is one appropriate situation for write() or writeln(): to dynamically include extra resources under certain conditions. For example, ads and third-party scripts frequently use these methods to dynamically insert the code into the page if JavaScript is supported (often using iframes, too).

Moving on, later in this chapter I'll specifically discuss the document.cookie property, along with the DOM manipulation properties and methods, but there are two more document properties to introduce here: title and compatMode. The title property of the document object stores the browser window's title for the current page. It can also be used to dynamically change the title:

```
document.title = 'New Title';
```

You might do this to change the browser's title when you also change the URL. As the title is used for the name of the corresponding bookmark, this allows you to create unique URLs with unique titles.

(As a reminder, the window object is implied, so you can use just document without referencing window.)

Finally, Chapter 2 walked through the issue of an HTML page's DOCTYPE and how that impacts the browser mode: Quirks or Standard. The operating mode is stored in document.compatMode. It will have the value *BackCompat* (short for "backward compatible") to represent Quirks mode and *CSS1Compat* for Standard mode. If you know of particular issues when the browser is in Quirks mode, you could use JavaScript to correct those problems. Or, you could use this as a debugging tool: making sure your page always runs in Standard mode.

# MANIPULATING THE DOM

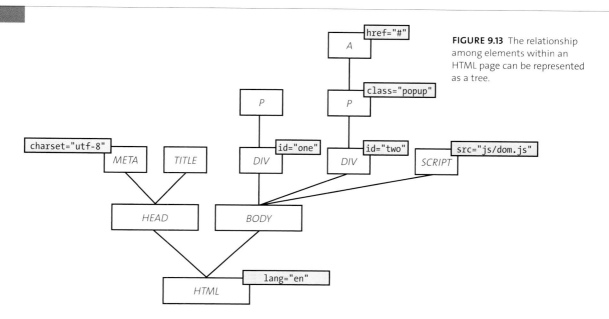

FIGURE 9.13 The relationship among elements within an HTML page can be represented as a tree.

The Document Object Model (DOM), first standardized by the World Wide Web Consortium (W3C) in 1998, is simply a way to represent and work with XML, XHMTL, and HTML data. By tapping into the DOM, it's relatively easy in JavaScript to find, access, and manipulate HTML elements, thereby dynamically altering the contents and presentation of an HTML page. Let's look at what the DOM is, in detail, how you can access page elements, how to manipulate elements, and how to dynamically alter the contents of the DOM itself.

## DOM FUNDAMENTALS

The DOM represents data as a tree, starting with a single trunk, known as the *root*. In an HTML page, that starting point is the HTML tag. From the root there are limbs, each of which is another element of the HTML page, so that every HTML element, and its properties and values, are represented by the DOM. **Figure 9.13** shows a simple visual representation of the following HTML:

```
<!doctype html>
<html lang="en">
<head>
    <meta charset="utf-8">
    <title>This Is The Title</title>
</head>
<body>
        <div id="one"><p>This is a paragraph.</p></div>
        <div id="two"><p>This is a paragraph with
    →   <a href="#" class="popup">a link</a>.</p></div>
    <script src="js/text.js"></script>
</body>
</html>
```

The elements represented in the DOM are called *nodes*. These nodes can have their own offshoots, which are also nodes. This structure is often described in familial ways: with *parents* having *child* nodes, nodes having *siblings*, and so forth. The root node, document in a Web page, has no parent and only one child: html.

Each node in the DOM is represented as an object. These objects have special properties that reflect the relationship each node has to its immediate family members. For example, the parentNode property points to the parent of the current object and childNodes is an array of objects pointing to the children of the current object. Looking at Figure 9.13, the parentNode of BODY is the HTML node, and BODY has three child nodes: DIV, DIV, and SCRIPT.

There are the firstChild and lastChild properties, as well as previousSibling and nextSibling. The firstChild of HEAD is the META node, which is also the previousSibling of the TITLE node.

Figure 9.13 only shows the HTML elements, but there are also text nodes. For example, TITLE has a child that is a text node that contains the string *This Is The Title*. The paragraph within the second DIV has both an A child node and a text child node (and the A has its own text child node). The children property represents the child nodes that are HTML elements, which excludes the text nodes that would be returned, along with the HTML nodes, by the childNodes property.

Each node has properties providing information about the node itself:

- nodeName
- nodeValue
- nodeType

For HTML elements, the nodeName is the HTML tag in all capital letters. For text nodes, the nodeName is #text. For the document node, the nodeName is #document.

The nodeType property will be a number:

- 1 for an HTML element
- 2 for text
- 8 for comments
- 9 for the document
- 10 for the HTML element

In theory, you can access individual DOM elements using combinations of these various properties. With the above HTML, in JavaScript, you would begin with document.documentElement, which returns the root element (here, HTML). This means that document.documentElement.lastChild references the BODY and document.documentElement.lastChild.children[0] references the first DIV.

You can continue on in this manner to navigate the entire DOM, but it quickly becomes tedious. Also, the presence of white space within the HTML will cause unexpected problems, as it gets represented in the DOM as a text node with an empty string value. Thus, document.documentElement.lastChild.children[0] references the first DIV, but document.documentElement.lastChild.childNodes[0] actually references an empty text node (because the children property only returns HTML elements but childNodes returns them all).

Fortunately, there are many easier alternatives for navigating the DOM.

## DOM SHORTCUTS

There are a handful of properties in the document object that act as shortcuts to important DOM elements:

- document.body refers to the HTML body
- document.forms is an array of every form in the page

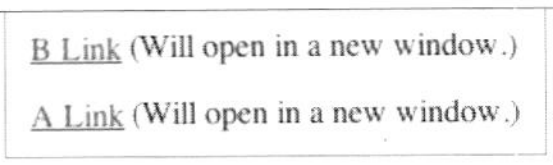

**FIGURE 9.14** The updated HTML page now has two links, although both are to the same page.

- document.images is an array of every image in the page

- document.links is an array of every link in the page (loosely stated)

For example, the first form in the page can be referenced using document.forms[0]. You can also use an element's name instead of a numeric index, which is normally more appropriate: document.images['someImageName'] or document.forms['theForm'].

## USING DOM MANIPULATION

Earlier in the chapter, I explained how to create accessible pop-up windows, but the code only worked for a specific link. Let's apply this new information to make a system that will automatically work on all links (later in the chapter you'll learn what you need to know so that you can specify which links should or should not be opened in new windows). The new HTML page (**Figure 9.14**) is an updated version of popupA.html, now called popups.html. It contains this code:

```
<p><a href="popupB.html" id="link" target="PopUp">B Link</a>
   (Will open in a new window.)</p>

<p><a href="popupA.html" id="link" target="PopUp">A Link</a>
   (Will open in a new window.)</p>
```

The HTML page will include popups.js , an update of popup.js, using the following sequence of steps.

**To create a dynamic, accessible pop-up:**

1. Open popup.js in your text editor or IDE, if it is not already.

2. Within the onload anonymous function, replace the call to document.getElementById() with a for loop:

```
for (var i = 0, count = document.links.length; i < count; i++) {
} // End of for loop.
```

This for loop will be used to access every link in the page. That number can be found by referring to the length property of document.links (since document.links is an array, it has a length property). This value is assigned to another variable, and the loop's condition will be TRUE so long as the counter variable, i, is less than the count.

3. Within the loop, add a click handler to the link:

```
document.links[i].onclick = createPopup;
```

Upon each iteration of the loop, `document.links[i]` will refer to the next link. Within the loop, an event handler is added to the link by assigning the `createPopup()` function to the link's `onclick` property.

4. Change the `createPopup()` function so that it takes the event as an argument:

```
function createPopup(e) {
```

In order to be able to handle multiple links dynamically—opening the appropriate HTML document for each, a reference to the target of the event is required. In other words, this function needs to be able to see which link triggered the event.

5. Within the `createPopup()` function, before the new window is opened, add:

```
if (typeof e == 'undefined') var e = window.event;
var target = e.target || e.srcElement;
```

This code, explained in Chapter 8, provides a reliable, cross-browser way to get both the event itself and the HTML element that triggered the event.

6. Change the creation of the pop-up window to:

```
var popup = window.open(target.href, 'PopUp',
⇢ 'height=100,width=100,top=100,left=100,location=no,
⇢ resizable=yes,scrollbars=yes');
```

The only change is the first argument, which is no longer hardcoded. Instead, with `target` representing the HTML element that triggered the event (i.e., the link that was clicked), its `href` property represents the HTML page that is the destination of that link.

Note that because the same window name is used for all links, only one popup window will ever be created, and each link will reuse it.

7. Save the file as popups.js, in a js directory next to popups.html, and test it in your Web browser.

## DOM METHODS

Using the various document properties can be a fine way to find some page elements, but built into the document object are two excellent methods that are more commonly used. To find a specific element, call the getElementById() method. This method was first introduced in Chapter 2. It has been supported by every major browser for years, so it's reliable, and rather fast, too. As long as there's a single element with the provided id value, this method will work. The getElementById() method returns null if no corresponding element can be found.

To find every element of a specific type, use getElementsByTagName(). It returns an array-like list of chosen elements (note the plural *Elements* in the method's name). Unlike getElementById(), getElementsByTagName() can be invoked on any element, so you can use a specific starting point to limit the scope of the search. For example, the next bit of code only retrieves the links found within the header:

```
var header = document.getElementById('header');
var hLinks = header.getElementsByTagName('a');
```

Or, written as one line:

```
var hLinks = document.getElementById('header').
  getElementsByTagName('a');
```

Because the variable returned by getElementsByTagName() can be treated like an array, you can use array syntax to reference individual elements. For example, this next bit of code points to the first link within the header:

```
document.getElementById('header').getElementsByTagName('a')[0];
```

That single line of code is the kind of thing that can be confusing to those new to JavaScript, but it's just a collapsing of multiple lines of code into one.

A newer method is getElementsByClassName(), which returns an array-like list of every element of any type that has the provided class name. The means that you could take popups.html, add a *popup* class value to links you want to appear in a new window, and then assign event handlers using:

```
var popupLinks = document.getElementsByClassName('popup');
for (var i = 0, count = popupLinks.length; i < count; i++) {
    popupLinks[i].onclick = createPopup;
} // End of for loop.
```

This function does not exist on versions of IE before 9, though, so you'd have to check for support for this method prior to trying to use it. Online you can find libraries for finding elements by class name that will work across all browsers.

## CSS SELECTORS

A relatively new way to find page elements in JavaScript is to use *CSS selectors*. CSS selectors refers to the syntax CSS has for identifying page elements, such as by HTML tag, id value, or class.

These can be combined in various ways:

- #header a (all links within the header)

- p.description (all paragraphs with a class of *description*)

- p.description > a (all links within all paragraphs that have a class of *description*)

With each new CSS standard (there are currently three), more and more selector possibilities are created.

### XPATH EXPRESSIONS

A much faster and more advanced alternative to CSS selectors are *XPath expressions*. Just as the DOM is a *representation* of an XML document (including HTML), XPath is a way to *navigate* an XML document. XPath allows you to look for elements by tag, class, relationships to other elements, and so forth. On the browsers that do support XPath, its performance can be exceptional.

On the other hand, browser support for XPath is inconsistent: the current versions of the major browsers support XPath 1.0, but newer XPath standards are less supported. And learning the XPath syntax is not for the faint of heart.

To use CSS selectors in JavaScript, you turn to either the querySelector() method or querySelectorAll(). The former returns only at most a single element (the first found that matches the criteria); the latter returns as many elements as meet the criteria. Both methods can be invoked on either the document object, or on a specific element. If you go the latter route, then the CSS selectors will only apply to elements that are children of that element:

```
// Returns all images with a class of thumbnail:
document.querySelectorAll('img.thumbnail');
// Returns the first link in the nav element with a class of selected:
document.getElementById('nav').querySelector('a.selected');
```

Browser support for these methods is pretty good, with only Internet Explorer versions prior to 8 not supporting them (and IE8 only supporting CSS2.1 selectors).

### CHANGING ELEMENTS

Once you have a reference to an HTML element, one way you can manipulate the DOM is to change the properties of that element. Many of the properties to be changed are just the attributes of the HTML element itself. For example, the popups.js code retrieved a reference to a link through an event handler and then made use of the link's href attribute. This means you could dynamically change an href value, too:

```
document.getElementById('someLink').href ='newpage.html';
```

Or, as a more practical example, after a form is submitted, it's sometimes best to disable the submit button to prevent a secondary submission (such as with an e-commerce site). To do that, just set the submit button's disabled property:

```
document.getElementById('submitButton').disabled = 'disabled';
```

**NOTE:** You should be wary of changing an element's id value, as other code may rely upon that value being both constant and unique.

There are a couple of properties that must be referenced in special ways: class and for (as in the label's for property). Both properties are also keywords in JavaScript, so you cannot do this:

```
document.getElementById('someDiv').class ='newClass'; // NO!
document.getElementById('someLabel').for ='someElem'; // NO!
```

Instead, use className and htmlFor:

```
document.getElementById('someDiv').className ='newClass'; // Yes!
document.getElementById('someLabel').htmlFor ='someElem'; // Yes!
```

You can also change HTML elements using special properties that are not actual HTML element attributes. You've already seen two: innerText and textContent. Both can be used to get or set the text value of an element, like the text found within a paragraph or a DIV. The textContent property is the W3C standard and works on multiple browsers, but is not supported on Internet Explorer; innerText works on most browsers, but not Firefox. Both properties can only return or set *text*: you cannot fetch or assign HTML using them. If you need to do that, use the innerHTML property:

```
document.getElementById('someP').innerHtml =
→ '<a href="somepage.html">link</a>';
```

The innerHTML property is reliable across all modern browsers except when it comes to updating HTML tables, so don't use it for that purpose. But you can also use the innerHTML property to fetch the HTML found within an element:

```
var original = document.getElementById('someDiv').innerHtml;
```

When using innerText, textContent, or innerHtml, understand that assigning a value to these properties completely replaces the existing text or HTML content. If you just need to add text or HTML, you can use concatenation:

```
document.getElementById('someP').innerHtml +=
→ '<a href="somepage.html">link</a>';
```

Also, you should only use innerHtml if you actually need to fetch or set HTML; otherwise, use innerText and textContent.

As a practical example of this, let's return to the idea of linking some text to the browser's Back button, via the window.history.back() method. To do that in a simple, progressively enhanced way, you would start by creating the message as just text:

```
Please <span id="backSpan">go back</span> to the previous window
→  and do what needs to be done.
```

Within the JavaScript, logically in a window load event handler, you could update the span, creating a click handler for that text:

```
window.onload = function() {
    if (typeof window.print == 'function') {
        var backSpan = document.getElementById('backSpan');
        backSpan.onclick = function() {
            window.print();
        }
    }
};
```

A more elaborate way to create elements and manipulate the DOM will be explained next. I will say here that using the innerHTML property is much faster than what you're about to learn, and should be preferred whenever possible.

### CREATING ELEMENTS

The final approach for manipulating the DOM is to actually manufacture, or just remove, HTML elements. Again, this route of creating elements and adding them to the DOM is slower than using innerHTML, but is sometimes required.

First, you can use the document.createElement() method to create an element of a given HTML type, assigning the result to a variable:

```
var p = document.createElement('p');
```

At this point, there is a new HTML paragraph element, but it is currently empty, with its default properties, and, most importantly, it's not part of the DOM, meaning it's not visible to the end user.

Next, you can set the various HTML and other properties to customize the element:

```
p.innerText = 'This is some text.';
p.className = 'enhanced';
```

(Remember to reference element classes using className, not class.)

Finally, you add the element to the DOM using one of several possible methods—`insertBefore()`, `appendChild()`, or `replaceChild()`, depending upon the desired end result. In any case, you'll at least need a reference to the element within which the new element will be placed. Let's say this new paragraph is going within a certain DIV:

```
var div = document.getElementById('someDiv');
```

To just add the paragraph to the DIV, use `appendChild()`, calling it on the destination element, providing the element to be appended as an argument:

```
div.appendChild(p);
```

That line formally adds the new paragraph element to the end of the DIV.

If the destination element already has other elements (i.e., children), and you do not want to add the new element at the end of the DIV (i.e., after all of the other children), use the `insertBefore()` method. Again, this is called on the destination element and its first argument is the element being added, but it takes a second argument, which is the element before which the new element should be placed:

```
div.insertBefore(p, document.getElementById('someP'));
```

A third option is to replace an existing element with another kind of element, using the `replaceChild()` method. It is called upon the destination element, and takes the new element as its first argument and the element to be replaced as its second:

```
div.insertBefore(p, document.getElementById('someImg'));
```

Note that you would likely not want to use this method if you're replacing one element with another element of the same kind, as it would just be easier and faster to replace the element's contents or attributes.

If you just need to add some text to a page, without creating a whole element, you can use the `createTextNode()` method:

```
var t = document.createTextNode('This is some text.');
```

Then you can add this text to the DOM where appropriate by using it as the first argument to `appendChild()`, `insertBefore()`, and `replaceChild()`. You would need to go this route when you're adding text to an element that has other children (because just using `innerText` and `textContent` would eradicate that other content).

You can also create new elements by copying existing ones, using the cloneNode() method:

```
var newDiv = document.getElementById('someDiv').cloneNode();
// Now manipulate newDiv.
```

This means that an alternative way of updating the page is to clone an element, update its properties and content (i.e., children), and then replace the original element with the modified clone. If you have a lot of changes to make, this approach only forces the browser to redraw the page (i.e., update the visually represented DOM) once. Note that cloning a node does not clone any event handlers that the original node might have.

Another way you can manipulate the DOM is to remove elements from the page by calling the removeChild() method on the parent element, providing the child to be removed as the argument:

```
div.removeChild(p);
```

Note that both objects used are references to the HTML elements, such as the value returned by getElementById(). You cannot just provide the id value of either element.

As a reminder, if you know the element to be removed but are unsure of its parent, use its parentNode property to find it:

```
var p = document.getElementById('someP');
var parent = p.parentNode;
parent.removeChild(p);
```

This can be simplified to just:

```
var p = document.getElementById('someP');
p.parentNode.removeChild(p);
```

With this new information in mind, let's implement a reliable "print this page" option. The HTML page is named print.html, and it contains some text within a DIV that has an id value of *main* (**Figure 9.15**). The HTML page includes the print.js JavaScript file, to be written in the subsequent steps. If JavaScript is enabled and printing is an option, a print button will be added (**Figure 9.16**).

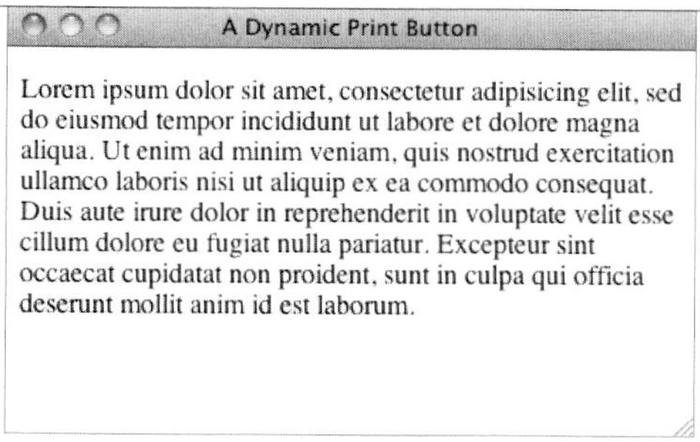

FIGURE 9.15 The HTML page, without the influence of JavaScript.

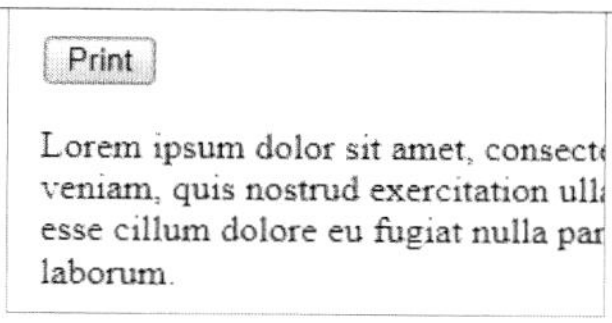

FIGURE 9.16 The dynamically added print button.

**To create a print button:**

1. Create a new JavaScript file in your text editor or IDE, to be named `print.js`.

2. Begin defining a function to be executed when the window loads:

```
window.onload = function() {
    'use strict';
```

3. Check for print capability:

```
if (typeof window.print == 'function') {
```

If the `window` object has a `print` property that is of type *function*, then a print button can be created.

4. Create a button element:

```
var printButton = document.createElement('button');
```

This line creates a new element of type `button`, assigning the result to the `printButton` variable.

5. Give the button some visible text:

```
if (printButton.textContent != 'undefined') {
    printButton.textContent = 'Print';
} else {
    printButton.innerText = 'Print';
}
```

The text written on a button actually goes between the HTML tags, as in:

```
<button>Print</button>
```

For this reason, the button's `textContent` or `innerText` property, depending upon the browser, must be assigned the visual text. If you'd rather, you could create an input of type `button`, with a value of *Print*.

6. Add a click event handler:

```
printButton.onclick = function() {
    window.print();
};
```

This anonymous function will be called when the click event occurs on the button. The contents of the function are just a call to the `window.print()` method.

7. Add the print button to the document:

```
document.body.insertBefore(printButton,
  → document.getElementById('main'));
```

The button is being added to the body, before the main DIV.

8. Complete the conditional begun in Step 3 and complete the function:

```
    } // End of IF.
}; // End of onload anonymous function.
```

9. Save the file as `print.js`, in a `js` directory next to `print.html`, and test it in your Web browser.

10. If possible, load the page on a device without print capability.

Barring that, just run it without JavaScript enabled to see the same result.

# JAVASCRIPT AND CSS

The definitions of both "modern browsers" and "progressive enhancement" involve three components: JavaScript, DOM manipulation, and CSS. Although JavaScript and CSS are two distinct technologies with different roles within the Web browser, the two can be used together to improve the user's experience.

Before getting into the particulars of CSS manipulations, I want to point out that you already saw a great way to change an element's styling: by altering its className attribute. In an ideal world, your style sheets define all the styling required by the page after any modifications, so just changing the classes as needed will suffice. If not, there are these other techniques.

And I have two caveats in advance. First, in the following pages, you'll learn how to use JavaScript and CSS together, but due to my poor visual design skills, you won't see gorgeous CSS. Second, this book in no way covers CSS in any detail; see a good CSS resource for more particulars.

## REFERENCING INDIVIDUAL STYLES

Once you have a reference to a browser element, you can get the element's current CSS styling through its style property:

```
var elem = document.getElementById('someElement');
// Use elem.style
```

The style property has its own properties for the various styles: height, width, backgroundColor, and so forth. To change any of the element's styling, assign a new value to the specific style:

```
elem.style.specificStyle = value;
```

One thing to watch for here is that you must use *camelCase* for all properties, even for those that would ordinarily have a hyphen:

```
elem.style.fontSize = '10em';
```

Second, when setting sizes in JavaScript, you must always specify the size unit (e.g., px, em, etc.).

The style property assigns the new value as an *inline style*, meaning that it will take precedence over any style rules defined elsewhere. This also means that when you read in the value of the style property, it only reflects inline styles, not all of the applicable styles.

```
> var elem = document.getElementById('tabLinks');
  undefined
> var styles = window.getComputedStyle(elem);
  undefined
> styles.fontSize;
  "14px"
```

To find all the applicable styles, you'll need to use different approaches for different browsers. As a change of pace, in this area, IE has the simplest solution: the currentStyle property:

```
var info = currentStyle.specificStyle;
```

For browsers that don't support currentStyle, there's the getComputedStyle() method of the window object:

```
var elementStyle = window.getComputedStyle(elem);
```

This method takes a reference to the element as its argument. The returned value can be treated as either an associative array or an object:

```
elementStyle['display']; // inline
elementStyle.display; // inline
```

Note that you can only read styles using this approach; they cannot be changed this way. Also, all sizes are returned with the size units: *10em*, not just *10* (**Figure 9.17**).

### HIDING AND SHOWING ELEMENTS

There are two CSS properties that can be manipulated to hide and show HTML elements: display and visibility. The difference between the two is in how the layout is affected. The visibility property does *not* affect the flow of elements before and after the element affected. Its two values are *visible* and *hidden*:

```
elem.style.visibility = 'hidden';
elem.style.visibility = 'visible';
```

Again, changing the visibility of an element will not impact the page's layout; there will just be an empty space where the element was.

FIGURE 9.18 The modal window contains HTML, styled by CSS, and appears within the browser window, but above the existing content.

Conversely, the `display` property will impact the layout, but exactly how depends upon the value it has. The possible values include *inline*, *block*, *inline-block*, and *none*:

```
elem.style.display = 'inline';
elem.style.display = 'none';
```

See a good CSS reference for descriptions of what these values mean.

You can also change the visibility of an element by altering its opacity. You'll see an example of that next.

## CREATING MODAL WINDOWS

One great use of JavaScript and CSS together is to create a new type of modal window, which you've probably seen many times over by now (**Figure 9.18**). These are modal windows, in that their appearance blocks the user from doing other things on the page, but unlike the dialogs first explained, these modal windows can be styled, and unlike creating a new browser window, these windows cannot be blocked using conventional window blocking. These modal windows do require CSS and JavaScript support, however. I'll explain how to create a modal window in the following sequence of steps. Unlike in most other examples, I'll walk through the HTML and CSS, too, as both are integral to the success of the system.

**To create a modal window:**

1. Create a new HTML file in your text editor or IDE, to be named `modal.html`:

```
<!doctype html>
<html lang="en">
<head>
    <meta charset="utf-8">
    <title>A Modal Window</title>
```

```
<!--[if lt IE 9]>
<script src="http://html5shiv.googlecode.com/svn/trunk/
    html5.js"></script>
<![endif]-->
<link rel="stylesheet" href="css/modal.css" id="css">
</head>
<body>
</body>
</html>
```

I'm using the basic HTML5 template, but you can use whatever HTML you want.

2. Create some static content:

```
<div><p>Lorem ipsum dolor sit amet...</p></div>
<div><p>Lorem ipsum dolor sit amet...</p></div>
```

The static content in the script are two DIVs, containing the Latin boiler-plate. You can change your content to something meaningful, if you'd prefer.

3. Create a DIV with an id value of *modal*:

```
<div id="modal"></div>
```

This DIV will be used to wrap all of the modal content. It will initially be hidden. You can place this DIV wherever you want; I've chosen to place it between the two existing DIVs.

4. Within the new DIV, add a DIV to be used to mask out the rest of the page:

```
<div id="modalMask"></div>
```

When the modal window is shown, the rest of the page needs to be "dis-abled," to give the modal window priority. This will be accomplished using an empty DIV that covers the entire window. This DIV must be placed within the *modal* DIV, so that it is also initially hidden.

5. After the mask, add a DIV to be used as the modal content:

```
<div id="modalContent"><p>This is modal content.</p>
→  <input type="button" id="closeModal" value="Close"></div>
```

This example uses a very simple bit of content. Do make sure that the modal window includes a button or link to close the window. Here, that input is given an id of *closeModal*.

6. Outside of the *modal* DIV, add a button to open the modal window:

```
<input type="button" value="Show Window" id="openModal">
```

Don't place this within the *modal* DIV, or else the user will never be able to open the window!

7. Make sure the HTML page includes a CSS file and a JavaScript file:

```
<link rel="stylesheet" href="css/modal.css">
```

```
<script src="js/modal.js"></script>
```

These will be written next.

8. Save the file as `modal.html`.

9. Create a new CSS file in your text editor or IDE, to be named `modal.css`.

10. Add the rules for the *modal* element:

```
#modal {
    display: none;
    position: absolute;
    left: 0px;
    top: 0px;
    width:100%;
    height:100%;
}
```

This is the DIV that wraps the entire modal content. It's initially not displayed but is positioned to use the entire browser window.

**11.** Add the rules for the *modalMask* element:

```
#modalMask {
    position: absolute;
    left: 0px;
    top: 0px;
    width:100%;
    height:100%;
    background-color: #eee;
    z-index: 1000;
    opacity: 0.9;
    filter:alpha(opacity=90);
    -moz-opacity: 0.9;
}
```

This DIV will also take up the entire browser window, but its opacity is set to 90% (using three different CSS properties, to work in all browsers) and its color is gray. Most importantly, it has a z-index value of 1000, which should place it on top of all the other page content. Look online if you're unfamiliar with the concept of a z-index.

**12.** Add the rules for the *modalContent* element:

```
#modalContent {
    position: relative;
    width:300px;
    margin: 15px auto;
    padding:15px;
    background-color: #fff;
    border:1px solid #000;
    text-align:center;
    z-index: 9999;
}
```

Finally, these rules style the actual modal window. The only critical value here is the z-index, which is set higher than any other element, including the mask.

13. Save the file as modal.css, within a css directory.

14. Create a new JavaScript file in your text editor or IDE, to be named modal.js.

15. Define the openModal() function:

```
function openModal() {
    'use strict';
    document.getElementById('closeModal').onclick =
    → closeModal;
    document.getElementById('modal').style.display =
    → 'inline-block';
    document.getElementById('openModal').onclick = null;
} // End of openModal() function.
```

The only step this function *has* to take is to set the display property of the *modal* DIV to *inline-block*. Doing so will reveal the entire DIV, including the mask layer and the modal content.

As an extra step, the event listeners on the two buttons—one for closing the window, the other for opening it—will be added and removed as needed. When the modal window is open, there becomes a need to listen for click events on the *closeModal* button, but there is no longer a need to listen for click events on the *openModal* button, so that listener can be removed.

16. Define the closeModal() function:

```
function closeModal() {
    'use strict';
    document.getElementById('openModal').onclick = openModal;
    document.getElementById('modal').style.display = 'none';
    document.getElementById('closeModal').onclick = null;
} // End of closeModal() function.
```

This code is the inverse of that in openModal().

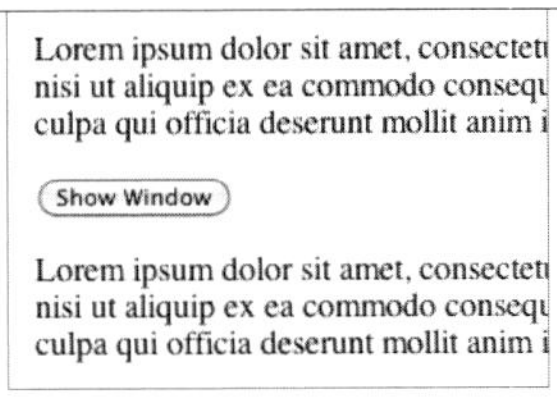

Lorem ipsum dolor sit amet, consectetu
nisi ut aliquip ex ea commodo consequ
culpa qui officia deserunt mollit anim i

( Show Window )

Lorem ipsum dolor sit amet, consectetu
nisi ut aliquip ex ea commodo consequ
culpa qui officia deserunt mollit anim i

**FIGURE 9.19** The content
without the modal window
being shown.

17. Establish functionality when the window loads:

```
window.onload = function() {
    'use strict';
    document.getElementById('openModal').onclick = openModal;
};
```

This function just needs to add the click handler to the *openModal* button.

18. Save the file as modal.js, within a js directory, and test it in your Web browser (**Figure 9.19**).

### REFERENCING STYLE SHEETS

Rather than manipulating individual styles, an alternative is to manipulate the whole page's style sheets. The document.styleSheets property stores a list of every style sheet in use by a page, including external CSS files and internally defined styles. If your style HTML elements use id attributes, you can also reference individual style sheets using document.getElementById():

```
<!-- HTML -->
<link rel="stylesheet" id="mainStyleSheet" href="css/style.css">
// JavaScript:
var mainCSS = document.getElementById('mainStyleSheet');
```

Once you have a reference to the style sheet, you can find its associated external file name (for external style sheets only) using its src attribute:

```
mainCSS.src; // 'css/style.css'
```

Most of the style sheet's properties are read-only, meaning they can't be modified, although you can disable an entire style sheet on the fly by setting its disabled property to *disabled* or true:

```
mainCSS.disabled = 'disabled'
```

Just by dynamically enabling and disabling style sheets, you can have a great impact on what the user sees. For example, you could enable a black-and-white style sheet for users accessing the site on grayscale devices, or a style sheet with just a few colors for other, more primitive devices. Later in this chapter, you'll see how to switch style sheets to let a user select the page's theme.

With a reference to a style sheet, you can create new rules using the `insertRule()` method. Its first argument is the new rule and its second is an index value, which is to say where in the style sheet the new rule is inserted:

```
mainCSS.insertRule('.hide: {visibility: none;}', 50);
```

As CSS rules apply differently based upon their order, the index position is significant.

To remove a style sheet rule, use `deleteRule()`, providing the index position of the rule to be removed:

```
mainCSS.deleteRule(5);
```

The `insertRule()` and `deleteRule()` methods work on most browsers but not on IE. IE instead uses `addRule()` and `removeRule()`. The `addRule()` method takes three arguments: the selector, the rule, and the index:

```
mainCSS.addRule('.hide', '{visibility: none;}', 50);
```

Generally speaking, I would recommend that CSS rules be permanent and hardcoded, but it's reasonable for high-end, CSS-driven sites to perform rule manipulation using JavaScript.

Finally, as a progressive enhancement example, you could have a page with a disabled style sheet by default, only to have it enabled if JavaScript is supported. Or, in that case, you can dynamically create a new set of style rules by using `createElement()`, creating an element of type *style*:

```
var s = document.createElement('style');
```

You would then need to establish its contents:

```
s.innerText = 'body {font-size: 90%;font-family: arial,sans-serif;}';
```

And finally, you can add the style sheet to the page by making it a child of the body:

```
document.body.appendChild(s);
```

# WORKING WITH COOKIES

Cookies, another technology invented at Netscape, has been integral to the progression of dynamic Web sites. HyperText Transfer Protocol (HTTP), the technology normally used for a Web browser to request a Web page, is a *stateless* protocol, meaning that when you go from page A on a site to page B on the same site, the server is unable to track that it's the same person—you—accessing both pages. This is a problem, as without a vehicle for maintaining state, there can be no user management (i.e., the ability to log in and log out), custom presentation of content, and only a limited sense of e-commerce. Fortunately, there are two ways of maintaining state: using *sessions* or *cookies*. Sessions can only be accomplished using a server-side technology, as sessions store the data itself on the server. Cookies, though, can be managed using a server-side technology or using JavaScript within the browser.

In layman's terms, cookies are just a Post-It note of information, stored in the user's browser, and associated with a particular Web site. When a visitor goes to a site, the site's server can send a cookie to the user's browser. After a cookie has been stored in the user's browser, it will be passed back to the server with subsequent page visits. It's important to know that cookies are only sent back to the same server from which they were originally received. A cookie sent from www.LarryUllman.com cannot read in a cookie sent to the same browser from www.example.com. This restriction has both a security and a performance benefit.

The cookie contains several discrete pieces of information:

- Its name

- Its value

- An expiration date and time

- A path where it is valid (defaults to the current path)

- Its domain (defaults to the current host)

The expiration date and time needs to be formatted as a UTC string (see Chapter 6, Complex Data Types). The *path* is the directory or directories on the server where the cookie is valid. For example, if your site is at www.example.com, a path of / makes the cookies available within the root directory and any subdirectories. If the path is set to /forums, then the cookie is only readable by the server when the user is visiting a page within www.example.com/forums, including any subdirectories.

With that information in mind, let's look at how to set, read, and remove cookies.

Cookies, whether used in JavaScript or a server-side technology, can be a wonderful convenience, but they do have their limitations. For starters, cookies are easily visible on the user's computer, so they should never be used to store sensitive information. Second, cookies can easily be manipulated by the end user, so the server side—the Web site—should always validate the cookie values, and use those values cautiously. Third, there is a limit as to how much information a single cookie can store (approximately 4 KB each), and as to how many cookies a single server can send to a single user. Finally, users can block cookies from being sent, either universally or individually.

With all of this in mind, I recommend that you treat cookies in JavaScript the same way you should treat JavaScript itself: as a way to provide enhanced functionality to the user. Applications where security is an issue should always use sessions, implemented using a server-side technology.

## CREATING COOKIES

Cookies in JavaScript are addressed through the `cookie` property of the `document` object. Creating a cookie is done using:

```
document.cookie = value;
```

The value needs to be of a specific syntax, starting with *cookieName=cookieValue*. For example, this next cookie could be used to save the user's preferred font size:

```
document.cookie = 'fontSize=14';
```

That sends a cookie using the default values for the expiration, path, and domain. To change any of those, add a semicolon, followed by other cookie property names and values: *expires*, *path*, and *domain*:

```
document.cookie = 'fontSize=14;expires=' + someDate.toGMTString() +
⟶ ';path=/subdirectory;domain=*.example.com';
```

You can set multiple cookies, assigning each to the same `document.cookie` property, so long as you use different cookie names:

```
document.cookie = 'fontSize=14';
document.cookie = 'color=3C9';
```

FIGURE 9.20 The value of
the document.cookie property
reflects both sent cookies.

```
>> document.cookie = 'fontSize=14';
   document.cookie = 'color=3C9';
   document.cookie;
   "fontSize=14; color=3C9"
```

This is possible because document.cookie is a special kind of property, with each additional assignment adding to the list of cookies, not replacing the previous ones.

The window.navigator.cookieEnabled property reflects whether cookies are enabled in the browser or not.

## READING COOKIES

Once you've set a cookie in JavaScript, you can read it in. Unfortunately, this is easier said than done in JavaScript. Whether you set one cookie or 12, the document.cookie property will represent every available cookie (**Figure 9.20**).

As you can see in the figure, multiple cookies are separated by semicolons, in *name=value* pairs. Thus, to read in every cookie, you must first break this string into its pieces:

```
var cookies = document.cookie.split(';');
```

Then you can loop through the cookies with a for loop:

```
for (var i = 0, count = cookies.length; i < count; i++) {
    // cookies[i] will be name=value
}
```

Within the for loop, you must break the individual cookie value—one *name=value* combination—into its pieces by splitting it on the equals sign. In a moment, you'll put this code to the test. Note that you cannot access the individual cookie properties—the expiration, path, and domain, as just access to the cookie itself validates that the cookie has not expired, and is available to the page in the current path and domain.

**TIP:** Unlike with cookies sent from a PHP script, which cannot be accessed until another page is loaded (or the same page reloaded), JavaScript cookies can be immediately retrieved.

## DELETING COOKIES

Deleting cookies in JavaScript is simply a matter of setting a cookie with the same name as the cookie you want to delete, but with no value and an expiration in the past, such as on the epoch:

```
document.cookie = 'fontSize=;expires=Thu, 01-Jan-1970 00:00:01 GMT';
```

For optimum reliability, the path and domain values should be the same as used when the cookie was created.

## CREATING A COOKIE LIBRARY

Because the syntax for creating and retrieving cookies is delicate, it's a good opportunity to make a library explicitly for this purpose. The following code will be similar in some ways to the utilities.js script created in Chapter 8. A subsequent example will make use of this library.

**To create a cookie library:**

1. Create a new JavaScript file in your text editor or IDE, to be named cookies.js.

2. Begin creating a new object named *COOKIE*:

   ```
   var COOKIE = {
   ```

   The COOKIE object will be the lone global variable created by this script.

3. Define the setCookie() method:

   ```
   setCookie: function(name, value, expire) {
       'use strict';
       var str = encodeURIComponent(name) + '=' +
       → encodeURIComponent(value);
       str += ';expires=' + expire.toGMTString();
       document.cookie = str;
   }, // End of setCookie() function.
   ```

   This function takes three arguments: the cookie's name, its value, and its expiration. The function then creates a string for the complete value, and assigns this to document.cookie. Note that I've skipped validation here, to keep the script shorter, but you should add that in the real world, including validating that the expire value is a Date object.

There's one new addition here: to ensure that the name and value are safe to store in the cookie, both are run through the encodeURIComponent() function. This function escapes potentially problematic characters to prevent server problems.

4. Start defining the getCookie() method:

```
getCookie: function(name) {
    'use strict';
    var len = name.length;
```

The getCookie() function will be the most complicated and important in this library. It takes one argument: the name of the cookie whose value should be returned. Within the function, the number of characters in the name is assigned to a variable, as it will be useful to know that information later in the function.

5. Split the cookie value on the semicolon:

```
var cookies = document.cookie.split(';');
```

The document.cookie property could store a single cookie, or a dozen, separated by semicolons. If only one cookie exists, split() will return an array of one element. If three cookies exist, then cookies will have three elements.

6. Begin looping through the cookies:

```
for (var i = 0, count = cookies.length; i < count; i++) {
    var value = (cookies[i].slice(0,1) == ' ') ?
    →   cookies[i].slice(1) : cookies[i];
```

The loop itself was already explained. What was not explained is that some browsers add a space in between the cookie values in document.cookie. This first line then assigns to the value variable either cookies[i], with the initial character sliced off (if that character is a space), or just cookies[i]. Written out, this is the same as:

```
if (cookies[i].slice(0,1) == ' ') {
    var value = cookies[i].slice(1);
} else {
    var value = cookies[i];
}
```

7. Decode the value:

```
value = decodeURIComponent(value);
```

The value variable at this point will be *name=value*. However, both pieces will have been encoded when sent, so they must be decoded now, using the corresponding decodeURIComponent() function.

8. Return the value if this is the right cookie:

```
if (value.slice(0,len) == name) {
    return cookies[i].split('=')[1];
} // End of IF.
```

The next step in the loop is to see if the current cookie value matches the name of the cookie the script is looking for. There are many ways of doing this: here I'm comparing a slice from the value, starting at 0 and going for len characters, to the name. If this conditional is TRUE, then the value should be returned by the function (which will also terminate the loop).

To find and return the value, I've used just one cryptic line of code. That is equivalent to:

```
var v = cookies[i].split('=');
return v[1];
```

The first line splits the *name=value* string into its two parts. The second line returns the second part.

9. Complete the for loop:

```
} // End of FOR loop.
```

FIGURE 9.21 The plain content, without any CSS formatting.

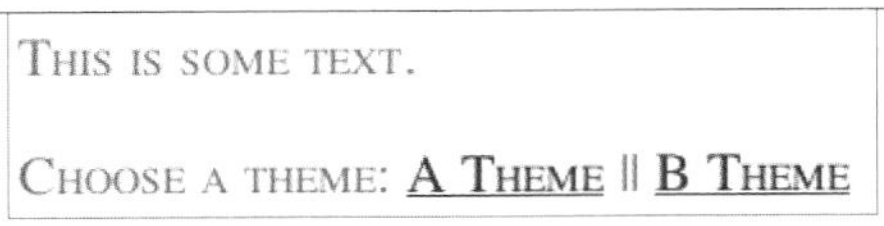

FIGURE 9.22 The same content, using one of the selected "themes."

This is some text.

Choose a theme: A Theme ‖ B Theme

THIS IS SOME TEXT.

CHOOSE A THEME: A THEME ‖ B THEME

10. Complete the getCookie() function:

```
    return false;
}, // End of getCookie() function.
```

The function always returns false if it gets to this point, which means that a matching cookie was not found.

11. Define the deleteCookie() function:

```
deleteCookie: function(name) {
    'use strict';
    document.cookie = encodeURIComponent(name) +
    →  '=;expires=Thu, 01-Jan-1970 00:00:01 GMT';
} // End of deleteCookie() function.
```

This function just takes a single argument: the name of the cookie being deleted.

12. Complete the COOKIE() definition:

```
}; // End of COOKIE declaration.
```

13. Save the file as cookies.js.

You'll want to place the script, or a copy of it, in the same directory as all the other JavaScript files you write in this chapter.

## USING THE COOKIE LIBRARY

As an example of using the new cookie library, let's tie into the information learned about CSS and create a system that allows the user to select the page's theme. The actual example will just change the colors and fonts, but CSS can make major stylistic changes of the same content. The page will not use any CSS when the user first arrives (**Figure 9.21**). Two links will let the user change the theme. When the user clicks on a link, not only is the theme set for the current viewing of the page (**Figure 9.22**), but a cookie will be sent as well, so that the same CSS is used upon subsequent visits. The end result is about 60 lines of JavaScript that combines event handling, default browser behavior prevention, cookies, and DOM manipulation!

The HTML page, to be named theme.html, has two links:

```
<p>Choose a theme: <a href="somepage.php?theme=a" id="aTheme">
  A Theme</a> || <a href="somepage.php?theme=b" id="bTheme">
  B Theme</a></p>
```

The HTML page will also include two JavaScript files: cookies.js, just written, and theme.js, to be explained in the next series of steps. You can download the requisite CSS files from the book's corresponding Web site (www.LarryUllman.com).

**To use cookies and custom CSS:**

1. Create a new JavaScript file in your text editor or IDE, to be named theme.js.

2. Begin defining the setTheme() function:

   ```
   function setTheme(theme) {
       'use strict';
       var css = null;
   ```

   The setTheme() function takes one argument, which will be the user's chosen theme (aka stylesheet). The function will use DOM manipulation to make the chosen theme active. Within the function, the css variable will represent the DOM element, which will end up being:

   ```
   <link rel="stylesheet" href="css/someTheme.css" id="cssTheme">
   ```

3. If the link element already exists, update it:

   ```
   if (document.getElementById('cssTheme')) {
       css = document.getElementById('cssTheme');
       css.href = 'css/' + theme + '.css';
   ```

   It's possible that the link element already exists on the page; that would be the case if the user is switching themes. If so, then the JavaScript only needs to change the href property of the element. The href value needs to be *css/*—because all style sheets are in the css folder—plus the value of theme, plus *.css*.

4. If no link element exists, create it:

```
} else {
    css = document.createElement('link');
    css.rel = 'stylesheet';
    css.href = 'css/' + theme + '.css';
    css.id = 'cssTheme';
    document.head.appendChild(css);
}
```

The first line within the block creates a new element of type *link*. The second assigns *stylesheet* to the element's rel property. The third assigns the href value. And the fourth creates the id value, so that the code in Step 3 can reference this new element when the user switches themes. Finally, the element is added to the DOM, specifically within the HTML head.

Alternatively, you could hardcode the link in the HTML, with an empty or simple CSS file, then just always update it, without creating a new link element.

5. Complete the function:

```
} // End of setTheme() function.
```

6. Begin defining the setThemeCookie() function:

```
function setThemeCookie(e) {
    'use strict';
    if (typeof e == 'undefined') e = window.event;
    if (e.preventDefault) {
        e.preventDefault();
    } else {
        e.returnValue = false;
    }
    var target = e.target || e.srcElement;
```

This function will be called when the user clicks a link. The function needs to store the selected theme in a cookie and then have the page be updated to use the new theme. To know which link was clicked, a reference to the event and the event target are required. This function also needs to prevent the default browser behavior, which would be the page following the actual link (to, for example, somepage.php?theme=a). All of this code is explained in Chapter 8.

7. Set the cookie:

```
var expire = new Date(); // Today!
expire.setDate(expire.getDate() + 7); // One week!
COOKIE.setCookie('theme', target.id, expire);
```

The cookie is created using the COOKIE.setCookie() function. The name of the cookie will be *theme* and its value will be the id value of the target: *aTheme* or *bTheme*. The cookie is set to expire in a week.

8. Update the theme and complete the function:

```
    setTheme(target.id);
    return false;
} // End of setThemeCookie() function.
```

To update the page for the new theme, the setTheme() function needs to be called, passing to it the new theme's identifier.

9. Create a function to handle the window's load event:

```
window.onload = function() {
    'use strict';
```

This function will need to add click handlers to the two links. It will also need to check the user's cookies to see if the user had previously selected a theme, which should be used now.

10. Add the click handlers:

```
document.getElementById('aTheme').onclick = setThemeCookie;
document.getElementById('bTheme').onclick = setThemeCookie;
```

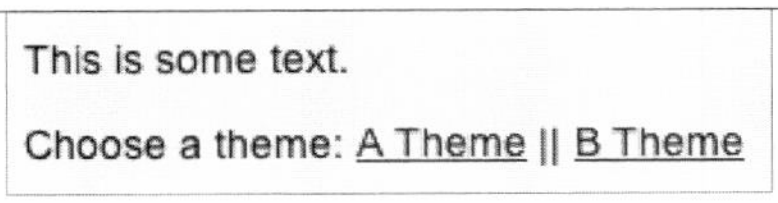

**FIGURE 9.23** The same content, using the other theme.

> This is some text.
>
> Choose a theme: <u>A Theme</u> || <u>B Theme</u>

When either link is clicked, the setThemeCookie() function will be called. If the user does not have JavaScript enabled, then the browser will be taken to, for example, somepage.php?theme=a. That PHP script could set the cookie instead.

**11.** Retrieve the cookie and set the theme, if appropriate:

```
var theme = COOKIE.getCookie('theme');
if (theme) {
    setThemeCookie(theme);
}
```

The first line uses the COOKIE.getCookie() function to get the value of the theme cookie. If that function returns a non-false value, then a theme was previously stored, and the page needs to be updated for the chosen theme. That could be done by just calling setTheme(), passing it the theme value. However, as written, the theme cookie will expire in a week. By calling the setThemeCookie() function here, the cookie will be renewed for another week (from today), and the page will be updated. This keeps the user's preferences retained so long as it hasn't been more than a week since the user accessed the page.

**12.** Complete the anonymous function:

```
};
```

**13.** Save the file as theme.js, within a js directory, and test it in your Web browser.

**14.** Click a link to switch themes (**Figure 9.23**).

**15.** Close your browser window, or even quit the browser, and then reopen the page to see your theme selection retained.

# USING TIMERS

One more area of functionality provided by the browser is the ability to create *timers*. I'm not talking about a timer in the sense of timing how long a process takes: for that, you can use the Date object and Date arithmetic, as explained in Chapter 6. No, here I'm speaking of a timer in the sense of a countdown timer, where you can tell JavaScript to execute some code after a certain period. To do that, call the setTimeout() function, providing a function to be called as the first argument and a number of milliseconds as the second:

```
setTimeout(function() {
    alert('It has been 2000 milliseconds!');
}, 2000);
```

(As you can see in this code, this is a good place to use anonymous functions, although you certainly don't have to.)

A variation on setTimeout() is setInterval(). It takes the same arguments but invokes the function repeatedly at every indicated interval:

```
// You will regret this:
setInterval(function() {
    alert('It has been 2000 milliseconds!');
}, 2000);
```

In short, the setTimeout() function creates a one-time timer; setInterval() creates a recurring timer.

To be clear, that is code you never want to execute, as it will continually create the alert every 2 seconds until...well, until you close the browser window. For this reason, whenever you use setInterval(), you should have some code in place that will eventually stop the timer. To do that, first assign the result of the setInterval() call to a variable:

```
var interval = setInterval(doThis, 10000);
```

Then, when appropriate, call the clearInterval() function, providing to it the timer identifier:

```
var n = 1;
function doThis() {
    alert('This is alert #' + n);
    n++;
    if (n == 5) clearInterval(interval);
}
```

With that function definition, the alert dialog will be created five times, approximately 10 seconds apart.

Timers created using setTimeout() can also be stopped by assigning its call to a variable and then providing that variable to the clearTimeout() function.

There is one gotcha when it comes to setting timers: the function is not guaranteed to be executed precisely upon the interval. The reason for this is that JavaScript runs using a single thread, meaning that JavaScript can only do one thing at a time. While time is elapsing for the timers, the user or browser might be triggering events that must also be handled by other JavaScript code. If the interval is up while JavaScript is busy handling another event, JavaScript will need to wait until a free moment to call the interval's associated function. In neither case will the function be called *before* the interval is up, but it may not be called immediately when the interval passes. (I'm simplifying this process a bit, but that's the general idea: events, including timer events, get queued up and are handled as soon as possible.)

There are a lot of good uses for timers, for a wide range of purposes. For example, animations and effects require timers (although complex animations should not be done with timers). This next bit of code will fade a DIV by decreasing its opacity incrementally from 100% to 0%:

```
var div = document.getElementById('someDiv');
var opacity = 1;
var fader = setInterval(function() {
    opacity -= .1; // Decrease the opacity.
    if (opacity >= 0) { // Stop at negative numbers.
```

```
        if (typeof div.style.opacity == 'string') { // Most browsers.
            div.style.opacity = opacity;
        } else { // IE
            div.style.filters = 'alpha(opacity=' + (opacity * 100) +
            → ')';
        }
    } else { // Stop the timer!
        clearInterval(fader);
    }
}, 100); // Every 100 milliseconds.
```

## (NOT) USING EVAL()

Another top-level (i.e., window) function with which you ought to be familiar is eval(). The eval() function takes a string as its lone argument and executes that as if it were JavaScript code. The following two lines have the same result:

```
alert('This is an alert.');
```

```
eval("alert('This is an alert.')");
```

To be clear, you would never use eval() on a literal string of text like that, as it'd be more efficient to just execute that JavaScript directly. The eval() function is actually used to evaluate a string of code that is unknown when the script is written:

```
eval(someVar);
```

Here, then, is why you shouldn't use eval(): it's terribly dangerous to blindly execute code that is unknown. Doing so leaves your scripts vulnerable to injection attacks: where a malicious user knowingly provides bad data in the hopes of learning something or causing harm. Code run through eval() has historically performed poorly, too, and is much harder to debug.

There are some legitimate uses of eval(), though. One traditional use was for converting the data returned by an Ajax request into a JavaScript object (to be explained in Chapter 11). But in today's JavaScript, there's almost always a better solution than using eval(), and you should be suspicious of code that invokes it.

That code is only a little bit tricky because of the two ways required to change the opacity; other than that, it's effectively a loop from 1 to 0, counting down by .1.

Another use of timers is to automatically update content, such as the current time, the weather, or a stock quote (i.e., a timer could be used to fetch a stock quote regularly). In Chapter 6, I discussed how the Date object can be used to show how much time is left in an online auction. Using a timer, you could regularly update the amount of time remaining. (In fact, the example in Chapter 15, PHP and JavaScript Together, will do exactly that.)

As another example, earlier in this chapter, I discussed using the URL hash value to mark a page's state, noting one problem: use of the Back and Forward buttons changes the URL, but doesn't trigger the JavaScript to execute again. The solution is to use a timer that watches for changes in the hash value:

```
var hash = window.location.hash;

var hashWatcher = setInterval(function() {

    if (window.location.hash != hash) { // Changed!

        updatePage();

    }

}, 1000); // Every second.
```

## REVIEW AND PURSUE

If you have any problems with these sections, either in answering the questions or pursuing your own endeavors, turn to the book's supporting forum (www.LarryUllman.com/forums/).

### REVIEW

- What three kinds of dialogs were discussed in this chapter?

- How do you create a new browser window?

- How do you change the browser's focus to another window? How do you take the focus off of the current window?

- How can you provide new windows in a *progressively enhanced* manner?

- What is the *same origin policy*?

- Through what object and property can you access the browser's history?

- How do you redirect the browser using JavaScript? How do you redirect the browser without leaving the previous page in the user's history?

- What is the significance of the `window.location.hash` property? How about `window.location.search`?

- How do you trigger the browser's print functionality? What should you be mindful of when it comes to offering this?

- In what property can you access the browser's window title?

- In what property can you see what mode—*Quirks* or *Standard*—the browser is running in?

- What is the DOM?

- What are some of the easiest ways to obtain a reference to HTML elements?

- What are CSS selectors? How do you use them?

- What are some of the ways that you can change existing HTML elements?

- How do you create new elements and add them to the DOM?

- What ways exist for manipulating CSS?

- How do you create and read cookies using JavaScript?

- What two functions are used to create timers and how do they differ? How do you stop a timer?

## PURSUE

- There's a lot of content presented in this chapter (a lot!), so practice some of the ideas using your browser's console interface. In particular, check out some of the properties named in the `window` and `document` objects, and try dynamically manipulating the DOM.

- If you've relied upon one of the dialog types in a project, rewrite that site's code to use a different, better window type instead.

- If you want, create a script that uses various window properties to report upon what JavaScript can know about the user's browser and screen.

- If you think you might have the need to communicate between two windows using JavaScript, use the information covered in this chapter to practice that. Or try it with iframes.

- Write a simple script that redirects the browser to another page, just to confirm that you know how to make that happen.

- Create a function that, on the window's load, checks the browser's compatibility mode and reports that.

- Research more about the DOM and DOM manipulation.

- Modify popups.js and popups.html so that only links with a specific class value trigger the createPopup() function.

- Rewrite popups.js using the getElementsByClassName() method if supported, and a fallback approach if not.

- If you are really comfortable with CSS, research more about *CSS selectors*.

- If you are adventurous and generally conversant with XML, investigate *XPath expressions*.

- Complete the "go back" link functionality so that it's accomplished in a progressively enhanced manner, similar to how the print functionality was created.

- Learn more about CSS, if you feel that's a weakness of yours. (Personally, I understand the concepts involved, but lack the design skills to use CSS well.)

- Update the cookies.js script to add the necessary validation.

- Update the cookies.js script so that the path and domain values can be passed to the setCookie() and deleteCookie() functions.

- Change `theme.html` so that a simple, or blank CSS file is always present, and then change `theme.js` to just update it.

- Implement your own timer example, such as the seconds since the epoch script from Chapter 8.

## WRAPPING UP

First, congratulations for getting through a long chapter, with tons of new information presented in it! There was a lot to cover because the browser is so important to JavaScript (which goes without saying). As you probably experienced, the examples that you can create have become more fully formed, making use of events, DOM manipulation, CSS, and so forth.

The most important things covered by this chapter were:

- Key members of the `window` and `window.document` objects

- Several ways to create new windows, from dialogs to actual browser windows to CSS layers

- How to navigate and manipulate the DOM

- How to interact with CSS

- The basics of timers

You also encountered a number of specific issues, such as accessing the browser history, connecting with the browser's print functionality, and creating cookies. Many of the examples were extremely practical, and occasionally advanced, putting together the right combination of HTML, CSS, and JavaScript. Progressive enhancement—improving the user's experience without leaving others behind—continues to be endorsed and demonstrated.

There really was a lot to this chapter, and hopefully you weren't overwhelmed. From here on out, the chapters become more focused on smaller topics and individual applications of JavaScript, starting in the next chapter, which goes into JavaScript and forms in greater detail, with lots of specific examples that you'll use every day.

# 10

# **WORKING** WITH FORMS

Forms are integral to the usefulness of the Web as they provide the primary interface for user interaction. In this book, forms have been used heavily ever since Chapter 2, JavaScript in Action, but this chapter is going to complete the coverage of the subject. To start, there are some more general form issues, but the meat of the chapter goes through aspects of using the various form element types. That section of the chapter will be more like a recipe book, with explicit code for performing specific tasks. The chapter concludes with a discussion of *regular expressions*. Although they aren't exclusive to forms, regular expressions are often used to validate textual form data, and you'll see exactly how.

# GENERAL FORM CONSIDERATIONS

Although the basics of forms have been well covered by now, I want to quickly reiterate a few key points, and perhaps introduce one or two new things.

First, as already explained, the best way to handle a form's submission is to add a submit handler to the form itself. Such an event is triggered when the user clicks on the submit button *or* when the user presses Enter/Return, which submits a form on some browsers. Thus, watching for a submit event is the most reliable and accessible approach. In very limited situations, you may want to perform validation when certain form elements change, but you should be careful when doing so, as change events can occur more often than may be appropriate for broad validation.

Historically, developers have sometimes created forms without a submit button: instead, the form would be submitted when a form element's value changes (such as by the selection of a drop-down menu). Understand that if you do this, then users without JavaScript cannot submit your form.

Speaking of accessibility, forms should always have a valid `action` attribute value, allowing the form data to go through to a real resource when JavaScript is not enabled. Of course, most of the examples in this book did not use a valid `action` attribute, but that's only because the focus was on the idea being introduced, and no actual page was being written to handle the form's submission anyway. On live sites, you must always create a fallback page that will handle the form's submission should the user not have JavaScript enabled.

You can change the `action` value dynamically using JavaScript:

```
document.getElementById('theForm').action = 'otherPage.php';
```

By doing so, you can have JavaScript-enabled users head to a different location than the non-JavaScript users upon the form's submission.

As a reminder, to prevent the form's submission to the server-side script, you can use the standard techniques for preventing any default event behavior (this would go within the form submission handler):

```
if (e.preventDefault) {
    e.preventDefault();
} else {
    e.returnValue = false;
}
return false;
```

First Name
Last Nam
Email Addre
Please fill out this field.

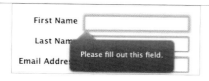

**FIGURE 10.1** An error message created by HTML5's built-in validation.

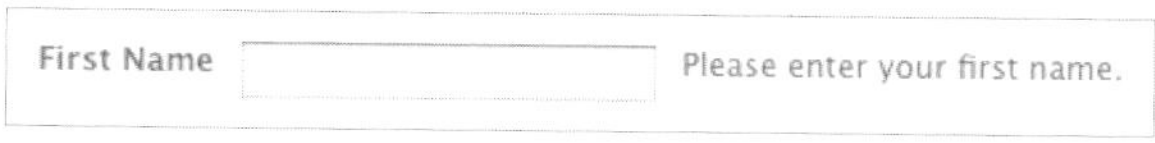
First Name
Please enter your first name.

**FIGURE 10.2** The error message created by a custom JavaScript function.

Returning `false` only works when the event handler was created using the DOM Level 0 approach; the other methods work with DOM Level 2 event handlers, on browsers that can use `addEventListener()` and those that can't (i.e., older IE), respectively.

You can, using JavaScript, actually force a form submission yourself, by calling the `submit()` method on the form element:

```
document.getElementById('theForm').submit();
```

Be aware that doing this does not actually trigger a submit event.

**TIP:** To place the browser focus on a form element, call the `focus()` method on that element when the page has loaded.

Lastly, as a reminder, HTML5, when supported by the browser, will perform validation based upon the input type and the properties assigned. This validation nicely includes visual error messages (**Figure 10.1**). If you're not using HTML5, or if the user's browser does not support HTML5, then you need to use DOM manipulation and CSS (i.e., the information taught in Chapter 9, JavaScript and the Browser) to provide attractive inline error messages (**Figure 10.2**). Let's create a function toward that end.

## CREATING ERROR MESSAGES

In order to do everything required, the function needs to take two arguments: the `id` value of the form element to which the error message is being applied and the error message itself. The function should then create a `span` containing the message and append the `span` after the target element. The function also needs to give this new `span` an `id` value, so that the function itself can check for its existence upon repeat calls (no need to create it if it's already there), and so that another function can remove that error message when appropriate. The function will also add the *error* class to the form element's label (see Figure 10.2).

**To add and remove error messages:**

1.  Create a new JavaScript file in your text editor or IDE, to be named errorMessages.js.

2.  Begin defining the addErrorMessage() function:

    ```
    function addErrorMessage(id, msg) {
        'use strict';
    ```

    The function needs to take the aforementioned two arguments.

3.  Get a reference to the form element, and check for the existence of the span:

    ```
    var elem = document.getElementById(id);
    var newId = id + 'Error';
    var span = document.getElementById(newId);
    if (span) {
        span.firstChild.value = msg;
    ```

    The problematic form element is the focus of the function, so a reference to that must first be garnered. Then the script starts looking at the error span. Its id value will be the id of the corresponding form element, plus the text *Error* (e.g., *firstNameError*). Next, the script checks if this element already exists. This allows for the possibility that the initial error message might say, for example, *Please enter your desired username.*, but a follow-up error message—using the same span—might say *That username is already taken.*

    If the span already exists, then its first child's value is updated to the message. As you'll see in Step 4, the span's first—and only—child will be a text node. Alternatively, you could update the span's innerText or textContent attribute, depending upon the browser.

**NOTE:** All of the code for the book is available to be downloaded from www.LarryUllman.com.

4. If the span does not exist, create one:

```
} else {
    span = document.createElement('span');
    span.id = newId;
    span.className = 'error'
    span.appendChild(document.createTextNode(msg));
```

The first line within the clause creates a new element (see Chapter 9 for more on this, if needed). The second line assigns to the element a proper id value. And the third line applies the *error* class to this span. Finally, a child node is added to this element. The child node is a text node, whose content will be the message. Again, you could set the span's innerText or textContent attribute, if you'd rather.

5. Add the span to the DOM:

```
elem.parentNode.appendChild(span);

elem.previousSibling.className = 'error';
```

The error message, stored in the span, shouldn't be added to the form element, but rather made a new sibling of the form element. To do that, append this new span to the form element's parent. This will work so long as each form element is within its own DIV or paragraph, as in:

```
<div><label for="firstName">First Name</label><input type=
    "text" name="firstName" id="firstName" required></div>
```

With that HTML, elem.parentNode refers to the DIV, so appending a new child results in:

```
<div><label for="firstName" class="error">First Name</label>
    <input type="text" name="firstName" id="firstName"
    required><span id="firstNameError">MESSAGE</span></div>
```

The second line in the code assigns the *error* class to the element's label (i.e., the element's previous sibling), as also shown in the HTML.

A simpler alternative would be to add the *error* class to the element's parent (e.g., a DIV), but that would only work if each form element has a unique parent and if that parent doesn't already have its own meaningful class.

6. Complete the main if-else and the function:

```
    } // End of main IF-ELSE.
} // End of addErrorMessage() function.
```

7. Begin defining the removeErrorMessage() function:

```
function removeErrorMessage(id) {
    'use strict';
```

This function takes the form element id as its lone argument. It needs to remove the span and remove the error class from the corresponding label. As you'll see in the following steps, this function will not directly reference the form element, but as the addErrorMessage() function takes the form element's id as its first argument, it's best to be consistent.

8. Get a reference to the span and check for its existence:

```
var span = document.getElementById(id + 'Error');
    if (span) {
```

There's no point in attempting to remove the element if it doesn't exist!

9. Remove the class from the label:

```
span.previousSibling.previousSibling.className = null;
```

This is similar to the code in Step 5, but this time the className property is being assigned the value null.

A possible problem with this system is that it assumes that the element's label does not have another class, as the addErrorMessage() function replaces the entire className value, and this function empties that value. At the end of the chapter, you'll see hints for how you can change this code to fix this potential issue.

FIGURE 10.3 The tooltip dynamically appears beside the form element when it receives the user's focus.

10. Remove the span:

```
span.parentNode.removeChild(span);
```

The first two parts of the code—span.parentNode—obtain a reference to the span's parent. Then the removeChild() method can be called on it, providing the element to be removed—the span—as its argument.

11. Complete the function:

```
    } // End of IF.
} // End of removeErrorMessage() function.
```

12. Save the file as errorMessage.js, in a js directory.

At the end of the chapter, you'll see how to use these two functions, if it's not already clear.

## CREATING TOOLTIPS

In order to minimize user errors, it's best to communicate expectations to the user while the form is being completed. If your design allows for it, you could add notes beside the form elements, but that approach can make the page look busy. An alternative is to use tooltips (**Figure 10.3**). Tooltips appear and disappear as needed, so that only one tooltip—for the element currently being addressed—is ever shown at a time.

From a design and programming perspective, a tooltip is a lot like a modal window (see Chapter 9) that does not block out the rest of the page. You would start by creating the tooltip as hardcoded HTML:

```
<div><label for="username">Username<span class="tooltip">
→  Usernames can only contain letters and numbers and must be
→  at least 4 characters long.</span></label><input type="text"
→  name="username" id="username" required></div>
```

For accessibility purposes, it's best to put the tooltip itself within the corresponding element label, but the span will be hidden on browsers that support that CSS, so placing the HTML there won't be as intrusive as it might originally look. Notice that the span has a class of *tooltip*, which will be used by both the CSS and the JavaScript:

```css
label { position: relative; }
.tooltip {
    display: block;
    visibility: hidden;
    position: absolute;
    left: 30em; top: 0; padding: 0.5em; width: 10em;
    border:solid 2px #425955;
    background-color: #BFBD9F;
}
```

When the tooltip is to be shown, the CSS for the tooltip will move it to the right of the form element itself, which is more natural and less impactful on the layout of the form. For that to work, the label itself must have a position value of *relative* (I'm far from a CSS expert, but that much I do know).

The CSS also hides all of the tooltips by setting the visibility property to *hidden*. If you want to make this system work for devices without JavaScript, you would have the tooltips be displayed by default, and then use JavaScript to hide them when the window is loaded.

The JavaScript now just needs to change the tooltip's visibility when the corresponding form element is moused over, or gains focus:

```javascript
document.getElementById('someFormElement').onmouseover = showTooltip;
document.getElementById('someFormElement').onfocus = showTooltip;
```

By watching for both events, the script recognizes both input device and keyboard-based events.

The tooltip should be hidden when the same element loses focus or the mouse leaves it:

```
document.getElementById('someFormElement').onmouseout = hideTooltip;
document.getElementById('someFormElement').onblur = hideTooltip;
```

Since there are four event listeners to be added to each element, it'd be easier if you create a function that does all this:

```
function addTooltipHandlers(elem) {
    elem.onmouseover = showTooltip;
    elem.onmouseout = hideTooltip;
    elem.onfocus = showTooltip;
    elem.onblur = hideTooltip;
}
```

All that remains are the showTooltip() and hideTooltip() functions. Each would take an event as an argument, and would use that event to dynamically change the element's visibility accordingly:

```
function showToolTip(e) {
    if (typeof e == 'undefined') e = window.event;
    var target = e.target || e.srcElement;
    target.previousSibling.lastChild.style.visibility = 'visible';
}
function hideToolTip(e) {
    if (typeof e == 'undefined') e = window.event;
    var target = e.target || e.srcElement;
    target.previousSibling.lastChild.style.visibility = 'hidden';
}
```

The trick to these two functions is that the form element triggers the events, but the span within the label needs to be changed. To get from the form element to the span, refer to previousSibling, which will be the label, then lastChild.

## DISABLING THE SUBMIT BUTTON

Chapter 9 included a quick bit of code that demonstrated how to disable a submit button, but it's a common enough need that it's worth repeating. Most frequently, the submit button is disabled to prevent accidental multiple submissions, especially when the act of submitting the form begins the payment processing step in an e-commerce site.

Disabling of the submit button is accomplished by setting the button's `disabled` property to *disabled*, or the Boolean `true`:

```
document.getElementById('submitButton').disabled = true;
document.getElementById('submitButton').disabled = 'disabled';
```

In situations like this, where a Boolean value is expected, that fact is that *any value* will count as TRUE, so both the string *disabled* and Boolean `true` have the same effect.

As an added feature, when disabling the submit button it'd be best to visually indicate the change and status to the user. This could be done by applying a CSS class to the button itself, by adding an element with a message beside the button, by changing the text printed on the button, or some combination of these. The second idea—adding a message—was just demonstrated, as it's the same technique used to create error messages for form elements. The other three ideas were demonstrated in Chapter 9, just not specific to a submit button. In fact, you could use a CSS-based modal window, as explained in that chapter, to create a new layer with a message, and also gray out the rest of the page, simultaneously blocking the user from clicking the button again and informing them of what's happening.

# TEXT INPUTS AND TEXTAREAS

Moving on, let's look at some specific form elements, what meaningful properties they have, and implement some common uses of them, when it comes to JavaScript. To start, there's the text input and the textarea.

## TEXT INPUT AND TEXTAREA BASICS

You can retrieve what the user entered into a text input or textarea by checking its value attribute:

```
var data = document.getElementById('comments').value;
```

The value attribute represents any text present in the element, whether it was entered by the user or preset. The value property also works for hidden and password inputs.

You can change the contents of a text input or textarea by assigning a new string to the element's value:

```
document.getElementById('someInput').value = 'new value';
```

You've already seen this in Chapter 8, Event Handling, in which the user was limited as to how much data could be typed in a textarea. In HTML5, you can finally use the maxlength property for textareas, too, although you should indicate to the user that a restriction is in place.

When it comes to validating text inputs and textareas, you can use string methods to check for a minimum length, or you can use regular expressions, when appropriate, which are covered at the end of the chapter.

If you have a preset (i.e., default) value for a text input or textarea, the validation routines have to take that into account, only passing the validation if the text input or textarea has a value that's not the original. There's a neat little trick for doing this: using the element's defaultValue property. I'll explain...

**TIP:** HTML5 will automatically validate against the default (i.e., placeholder) value.

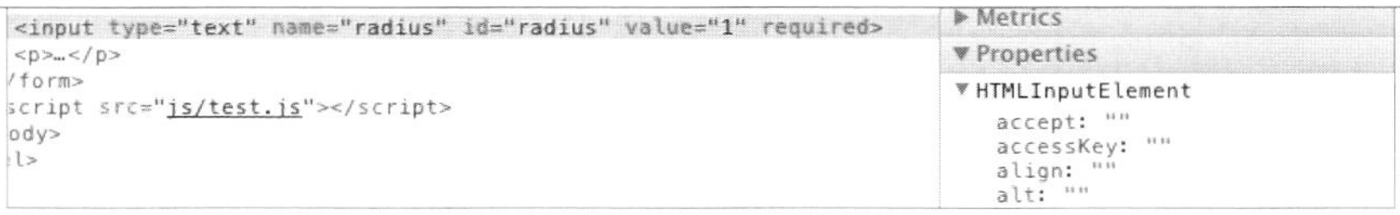

FIGURE 10.4 Just a few of the properties that exist for the text input.

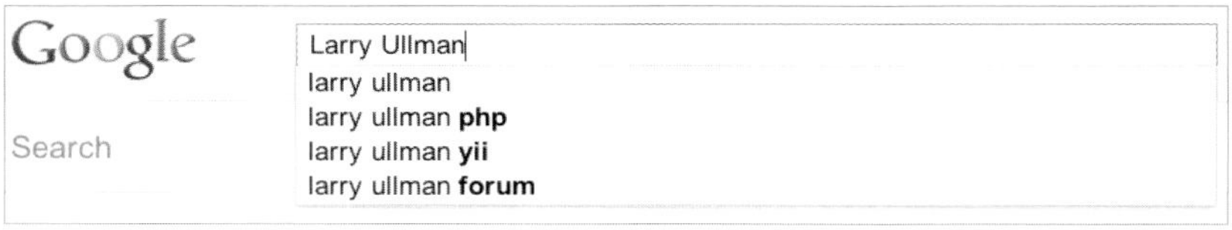

FIGURE 10.5 Google's Suggest feature, updated as the user types.

If you inspect an HTML element in your browser's console window (**Figure 10.4**), you'll see many more properties than commonly used. One of these is defaultValue. This property represents the value assigned to the value attribute, as in:

```
<input type="text" name="radius" id="radius" value="1" required>
```

With this in place, you can validate against the default value during the validation process:

```
if (elem.value == elem.defaultValue) {
    addErrorMessage(elem.id, 'Please enter a value');
}
```

## IMPLEMENTING AUTOCOMPLETE

A common, dynamic use of JavaScript and text inputs is to provide suggestions as the user types, a feature known as *autocomplete*. I remember first seeing this implemented as Google Suggest (**Figure 10.5**) back when it was in Google Labs, and was absolutely blown away. Autocomplete enhances the user experience in many ways. First, it saves the user from typing, which means it also saves the user from making a mistake. Second, depending upon how the autocomplete is implemented, it either puts forth the available results or the results that are most likely useful. For example, a human resources tool for finding an employee's record may only offer up actual employee names, whereas Google's autosuggest provides the most common search terms, based upon what you've typed.

There are three hurdles to overcome with respect to autocomplete functionality. The first is the searching algorithm. If you're performing a browse, that's not too hard or too slow (e.g., when the user types *ac*, *ace* and *active* would come up, but not *didactic*). If you want a true search, where the letters could be found within the results, that takes a bit more effort (e.g., *ac* would apply to *didactic*). The second hurdle is where the data comes from. If there's a relatively small data set to be searched, then it would make sense to create that set as a JavaScript array, stored within the browser. If there's a large data set, then you'd want to fetch the data on the fly, using Ajax (see Chapter 11, Ajax). The third hurdle is more minor: displaying the suggestions in a reliable, cross-browser way.

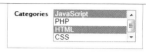

**FIGURE 10.6** A select menu with multiple options selected.

Taking these three hurdles together, a good autocomplete is complicated enough that you may want to use a framework or library for this purpose. You'll see multiple examples of this in Chapter 13, Frameworks.

## SELECT MENUS

The select menu is like the text input, textarea, password, and hidden input in that the value selected by a user is available through the value attribute:

```
var data = document.getElementById('selectMenu').value;
```

But unlike with those other elements, you cannot change the select menu's value by assigning something new to this attribute. Instead, you must change the menu's selectedIndex attribute to alter the selected value. This property reflects which item in the list, indexed beginning at 0, is selected. The following code changes the selection to the second item:

```
document.getElementById('selectMenu').selectedIndex = 1;
```

As an added complication, select menus can be set to allow for multiple selections (**Figure 10.6**):

```
<select name="categories" id="categories" multiple>
```

When multiple options are selected, the value attribute will only represent the *first* selected value, as will selectedIndex. To retrieve *every* selected value, you must loop through all of the options and find the ones that were selected. To access every option, refer to the select menu's options property. The options property is an array, meaning it has a length attribute, usable in a for loop:

```
for (var i = 0, count = elem.options.length; i < count; i++) {
    // Use elem.options[i].
}
```

For each option, there are selected, value, and text properties. For example, to pull out every selected value, you would use this code:

```
var selected = [];
for (var i = 0, count = elem.options.length; i < count; i++) {
    if (elem.options[i].selected) {
        selected.push(elem.options[i].value);
    }
}
```

## VALIDATING SELECT MENUS

To validate that a select menu was changed by the user, just confirm that the element's selectedIndex property does not equal -1. This works whether the menu allows for only a single selection or for multiple selections. If the select menu allows for multiple selections, you can use the previous code to retrieve all the values, and then get the length of the selected array to see how many selections were made. If the select menu has an initial option used as a prompt (in which case it probably doesn't allow for multiple selections), you would want to make sure that the selectedIndex is not 0.

## CREATING DYNAMIC SELECT BOXES

A common, dynamic use of select menus that requires JavaScript are linked select menus, where the selection of an option in the first changes the possible options in the second. For example, the first might list car makes and the linked, car models.

**TIP:** The data for the second select menu could be fetched from the server using Ajax, thereby minimizing the amount of data that must first be transmitted to the client.

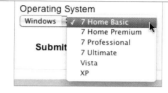

FIGURE 10.7 The select menu as it appears for users without JavaScript.

FIGURE 10.8 The options in the second menu will change based upon the value selected in the first.

Pulling this off requires a change event on the first select menu. In the event handler, change the options of the second menu based upon the selected value in the first. There are a couple of ways of doing just that. *In theory*, a simple solution is to assign the options as HTML to the select menu's innerHTML property. This *should* work because a select menu is an element that can contain HTML (specifically, option elements). Unfortunately, this has been a bug in Internet Explorer since the beginning of time (well, Web development time), and as it's still not working in IE9, a more involved approach is required, as you'll see in the following steps.

For the specific example, the user will select an operating system. In the default presentation, without use of JavaScript, the user will see one longer select menu, with the options grouped by general type (**Figure 10.7**). For users with JavaScript enabled, the menus will be progressively enhanced by spreading the options over two menus (**Figure 10.8**). The second menu's options will always be based upon the selection in the first menu.

The important initial HTML is:

```
<div><label for="os">Operating System</label><select name="os" id="os">
    <option>Choose</option>
    <optgroup label="Windows">
        <option value="7 Home Basic">7 Home Basic</option>
        <option value="7 Home Premium">7 Home Premium</option>
        <option value="7 Professional">7 Professional</option>
        <option value="7 Ultimate">7 Ultimate</option>
        <option value="Vista">Vista</option>
        <option value="XP">XP</option>
```

```
    </optgroup>
    <optgroup label="Mac OS X">
        <option value="10.7 Lion">10.7 Lion</option>
        <option value="10.6 Snow Leopard">10.7 Snow Leopard</option>
        <option value="10.5 Leopard">Leopard</option>
        <option value="10.4 Tiger">Tiger</option>
    </optgroup>
<select></div>
```

You can find this code in the os.html file in the downloadable code. This page also includes the os.js file, to be written in the following steps.

**To create linked select menus:**

1. Create a new JavaScript file in your text editor or IDE, to be named os.js.

2. Begin defining the updateMenu() function:

```
function updateMenu() {
    'use strict';
```

This function does not need to take any arguments as it's already known exactly what HTML elements will be used within this function.

3. Get references to the two select menus:

```
var os = document.getElementById('os');
var os2 = document.getElementById('os2');
```

The second menu will be dynamically created in the initializing function.

4. Create an empty variable:

```
var options = null;
```

This variable will be used to store the second menu's options, based upon the selection in the first menu. The variable is initially assigned a null value, so that it can be used as an indicator later in the script.

5. Empty the second menu:

```
while (os2.firstChild) {
    os2.removeChild(os2.firstChild);
}
```

Because the second menu could be used multiple times—for example, a user first selects *Windows*, then changes the first menu to *Mac OS X*, this function must first make sure there are no options in the second menu, prior to dynamically adding the appropriate ones. To clear out all the options, use a loop. The while loop will continue to execute so long as the element (os2) has a child element (and, if it has at least one child, then it has a firstChild). Within the while loop the first child is removed. Once the element is empty—has no children—the condition will be FALSE.

> **TIP:** This while loop construct can be used to clear the children from any element type.

6. Assign the proper options for the second menu based upon the selected value of the first:

```
if (os.value == 'Windows') {
    options = ['7 Home Basic', '7 Home Premium',
    →  '7 Professional', '7 Ultimate', 'Vista', 'XP'];
} else if (os.value == 'Mac OS X') {
    options = ['10.7 Lion', '10.6 Snow Leopard',
    →  '10.5 Leopard', '10.4 Tiger'];
}
```

The first condition checks if the value of the first select menu equals *Windows*. If this is TRUE, then options is assigned a new array of values. If the first menu's value equals *Mac OS X*, then options is assigned a different array of values.

7. If there are options, enable the second menu:

```
if (options) {
    os2.disabled = false;
```

If the options variable now has a TRUE value, then the second menu needs to be enabled (because it's initially disabled, as you'll soon see).

8. Add the new options to the menu:

```
for (var i = 0, count = options.length; i < count; i++) {
    var opt = document.createElement('option');
    opt.text = opt.value = options[i];
    os2.appendChild(opt);
}
```

To add each new option to the select menu, loop through the options array. Within the loop, a new element is created, of type *option*. Then the element's text and value properties are assigned the current array value (e.g., *7 Home Basic*). This one line is just a shortcut for:

```
opt.text = options[i];
opt.value = options[i];
```

This shortcut works because assignment works from right to left: The value on the far right—options[i]—will be assigned to the variable on its immediate left—opt.value, which will then be assigned to the variable on its immediate left—opt.text.

Finally, the new element is added to the menu.

9. Complete the options if-else if and the function:

```
    } else {
        os2.disabled = true;
    }
} // End of updateMenu() function.
```

If the user, for whatever reason, goes back and selects the first option from the first menu, which is *Choose*, then the second menu needs to be disabled and show no values. The values will have already been cleared out by this function, and since options was not assigned a new array of values if the user didn't select *Windows* or *Mac OS X*, the only thing left to do is disable the menu.

10. Begin defining the initializing function:

```
window.onload = function() {
    'use strict';
```

11. Clear out the first menu's options:

```
var os = document.getElementById('os');
while (os.firstChild) {
    os.removeChild(os.firstChild);
}
```

If JavaScript is enabled, then the original menu will be replaced with a more specific one, once the window has loaded. First, though, the original values have to be removed, using the code already explained.

12. Add the new options:

```
var options = ['Choose', 'Windows', 'Mac OS X'];
for (var i = 0, count = options.length; i < count; i++) {
    var opt = document.createElement('option');
    opt.text = opt.value = options[i];
    os.appendChild(opt);
}
```

This is the same code as that in the updateMenu() function, just using different values.

13. Add a change event handler to the menu:

```
os.onchange = updateMenu;
```

FIGURE 10.9 The options in the second menu when *Mac OS X* is selected in the first.

14. Create the second menu:

```
var os2 = document.createElement('select');
os2.id = 'os2';
os2.disabled = true;
os.parentNode.appendChild(os2);
```

To create the second menu, first an element of type *select* is created. It is then assigned a unique id value, and initially disabled. It should be placed next to the original select menu, so it's appended to that menu's parent.

15. Complete the function:

```
};
```

16. Save the file as os.js, in a js directory, and test it in your Web browser (**Figure 10.9**).

## CHECKBOXES

Checkboxes have not been given much attention in this book thus far. Unlike the text inputs and textareas, users do not enter data through a checkbox but just toggle its state: checked or not checked. The state of any checkbox can be found by looking at its checked property, which will be either true or false:

```
var which = document.getElementById('someCheckbox').checked;
```

You can programmatically check a box by assigning true (or the string *checked*) to that property:

```
which.checked = true;
```

You can fetch the checkbox's value through the value property:

```
if (which.checked) {
    var value = document.getElementById('someCheckbox').value;
}
```

One use of checkboxes and JavaScript is to have JavaScript take some action when a given checkbox is checked. For example, some sites will disable the submit button—prevent the submission of the form—until the user has actively indicated agreement to some terms (that, without a doubt, the user never read) by clicking a checkbox:

```javascript
window.onload = function() {
    var termsBox = document.getElementById('termsCheckbox');
    termsBox.onclick = function() {
        document.getElementById('submit').disabled = false;
    };
};
```

That's the quick and dirty version, which wouldn't re-disable the submit button if the user, for whatever reason, unchecked the box. If you want to be more formal, you would set a change event handler for the checkbox, and then enable or disable the submit button based upon the checkbox's checked value. You'll see an example of this at the end of the chapter.

A checkbox is also often used on e-commerce sites to provide a quick way of equating the shipping address with the billing address. That code would be along the lines of:

```javascript
window.onload = function() {
    document.getElementById('sameAsBilling').onclick = copyBilling;
};
function copyBilling() {
    document.getElementById('shippingStreet1').value =
    → document.getElementById('billingStreet1').value;
    // Repeat for all elements!
}
```

That code will work easily for the text inputs (although, again, you could more specifically watch for change events and then look at the checked property). For a select menu, you can use the following, so long as both menus have the same options in the same order:

Create Your Own Pizza
Toppings ☑ All/None

☑ Ham ☑ Mushrooms ☑ Onions ☑ Sausage ☑ Green Peppers

[ Submit ]

```
document.getElementById('shippingState').selectedIndex =
→  document.getElementById('billingState').selectedIndex;
```

One last common use of checkboxes (as far as something that needs to be scripted) is to have a checkbox act as a master to a number of other checkboxes (**Figure 10.10**). This has never been that hard, but by tapping into *CSS selectors* (see Chapter 9), it's even easier now. The relevant HTML is:

```
<input type="checkbox" name="toggle" id="toggle" value="toggle">
→  All/None

<p><input type="checkbox" name="ham" id="ham" value="ham">
→  Ham <input type="checkbox" name="mushrooms" id="mushrooms"
value="mushrooms"> Mushrooms <input type="checkbox" name="onions"
→  id="onions" value="onions"> Onions <input type="checkbox"
→  name="sausage" id="sausage" value="sausage"> Sausage
→  <input type="checkbox" name="greenPeppers" id="greenPeppers"
→  value="greenPeppers"> Green Peppers </p>
```

You can find this code in the `pizza.html` file in the downloadable code. This page also includes the `pizza.js` file, to be written in the following steps.

**To create a master checkbox:**

1. Create a new JavaScript file in your text editor or IDE, to be named `pizza.js`.

2. Begin defining the `toggleCheckboxes()` function:

   ```
   function toggleCheckboxes () {
        'use strict';
   ```

3. Get the master checkbox's checked value:

   ```
   var status = document.getElementById('toggle').checked;
   ```

   The value of all the other checkboxes will match that of the master, so this value is fetched and assigned to a variable for repeated use later.

4. Get all the checkboxes:

```
var boxes = document.querySelectorAll('input[type="checkbox"]');
```

Historically, finding all the checkboxes on a page could be cumbersome, as you couldn't use getElementById(), which requires unique id values (or, you'd have to know all the individual id values in advance and get each one separately). One solution is to use *CSS selectors*, introduced in Chapter 9. The specific selector, which comes from CSS 2.1, selects every input element whose type attribute equals *checkbox*. This selector, and the querySelectorAll() method, will work on all modern browsers. The alternative would be to invoke getElementsByTagName(), selecting all the inputs, and then check the each input's type within the loop (Step 5).

5. Loop through *almost every* checkbox and update its checked property:

```
for (var i = 1, count = boxes.length; i < count; i++) {
  boxes[i].checked = status;
} // End of FOR loop.
```

The querySelectorAll() method will return the matching elements in the order they appear in the browser. Since the master checkbox appears first, and there's no need to touch its checked property, the loop starts with the second checkbox, by initializing i at 1. Within the loop, the current checkbox's checked property is assigned the value of status.

6. Complete the function:

```
} // End of toggleCheckboxes() function.
```

7. Create the event handler once the window has loaded:

```
window.onload = function() {
    'use strict';
    document.getElementById('toggle').onchange =
      toggleCheckboxes;
};
```

8. Save the file as pizza.js, in a js directory, and test it in your Web browser.

# RADIO BUTTONS

Radio buttons are quite similar in functionality to checkboxes, but the user is restricted to only selecting one radio button in each group. As with checkboxes, the checked property has a Boolean value indicating if the given element is checked. Unlike checkboxes, you cannot just grab a reference to a specific radio button and look at its checked property, but rather you have to loop through all the radio buttons in a group to find the checked one (much as you would loop through every option in a select menu when multiple options might be checked). This is complicated because a group of radio buttons must have the same name attribute value—to allow only one to be checked—but id values, by definition, must be unique within a page. A solution is to use the getElementsByName() method, which is like getElementsByTagName():

```
<!-- HTML: -->
<input type="radio" name="gender" value="Male"> Male
  <input type="radio" name="gender" value="Female"> Female
// JavaScript:
var radios = document.getElementsByName('gender');
for (var i = 0, count = radios.length; i < count; i++) {
    // Do something with radios[i].
}
```

When a radio button is checked, you can use its value property to get the value of the particular user selection. To validate that the user did select at least one radio button, use a flag variable:

```
var radios = document.getElementsByName('gender');
var selected;
for (var i = 0, count = radios.length; i < count; i++) {
    if (radios[i].checked) {
        selected = radios[i].value;
        break;
    }
}
if (selected) { // OK!
```

By the end of that code, the `selected` variable will still be `null` if no radio button was selected, or have the value of the actual selection.

In terms of dynamic effects with radio buttons, much of what you'd do could parallel that done with checkboxes. The most interesting modern use of radio buttons, in my opinion, is as a star rating system as many sites have (**Figure 10.11**). Because users can only select one in a group of radio buttons, it makes a good choice for a rating system (you could also use a select menu). By adding some JavaScript and CSS, you can turn the boring buttons into visual stars, providing excellent feedback to the user as he or she rates whatever is being rated. And because the basic functionality is in the radio buttons, it degrades nicely across all browsers. There's too much CSS to make such an example useful for this book, but look online for tutorials if you're curious (the JavaScript itself shouldn't be too hard for you by this point).

**FIGURE 10.11** This star rating system (at Amazon) is created by applying CSS and JavaScript to radio buttons.

**FIGURE 10.12** A file input on IE, with a bit of styling.

## HANDLING FILE UPLOADS

The last form element type to discuss is the file input, which provides a way for the user to upload a file from his or her computer to the server (**Figure 10.12**). This discussion will be short, though, as using traditional HTML (as opposed to HTML5) offers little that can be done with file inputs. (More dynamic file-related functionality can be accomplished using a Flash or Java plug-in, or an iframe.)

What you *can* do in JavaScript is access the standard HTML properties of the file input, such as its class (i.e., `className`). You can also access the input's `value` property, which will be populated once the user has selected a file to be uploaded. However, as a security measure, the value will be something like `C:\fakepath\` *actualFileName*`.ext`. For example, when using Safari on a Mac, which doesn't even have a `C:\` directory, if the `somefile.txt` file is selected, then the input's value will be `C:\fakepath\somefile.txt`. This is a good thing, as it prevents JavaScript from learning anything about the user's file system. Still, you can use JavaScript to validate that a file was at least selected. You cannot set the value of a file input, which is illogical considering the lack of access to the file system.

File inputs are styled, and even behave, to a lesser degree, differently from one browser and operating system to the next. You can use CSS and JavaScript to standardize this, although that's not terribly interesting in JavaScript terms.

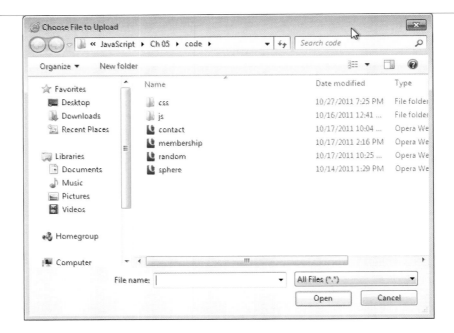

The events that the file input triggers—that you may want to watch for—are: change, focus, and blur. You would think that the file input would trigger a click event, but it doesn't. Oddly, you *can* call the click() method on the element:

```
document.getElementById('fileInput').click();
```

On all browsers but Firefox, doing this will open the file selection dialog, as if the user had clicked on the input manually (**Figure 10.13**). Firefox does not do this, and there's a strong argument that you shouldn't even attempt this unless it's clearly the user's intent to select a file on her or his computer—which, of course, the user can indicate by just clicking on the file input him or herself.

HTML5 makes it possible for a user to upload multiple files through a single file input and has other file uploading features. With some fancy JavaScript, you can replicate multiple-file capability by dynamically creating a new file input each time the user selects a file to be uploaded.

# REGULAR EXPRESSIONS

Regular expressions are an amazingly powerful (but tedious) tool available in most of today's programming languages and even in many applications. Think of regular expressions as an elaborate system of matching patterns. You first write the pattern and then use one of JavaScript's built-in functions to apply the pattern to a value (regular expressions are applied to strings, even if that means a string with a numeric value). Whereas a string function could see if the name *John* is in some text, a regular expression could just as easily find *John*, *Jon*, and *Jonathon*. Regular expressions are available in most languages and technologies: learn how to use them once and you can use them almost anywhere!

Because the regular expression syntax is so complex, while the functions that use them are simple, the focus over these pages will be on mastering the syntax in little bites. There are different kinds of regular expressions; JavaScript supports Perl-Compatible Regular Expressions (PCRE), the most common type.

## WHAT ARE REGULAR EXPRESSIONS?

Regular expressions are merely the application of a pattern to a value. In JavaScript, the pattern itself is represented as a RegExp object. Through different methods of the RegExp and String objects, you can apply that pattern to any value you need, whether it's user data or that coming from another server.

As an example of why a regular expression is useful, let's think about a valid email address, a surprisingly hard value to validate. There's no point in getting into the full technical details, but an email address is generally of the syntax: *name@domain*. Looking at that, three things are already known: there has to be exactly one @; it cannot be the first character; and it cannot be the last character. You could use the indexOf() method to confirm these three qualities, but email addresses are more demanding than that.

The *name* part can contain any letters, case-insensitive, plus numbers, a dash, and a period. But the name cannot contain a space and certain other characters. So validating the name part has just become much harder. The *domain* can also contain those same characters and *must* contain at least one period (as in *example.com*). Moreover, only 2 to 6 letters can come after the final period, from *.tr* for Turkey or *.museum*. In theory, you might be able to validate all of these conditions using the String methods, but the code would be both laborious and slow. A regular expression can validate all of those conditions in one pattern.

For a more pedestrian example, think about the format of the United States zip code: it can be either exactly five digits (*12345*) or five+four (*12345-6789*). Either is valid, and the same regular expression can immediately validate both.

## CREATING A REGULAR EXPRESSION

Unlike in other languages, a regular expression in JavaScript is a specific type, just like Number, String, or Date. As with most value types in JavaScript, there are two ways to create a regular expression value. The first, and preferred, approach is to create a literal regular expression, accomplished by placing the regular expression pattern between forward slashes:

```
var regexp = /pattern/;
```

Understand up front that the pattern is not to be quoted. For example, the pattern for matching a U.S. zip code is:

```
var zip = /^\d{5}(-\d{4})?$/;
```

That code may seem like madness to you (and this is a relatively easy regular expression), but you'll understand it shortly.

After the closing slash you can place flags that impact how the regular expression behaves. The easiest to understand is *i*, which makes the pattern case-insensitive. Thus, each of these three patterns match a letter, case-insensitive:

```
var letter = /[A-Za-z]/;
var letter = /[A-Z]/i;
var letter = /[a-z]/i;
```

The second way to create a regular expression is to create a new object of type RegExp. Just as you should never create a String by formally making a String object, you'll rarely want to create a RegExp object—and doing so brings up other syntactical issues, so you won't see that approach in this book.

## REGULAR EXPRESSION FUNCTIONS

Once you have a regular expression object, you can use it to compare that pattern to a string. There are four methods used for this purpose:

- test(), available to RegExp objects
- exec(), available to RegExp objects
- search(), available to String objects
- match(), available to String objects

Assuming you've created the regular expression as the variable r, and you're testing the string value s, these functions would be used like so:

```
r.test(s);
r.exec(s);
s.search(r);
s.match(r);
```

As you can see, it's largely a matter of either calling a RegExp method and providing the string as the argument, or calling a String method and providing the regular expression as the argument.

The test() method is perhaps the most commonly used method for testing regular expressions. It's also the fastest. This method returns a Boolean value indicating if a match was made or not.

The search() method of the String object can be used similarly, as it behaves like indexOf(). If part or all of the string matches the regular expression, search() returns the first indexed position where the match begins. It returns -1 if no match was made. Unlike indexOf(), you cannot indicate a position to start the search (i.e., the search will always start at the beginning).

The exec() method is slower than test() as it returns the match that was found (in more complicated regular expressions, there are multiple matches). If you only need to confirm if a match was made, which is normally the case with a regular expression for validation purposes, you should use test() instead of exec(). If no match was made, exec() returns null.

```
>> var zip = /^\d{5}(-\d{4})?$/;
>> zip.test('12345');
   true
>> zip.test('12345-6789');
   true
>> zip.test('1234b');
   false
```

The `match()` method is like `exec()` for basic usage, but differs when using *groupings*, a more advanced subject not being discussed here.

Also, the `split()` method of the `String` object can take a regular expression as the argument for the separator. This allows you to, say, split some text based upon HTML elements found within it. The `replace()` method of the `String` object can take a regular expression to find the data to be replaced.

For the purposes of the rest of this chapter, while learning regular expressions, I'd recommend that you use the console interface of your browser, as you'll see in several of the images. In that environment, you don't have to create actual variables, but doing so allows you to easily reuse the regular expressions or the strings (**Figure 10.14**).

## DEFINING SIMPLE PATTERNS

Using one of JavaScript's regular expression functions is easy; defining patterns to use is hard. There are lots of rules for creating a pattern. You can use these rules separately or in combination, making your pattern simple or complex. To start, then, you'll see what characters are used to define a simple pattern. I'll define patterns in **bold** and will indicate what the pattern matches in *italics*. You can test any of these using your browser's console window, as in Figure 10.14.

The first type of character you will use for defining patterns is a *literal*. A literal is a value that is written exactly as it is interpreted. For example, the pattern **a** will match the letter *a*, **ab** will match *ab*, and so forth. Therefore, assuming a case-insensitive search is performed, **rom** will match any of the following strings, since they all contain *rom*:

- CD-ROM

- Rommel crossed the desert.

- I'm writing a bildungsroman.

Along with literals, your patterns will use *meta-characters*. These are special symbols that have a meaning beyond their literal value (**Table 10.1**). While **a** simply means *a*, the period (.) will match any single character except for a newline (. matches *a*, *b*, *c*, the underscore, a space, etc., just not \n). To match any meta-character, you will need to escape it, much as you escape a quotation mark to print it. Hence **\.** will match the period itself. So **1.99** matches *1.99* or *1B99* or *1299* (a 1 followed by any character followed by 99) but **1\.99** only matches *1.99*.

**TABLE 10.1** Meta-Characters

| CHARACTER | MEANING |
| --- | --- |
| \ | Escape character |
| ^ | Indicates the beginning of a string |
| $ | Indicates the end of a string |
| . | Any single character except newline |
| \| | Alternatives (or) |
| [ | Start of a class |
| ] | End of a class |
| ( | Start of a subpattern |
| ) | End of a subpattern |
| { | Start of a quantifier |
| } | End of a quantifier |

Two meta-characters specify where certain characters must be found. There is the caret (^), which marks the beginning of a string. There is also the dollar sign ($), which marks the conclusion of a string. Accordingly, **^a** will match any string beginning with an *a*, while **a$** will correspond to any string ending with an *a*. Therefore, **^a$** will only match *a* (a string that both begins and ends with *a*), equivalent to:

```
if (str == 'a') {
```

These two meta-characters—the caret and the dollar sign—are crucial to validation, as validation normally requires checking the value of an entire string, not just the presence of one string in another. For example, using an email- matching pattern without those two characters will match any string *containing* an email address. Using an email-matching pattern that begins with a caret and ends with a dollar sign will match a string that contains *only* a valid email address.

Regular expressions also make use of the pipe (|) as the equivalent of *or*: **a|b** will match strings containing either *a* or *b*. (Using the pipe within patterns is called *alternation* or *branching*.) So **yes|no** accepts either of those two words in their entirety (the alternation is *not* just between the two letters surrounding it: *s* and *n*).

FIGURE 10.15 Three different
simple regular expressions,
tested in the browser.

```
>> var regexp = /cat/;
>> regexp.test('catastrophe');
   true
>> regexp.test('Cat');
   false
>> var regexp = /^cat/;
>> regexp.test('my cat left');
   false
>> var regexp = /col(o|ou)r/;
>> regexp.test('I like the color blue.');
   true
```

Once you comprehend the basic symbols, then you can begin to use parentheses to group characters into more involved patterns. Grouping works as you might expect: **(abc)** will match *abc*, **(trout)** will match *trout*. Think of parentheses as being used to establish a new literal of a larger size. Because of precedence rules in Perl-Compatible Regular Expressions, **yes|no** and **(yes)|(no)** are equivalent. But **(even|heavy\-) handed** will match either *evenhanded* or *heavy-handed*.

**To use simple patterns:**

1. Load a console in your Web browser, if it is not already.

2. Check if a string contains the letters *cat*.

   To do so, use the literal **cat** as the pattern and any number of strings as the subject. Any of the following would be a match: *catalog, catastrophe, my cat left*, etc. For the time being, use all lowercase letters, as **cat** will not match *Cat*.

   Remember to use delimiters around the pattern as well (see the figures).

3. Check if a string starts with *cat*.

   To have a pattern apply to the start of a string, use the caret as the first character (**^cat**). The sentence *my cat left* will not be a match now.

4. Check if a string contains the word *color* or *colour* (**Figure 10.15**).

   The pattern to look for the American or British spelling of this word is **col(o|ou)r**. The first three letters—*col*—must be present. This needs to be followed by either an *o* or *ou*. Finally, an *r* is required.

**TIP:** If you are looking to match an exact string, without any flexibility, you should always use the indexOf() method, or an equality comparison, which are much faster.

## USING QUANTIFIERS

You've just seen and practiced with a couple of the meta-characters, the most important of which are the caret and the dollar sign. Next, there are three meta-characters that allow for multiple occurrences: **a*** will match zero or more *a*'s (no *a*'s, *a*, *aa*, *aaa*, etc.); **a+** matches one or more *a*'s (*a*, *aa*, *aaa*, etc., but there must be at least one); and **a?** will match up to one *a* (*a* or no *a*'s match). These meta-characters all act as quantifiers in your patterns, as do the curly braces. **Table 10.2** lists all of the quantifiers.

**TABLE 10.2** Quantifiers

| CHARACTER | MEANING |
|---|---|
| ? | 0 or 1 |
| * | 0 or more |
| + | 1 or more |
| {x} | Exactly x occurrences |
| {x,y} | Between x and y (inclusive) |
| {x,} | At least x occurrences |

To match a certain quantity of a thing, put the quantity between curly braces ({}), stating a specific number, just a minimum, or both a minimum and a maximum. Thus, **a{3}** will match *aaa*; **a{3,}** will match *aaa*, *aaaa*, etc. (three or more *a*'s); and **a{3,5}** will match just *aaa*, *aaaa*, and *aaaaa* (between three and five). When using curly braces to specify a number of characters, you must always include the minimum number. The maximum is optional: **a{3}** and **a{3,}** are acceptable, but **a{,3}** is not.

Note that quantifiers apply to the thing that came before it, so **a?** matches zero or one *a*'s, **ab?** matches an *a* followed by zero or one *b*'s, but **(ab)?** matches zero or one *ab*'s. Therefore, to match *color* or *colour*, you could also use **colou?r** as the pattern.

```
>> var regexp = /c.+t/;
>> regexp.test('coefficient');
   true
>> regexp.test('doctor');
   false
>> var regexp = /^cats?$/;
>> regexp.test('cat');
   true
>> regexp.test('cats');
   true
>> regexp.test('I like cats.');
   false
```

**FIGURE 10.16** Two more complicated and flexible regular expressions.

**To use simple patterns:**

1.  Load a console in your Web browser, if it is not already.

2.  Check if a string contains the letters *c* and *t*, with one or more letters in between.

    To do so, use **c.+t** as the pattern and any number of strings as the subject. Remember that the period matches any character (except for the newline). Each of the following would be a match: *cat*, *count*, *coefficient*, etc. The word *doctor* would not match, as there are no letters between the *c* and the *t* (although *doctor* would match **c.\*t**).

3.  Check if a string matches either *cat* or *cats* (**Figure 10.16**).

    To start, if you want to make an exact match, use both the caret and the dollar sign. Then you'd have the literal text *cat*, followed by an *s*, followed by a question mark (representing 0 or 1 *s*'s). The final pattern—**^cats?$**— matches *cat* or *cats* but not *my cat left* or *I like cats*.

4.  Check if a string ends with *.33*, *.333*, or *.3333*.

    To find a period, escape it with a backslash: **\.**. To find a three, use a literal **3**. To find a range of 3's, use the curly braces (**{}**). Putting this together, the pattern is **\.3{2,4}**. Because the string should end with this (nothing else can follow), conclude the pattern with a dollar sign: **\.3{2,4}$**.

    Admittedly, this is kind of a stupid example (not sure when you'd need to do exactly this), but it does demonstrate several things. This pattern will match lots of things—*12.333*, *varmit.3333*, *.33*, look *.33*—but not *12.3* or *12.334*.

5.  Match a five-digit number.

    A number can be any one of the numbers 0 through 9, so the heart of the pattern is **(0|1|2|3|4|5|6|7|8|9)**. Plainly said, this means: a number is a 0 or a 1 or a 2 or a 3.... To make it a five-digit number, follow this with a quantifier: **(0|1|2|3|4|5|6|7|8|9){5}**. Finally, to match this exactly (as opposed to matching a five-digit number within a string), use the caret and the dollar sign: **^(0|1|2|3|4|5|6|7|8|9){5}$**.

    This, of course, is one way to match a United States zip code as five digits.

## LEARNING MORE ABOUT REGULAR EXPRESSIONS

Because the rules for creating regular expressions are so complex, I've done my best to simplify the topic here, with an emphasis on the most important bits. When just using regular expressions for form validation, this information will suffice, providing better security and data integrity without making your brain hurt (hopefully). In time, there are other things to learn when it comes to regular expressions. Just the patterns themselves can be expanded, using *back references* and *look-aheads* and *look-behinds* and all sorts of crazy things. You can also, in the JavaScript code, find specific matches. For example, a regular expression can match a zip code and simultaneously break that code into its five digits and its "plus four." You can also use regular expressions in replacements: swapping out a matched pattern with some other text. That idea is useful, for example, to dynamically turn valid URLs into active HTML links.

Once you feel comfortable with the basics of regular expressions, you can start looking into these other topics.

## USING CHARACTER CLASSES

As the last example demonstrated, relying solely upon literals in a pattern can be tiresome. Having to write out all those digits to match any number is silly. Imagine if you wanted to match any four-letter word: ^(a|b|c|d...){4}$ (and that doesn't even take into account uppercase letters)! To make these common references easier, you can use *character classes*.

Classes are created by placing characters within square brackets ([]). For example, you can match any one vowel with [aeiou]. This is equivalent to (a|e|i|o|u). Or you can use the hyphen to indicate a range of characters: [a-z] is any single lowercase letter and [A-Z] is any uppercase, [A-Za-z] is any letter in general, and [0-9] matches any digit. As an example, [a-z]{3} would match *abc*, *def*, *oiw*, etc.

Within classes, most of the meta-characters are treated literally, except for four. The backslash is still the escape, but the caret (^) is a negation operator when used as the first character in the class. So [^aeiou] will match any non-vowel. The only other meta-character within a class is the dash, which indicates a range. (If the dash is used as the last character in a class, it's a literal dash.) And, of course, the closing bracket (]) still has meaning as the terminator of the class.

Regular expressions are amazing and powerful, but they are expensive in terms of code execution. To minimize the impact on your script's performance, only use a regular expression if you absolutely must. There are many times where a string method will do the trick, or where simply checking the length of a string is good enough for client-side validation.

When you do use regular expressions, assign the pattern to a variable (i.e., create a regular expression object) when that regular expression might be tested multiple times by the same script. This way the browser can optimize the performance.

Smart regular expression patterns are also written to "fail fast." This is to say that invalid values will be ruled out quickly, such as a URL not beginning with *http*.

Finally, alternation (using the pipe) can adversely affect performance, too. If you can, use a character class instead. When you do have to use alternation, try to keep it to as few characters as possible, so that JavaScript does not have to consider quite so many possibilities when analyzing the validity of a string.

Naturally, a class can have both ranges and literal characters. A person's first name, which can contain letters, spaces, apostrophes, and periods, could be represented by [A-z '\.] The period doesn't need to be escaped within the class, as it loses its meta-meaning there, but I generally err on the side of escaping potentially problematic characters just to be safe.

Along with creating your own classes, there are six predefined classes that have their own shortcuts (**Table 10.3**). The digit and space classes are easy to understand. The *word* character class doesn't mean "word" in the language sense but rather as in a string unbroken by spaces or punctuation. You should be aware that the word class is only meaningful when using non-accented Latin characters (A through Z). Other languages, which don't use or aren't limited to that letter range, can have "words" using other character combinations.

**TABLE 10.3** Character Classes

| CLASS | SHORTCUT | MEANING |
|---|---|---|
| [0-9] | \d | Any digit |
| [\f\r\t\n\v ] | \s | Any white space |
| [A-Za-z0-9_] | \w | Any word character |
| [^0-9] | \D | Not a digit |
| [^\f\r\t\n\v ] | \S | Not white space |
| [^A-Za-z0-9_] | \W | Not a word character |

Using this information, the five-digit number (aka, zip code) pattern could more easily be written as **^[0-9]{5}$** or **^\d{5}$**. As another example, **can\s?not** will match both *can not* and *cannot* (the word *can*, followed by zero or one space characters, followed by *not*).

**To use character classes:**

1. Load a console in your Web browser, if it is not already.

2. Check if a string is formatted as a valid United States zip code (see Figure 10.14). A United States zip code always starts with five digits (**^\d{5}**). But a valid zip code could also have a dash followed by another four digits (**-\d{4}$**). To make this last part optional, use the question mark (the 0 or 1 quantifier). This complete pattern is then **^(\d{5})(-\d{4})?$**. To make it all clearer, the first part of the pattern (matching the five digits) is also grouped in parentheses, although this isn't required in this case.

3. Check if a string contains no spaces.

    The **\S** character class shortcut will match non-white space characters. To make sure that the entire string contains no spaces, use the caret and the dollar sign: **^\S$**. If you don't use those, then all the pattern is confirming is that the subject contains at least one non-space character.

FIGURE 10.17 This more
strict pattern is a pretty good,
although not perfect, validation tool for an email address.

```
>> var regexp = /^[\w.-]+@[\w.-]+\.[A-Za-z]{2,6}$/
>> regexp.test('I like cats.');
   false
>> regexp.test('email@example.com');
   true
>> regexp.test('some-user9@example.co.uk');
   true
```

4. Validate an email address (**Figure 10.17**).

   The pattern **^[\w.-]+@[\w.-]+\.[A-Za-z]{2,6}$** provides for reasonably good email validation. It's wrapped in the caret and the dollar sign, so the string must be a valid email address and nothing more. An email address starts with letters, numbers, and the underscore (represented by **\w**), plus a period (.) and a dash. This first block will match *larryullman*, *larry77*, *larry.ullman*, *larry-ullman*, and so on. Next, all email addresses include one and only one @. After that, there can be any number of letters, numbers, periods, and dashes. This is the domain name: *larryullman*, *smith-jones*, *amazon. co* (as in *amazon.co.uk*), etc. Finally, all email addresses conclude with one period and between two and six letters. This accounts for *.com*, *.edu*, *.info*, *.travel*, etc. This email address validation pattern is pretty good, although not perfect. It will allow some invalid addresses to pass through (like ones starting with a period or containing multiple periods together). However, a 100 percent foolproof validation pattern is ridiculously long, and frequently using regular expressions is really a matter of trying to exclude the bulk of invalid entries without inadvertently excluding any valid ones.

## USING **BOUNDARIES**

*Boundaries* are shortcuts for helping to find, um, boundaries. In a way, you've already seen this: using the caret and the dollar sign to match the beginning or end of a value. But what if you wanted to match boundaries within a value?

The clearest boundary is between a word and a non-word. A "word" in this case is not *cat*, *month*, or *zeitgeist*, but in the \w shortcut sense: the letters A through Z (both upper- and lowercase), plus the numbers 0 through 9, and the underscore. To use words as boundaries, there's the \b shortcut. To use non-word characters as boundaries, there's \B. So the pattern \bfor\b matches *they've come for you* but doesn't match *force* or *forebode*. Therefore \bfor\B would match *force* but not *they've come for you* or *informal*.

# PUTTING IT ALL **TOGETHER**

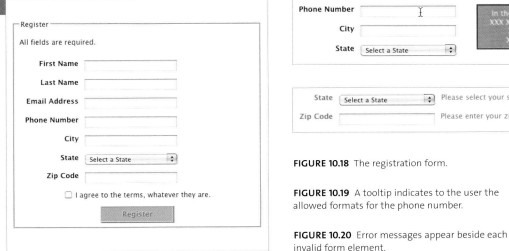

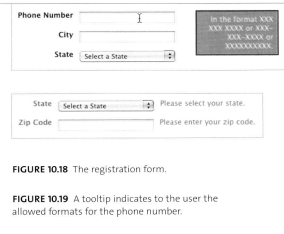

**FIGURE 10.18** The registration form.

**FIGURE 10.19** A tooltip indicates to the user the allowed formats for the phone number.

**FIGURE 10.20** Error messages appear beside each invalid form element.

A fitting conclusion to this chapter is to take all the form information, the ability to create error messages, and the newfound knowledge of regular expressions to create one complete example. The specific example will be a registration page (**Figure 10.18**). JavaScript will then be layered on top to:

- Disable the submit button until the user agrees to the terms (by checking that box).

- Provide a tooltip for the format of the phone number (**Figure 10.19**).

- Validate the form, partially using regular expressions.

- Report errors inline (**Figure 10.20**).

- Just a snippet of the HTML form is:

```
<div class="two"><label for="firstName">First Name
→ </label><input type="text" name="firstName" id="firstName"
→ required></div>

<div class="two"><label for="lastName">Last Name</label>
→ <input type="text" name="lastName" id="lastName"
→ required></div>

<div class="two"><label for="email">Email Address
→ </label><input type="email" name="email" id="email"
→ required></div>
```

```
<div class="two"><label for="phone">Phone Number
 →  <span class="tooltip">In the format XXX XXX XXXX or
 →  XXX-XXX-XXXX or XXXXXXXXXX.</span></label>
 →  <input type="text" name="phone" id="phone" required></div>
<div class="two"><label for="city">City</label>
 →  <input type="text" name="city" id="city" required></div>
<div class="two"><label for="state">State</label>
 →  <select name="state" id="state">
    <option value="">Select a State</option>
    <option value="AL">Alabama</option>
```

You can download the complete HTML page, along with the requisite CSS, from www.LarryUllman.com.

For the JavaScript, the example is going to use the utilities.js script from Chapter 8 to help with the event listener registration. Within it, three function definitions will be added: enableTooltips(), showTooltip(), and hideTooltip(). You can see the utilities.js script in the downloads (within the Ch10/js folder) for specifics, if you don't know how to define those yourself. You could also define the addErrorMessage() and removeErrorMessage() functions there, too. (And, at that point, those functions could be written to use the U.$() shortcut.)

Therefore, the HTML page needs to include these three JavaScript files, in this order:

- utilites.js

- errorMessages.js

- register.js

The last one will be written in the following steps.

**To create a fully formed form:**

1. Create a new JavaScript file in your text editor or IDE, to be named register.js.

2. Begin defining the validateForm() function:

```
function validateForm(e) {
    'use strict';
    if (typeof e == 'undefined') e = window.event;
```

The function does need to take the event as an argument, in order to prevent the default browser behavior—the submission of the form to the server—should an error occur.

3. Get the form element references:

```
var firstName = U.$('firstName');
var lastName = U.$('lastName');
var email = U.$('email');
var phone = U.$('phone');
var city = U.$('city');
var state = U.$('state');
var zip = U.$('zip');
var terms = U.$('terms');
```

I'm getting references to every form element, although they won't all be validated within this function (to save space in the book). Instead of using document.getElementById(), U.$() is being used, which is a shortcut defined in the utilities.js script. For each, the variable's value is the element itself, not just its value. A couple of the elements will be validated based on a property other than value and it's best to be consistent.

4. Create a flag variable:

```
var error = false;
```

This variable will be used to confirm whether or not the form was completed properly. It's initially set to false, indicating that no errors have occurred.

5. Validate the first name:

```
if (/^[A-Z \.\-']{2,20}$/i.test(firstName.value)) {
    removeErrorMessage('firstName');
} else {
    addErrorMessage('firstName', 'Please enter your first
  → name.');
    error = true;
}
```

The first name is being validated using a regular expression. The specific expression allows for any letter, case-insensitive, plus a space, a period, and a hyphen. The value must be between 2 and 20 characters long. If the result returned by test() is true, this condition will be TRUE, and the removeErrorMessage() function is called in case an error was previously added. If the value does not pass the test, then the addErrorMessage() function is called and the error variable is assigned the value true.

6. Validate the email address:

```
if (/^[\w.-]+@[\w.-]+\.[A-Za-z]{2,6}$/.test(email.value)) {
    removeErrorMessage('email');
} else {
    addErrorMessage('email', 'Please enter your email
 ⇥   address.');
    error = true;
}
```

The email address pattern has already been explained, and while not flawless, is sufficiently strict.

7. Validate the phone number:

```
if (/\d{3}[ \-\.]?\d{3}[ \-\.]?\d{4}/.test(phone.value)) {
    removeErrorMessage('phone');
} else {
    addErrorMessage('phone', 'Please enter your phone
 ⇥   number.');
    error = true;
}
```

The phone number pattern requires three digits, three digits, and then four digits. To allow for some flexibility, between those groupings one space, hyphen, or period is allowed, but is not required.

**8.** Validate the state:

```
if (state.selectedIndex != 0) {
    removeErrorMessage('state');
} else {
    addErrorMessage('state', 'Please select your state.');
    error = true;
}
```

The state element is a select menu, so it can be validated by checking that its selectedIndex property is not 0 (i.e., an option other than the first one has been selected).

**9.** Validate the zip code:

```
if (/^\d{5}(-\d{4})?$/.test(zip.value)) {
    removeErrorMessage('zip');
} else {
    addErrorMessage('zip', 'Please enter your zip code.');
    error = true;
}
```

This pattern was also explained earlier.

**10.** If an error occurred, prevent the default behavior:

```
if (error) {
    if (e.preventDefault) {
        e.preventDefault();
    } else {
        e.returnValue = false;
    }
    return false;
}
```

**11.** Define the toggleSubmit() function:

```
function toggleSubmit() {
    'use strict';
    var submit = U.$('submit');
    if (U.$('terms').checked) {
        submit.disabled = false;
    } else {
        submit.disabled = true;
    }
} // End of toggleSubmit() function.
```

This is the more proper implementation of code explained earlier. If the terms checked value is true, then the submit button is enabled. Otherwise, the submit button is disabled.

**12.** Establish the initial functionality:

```
window.onload = function() {
    'use strict';
    U.addEvent(U.$('theForm'), 'submit', validateForm);
    U.$('submit').disabled = true;
    U.addEvent(U.$('terms'), 'change', toggleSubmit);
    U.enableTooltips('phone');
};
```

Several things need to be done when the window has loaded. First, an event handler has to be registered on the form's submission. Second, the submit button should be initially disabled. Third, a change event handler has to be registered on the terms checkbox (which will enable the submit button). And, fourth, the tooltips need to be activated on the phone number.

**13.** Save the file as register.js, in a js directory, and test it in your Web browser.

# REVIEW AND PURSUE

If you have any problems with these sections, either in answering the questions or pursuing your own endeavors, turn to the book's supporting forum (www.LarryUllman.com/forums/).

## REVIEW

- What event should you almost always use to handle form submissions and why?

- Why should you always use a submit button (or image)?

- What property do you use to fetch or set the value of a text input or textarea? On what other elements does that same property work for retrieving and setting values?

- How do you create linked select menus?

- How do you confirm that a checkbox was checked?

- What code is required to find out which radio button was checked?

- What JavaScript functions can be used to test a regular expression?

- How do you match a literal character or string of characters?

- What are meta-characters? How do you escape a meta-character?

- What meta-character do you use to bind a pattern to the beginning of a string? To the end?

- How do you create subpatterns (aka groupings)?

- What are the quantifiers? How do you require 0 or 1 of a character or string? 0 or more? 1 or more? Precisely X occurrences? A range of occurrences? A minimum of occurrences?

- What are character classes?

- What meta-characters still have meaning within character classes?

- What shortcut represents the "any digit" character class? The "any white space" class? "Any word"? What shortcuts represent the opposite of these?

## PURSUE

- Update an older example in the book to use the errorMessages.js script.

- Update errorMessages.js so that it allows for the form element's label to have more than one class. HINT: Use concatenation to add the *error* class, and remove the error class by slicing off the text after the last space in the className value (because multiple classes are represented as class="someClass error").

- Change the addTooltipHandlers() function so that it also applies appropriate event listeners to the form's label. HINT: Start by changing the function so that it takes the element's id value as its argument, then either give each label an id value of id + 'Label', or use the previousSibling reference, as in the showTooltip() and hideTooltip() functions.

- Create some code for disabling the submit button while simultaneously implementing some of the suggested additions: changing the button's class or text, adding a message button beside it, or creating a modal window.

- Change the addTooltipHandlers() function so that it uses addEventListener(), attachEvent(), and the corollary remove event functions instead of the DOM Level 0 approach.

- Modify os.js so that one function actually updates the menu. The function would need the menu's id as one argument, and the array of options as the second. The function would then clear out all the existing options and add the new ones. The initializing and updateMenu() functions could then both call this new function, providing those two values.

- Create another pair of linked select menus. Or, for a bigger challenge, create three linked menus.

- Fully implement the example where clicking a checkbox copies the information from one form to another form.

- Research how you can use CSS and JavaScript to customize the look, and to a lesser degree, the behavior, of file inputs.

- Apply regular expressions to some of the examples from previous chapters.

- Search online for a PCRE "cheat sheet" (JavaScript or otherwise) that lists all the meaningful characters and classes. Print out the cheat sheet and keep it beside your computer.

- Practice, practice, practice with regular expressions!

- Complete the `register.js` `validateForm()` function to validate the other form elements.

## WRAPPING **UP**

Even though forms have been used ever since Chapter 2, there was still plenty to be covered in this chapter. You learned a few more things about specific form elements, and picked up lots of useful, real-world code...

- Creating inline error messages

- Unobtrusive tooltips

- Manipulating the submit button

- Scripting linked select menus

- Making a master checkbox

These examples involved a combination of the material covered to this point: event handling, DOM manipulation, interacting with CSS, and more.

The chapter also covered regular expressions, a more advanced but highly useful topic. At the end of the chapter, regular expressions, and the other topics, were all put together to professionally and reliably validate a registration form. Hopefully, by now you should feel fairly comfortable with using modern JavaScript for many of today's uses.

The next two chapters round out the coverage of what I'd call standard JavaScript. Next, Chapter 11 takes things in a slightly different direction: interacting with the server using Ajax.

# 11

# AJAX

As suggested in Chapter 1, (Re-)Introducing JavaScript, Ajax is one of the most important developments in the history of both JavaScript and Web development. Simply put, Ajax is the process of having JavaScript in the browser make a behind-the-scenes request of the server, in order to retrieve additional information or cause a server-side reaction. For example, the request may retrieve a set of data to be displayed, see if a username is available, or update a record in the database. While this is happening, the user could be unaware of the transaction, still using the page that was originally loaded. Grasping the concept, and benefits, of Ajax can sometimes be hard, and Ajax creates additional debugging challenges, but mastering Ajax pays off, and in this chapter you'll learn everything you need to know, while simultaneously picking up plenty of usable code.

# AJAX BASICS

With just a few lines of the right code, Ajax is not difficult to implement, so the chapter begins with the fundamentals. After this initial section, you'll turn to the server side of things, and then practice Ajax with a multitude of real-world examples.

## UNDERSTANDING AJAX

Chapter 1 provided a detailed description of what Ajax is. If you're still unsure, then return to that chapter, or search online for some live demos (undoubtedly, you've witnessed dozens, if not hundreds, of Ajax-enabled sites by now, although you may not have known it).

In terms of actual JavaScript code, performing an Ajax request begins with these three steps:

- Creating an Ajax object
- Making the request
- Handling the server response

The next few pages will cover these basics, and then you'll learn how to:

- Include data with the request
- Debug Ajax transactions
- Handle different types of server responses

There also needs to be the actual server-side resource that JavaScript will communicate with. As PHP is my preferred server-side language, you'll see many PHP-based examples, especially toward the end of the chapter. But for the sake of demonstrating the initial ideas, a simple text file on the server can represent the server-side resource, and its contents will end up being the server response.

## CREATING AN AJAX OBJECT

The Ajax process begins with an object through which the communications can occur. I'll refer to this as an "Ajax" object, although you'll also see it called an "XHR" object, short for *XML HTTP Request*, or just some variation on those key words. These terms reflect that JavaScript is being used to make a request of another resource using the HyperText Transfer Protocol (HTTP). Originally, the returned data was in eXtensible Markup Language (XML) format, although that's much less often the case today.

## AJAX AND PROGRESSIVE ENHANCEMENT

Like with anything accomplished via JavaScript, you have to be mindful of the possibility that some users might not have JavaScript enabled. With Ajax, which requires JavaScript to both perform the request and update the page with the results, creating a non-JavaScript version is actually fairly easy if you work backward. I won't waste precious book space demonstrating these non-JavaScript alternatives in this chapter, but let's take a quick look at a couple of logical examples so you will know how (Chapter 15, PHP and JavaScript Together, will implement much of this).

One broad use of Ajax is to fetch data from the server and update the page with that information. The fallback option in such a situation would be to just create another HTML page that shows the data without using JavaScript. The first page would link to that other page, and JavaScript could progressively enhance the link by making it trigger the Ajax call instead of taking the browser to that other page.

The other broad use of Ajax is to send data to the server, for example, from a contact form or during a registration script. In these cases, you would have the form's submission continue to the server-side script when Ajax is not possible, and use Ajax to interrupt that submission when JavaScript is enabled.

You should also remember that search engines cannot see dynamic content created by JavaScript. If the content being fetched by Ajax needs to be indexed to appear in search results, the content must also be available in a non-dynamic way, such as on a linked secondary page, as already explained.

Ajax does require that the user be online, although with HTML5's ability to use local storage, this can be overcome (assuming that HTML5 is an option). And, as explained in Chapter 9, JavaScript and the Browser, unless extra steps are taken, dynamic changes made by JavaScript cannot be bookmarked, nor are those changes reflected in the browser's history. At the end of the chapter, I discuss the solution to these problems.

Every browser has defined an XMLHttpRequest object with the required functionality, but as you've probably come to expect by now, the particulars of creating an instance of that object varies just slightly from browser to browser.

To create an Ajax object reliably for all browsers, use this code:

```
var ajax;
if (window.XMLHttpRequest) {
    ajax = new XMLHttpRequest();
} else if (window.ActiveXObject) { // Older IE.
    ajax = new ActiveXObject('MSXML2.XMLHTTP.3.0');
}
```

The XMLHttpRequest object exists in all non-IE browsers, and in Internet Explorer since version 7. Older versions of IE must create a new ActiveXObject, providing *MSXML2.XMLHTTP.3.0* as the argument. This code will work on IE as old as version 5 (you'll see slight variations on this value in various bits of code and other resources). The good news is that once you've created the Ajax object, regardless of how, you can use it in exactly the same way.

Because this is code you'll use many times over, it makes sense to put it into its own function, defined in a separate file, to be named ajax.js:

```
function getXMLHttpRequestObject() {
    var ajax = null;
    if (window.XMLHttpRequest) {
        ajax = new XMLHttpRequest();
    } else if (window.ActiveXObject) { // Older IE.
        ajax = new ActiveXObject('MSXML2.XMLHTTP.3.0');
    }
    return ajax;
}
```

All of the examples in the rest of this chapter would then include this script. You would use the function like so:

```
var ajax = getXMLHttpRequestObject();
```

Because `ajax` will have a `null` value if an `XMLHttpRequest` object could not be assigned to it, if you want to be extra careful, your code could then verify that the Ajax object has a non-FALSE value before attempting to use it:

```
if (ajax) {  // Use it!
```

## IDENTIFYING A RESULT HANDLER

Once you have an Ajax object, the next step you should take is to identify the result handler for that object. This is the function that will be called during the Ajax transaction. To associate the function with the Ajax call, assign the function to the object's onreadystatechange property:

```
ajax.onreadystatechange = handleStateChange;
```

You can also use an anonymous function here, and you'll see both approaches in this chapter.

## MAKING A REQUEST

With the Ajax object created and the response handling function identified, it's time to perform the actual request. To make an Ajax request, you first call the open() method of the object, providing the type of request to make as the first argument, the URL of the server resource as the second, and the value `true` as the third:

```
ajax.open('GET', 'http://www.example.com/page.php', true);
```

The most common request types are GET and POST. GET requests are the standard method for requesting any HTML page; it's the type of request a browser makes when you click on a link. Philosophically, *GET requests are best used to fetch data*. POST requests are the standard method for form submissions (aside from search engine forms, which normally use GET). Philosophically, *POST requests are intended to cause a server change or reaction*. Put another way, GET is for requests that should be common and repeatable, even bookmarkable; POST is for unique requests, not intended to be repeated, such as the updating of a specific database record or the submission of a contact form (in either case, the general concept will be repeated, but the specifics would differ). Note that the method type should be in all capital letters.

The URL can be either absolute or relative (see Chapter 2, JavaScript in Action), but must be accurate. If you're running the page http://www.example.com/page.html, then the values *http://www.example.com/page.php* or just *page.php* will both work, assuming that page.php and page.html are within the same directory.

There are two common problems and points of confusion when it comes to the URL. The first involves the *same-domain policy*, explained in Chapter 9. As a security measure, JavaScript in the browser is prevented from making requests of resources on another domain. This means that http://www.example.com/page.html cannot make a request of http://shop.example.com/page.php or http://www.LarryUllman.com/page.php. At the end of the chapter, I discuss different ways to circumvent this restriction, when appropriate.

The second issue is that Ajax requests must be made through a server in order to work. This means that the HTML page with the JavaScript in it must also be loaded through a URL (i.e., http://*something*). If your request is returning a 0 status code (more on status codes later), or is returning PHP code instead of data, you probably are not making the request through a URL. If you don't have a live Web site on which you can test the examples in this chapter, then I would recommend installing an all-in-one package such as XAMPP for Windows (www.apachefriends.org) or MAMP for Mac OS X (www.mamp.info) in order to use your desktop computer as a server.

The third argument to the open() method indicates whether the request should be made *asynchronously* or *synchronously*. The default is true, which correlates to asynchronously, but you should explicitly provide it anyway. During asynchronous requests, other JavaScript code can be executed, such as that handling other events, while the JavaScript awaits the server response. In very rare circumstances you will want to perform a synchronous request, as doing so prevents JavaScript from doing anything else while the request is being made and processed, including handling user-based events (you'll see one practical example of a synchronous request in this chapter). If you were to perform a synchronous request, you wouldn't create a function to handle readyState changes, as the script waits for the server response before doing anything else anyway.

The open() method takes optional fourth and fifth arguments, representing a username and password, respectively. Both would be necessary if the resource is protected by HTTP authentication. However, to use these arguments, you'd need access to those values in your JavaScript code. The only secure way to do that would be to have the user input those values so they are not hardcoded in the page's source.

The final step is to actually send the request, by calling the send() method:

```
ajax.send(null);
```

For the time being, use the value null as the only argument to this method, which represents the data to be included in the request.

Once a request has been sent, but before it has been completed, you can cancel it by invoking the object's abort() method. You could set a timer (see Chapter 9) that aborts the request if it takes too long:

```
ajax.open('GET', 'http://www.example.com/page.php', true);
var ajaxAbortTimer = setTimeout(function() {
    if (ajax) {
        ajax.abort();
        ajax = null;
    }
}, 5000); // Five seconds.
```

That code creates an anonymous function that will be called after 5 seconds. Within the function, if the ajax object still has a non-FALSE value, it's assumed that the request is still being made and should now be aborted. When the request is aborted or completed, ajax would be assigned a FALSE value, such as null, to indicate that the request is no longer active. You would also want to indicate the problem to the user in some way.

## HANDLING THE SERVER RESPONSE

Once an asynchronous Ajax request has been made, the function assigned to the onreadystatechange property of the Ajax object will be called whenever the object's readyState property changes. There are five possible values for this property, in this order of execution:

- 0, unsent
- 1, opened
- 2, headers received
- 3, loading
- 4, done

For example, immediately after sending the request, the value would be 1, then 2, then 3, and finally, 4. At that point, this function will be used to handle the server's response, but understand that the function will be called during each phase of the process.

In the function that handles readyState changes, you can check the readyState property and react accordingly. For example, a value of 4 means the process has been completed and the page can make use of the results. Other values means the Ajax request is still being processed, in which case the script could do nothing, or could show a "Loading..." message to the user:

```
if (ajax.readyState == 4) {
    // Handle the response.
} else {
    // Show the 'Loading...' message or do nothing.
}
```

Alternatively, you could create the "Loading..." message after calling the open() method, and then hide the message when the readyState equals 4.

When the readyState value equals 4, the Ajax request has come full circle, but there's one more check to make before trying to handle the response: confirming that the response was good. To do that, check the object's status property, which represents the server's response code for the resource. These are server HTTP codes, which include:

- 200, OK
- 301, Moved Permanently
- 304, Not Modified
- 307, Temporary Redirect

- 401, Unauthorized
- 403, Forbidden
- 404, Not Found
- 500, Internal Server Error

You don't have to memorize, or even address every single probability. When the status code is in the 200's, the resource was found and able to be loaded. If the status code is 304, the browser already has a cached version that can be used. All other codes are problematic.

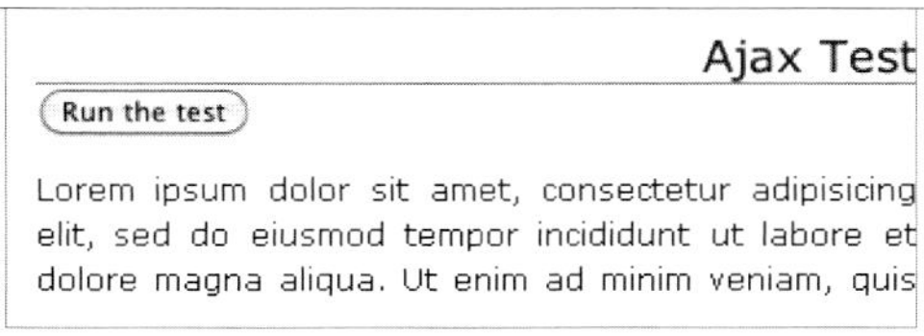

FIGURE 11.1 The content shown below the button will be retrieved from another file via Ajax.

Putting this code together, the handling function begins with this skeleton:

```
if (ajax.readyState == 4) {
    if ( (ajax.status >= 200 && ajax.status < 300)
    || (ajax.status == 304) ) {
        // Handle the response.
    } else {
        // Status error!
    }
}
```

Depending upon the specific use of Ajax, if a problematic status code is returned, you could reenact the default browser behavior: redirect the browser to the non-Ajax page, actually submit the form, and so forth.

The statusText property represents the string message returned by the server, corresponding to the status code. You can use that in any error reporting.

When the function is ready to handle the server response, it can look into one of two properties to find the response data: responseXML and responseText. The former is used when the returned data is in XML format, and will be explained later in the chapter. The responseText property will be populated when XML data was not returned, and therefore will be used most of the time. This property just stores a string, and can be used like any other string. You'll see an example shortly.

One you are done with the Ajax object—and it won't be used again by the script—you should clear it out by assigning it a null value:

```
ajax = null;
```

This frees up the browser resources required by the object.

To test the information covered so far, this next example will simply request a resource and write the received response to the page (**Figure 11.1**). The relevant HTML is:

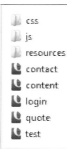

FIGURE 11.2 The directory structure for this chapter, with all Ajax requests being made of files stored in the resources directory.

```
<div><button type="button" id="btn">Run the test</button><br>
<p id="output"></p></div>
```

I would put this in a file named test.html, which would include both the ajax.js script (the contents of which were just shown) and then test.js, to be written in the following steps. You'll also need to create a plain text file named test.txt, and you can place any amount of HTML or text in it. Store this text file in a resources directory, to keep it separate from the other files (**Figure 11.2**).

**To test Ajax:**

1. Create a new JavaScript file in your text editor or IDE, to be named test.js.

2. Begin defining an anonymous function for when the page has loaded:

```
window.onload = function() {
    'use strict';
```

All of the work will actually take place within this function, which avoids polluting the global namespace. For brevity sake, I'm also using DOM Level 0 event handlers, but you can change that code, if you'd prefer.

3. Create the Ajax object:

```
var ajax = getXMLHttpRequestObject();
```

This assumes that the ajax.js script is included prior to the page loading.

4. Begin creating the onreadystatechange function:

```
ajax.onreadystatechange = function() {
    if (ajax.readyState == 4) {
```

This anonymous function will be called when the object's readyState property changes. Within the function, a conditional checks the value of the readyState, as the only important value is 4.

**NOTE:** All of the code for the book is available for download from www.LarryUllman.com.

Ajax Test

Run the test

Not Found

**FIGURE 11.3** The result if the server returned a poor status code.

5. If the correct status code was returned, update the page with the response:

```
if ( (ajax.status >= 200 && ajax.status < 300)
|| (ajax.status == 304) ) {
    document.getElementById('output').innerHTML =
    ⇢ ajax.responseText;
```

If the status code has a value within the 200's, or a value of 304, then the `innerHTML` property of the output element in the HTML is assigned the entire value of the returned response.

For security reasons, you don't want to be in this habit of blindly requesting data via Ajax and inserting it into the page as HTML. If someone were to hack the system, the server resource could return malicious HTML, which is to say HTML with JavaScript. Such data, when assigned to the `innerHTML` property, would execute the JavaScript. To prevent that, when possible, you should assign the data to an `innerText` or `textContent` property instead, or first search the response to make sure it does not include the text *<script* (case insensitive).

6. Report the status text if a different status code was returned:

```
} else {
    document.getElementById('output').innerHTML = 'Error: ' +
    ⇢ ajax.statusText;
}
```

If the conditional in Step 5 is FALSE, this `else` clause applies, showing the textual version of the status code (**Figure 11.3**). You would not want to reveal this to an actual user, but instead either show a generic error message or allow the non-Ajax process to proceed (you'll see examples of that shortly).

7. Complete the onreadystatechange function:

```
    } // End of readyState IF.
}; // End of onreadystatechange anonymous function.
```

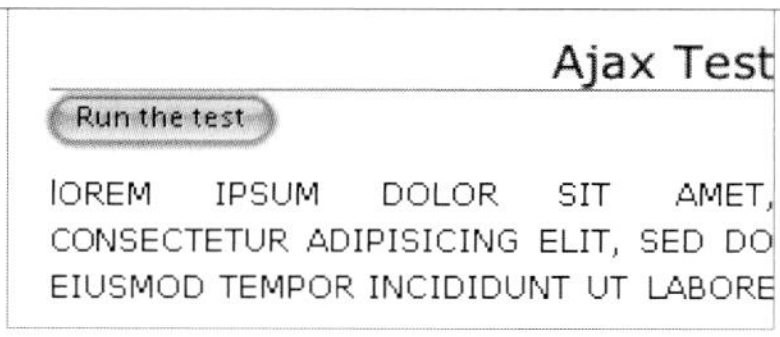

Ajax Test

FIGURE 11.4 The updated contents of the text file are reflected in the updated Web page.

Ajax Test

Run the test

IOREM IPSUM DOLOR SIT AMET, CONSECTETUR ADIPISICING ELIT, SED DO EIUSMOD TEMPOR INCIDIDUNT UT LABORE

You'll notice that I'm not clearing out the Ajax object (by assigning it a null value), as I expect to reuse it.

8. Invoke the Ajax request when the button is clicked:

```
document.getElementById('btn').onclick = function() {
    ajax.open('GET', 'resources/test.txt', true);
    ajax.send(null);
}; // End of onclick anonymous function.
```

To invoke the request, first open it, then call send().

9. Complete the onload function:

```
}; // End of onload anonymous function.
```

10. Save the file as test.js, in a js directory, and test it in your Web browser (Figure 11.1).

Again, you'll need to have created test.txt, with any text or HTML in it.

11. Change the contents of test.txt, and click the button to test the results (**Figure 11.4**).

If you don't immediately see the altered contents displayed, your browser is probably caching the results, and I'll explain how to work around that later in the chapter. For now, reloading the browser first should do the trick.

## SENDING DATA

Once you know how to retrieve data from a server resource, the next thing to learn is how to send data to the server. The data transmitted could be used to impact the data returned (e.g., to fetch the employees in a specific department, the Ajax request would send a department identifier to the server). In other situations, the data sent would be validated by the server, such as the availability of a username.

Or, the data sent could trigger a server reaction, like the posting of comments to a message board.

There are a couple of ways to send data to the server as part of the request. The first option is to append the data to the URL. The data should be structured in *name=value* pairs, with multiple pairs separated by ampersands. To guarantee the data is safe to use in the request, wrap it in encodeURIComponent() calls:

```
ajax.open('GET', 'http://www.example.com/somepage.php?id=' +
→ encodeURIComponent(id), true);
```

A slightly better alternative is to provide the data as the lone argument to the send() method (in place of null):

```
var data = 'email=' + encodeURIComponent(email) + '&password=' +
→ encodeURIComponent(password);
ajax.open('GET', 'http://www.example.com/somepage.php', true);
ajax.send(data);
```

The end result is the same for both approaches, but the latter code is cleaner.

Because the GET method is being used, the receiving PHP script can access the sent data in $_GET['email'] and $_GET['password'], respectively.

When you're making a POST request, you must provide the data to the send() method, as opposed to appending it to the URL. And, when using POST, for improved reliability, you should indicate (to the server), the content type being sent. You can do this by calling the setRequestHeader() method of the Ajax object. Its first argument is the name of the header and the second is the value. To identify the proper data encoding, use this:

```
ajax.setRequestHeader('Content-Type',
→ 'application/x-www-form-urlencoded');
```

To be clear, you would want to do this prior to sending the request:

```
var data = 'email=' + encodeURIComponent(email) + '&password=' +
→ encodeURIComponent(password);
ajax.open('POST', 'http://www.example.com/somepage.php', true);
ajax.setRequestHeader('Content-Type',
→ 'application/x-www-form-urlencoded');
ajax.send(data);
```

Here, because the POST method is being used, the receiving PHP script can access the sent data in $_POST['email'] and $_POST['password'], respectively.

As you can see, the structure of the data is the same whether you make GET or POST requests, but, as was explained earlier, there are times when it's appropriate to make GET requests and times when it's proper to use POST. There is also a limit as to how much data can be transmitted via GET, somewhere in the range of 2-4 KB, depending upon the browser.

An alternative way to send data to the server is to create a FormData object:

```
var data = new FormData();
```

Then add each item by calling the append() method of the FormData object, providing a name and a value:

```
data.append('email', email);
data.append('password', password);
```

When using this approach, note that you don't need to invoke ecnodeURIcomponent(), as the data will be encoded automatically. You also don't need to set the *Content-Type*.

Finally, provide the data object to the send() method:

```
ajax.send(data);
```

FormData is not supported by all browsers yet; you can test for its availability in order to create the data in a reliable way:

```
if (typeof FormData == 'function') {
    // Create data as FormData.
} else {
    // Create data as name=value pairs.
    // Add Content-Type header, if POST.
}
ajax.send(data);
```

**FIGURE 11.5** The results of directly accessing the Ajax resource in the browser.

When transmitting data to, or from, the server, be aware of any security implications. Just because the request is being made behind the scenes does not mean that the data is being transmitted secretly or securely. In cases where higher security is required, the server resource can be accessed over HTTPS (assuming the server supports that).

## BASIC DEBUGGING

The hardest aspect to Ajax, in my opinion, is that debugging can be a bit more difficult. But with the right tools and approach, this, too, is manageable.

The first thing you should always do is to test the server-side resource to confirm the data being sent back to the JavaScript. Not only should you do this as a debugging step, but I recommend that you do this immediately after creating the server-side resource, in order to confirm that there are no problems prior to writing any JavaScript. Many server-side resources can be tested by merely loading them directly in your browser. The net effect of loading the resource will often be the same as the response received by the JavaScript. In the previous example, a simple text file was being used, so loading that in your browser just shows the contents of the text file (**Figure 11.5**). This is good to confirm, though. With PHP scripts, or other dynamic, server-side tools, you'll want to load them to make sure they are working properly. Too many of my initial Ajax attempts have failed because the PHP script had an error in it, an error I would have caught had I just tested the script first. In all cases, always make sure that you are loading your Ajax page, and therefore the resource, through a URL (http://*something*).

If the PHP script (or other server-side resource) needs to receive some data in order to work, testing it can be a bit more challenging. If a GET request is being made of the script, then you can append that data to the URL yourself, as in: http://www.example.com/somepage.php?name=value&name2=value2. If data is being sent to the server-side resource via POST, you'll need to post data to it, which isn't as simple. One way to do that would be to have a form send the data to the PHP script. In fact, if you're using progressive enhancement, you should already have that process in place: just test the submission of the form data to the PHP script without involving JavaScript at all. In any case, testing the server-side resource should always be the first step before adding the JavaScript code. Or, if you forgot to do that, it should be your first debugging step.

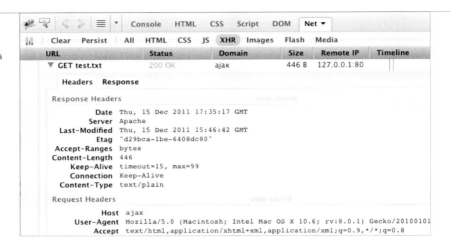

**FIGURE 11.6** The network monitor clearly shows the data sent and received as part of a request.

The second thing you should do to debug Ajax processes is use a *network monitor*. Firebug, and some browser tools such as Opera's Dragonfly and Safari's Web Inspector, have one built in. The network monitor can verify that a request was made, show what data was transmitted in the request, and show what data was returned in the response (**Figure 11.6**). Almost always, this will reveal the cause of the problem. Or, if not, the network monitor will clue you in as to whether the problem is in the request or in the response. From there, you can apply debugging techniques to the JavaScript or PHP, accordingly.

When you begin using different data formats, such as JSON and XML, you'll want to verify the integrity of the data itself. It's possible, if not likely, that the server is returning a positive response, but that the data isn't properly formatted, making it unusable in the JavaScript code. You can validate JSON data using JSONLint (http://jsonlint.com). You can validate XML using any number of validators found by searching online using the terms *XML Validator*.

Another thing to be aware of is when the same page might make multiple Ajax requests. You can use a single Ajax object only if a page has a single request to make. However, if multiple and different requests are required, possibly at the same time, you'd want to use multiple Ajax objects to avoid conflict.

Finally, debugging can be made more challenging because of the browser's natural attempts to cache data. To improve performance, and therefore the user's experience, the browser will cache downloaded resources whenever possible. This includes everything from images to CSS to JavaScript to HTML. By storing a resource locally, the browser will not need to download the resource again when the resource is used in subsequent requests. For example, when a user goes to a Web page, the browser will download and then cache the CSS file in use by that page. When the user goes to another page on that same site, which uses the same CSS script, the browser can utilize the cached version instead of downloading it again.

This is relevant to Ajax because the browser will attempt to cache the results of the Ajax request. You may have already seen this with the previous example. If the browser is caching the request, changes made to the server-side resource won't immediately be reflected, which will make debugging even harder. There are several ways of overcoming this obstacle. The first is to disable the cache in the browser (**Figure 11.7**). This solution is simple and only affects your experience.

Another solution, which will affect everyone using the same server-side resource, is to have that resource indicate that the request should not be cached. In PHP, this is done by sending a *Cache-Control* header:

```php
<?php
header('Cache-Control: no-cache');
```

Again, this will prevent all browsers from caching the request, which isn't always appropriate.

A third option is to make each request seem to be unique, even if it's not. A common way to do that is to add a random value to the requested URL, such as a timestamp:

```
var url = 'http://www.example.com/somepage.php?stamp=' +
    new Date.getTime();
ajax.open('GET', url, true);
```

Because each request will have a different and unique URL, there will never be a previously cached version that can be used in lieu of making the request again.

I'm presenting the issue of caching here as a debugging one, as caching can trip you up. In terms of development, there are situations where you would want to prevent anyone from caching a server-side resource. For example, say the resource is returning a stock quote. During the hours that the stock market is open, such a request should not be cached, as the returned response would differ from one request to the next, although the request itself would always look to be the same. For most situations, though, caching is a valuable tool that enhances the performance of both the Web site in the client and the Web server itself. Caching should not be overridden without due consideration.

**FIGURE 11.7** On Safari, use the Develop menu to disable the cache.

The first example just received plain text back from the server, which is an ideal route when the server is only returning a simple response. But when a lot of information, or just more complex data, is being returned, other data formats are required. The original data format for Ajax requests was XML, to be discussed first. Over time, the JSON format has become more popular, as it is, by definition, more natural to JavaScript, and therefore easier to use. In the discussion of these formats, a text file will still be used as the resource. After this section, you'll learn what you need to know to send XML and JSON dynamically from a server, specifically using a PHP script.

### XML

The XML format is quite similar to HTML, with tags surrounding values to define meaning. XML always has one root element that encompasses the entire data set. As in HTML, XML tags can also have attributes, providing additional information. Unlike with HTML, XML tags can be entirely made up by you:

```
<book>
    <chapter id="1">(Re-)Introducing JavaScript</chapter>
    <chapter id="2">JavaScript in Action</chapter>
</book>
```

That's a fairly simple snippet of XML, but that's really all there is to it. You just have to make sure that the XML is well formed: all opened tags are closed and all tags are properly nested. You should use all lowercase letters for your tags, too.

When using an `XMLHttpRequest` object to fetch XML, the returned data will automatically be represented in JavaScript as a DOM tree. This means you can use many of the same techniques explained in Chapter 9 to navigate that data. If an Ajax request fetched the above XML data, you can first get a reference to the response:

```
var data = ajax.responseXML;
```

Form there, you can use `documentElement` to access the root, then the `first-Child`, `nextSibling`, `childNodes`, and other properties to navigate the data. One trick about XML data is that the blank space between tags gets represented as an empty text node (in the above, book has three children). And, to get the value of a node, you must use nodeValue. The end result can be quite wordy. This bit of code points to the value *(Re-)Introducing JavaScript*:

```
documentElement.firstChild.nextSibling.firstChild.nodeValue
```

When you know there are a number of records represented by the XML, each with the same tag name, the easiest way to grab them all is to use the getElementsByTagName() method:

```
var chapters = data.getElementsByTagName('chapter');
```

You can then loop through the records:

```
for (var i = 0, count = chapters.length; i < count; i++) {
    // Use chapters[i].
}
```

To fetch the value of an attribute, use the getAttribute() method, providing it with the attribute name. To get the value of an individual tag, use firstChild.nodeValue:

```
for (var i = 0, count = chapters.length; i < count; i++) {
    // Use chapters[i].getAttribute('id')
    // Use chapters[i].firstChild.nodeValue
}
```

If you want to try applying this new information, just create a text file that contains some XML, and name it test.xml. To clearly indicate that the file contains XML data, it must begin with the XML declaration:

```
<?xml version="1.0" encoding="utf-8" standalone="yes" ?>
<book>
    <chapter id="1">(Re-)Introducing JavaScript</chapter>
    <chapter id="2">JavaScript in Action</chapter>
</book>
```

Then update `test.js` to make a request of this new file. Finally, modify the function that handles the `readyState` changes so that it fetches the data from `responseXML`, gets the relevant elements from that data by calling `getElementsByTagName()`, and then loops through those to obtain the individual values. If these instructions aren't immediately clear, all of this code can be found in the `test.js` script, available in the downloads from the book's Web site.

### JSON

While XML has been a standard format for representing data for years, it's not without its negatives. First, XML as a format is bulky: representing the four-digit year 2012 requires all of the characters in `<year>2012</year>`. Second, parsing XML data, while not hard, does require compound constructs like `chapters[i].firstChild.nodeName`. Also, XML is not native to JavaScript, and performance can be an issue.

Douglas Crockford, one of JavaScript's founding fathers, realized that JavaScript already had a good format for representing data. This format is both terse and easily navigable in JavaScript: JavaScript's Object Notation (JSON). The same earlier XML can be represented as a JavaScript object like so:

```
var chapters = {
    1: {
        title: '(Re-)Introducing JavaScript'
    },
    2: {
        title: 'JavaScript in Action'
    }
};
```

As you know, with object notation, you can now simply use `chapters[1].title` to get to *(Re-)Introducing JavaScript*.

In theory, if you were to take that same data, without assigning it to a variable, and place it in a text file, it would be in JSON format. However, JSON suggests that you quote all properties and values, using double quotation marks:

```
{
"1": {"title": "(Re-)Introducing JavaScript"},
"2": {"title": "JavaScript in Action"}
}
```

(The data could be compressed even further so it required even fewer characters to represent.)

> **NOTE:** JSON is not exactly the same as a JavaScript object, because it cannot represent some things, such as functions or regular expressions.

In terms of Ajax, there's only one trick to turning JSON data into something usable: it has to be parsed as JavaScript code. To start, get the data from the responseText property of the Ajax object (there is no *responseJSON* property):

```
var data = ajax.responseText;
```

## SENDING XML OR JSON TO THE SERVER

All of the examples in this chapter send plain text data to the server, which will often be the case. You can, however, send data to the server in other formats, such as XML or JSON. To do that, you'll first need to indicate to the server the proper content type:

```
ajax.setRequestHeader('Content-Type', 'text/xml');
```

or

```
ajax.setRequestHeader('Content-Type', 'application/json');
```

Next, you'll need to generate data in the right format. You can create XML by either creating literal strings of XML data, or by creating elements and nodes. The latter generates more reliable XML but requires more work (search online for specifics).

If you have data that you want to turn into JSON format, you can use the JSON.stringify() method:

```
data = JSON.stringify(data);
```

This method will be defined by your browser, or is available in the json2.js library.

In any case, the data must be in a format that's understandable—and expected—by the server-side resource.

Historically, the text was turned into a JavaScript object by running it through eval(), which executes a bit of code:

```
var data = eval('(' + data ')');
```

To make the intent clear, parentheses needed to be wrapped around the data. As mentioned in Chapter 9, it's actually quite a bad thing to use the eval() function. Because this function executes a string as if it's JavaScript code, eval() could introduce a major security hole. Quickly enough, Crockford came up with a better solution: a JSON library that turned JSON data into a usable JavaScript object while still making any data provided safe to run through eval(). Eventually, the JSON library was incorporated into the browser so that you can now use JSON.parse() instead of eval():

```
var data = JSON.parse(data);
// Use data[1].title
```

The JSON object, and its parse() method, have been supported in most browsers for several versions now. Unfortunately, it was only added in IE as of version 8. For older versions of IE, you must first include a JSON parsing library, such as json2.js (Crockford's update of his original), available at www.json.org. Once you've copied that library to your JavaScript directory, you can include it in your HTML page:

```
<script src="js/json2.js"></script>
```

A great feature of this library is that it will only define a new JSON object if one doesn't already exist. If you'd rather, you could have JavaScript dynamically load the library if the JSON object doesn't exist already:

```
if (typeof JSON == 'undefined') {
    var script = document.createElement('script');
    script.src = 'js/json2.js';
    // Add it to the HTML head:
    document.getElementsByTagName('head')[0].appendChild(script);
}
```

If you want to try applying this new information, just create a text file that contains some JSON data, and name it `test.json`. Then update `test.js` to make a request of this new file. Finally, modify the function that handles the `readyState` changes so that it fetches the data from `responseText`, parses it using `JSON.parse()`, and then uses object notation to access the individual values. Of course, you'll need to include the JSON parsing library in the HTML page. Again, if these instructions aren't immediately clear, all of this code can be found in the `test.js` script, available in the downloads from the book's Web site.

## THE **SERVER-SIDE SCRIPT**

The examples thus far only used a simple text file, but in the real world, you'll use a more dynamic server-side resource. For me, that's normally a PHP script. I'll quickly explain how a server-side PHP script would be written so that it may return plain text, XML, or JSON. In all cases, the most important thing to remember is that the PHP script will only be accessed by the JavaScript, so it shouldn't include or output any HTML (unless the script is returning HTML as part of a text response). Also, remember to test PHP scripts to make sure they work, prior to hooking them into the JavaScript.

As a warning, the content to follow does assume some familiarity and comfort with PHP. If you're using a different server-side technology, use that instead. If you don't yet know PHP, you'll probably want to learn, and I would selfishly recommend my book *PHP for the Web: Visual QuickStart Guide, 4th Edition* (Peachpit Press).

### RETURNING PLAIN TEXT

Returning plain text from a PHP script is just a matter of having PHP print whatever text should be sent back to the JavaScript:

```php
<?php // Nothing before this!
echo 'This is some text being printed';
?>
```

Normally, the PHP script will use some logic and perhaps a database call to determine the text to be returned. This text might indicate the availability of a username:

```php
<?php
if (/* username is available */) {
    echo 'AVAILABLE';
} else {
    echo 'UNAVAILABLE';
}
?>
```

The JavaScript code would then see if ajax.responseText equaled *AVAILABLE* or *UNAVAILABLE*. (In situations like this I prefer to return status indicators using all capital letters, as if they were constants.)

Although plain text is really only best for a limited amount of data, you can send multiple pieces if each is separated by a unique character—one that would not be in the data itself—such as the pipe. Here, then, is a single employee's record:

```php
<?php
// Validate the employee ID, received by this page!
// Get the employee record from the database.
// Return the record:
echo "{row['first_name']}|{row['last_name']}|{row['email']}";
?>
```

Within the JavaScript, you can split the incoming text on the same character in order to access the individual parts:

```javascript
var employee = ajax.responseText.split('|');
// Use employee[0], employee[1], and employee[2]
```

## RETURNING XML

Having a PHP script return XML data is not that hard. The first thing the script has to do is send a *Content-Type* header to indicate that XML data is to follow:

```php
<?php // Nothing before this!
header('Content-Type: text/xml');
```

This should be the first line in the PHP code, after the opening PHP tag.

Next, XML documents begin with a declaration that should be printed by the PHP script:

```php
echo '<?xml version="1.0" encoding="utf-8" standalone="yes" ?>';
```

A version value of 1 is just fine, but do make sure that the encoding indicated matches that actually being used by the PHP script itself (i.e., used by the application in which you created this PHP script). For technical reasons, you should have PHP print the declaration, as in the above, rather than trying to hardcode the literal text into the script.

Next, all XML data requires one root element. This can be called virtually anything:

```php
echo '<comments>';
```

As with all data being returned to JavaScript by PHP, the data is "returned" by just printing it out (so that it would appear in the Web browser, if the script were to be accessed directly).

Normally, the data being returned by the PHP script will come from the database. Database records are fetched in a while loop; thus, you can create the XML in the loop:

```php
$q = 'SELECT comment, email, date_submitted FROM comments ORDER BY
   date_submitted DESC';
$r = mysqli_query($dbc, $q);
while ($row = mysqli_fetch_array($r)) {
    echo "<record>
        <comment>{$row['comment']}</comment>
        <email>{$row['email']}</email>
```

```
        <date>{$row['date']}</>{$>
    </record>\n";
}
```

Finally, the PHP script needs to close the root element:

```
echo '</comments>';
```

### RETURNING JSON

To return JSON data from a PHP script, you start by sending the appropriate *Content-Type* header:

```
<?php
header('Content-Type: application/json');
```

After that, the PHP script needs to print the JSON data. Because the JSON syntax can be difficult to accurately create, the easiest solution is to build up an array of data, and then convert that data into JSON:

```
$data = array();
$q = 'SELECT comment, email, date_submitted FROM comments ORDER BY
⇒  date_submitted DESC';
$r = mysqli_query($dbc, $q);
while ($row = mysqli_fetch_array($r)) {
    $data[] = $row;
}
echo json_encode($data);
```

The json_encode() function has been part of PHP since version 5.2. If you're using an older version of PHP, you'll need to install a JSON library instead. The one now built into PHP comes from PECL (http://pecl.php.net), the Zend Framework has its own JSON library (http://framework.zend.com), and there are other JSON libraries out there. In any case, whatever JSON library you use, convert the data to JSON and print it.

# AJAX EXAMPLES

To wrap up this chapter, let's put this knowledge to the test with several real-world, practical uses of Ajax. With some examples, I'll discuss the premise and the solution, without fully implementing it. With others, I'll cover the most pertinent details. By the end of the chapter, you should be well able to mix and match the ideas and features to suit your needs. Again, I recommend that you download the corresponding files from www.LarryUllman.com, which include the full code.

## SHOWING PROGRESS

In Ajax processes that could take longer to execute, it's a good idea to indicate to the user that something is happening, particularly if you'd rather the user not do anything else in the interim. Unlike with the other event handling examples you have seen, Ajax processes can take longer because a lot of data must be validated and then sent to the server, or because a lot of data is being returned by the server and the DOM must then be heavily manipulated. For whatever delay, via CSS and DOM manipulation, it's easy to indicate that something is happening.

First, you should decide whether you want to use an image, some text, or both. You can even use a modal window, if you want (see Chapter 9). To quickly generate your own custom animated GIF, head to Ajaxload (www.ajaxload.info). Once you've done that, you have two options:

- Add the appropriate HTML to the page, initially hide the image using CSS, and show it when appropriate

- Add the HTML dynamically when it's time

For example, say you've added an animated GIF to the Web page:

```
<img src="images/ajax-loader.gif" id="loader">
```

And the CSS hides this image:

```
#loader { visibility: hidden; }
```

The Ajax process would then start by showing this image:

```
loader.style.visibility = 'visible';
ajax.open('GET', 'http://www.example.com/somepage.php', true);
ajax.send(null);
```

If data is being validated before the request is made, you could reveal the animated GIF before the validation even occurs.

In the function that handles the `readyState` change, after the response has been received and addressed, you simply hide the image again:

```
loader.style.visibility = 'hidden';
```

When running this code on your own computer, or with simple demonstrations, the animation may only appear for a moment. To get a fuller effect, you can delay the Ajax call using a timer (see Chapter 9):

```
var ajaxTimer = setTimeout(function() {

    ajax.open('GET', 'http://www.example.com/somepage.php', true);

    ajax.send(null);

}, 1000); // Wait one second!
```

Again, this time is only to delay the demonstration; you wouldn't want to use a timer to delay the request on a live site.

Thus far, you've only been made aware of and used a single Ajax-related event: the changing of the `readyState` value. There are four others that you can watch for:

- progress
- load
- error
- abort

The progress event is triggered when the Ajax request is being made, and will be triggered one or more times, depending upon how long it takes to complete the request. Within that event handler, the event object's `total` property will reflect the total number of bytes to be transferred and `loaded` will reflect the total bytes already received. Thus, you can use these two properties to determine how much of the transaction has occurred:

```
ajax.onprogress = function(e) {

    if (typeof e == 'undefined') e = window.event;

    var pct = e.loaded/e.total;

}
```

Although not demonstrated in this book, it is possible to upload a file via Ajax. One solution is to use a `FormData` object. But as already mentioned, `FormData` is not supported by all browsers. The most common solution is to use a hidden iframe for this purpose. If you search online, you'll find many tutorials explaining exactly how.

Understand, however, that Ajax requests normally happen very quickly; watching for progress events will only be meaningful on lengthy requests.

The load event is equivalent to the `readyState` being changed to 4. The other two events may or may not ever occur, but could be used to handle errors or do something different should a slow request be aborted.

Note that these handlers, like the `readystatechange` handler, need to be assigned before calling the `open()` method.

## COMPLETING THE LOGIN EXAMPLE FROM CHAPTER 2

To bring things full circle, it's time to add the Ajax layer to the login example begun in Chapter 2. The JavaScript script will take the username and password from the form and pass them to a server-side script for validation. The PHP script will only return a simple text message indicating the validation of the submitted values. The focus in the following steps is just to add server-side validation of the form data; there are many ways you can improve upon this example, and you'll see notes accordingly.

**To complete the login example:**

1.  Include the `ajax.js` script in `login.html`:

    ```
    <script src="js/ajax.js"></script>
    ```

    This is the only change needed in the HTML file.

2.  Within `login.js`, if the minimum validation is passed, create an Ajax object:

    ```
    if ( (email.value.length > 0) && (password.value.length > 0) ) {
        var ajax = getXMLHttpRequestObject();
    ```

FIGURE 11.8 For demonstration purposes, an alert reports
upon the Ajax result.

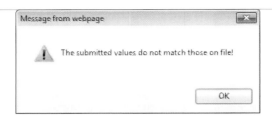

The original script performed a minimum of validation. If you wanted, you could use the information taught since then, such as regular expressions from Chapter 10, Working with Forms, to make the validation more stringent. In any case, if the data passes this validation, then the Ajax request will be made.

3. Begin creating the readyState change handling function:

```
ajax.onreadystatechange = function() {
    if (ajax.readyState == 4) {
        if ( (ajax.status >= 200 && ajax.status < 300)
        || (ajax.status == 304) ) {
```

4. Use an alert to report upon the results:

```
if (ajax.responseText == 'VALID') {
    alert('You are now logged in!');
} else {
    alert('The submitted values do not match those on file!');
}
```

The server-side PHP script will just be returning (i.e., printing) a simple text message: *VALID* or *INVALID*. Either way, alerts are used to report upon the results (**Figure 11.8**). For a more professional interface, if the response was *VALID*, you could hide the form and show other content (you'll see an example of this with a contact form shortly). If the response was *INVALID*, you could add an error message to the page.

5. Complete the readyState change handling function:

```
            } else { // Bad status!
                document.getElementById('theForm').submit();
```

```
        } // End of status IF-ELSE.
      } // End of readyState IF.
}; // End of function assignation.
```

If, for whatever reason, the server returned a status code not among the proper values, then the form needs to be actually submitted to the server-side script for processing. This would be the server-side script identified by the action attribute of the form, which is different than the Ajax script (e.g., one would include HTML, the other wouldn't).

6. Send the request, passing along the data:

```
ajax.open('POST', 'resources/login.php', true);
ajax.setRequestHeader('Content-Type',
    'application/x-www-form-urlencoded');
var data = 'email=' + encodeURIComponent(email.value) +
    '&password=' + encodeURIComponent(password.value);
ajax.send(data);
```

The request will be made using POST, which is standard for a login form. Then the *Content-Type* header is sent, so that the data to follow is properly handled (this is necessary when using POST and passing data). Next, the data is created as a string of *name=value* pairs, with the values run through encodeURIComponent() for security. Finally, the send() method is called.

7. Change the next return statement to return false:

```
return false;
```

Originally, the JavaScript would have returned true here to allow the form's actual submission to go through. Now, Ajax is sending the data to the server, and false should be returned instead.

8. Save login.js.

9. Create a PHP script named login.php, in a resources directory:

```
<?php # login.php
if ( isset($_POST['email'], $_POST['password'])
```

**FIGURE 11.9** Now correctly
logged in, via Ajax!

**FIGURE 11.10** The data in this
contact form will be submitted
to the server via Ajax.

**FIGURE 11.9** Now correctly
logged in, via Ajax!

**FIGURE 11.10** The data in this
contact form will be submitted
to the server via Ajax.

```
        && ($_POST['email'] == 'test@example.com')
        && ($_POST['password'] == 'securepass') ) {
            echo 'VALID';
    } else {
        echo 'INVALID';
    }
    ?>
```

The PHP script needs to validate the incoming data and compare it to that
stored on the system. Then the script prints just a single word that indicates
the results. For simplicity sake, I've hardcoded the proper values into this
script. In the real world, you'd tie the validation to a database. If you have
basic PHP and MySQL skills, that should not be hard for you to implement.

You could also begin a session in the PHP script upon a successful login. The
session won't impact the page the user is currently viewing, but when the
user accesses subsequent pages, the session will be active.

10. Test the system in your Web browser (**Figure 11.9**).

## CREATING AN AJAX CONTACT FORM

For this next example, an Ajax layer will be applied to a contact form (**Figure 11.10**).
Again, the PHP script on the server will only return a simple message indicating
the result. Within the JavaScript, I'll demonstrate two new tricks. The first will be
a quick method for creating Ajax data out of multiple form elements. The second
will be how to use a non-anonymous function to handle the readyState changes.

The relevant HTML is:

```
<form action="#" method="post" id="theForm">

    <fieldset><legend>Contact</legend>

    <p>All fields are required.</p>

    <div class="two"><label for="name">Name</label>
     → <input type="text" name="name" id="name" required></div>

    <div class="two"><label for="email">Email</label>
     → <input type="email" name="email" id="email" required></div>

    <div class="two"><label for="comments">Comments</label>
     → <textarea name="Comments" id="Comments" required>
     → </textarea></div>

    <div class="one"><input type="submit" value="Submit"
     → id="submit"></div>

    </fieldset>

</form>
```

This page includes the ajax.js script, and contact.js, to be written in the following steps.

**To create an Ajax-based contact form:**

1. Create a new JavaScript file in your text editor or IDE, to be named contact.js.

2. Begin defining the handleAjaxRequest() function:

```
function handleAjaxResponse(e) {
    'use strict';
    if (typeof e == 'undefined') e = window.event;
    var ajax = e.target || e.srcElement;
```

In the previous examples, when using an anonymous function to handle the readyState changes, the ajax variable was already available within that function (because of variable scoping). When you use a separate function to handle this event, the ajax variable will not be accessible, unless you were to make it global. The workaround is simple, however: get the object that was the target of the event, using code you've seen many times over by now. The object that is the target of the event will be the same XMLHttpRequest object.

3. Update the page with the script's response:

```
if (ajax.readyState == 4) {
    if ( (ajax.status >= 200 && ajax.status < 300)
    || (ajax.status == 304) ) {
        document.getElementById('contactForm').innerHTML =
        ⇒  ajax.responseText;
```

If there was a positive response, the form will be replaced with the response (there is a DIV with an id of *contactForm* that surrounds the form itself).

4. Complete the handleAjaxResponse() function:

```
        } else { // Status error!
            document.getElementById('theForm').submit();
        }
        ajax = null;
    } // End of readyState IF.
} // End of handleAjaxResponse() function.
```

If the server returns a bad response code, then the form will actually be submitted to the server-side script. In either case, the Ajax object is then cleared out.

5. Begin an anonymous function for handling the window load:

```
window.onload = function() {
    'use strict';
    var ajax = getXMLHttpRequestObject();
    ajax.onreadystatechange = handleAjaxResponse;
```

The Ajax object is created here so that it can be quickly used when the form is submitted.

6. Add an event handler to the form's submission:

```
document.getElementById('theForm').onsubmit = function() {
```

7. Create the data to be sent to the server:

```
var fields = ['name', 'email', 'comments'];
var data = [];
for (var i = 0, count = fields.length; i < count; i++) {
    data.push(encodeURIComponent(fields[i]) + '=' +
    ➝ encodeURIComponent(document.getElementById(fields[i]).
    ➝ value));
}
```

This shortcut code makes it quick and easy to send all the form's data to the server. First, an array is filled with the id values of the form elements to be passed to the server. Then an empty array is created, which will represent the data itself. The loop then goes through the array of elements.

Within that loop, an element is added to the data array. That element's value will simply be *name=value*, where the name comes from the `fields` array and the value comes from the corresponding form element. Both are passed through encodeURIComponent() for security. When the loop is done, there will be three *name=value* pairs stored in `data`.

For added security, you could include basic validation—that some value was provided for the element—within the loop.

The message has been sent.

**FIGURE 11.11** Upon a successful Ajax request, the form will be replaced with a message.

8. Invoke the Ajax request:

```
ajax.open('POST', 'resources/contact.php', true);
ajax.setRequestHeader('Content-Type',
   'application/x-www-form-urlencoded');
ajax.send(data.join('&'));
```

The final step in making the data appropriate for the request is to convert the data array into a string, with each *name=value* pair separated by an ampersand. The join() method can do just that.

9. Complete the onsubmit anonymous function:

```
    return false;
}; // End of onsubmit anonymous function.
```

The value false is returned to prevent the actual submission of the form.

10. Save the file as contact.js, in a js directory.

11. Create the contact.php script.

The PHP script would perform basic validation and then use the submitted data in the mail() function:

```
mail('youremail@example.com', 'Contact Form Submission',
   $body, $from);
```

The $body value would come from $_POST['comments'], after running it through sanitizing functions to make it safe. The $from value would come from $_POST['email'], after confirming that it's a syntactically valid email address. If you're unsure of how to do that, you can ask me for help in my support forums (www.LarryUllman.com/forums/).

12. Test in your Web browser (**Figure 11.11**).

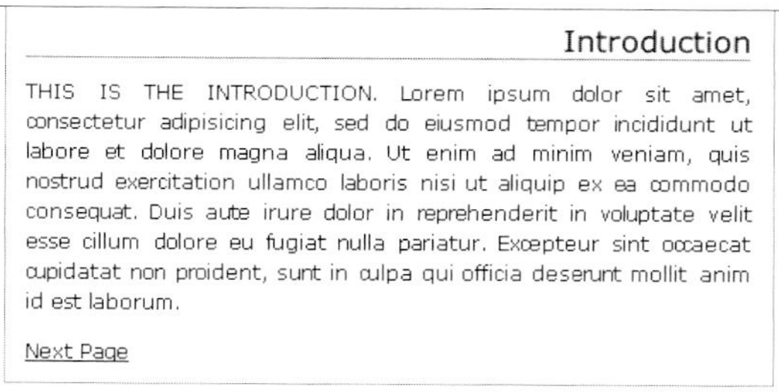

THIS IS THE INTRODUCTION. Lorem ipsum dolor sit amet, consectetur adipisicing elit, sed do eiusmod tempor incididunt ut labore et dolore magna aliqua. Ut enim ad minim veniam, quis nostrud exercitation ullamco laboris nisi ut aliquip ex ea commodo consequat. Duis aute irure dolor in reprehenderit in voluptate velit esse cillum dolore eu fugiat nulla pariatur. Excepteur sint occaecat cupidatat non proident, sunt in culpa qui officia deserunt mollit anim id est laborum.

Next Page

**FIGURE 11.12** This content, shown when the user first arrives, is the only content that has to be initially downloaded.

## PRELOADING DATA

The next example will use Ajax in a slightly different way: to preload content that the user would presumably need to see in short order. As how quickly a Web page is loaded depends partially on how much data is being downloaded, a page can load more quickly when it contains less data. Surely, you could trim out some of the fat, but if there's any content that won't be visible immediately but might be needed in time, that content is a good candidate to be loaded via Ajax. Logical examples include content shown in tabs, accordions, HTML tables, or even upon the user scrolling down the page (i.e., you could load elements in the top half of the page first, and then load more content subsequently).

For the specific example, the page will display an initial page of content, intended to be part of a series (**Figure 11.12**). As soon as the page has loaded, the next bit of content will be retrieved, making it available for immediate display when the user clicks the link. The relevant HTML is simply:

```
<div><h1 id="title">Introduction</h1><p id="content">THIS IS THE
    INTRODUCTION. Lorem ipsum...</p>
<p><a href="view.html" id="nextLink">Next Page</a></p></div>
```

This page includes the ajax.js script, and content.js, to be written in the following steps.

**To preload data:**

1. Create a new JavaScript file in your text editor or IDE, to be named content.js.

2. Begin defining a function to be called when the window has loaded:

```
window.onload = function() {
    'use strict';
```

This one function will do all the work.

3. Create two variables for tracking the pages:

```
var pages = ['model', 'view', 'controller'];
var counter = 0;
```

The page begins with some introductory text, as shown in Figure 11.12. The next three pages, in order, discuss the Model, the View, and the Controller: the three parts of the MVC approach. Each keyword is stored in the correct order in an array and a counter is initialized to 0. This counter will be used to know what page to fetch and display next.

4. Fetch the next bit of content:

```
var ajax = getXMLHttpRequestObject();
ajax.open('GET', 'resources/content.php?id=' + pages[counter],
→ false);
ajax.send(null);
```

The request will be made of content.php, passing that script an id value to indicate which bit of content should be requested. Note that this system is going to use a *synchronous* request, as clicking the link won't be meaningful until the new content has been loaded. Alternatively, you could perform an asynchronous request (so as not to prevent other user interactions), but disabled the link until the next bit of content has been loaded.

5. Get the data:

```
var title = ajax.responseXML.getElementsByTagName
→ ('title')[0].firstChild.nodeValue;
var content = ajax.responseXML.getElementsByTagName
→ ('content')[0].firstChild.nodeValue;
```

As this is a synchronous request, the data can be immediately fetched, instead of using a readyState function. The data itself will be in XML format, like:

```
<item>
    <title>The View Component</title>
    <content>Lorem ipsum dolor sit amet.</content>
</item>
```

To get the individual values out, use the getElementsByTagName() method. This method always returns an array, even if it's an array of one element. Consequently, that call must be followed by [0]: the array notation for the first item. Thus, ajax.responseXML.getElementsByTagName('title')[0] will represent <title>The View Component</title>. To get the actual value out, you must again use firstChild—pointing to the text node—and nodeValue.

6. Start creating the link click handler:

```
var nextLink = document.getElementById('nextLink');
nextLink.onclick = function() {
    document.getElementById('title').innerHTML = title;
    document.getElementById('content').innerHTML = content;
```

When the link with an id of *nextLink* is clicked, the page should be updated with the new content. That's accomplished by assigning the corresponding variables to the innerHTML properties of the HTML elements. You could use innerText and textContent with the title, if you want to be more precise and restrictive.

7. Increment and then check the counter:

```
counter++;
if (counter == 3) {
    nextLink.parentNode.removeChild(nextLink);
    ajax = null;
```

To retrieve the next bit of content, the counter has to be incremented (to point to the next item in the pages array). However, there are only three pages of content: when the counter equals 3, the process should stop. In that case, the link is also removed and the Ajax object is cleared out.

8. If the counter does not equal 3, request the next chunk of content:

```
} else { // Get the next bit of content:
    ajax.open('GET', 'resources/content.php?id=' +
      pages[counter], false);
    ajax.send(null);
```

```
title = ajax.responseXML.getElementsByTagName
→   ('title')[0].firstChild.nodeValue;

content = ajax.responseXML.getElementsByTagName
→   ('content')[0].firstChild.nodeValue;
}
```

This code repeats the earlier code, fetching the next page of content.

9. Complete the onclick anonymous function:

```
return false;
}; // End of onclick anonymous function.
```

The value false is returned to prevent the actual request of the linked page.

10. Complete the onload anonymous function:

```
}; // End of onload anonymous function.
```

11. Save the file as contact.js, in a js directory.

## PRELOADING IMAGES

If you would like to preload images, there's an easier, non-Ajax solution: just create a new image element with the file to be loaded as the src:

```
var temp = document.createElement('image');
temp.src = 'images/someimage.png';
```

As soon as that line of code is executed, someimage.png will be loaded by the browser. Because this code will presumably be executed after the page has loaded, the additional loading of the new image will not impede the loading of the original content. You can then swap in this new image, or add it to the page, when needed. To have the code react once the new image has loaded, just attach a load event handler to the new image.

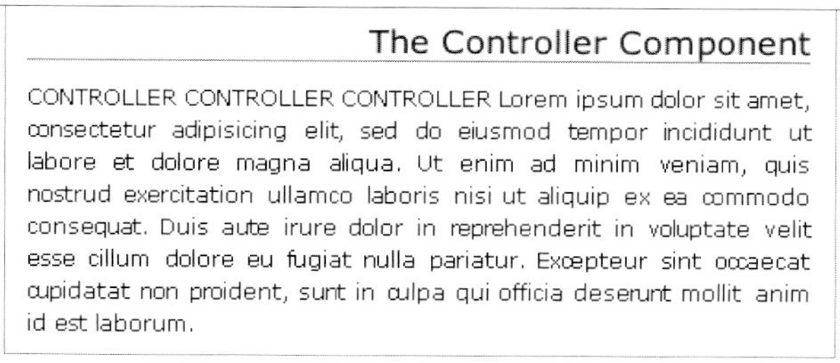

The Controller Component

CONTROLLER CONTROLLER CONTROLLER Lorem ipsum dolor sit amet, consectetur adipisicing elit, sed do eiusmod tempor incididunt ut labore et dolore magna aliqua. Ut enim ad minim veniam, quis nostrud exercitation ullamco laboris nisi ut aliquip ex ea commodo consequat. Duis aute irure dolor in reprehenderit in voluptate velit esse cillum dolore eu fugiat nulla pariatur. Excepteur sint occaecat cupidatat non proident, sunt in culpa qui officia deserunt mollit anim id est laborum.

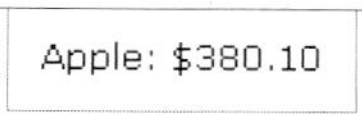

Apple: $380.10

**FIGURE 11.13** The last page of dynamically drawn content, with the link now removed.

**FIGURE 11.14** This page retrieves the latest price for a stock, showing it in the browser, and updating it every minute.

**12.** Create the `content.php` script.

The PHP script would perform basic validation of `$_GET['id']` and then return the correct XML. See the code in the downloadable file if you need direction.

**13.** Test in your Web browser (**Figure 11.13**).

## STOCK QUOTES WITH TIMER

For the last example in this chapter, let's create a page that displays a stock quote (**Figure 11.14**). The HTML page itself will be simple, the most important part being:

```
<p>Apple: $<span id="quote"></span></p>
```

This page also includes the `ajax.js` script, and `quote.js`, to be written in the following steps.

To retrieve the quote, I will use a Google page that returns the data for a stock in JSON format. However, because of the *cross-domain policy restriction* (see the sidebar on the next page), Ajax cannot directly access that Google page. The solution in this case will be to have the JavaScript access a PHP script on the same domain, and that PHP script will access the Google page using a URL access utility named cURL. PHP and cURL do not have the same cross-domain restriction. The Google page returns the data in JSON format, and the PHP script will also return the data in JSON format.

In order to automatically update the stock quote, without any user interaction, a timer will be used to call the PHP script every minute. Remarkably, all of this functionality requires comparatively little code.

## CROSSING DOMAINS

As mentioned in Chapter 9, browsers rightfully prevent JavaScript from retrieving data from other domains. This protects the end user, which is always the first goal. However, if you do need to retrieve data from a reliable source on another domain, there are options.

The first is to use a *proxy script* as in this example: the PHP script acts as an agent between the JavaScript in the client and the data on the other domain. This is a common solution, but be aware that it deliberately undercuts the browser's security measures and adds stress to the server. It would be most prudent to have your PHP script validate the returned data as thoroughly as possible before returning it to the JavaScript.

Another solution is to use an iframe within the client itself. A page can include an iframe whose source is on another domain.

One more solution is to use something called JSON-P, short for "JSON with Padding" (www.json-p.org). Whereas there's a restriction on having JavaScript request a resource from another domain, browsers do allow script tags to reference other domains. To take advantage of this capability, the script tag just needs to load a resource that contains JSON. However, JSON cannot be used as the root of a script block (i.e., there's no executable code in pure JSON). The work-around is to associate a function call with the request. When the JSON data is returned, that function will be called:

```
<script src="http://other.example.edu/resource?jsonp=parse"></script>
```

The function, parse() in the above, is defined in your JavaScript. When that server responds, the JSON data will be immediately sent to the parse() function in your code, which can then parse and handle the data as needed. The function should also perform all the necessary error handling.

An alternative solution still under development is Cross-Origin Resource Sharing (CORS). This is a proposed extension of the XMLHttpRequest object that would allow cross-domain requests under the proper circumstances.

### To create stock ticker:

1. Create a new JavaScript file in your text editor or IDE, to be named quote.js.

2. Begin defining a function to be called when the window has loaded:

```
window.onload = function() {
    'use strict';
```

Again, this one function will do all the work.

3. Create the Ajax object:

```
var ajax = getXMLHttpRequestObject();
```

4. Begin defining the onreadystatechange function:

```
ajax.onreadystatechange = function() {
    if (ajax.readyState == 4) {
        if ( (ajax.status >= 200 && ajax.status < 300)
        || (ajax.status == 304) ) {
```

This code should be quite familiar by this point.

5. Update the page with the new quote:

```
var data = JSON.parse(ajax.responseText);
var output = document.getElementById('quote');
if (output.textContent !== undefined) {
    output.textContent = data[0].l;
} else {
    output.innerText = data[0].l;
}
```

The first step is to parse the JSON data to make it a usable object (you could validate the response here as well). The next step is to update the quote span's contents with the latest stock price. To do that, assign a new value to either textContent or innerText. The Google page returns an array of objects: one object for each stock quote requested. Even if you only request one quote, you still get an array. Hence, the code needs to obtain a reference to the first object, which is data[0]. The specific property that shows the last price of the stock is a lowercase *l*, so data[0].l is the complete reference to the latest price for the one stock.

6. Complete the onreadystatechange anonymous function:

```
        } // End of status IF.
    } // End of readyState IF.
}; // End of onreadystatechange anonymous function.
```

7. Make an Ajax request to get the first quote:

```
ajax.open('GET', 'resources/quote.php', true);
ajax.send(null);
```

The page will start out without any stock quote at all. To fix that, an immediate request is made.

8. Within a timer, perform the request again, every minute:

```
var stockTimer = setInterval(function() {
    ajax.open('GET', 'resources/quote.php', true);
    ajax.send(null);
}, 60000);
```

The timer will call the anonymous function every minute, or 60,000 milliseconds. The function itself just resends the Ajax request.

9. Complete the onload anonymous function:

```
}; // End of onload anonymous function.
```

10. Save the file as quote.js, in a js directory.

11. Create the quote.php script, to be stored in a resources directory:

```
<?php # quote.php
header('Content-Type: application/json');
$curl = curl_init('http://www.google.com/finance/
    info?infotype=infoquoteall&q=AAPL');
curl_setopt($curl, CURLOPT_RETURNTRANSFER, 1);
$result = curl_exec($curl);
curl_close($curl);
print substr($result,3);
?>
```

Using cURL with PHP is a bit of an advanced topic—I discuss it in my *PHP 5 Advanced: Visual QuickPro Guide* (Peachpit Press), but I'll explain this code.

First, because the PHP script is returning JSON data, the proper *Content-Type* header must be sent. Then the cURL request is initialized, providing the specific URL to access. The `curl_setopt()` line tells cURL to return the request response so that it may be assigned to a variable, which is what happens on the next line when the cURL request is executed. Finally, the response itself has to be printed so that the JavaScript receives it. Because the Google response begins with a space and //, I chop those off first.

If your version of PHP doesn't support cURL, or if you'd rather not mess with all this, you can just create a text file with the stock quote in it as JSON data and then update that file every minute. The JSON data, to match what quote.js expects, would be:

```
[{"l": "380.10"}}]
```

12. Test in your Web browser (**Figure 11.15**).

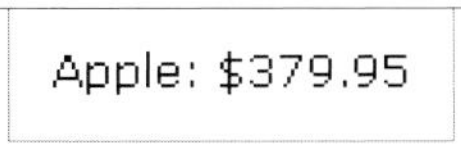

Apple: $379.95

**FIGURE 11.15** The stock price has been updated automatically.

# REVIEW AND PURSUE

If you have any problems with these sections, either in answering the questions or pursuing your own endeavors, turn to the book's supporting forum (www.LarryUllman.com/forums/).

## REVIEW

- How do you create an Ajax object?

- What are the arguments to the open() method?

- When should you make GET requests and when should you make POST requests?

- Why is it critical to load an HTML page through a URL when the JavaScript will be making an Ajax request?

- What is the difference between an *asynchronous* request and a *synchronous* one?

- What is the significance of the readyState property? What readyState value is most important?

- What two properties should you check to confirm that it's time to handle the server response (and what values should those properties have)?

- What method actually begins the Ajax request?

- How do you send data as part of the request? Note: There are multiple answers.

- What Ajax debugging techniques should you deploy when you have problems with Ajax?

- What is *caching* and how does it affect Ajax processes?

- How do you handle XML data using JavaScript? How do you handle JSON data?

- How do you write a PHP script that just returns plain text? What about XML? JSON?

- How do you repeatedly perform an Ajax request, every minute or some other interval? How do you delay performing an Ajax request?

## PURSUE

- For a more time-consuming challenge, complete the examples in this chapter so that they are all progressively enhanced versions that will work well with JavaScript disabled. If you have trouble doing so, see the code in Chapter 15.

- Change any example to use DOM Level 2 event handling instead of DOM Level 0.

- Update the test.js example so that it displays a "Loading..." message or an animated GIF while the Ajax request is occurring.

- Rewrite test.js to work with XML data. Try it with different XML data sets.

- Rewrite test.js to work with JSON data. Try it with different JSON data sets.

- Update login.js to hide the form after the user has logged in. Also have the JavaScript show an error message upon the submission of improper credentials, letting the user try again.

- If you already have an appropriate database, and are comfortable with PHP and MySQL, rewrite login.php to compare the submitted credentials against the database.

- Flesh out the `contact.php` script so that it may be used as a part of a contact form on a live site.

- Modify `quote.html` and `quote.js` so that it retrieves multiple stock quotes.

## WRAPPING **UP**

Although there's still one more chapter in this second part of the book, this chapter on Ajax concludes coverage of what I would describe as the most fundamental aspects of modern JavaScript. The rise and ubiquitous implementation of Ajax has given today's JavaScript its due as a reliable way to enhance the user experience.

The first half of the chapter covered the basics of Ajax, from creating an object, to making the request, to sending data to the server-side resource. You also learned about the three main formats for data—plain text, XML, and JSON—how to create them using PHP, and how to handle them in JavaScript. In the process, you developed a simple test example. You can use that test script to practice any type of Ajax request, while you're learning now or when developing something new in the future.

You also read through the fundamental steps for debugging Ajax processes. You should take these to heart:

- Test the server-side resource by itself.

- Make sure you're running everything through a URL.

- Watch requests in a network monitor.

- Be aware that caching may trip up your debugging efforts.

The last half of the chapter walked through many examples, describing both the theories and the most critical pieces of code. Hopefully, by now you have a sound sense of what Ajax is and can apply this knowledge—and the code—to your current projects.

In the next chapter, the last for Part 2 of the book, you'll learn about *error management*, a hallmark of the professional programmer.

# ERROR
# MANAGEMENT

One of the most profound differences between the beginning programmer and the expert is *error management*. Certainly errors will occur regardless of the skill level of the programmer, as the user causes many problems. But the more seasoned developer does a markedly better job of handling errors when they do occur. In this chapter, you'll learn three ways to prevent and deal with errors. The first is called *exception handling*, and takes advantage of JavaScript's built-in syntax: try...catch. The second approach is the use of *assertions*, which is an easy debugging tool utilized while writing code. Building on that concept, the chapter concludes with an introduction to *unit testing*.

# CATCHING AND THROWING ERRORS

Most of the examples in the book have a basic if-else construct watch for errors:

```
if (/* something good */) {
    // Do this.
} else {
    // Error!
}
```

This approach is sufficient for simple blocks of code, but with more complex situations, especially in Object-Oriented Programming (OOP), there is a better system—*exception handling*, involving the try and catch statements. Over the next several pages, you'll learn these two terms, plus throw and finally.

## CATCHING ERRORS

The syntax for a try...catch block is:

```
try {
    // Lots of code.
} catch (error) {
    // Use error.
}
```

This may seem to be virtually the same as the if-else approach, but a key difference is that a single catch can handle any error that occurs within any number of lines of code. For example:

```
try {
    doThis();
    doThat();
} catch (error) {
    // Use the error somehow.
}
```

## CATCHING BY TYPE

The code in this chapter demonstrates the basics of catching exceptions, with one catch block handling all of the exceptions that could occur within a try block. But exceptions can also be caught by specific type. For example, standard JavaScript code can throw a TypeError exception when the wrong type of object is used or a RangeError exception when a number surpasses the range of allowed values. As these are clearly different problems, you can handle them individually. To do that, use multiple catch blocks, indicating what type of exception each block should catch. To catch a specific type of exception, use the instanceof operator with a conditional:

```
try {
    // Lots of code.
} catch (ex if ex instanceof TypeError) {
    // Use error.
} catch (ex if ex instanceof RangeError) {
    // Use error.
}
```

Once you know how to create your own object types, discussed in Chapter 14, Advanced JavaScript, you can have your code catch your own custom types of exceptions, too.

When an error occurs within the try block (the section between the curly braces), programming flow immediately moves to the catch block. In the previous bit of code, this means that if the doThis() call causes an error, the doThat() call will never be made. If no errors occur within the try block, then the catch block will not be executed at all.

Within the catch block, you can use the error to respond accordingly. As you might come to expect by now, as almost everything in JavaScript is an object, the error variable will also be an object. In fact, in OOP, the errors involved in try...catch blocks are normally called *exceptions*, which is just an object representation of an error. (Now that I've introduced the term *exception*, I'll use that, and the variable ex, largely from here on.) Unless otherwise specified (see the sidebar), the specific type of object will be Error. This object will always have these two useful properties:

- name, which stores the error type

- message, which stores the error message

(Other browsers may provide other Error object properties.)

Using this information, a catch block might just log errors to the console:

```
console.log(error.name + ': ' + error.message + '\n');
```

Understand that the exception variable in the catch block is like a function parameter, and will only exist within that catch block.

### FINALLY CLAUSE

An addition you can make to the try…catch structure is the finally clause. It always comes last:

```
try {
    // Lots of code.
} catch (ex) {
    // Use ex.
} finally {
    // Wrap up.
}
```

The code in the finally block will always be executed, whether or not there was an error. The finally block is normally used to perform cleanup: that which always needs to be done, regardless of what happened beforehand. For example, the code in the finally clause could remove error handlers or assign a null value to a no-longer-needed Ajax object.

Neither the catch nor the finally block is required, but you must have at least one of the two. If you write code in a try block with an exception that is not caught, the exception will be reported to the user like a standard error without a try…catch. If, for some reason, you don't want to do anything with the exceptions that occur, then you can just create an empty catch block:

```
try {
    // Lots of code.
} catch (ex) {
}
```

## THROWING EXCEPTIONS

The code thus far is predicated upon the idea of JavaScript raising the exception when a problem occurs. You can also trigger your own exceptions, to be caught by a catch block. Doing so uses the throw statement:

```
throw something;
```

The *something* part can be a number, a string, or an Error object:

```
throw 2; // Assumes 2 is meaningful in the catch.
throw 'No such HTML element!';
throw new Error('No such HTML element!');
```

If you want, you can also throw a custom exception object, but it should have the name and message properties, as those are expected by most catch blocks:

```
var error = {name: 'Division Error', message: 'Cannot divide
→  by zero.'};
throw error;
```

You can condense these two lines into one:

```
throw {name: 'Division Error', message: 'Cannot divide by zero.'};
```

All that being said, it's generally best to throw Error objects, as you can consistently write catch blocks to use the name and message properties that way. As an added bonus, Error objects may have additional useful properties in some browsers.

Often, the code within a try block will throw an exception when a function call fails, likely because the function did not receive the proper arguments. You can write your own functions to throw exceptions, too:

```
function $(id) {
    'use strict';
    if (typeof id != 'undefined') {
        return document.getElementById(id);
    } else {
```

```
        throw Error('The function requires one argument.');
    }
}
```

Then, the try block might look like:

```
try {
    var elem = $();
    elem.innerHTML = '<p>blah</p>';
} catch (ex) {
    console.log('Could not update the element because: ' +
    → ex.message + '\n');
}
```

With that code, no attempt will be made to update the element's innerHTML property, because the function will have thrown an exception, moving focus to the catch.

## PUTTING IT ALL TOGETHER

There are many good and common uses of try…catch. In this next bit of code, the getXMLHttpRequestObject() function from Chapter 11, Ajax, will be updated. Specifically, the code will try to create an ActiveXObject, and catch any exception that occurred if it could not be created.

**To use try and catch:**

1. Open ajax.js in your text editor or IDE.

2. Replace the line that creates the new ActiveXObject with:

```
try {
    ajax = new ActiveXObject('MSXML2.XMLHTTP.3.0');
} catch (ex) {
    console.log('Could not create the ActiveXObject: ' +
    → error.message + '\n');
}
```

Now the attempt to create the `ActiveXObject` is placed within a `try` block. If that attempt fails, the exception will be caught and reported. You could extend this approach so that it attempts to create different kinds of `ActiveXObjects`, starting with the most current version possible—*MSXML2.XMLHTTP.6.0*—and working your way backward to a version that's supported.

3. Save the file as `ajax.js`.

To test this updated version, rerun any of the examples from the previous chapter.

## USING **ASSERTIONS**

A precursor to true *unit testing*—to be discussed next—is the *assertion*. Unlike the `try...catch` structure just discussed, intended to more gracefully handle errors that *might* occur, assertions and unit testing are designed to flag errors that *shouldn't* occur. In programming, an assertion is code that basically says: *Confirm that this is the case.* Assertions are easy to use, and can quickly aid debugging while you're developing a project. Assertions, like unit testing, will also minimize bugs in the final code you put out.

JavaScript doesn't have a predefined assertion method, but you can write one yourself, or use Firebug, which has its own assertion method. Let's take a quick look at both.

### CREATING AN ASSERTION FUNCTION

Your own assertion function could be defined like so:

```
function assert(expression, message) {
    if (!expression) throw {name: 'Assertion Exception',
       message: message};
}
```

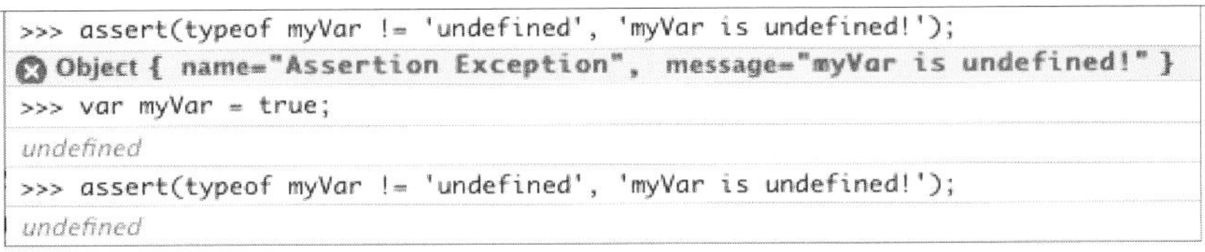

FIGURE 12.1 The assertion
function triggers an exception
when an assertion fails.

```
>>> assert(typeof myVar != 'undefined', 'myVar is undefined!');
⊗ Object { name="Assertion Exception", message="myVar is undefined!" }
>>> var myVar = true;
undefined
>>> assert(typeof myVar != 'undefined', 'myVar is undefined!');
undefined
```

Let's look at how that function would be used and then I'll explain it in detail.
The following code asserts that the variable myVar is not undefined (**Figure 12.1**):

```
assert(typeof myVar != 'undefined', 'myVar is undefined!');
```

The first argument is an expression to be evaluated: What condition do you
want to assert is TRUE? The second argument is the message to be displayed if the
expression *is not evaluated as TRUE*. The combination of that specific assert()
function call and the assert() function definition equates to:

```
if (!(typeof myVar != 'undefined')) {
    throw {name: 'Assertion Exception', message: 'myVar is
    ⇒  undefined'};
}
```

Once you've defined your own assert() function, you can use it to quickly add
checks to your code as you write:

```
var radius = document.getElementById('radius').value;
assert((typeof radius == 'number'), 'The radius must be a number.');
volume = (4/3) * Math.PI * Math.pow(radius, 3);
assert(!isNaN(volume)), 'The volume is not number.');
```

The logic on the last assertion is a bit backward: The goal is to confirm that the
volume variable *is* a number, so the isNaN() function should return false. To assert
that condition, precede the function call by the negation operator.

Because the assert() function throws an exception, that block of code could
be wrapped in a try...catch block.

Note that these assertions should not be part of any live code, for three reasons.
First, users shouldn't be privy to error messages (in fact, in a proper site, users
shouldn't see JavaScript errors at all). Second, there's no reason to have the user

download all that extra code. And third, as mentioned in the introduction to this section, assertions are intended to catch improbable or unlikely problems (i.e., bugs). You would not, for example, use assertions to validate user input.

### ASSERTIONS IN FIREBUG

If you're already using Firebug, you can invoke its `assert()` method as a debugging tool. It's defined as part of the `console` object:

```
var radius = document.getElementById('radius').value;
console.assert(typeof radius == 'number'), 'The radius must be a
    number.');
volume = (4/3) * Math.PI * Math.pow(radius, 3);
console.assert(!isNaN(volume)), 'The volume is not number.');
```

The `console.assert()` method works exactly like the one just defined, taking an expression as its first argument and a message as its second.

## UNIT TESTING

*Unit testing* is a relative newcomer to programming, but is an approach that many developers have embraced as it can make developing larger applications much more reliable. The premise of unit testing is that you define tests to confirm that particular bits of code work as needed. The tests should be as atomic as possible (i.e., specific and small). As with assertions, unit tests should check that code works as intended; unit tests are not for validating user input or for gracefully handling problems that could possibly arise during the live execution of a site (e.g., a server-side resource being unavailable for an Ajax call).

As the scope of the application increases, and as you add and modify the code, you continue to write tests for the new code, while still checking all of the original code against the existing tests, too. By doing this, you ensure that the introduction of new and modified code doesn't break something that was previously working. Moreover, unit testing will often improve the code you write from the get-go, as you'll begin thinking in terms of all possibilities, not just the expected ones.

The best way to implement unit testing is to use one of the many libraries available for the purpose. The first was JSUnit (www.jsunit.net), but it is no longer actively maintained. If you're already using a framework like jQuery or YUI, both of which are discussed in the next chapter, there are unit-testing plug-ins or components for those. For this chapter, I've decided to demonstrate jsUnity (http://jsunity.com), which is an updated version of JSUnit. There are many unit-testing options out there, and I seriously considered both Jasmine (http://pivotal.github.com/jasmine/) and Selenium (http://seleniumhq.org), but I find that jsUnity provides a good yet gentle introduction to the concept.

### SETTING UP JSUNITY

The first thing you'll need to do is download the jsUnity library. You can do so by clicking the link on the jsUnity home page. The download is a single JavaScript file, to be included in the HTML page to be tested:

```
<script src="js/jsunity-0.6.js"></script>
```

Logically, you would include this after the page's key JavaScript code. The tests themselves would then be defined in another script. You'll see an example of all of this in just a few pages.

### DEFINING TESTS

The best way to define a series of tests is to create a *suite* of tests. You can do so in many ways, such as defining an encompassing function:

```
var myTests = function() {
};
```

Within that function, create subfunctions that represent the individual tests:

```
var myTests = function() {
    function testThis() {
    }
};
```

Note that all test functions must have a name that begins with "test."

Within each test, use one of jsUnity's assertion methods. There's no simple assert() method, but you can use the more specific:

- assertTrue()
- assertFalse()
- assertIdentical()
- assertNotIdentical()
- assertEqual()
- assertNotEqual()
- assertMatch()
- assertNotMatch()
- assertTypeOf()
- assertNotTypeOf()
- assertInstanceOf()
- assertNotInstanceOf()
- assertNull()
- assertNotNull()
- assertUndefined()
- assertNotUndefined()
- assertNaN()
- assertNotNaN()

For example, jsUnity versions of earlier code would be:

```
jsUnity.assertions.assertNotUndefined(myVar);
jsUnity.assertions.assertTypeOf('number', radius);
jsUnity.assertions.assertNotNaN(volume);
```

As you can see, all of the assertion functions are defined within jsUnity.assertions.

To reiterate, unit tests should be as particular as possible. Unit tests should also cover the full range of possibilities. This means that tests should confirm appropriate results when code is executed properly, as well as the appropriate—but different—results when code is executed improperly. You'll see a concrete example of this later in the chapter.

## RUNNING TESTS

Once you've defined the tests, you can execute them by invoking the run() method:

```
var results = jsUnity.run(myTests);
```

After all the tests have run, the results variable will have several properties that reflect the results:

- `total`, the number of tests run

- `passed`, the number of tests passed

- `failed`, the number of tests that failed

- `duration`, the time it took to execute the tests, in milliseconds

This is a good start, but these results alone do not indicate *which* tests passed and which ones failed. To do that, you need to define a logging function.

## LOGGING RESULTS

To create a logging function that reports upon the results of the tests, assign a function definition to the `jsUnity.log` property:

```
jsUnity.log = function(message) {
    // Do something with message.
};
```

The function takes a string as its lone argument. This string will differ based upon the current stage of the testing, including reporting on the overall results. You could send this message to the console or dynamically add it to the Web page.

## SETTING UP AND TEARING DOWN

The last thing to know, before getting into an actual example, is how to prepare for tests. Many times, tests expect certain things to have occurred in order for the test to be viable. For example, if functions are triggered after a user action, you could manually trigger those functions as a setup step instead. This step can also be used to adjust for scoping issues: making necessary variables available to the tests.

The `setUp()` function can be used to perform some tasks before the tests are run. The corresponding `tearDown()` function will perform tasks after the tests run. Each can be defined within the test suite:

```
var myTests = function() {
    function setUp() {
        // Do these things.
    }
```

```
    function tearDown() {
        // Now do these.
    }
    function testThis() {
    }
};
```

## PUTTING IT TOGETHER

To put all this information together, let's create some unit tests for the utilities library first defined in Chapter 8, Event Handling. That library has two functions I want to test: $(), which is a shortcut to document.getElementById(), and setText(), for setting the textContent or innerText property of an element. To define the tests, you have to think about what the code should do when used properly or improperly.

The HTML page just needs a couple of paragraphs:

```
<p id="output"></p>
<p id="results"></p>
```

The first will be used for the tests; the second will be used to display the test results.

The HTML page needs to also include the utilities.js script (i.e., the code being tested), the jsUnity library file, and a third file, which defines and runs the tests. It will be written in the following steps.

**To perform unit testing:**

1.  Create a new JavaScript file in your text editor or IDE, to be named tests.js.

2.  Begin defining a suite of tests:

    ```
    var myTests = function() {
        'use strict';
    };
    ```

    The myTests object stores all of the tests. The four following function definitions should go within this anonymous function.

    No setting up or tearing down is necessary in this case.

3. Define the first test:

```
function testGetElement() {
    jsUnity.assertions.assertNotNull(U.$('output'));
}
```

This test confirms that the $( ) function returns a value that is not null when provided with a proper element ID. In other words, when used properly $( ) returns a good result. Because this particular function returns an element reference, and that element could be of many different types—paragraph, input, and so forth—it's not possible to test that the result is of a specific type.

4. Define the second test:

```
function testGetInvalidElement() {
    jsUnity.assertions.assertNull(U.$('doesNotExist'));
}
```

The second test confirms that the function returns null if an invalid element ID is provided.

These two tests combine to cover two possibilities. You could add another test that validates the result when no argument is provided to the $( ) function.

5. Define the third test:

```
function testSetText() {
    jsUnity.assertions.assertTrue(U.setText('output', 'test'));
}
```

The setText( ) function returns a Boolean indicating if it could or could not assign a value to the textContent or innerText property of the provided element. This first test confirms that the value true is returned when the function is provided with a valid element and a string.

6. Define the fourth test:

```
function testCannotSetText() {
    jsUnity.assertions.assertFalse(U.setText('doesNotExist',
        'test'));
}
```

The focus in this chapter is on using a unit-testing library for the purpose of testing a single page of code. To run the tests, the page itself is loaded in a browser. Some unit-testing frameworks and tools make it possible to simultaneously test your JavaScript on multiple browsers or in other ways:

- Tutti (`http://tuttijs.com`)
- Yeti, part of YUI (`http://yuilibrary.com/projects/yeti/`)
- TestSwarm (`http://swarm.jquery.org/`)
- JsTestDriver (`http://code.google.com/p/js-test-driver/`)
- Selenium (`http://seleniumhq.org`)

These tools are far more complicated than jsUnity and other simple libraries, but mastery of them can make large-scale and complex JavaScript applications much more reliable.

I should also mention that John Resig, creator of jQuery, has created Dromaeo (`http://dromaeo.com`) for JavaScript performance testing. And, as a reminder, using tools like JSLint can help catch many actual or potential problems.

This test confirms a result of `false` when an invalid element ID is provided. At this point, two possibilities for the `setText()` function are covered. You could also write tests for misuses of the function, such as a failure to provide both arguments or failure to provide the right types of arguments.

7. Create the `log()` function:

```
jsUnity.log = function(message) {
    U.$('results').innerHTML += '<p>' + message + '</p>';
};
```

The `log()` function in this case will add a paragraph containing the specific message to the results paragraph's `innerHTML` property.

8. Run the tests:

```
jsUnity.run(myTests);
```

As the logging function will report upon the results automatically, there's no need to assign the results of the tests to a new variable.

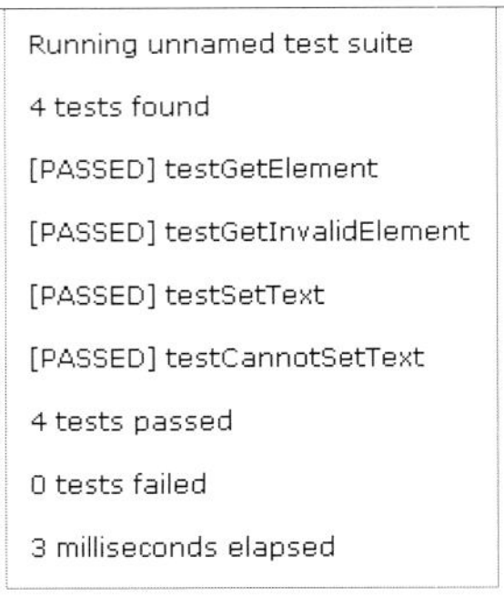

```
Running unnamed test suite
4 tests found
[PASSED] testGetElement
[PASSED] testGetInvalidElement
[PASSED] testSetText
[PASSED] testCannotSetText
4 tests passed
0 tests failed
3 milliseconds elapsed
```

**FIGURE 12.2** All four tests were successful.

9. Save the file as `tests.js` and run the HTML page in your Web browser (**Figure 12.2**).

If any tests failed, you would need to revisit the tested code to see why (i.e., look at the code in the utilities library).

## REVIEW AND PURSUE

If you have any problems with these sections, either in answering the questions or pursuing your own endeavors, turn to the book's supporting forum (`www.LarryUllman.com/forums/`).

### REVIEW

- What is the syntax for using try...catch? What about try...`finally`, with or without a `catch` block?

- What are the advantages of try...catch over using `if-else`?

- What is an *exception*?

- What are *assertions*? How are they used?

- What is *unit testing*? How is it used?

- When should you use exception handling and when should you use assertions or unit testing?

### PURSUE

- Go back and apply exception handling to other code developed in the book or that you developed on your own.

- If you're curious, investigate what other `Error` object properties each browser provides.

- Update `ajax.js` so that it attempts to create an `ActiveXObject` of type *MXSML2.XMLHTTP.6.0* first, and then attempts to create older versions if an exception was thrown.

- Go back and apply assertions or unit testing to code developed in the book or that you developed on your own.

- Add more tests to tests.js to check the results when no arguments, or the wrong type of arguments, are provided to the $() and setText() functions.

- Update all the functions in the utilities.js file so that the functions always deliberately return a value. Write tests for all the possible contingencies.

- If you're feeling confident with what you learned about unit testing in this chapter, investigate the subject more, particularly looking into other testing frameworks.


## WRAPPING **UP**

In this chapter, you learned some new techniques for gracefully handling errors and for catching for bugs as you write code. The hallmark of the professional programmer is *error management*, and *exception handling* via the try…catch block is an important tool toward that end. Any error that occurs within multiple lines of code, placed within a try block, can be handled by the same catch. A finally clause can perform wrap-up as needed.

You also saw two ways of testing your code as you write it: assertions and unit testing. Both are meant to flag the unexpected occurrence during the development process. Assertions are easy to comprehend and are a fundamental building block of unit testing itself. Unit testing, at its most basic level, applies simple tests to confirm that code works as it should under various circumstances. As you develop and expand your software, write more tests, and continue to execute them all, to better guarantee that bugs are not being introduced.

This chapter concludes Part 2 of the book, which covers all of the fundamental aspects of programming in JavaScript. The next chapter is one of three in Part 3: Next Steps. Those chapters introduce ways to expand upon the core principles that you've now learned.

# 13

# FRAMEWORKS

The rise of frameworks is one of the reasons for JavaScript's larger role in today's Web, and you can't fully appreciate modern JavaScript without learning frameworks, too. In this chapter, you'll be introduced to two of the most popular frameworks—jQuery and the Yahoo! User Interface (YUI) Library. You'll pick up the fundamentals for using both, and see a couple of specific add-ons for each. The chapter begins, though, with a discussion of how you should select a framework, as well as the arguments for and against them in general.

# CHOOSING A FRAMEWORK

Once you've decided to learn a framework, the natural question is: Which framework? Clearly, jQuery is the current dominant JavaScript framework, and it would be a reasonable decision to just start with it. But other frameworks that exist today have their own strengths, and new frameworks will come along, so it's worth identifying the criteria for selecting what framework to learn and use.

I would start with browser support, making sure that the framework supports the types and versions of the browsers that your site needs to support. Most frameworks support a very similar range of browsers, but it's worth checking into regardless. I would also research the framework's license. Again, almost all frameworks can be used for free, but you shouldn't assume that's the case.

Perhaps this is because I'm a writer, or because I've had my fair share of struggles trying to learn poorly documented subjects, but the quantity and quality of documentation is my next criterion. If you can't figure out how to use a framework, it's of little use. This includes not just the official documentation but the number, and clarity, of online tutorials that exist. On a similar note, having a community where you can turn to for help and advice will make a big difference, particularly when you get into more complicated uses of frameworks.

Next, I would look at the viability and extensibility of the framework, with the latter often impacting the former. It's hard to tell if a new framework is going to last, but you don't want to waste time mastering a new framework only to have it dry up within the next few months. Knowing that Yahoo! is behind YUI is an argument in its favor (not that companies don't sometimes abandon products, too). The viability of a framework is improved if it's designed to be extensible, as that encourages community involvement. It also means that if a framework can't do what you need it to out of the box, there may be a plug-in that will serve that role, or you could (in theory) write one yourself.

Finally, the framework has to feel right to you. There are easily a half-dozen or more frameworks that meet the above criteria, but you might be more inclined toward one particular framework than another, for no explicable reason. That's perfectly reasonable and justification enough for not trying to identify the "best" framework.

The most important thing to remember when using JavaScript frameworks is that *you're still programming in JavaScript*. This will always be the case, and is a point that can get lost thanks to the ease of frameworks like jQuery. Sound knowledge of JavaScript is required to use a framework, and anyone who says otherwise is quite mistaken. Learning to use a framework is largely a matter of learning how to translate something you'd do in straight JavaScript into framework-based code.

## SHOULD YOU USE A FRAMEWORK?

Just because frameworks are popular and useful doesn't mean you *should* use them, at least not all the time. The arguments for using a framework include faster development, better code testing, and much better cross-browser reliability. Especially when you get into more complex concepts, frameworks will allow you to implement the desired functionality in a fraction of the time it would take you to do so from scratch. Further, no matter how good you are about testing the code you write, a popular framework will have been put to the test much more thoroughly. Toward that end, you should expect the framework to work very, very well on the range of browsers that it supports.

An argument against using a framework is the initial time required to learn the framework. Today's frameworks are fairly approachable, but you will need to spend hours learning how to do something you could do using straight JavaScript in minutes. The counter argument is that once you've mastered a framework, you'll spend minutes writing code that would have otherwise taken you hours.

Secondarily, there is a code bloat factor, in that the user will have to download a significant amount of code on sites that use frameworks. Undoubtedly much of that code will define functionality that won't be used by the particular site, which is a waste of bandwidth, bad for performance, and so forth. Better frameworks ameliorate this problem by allowing you to create custom versions of the framework, supporting only the features you need. And, with today's faster connection speeds, it's not unreasonable for the user to download more and more code. Still, with more and more mobile users, and many users in countries with slower access speeds, you ought to be prudent about what the user is being forced to download.

It's important for today's JavaScript programmers to be conversant with at least one framework, but you should still question, on each project, whether a framework is appropriate. The first criterion for when to use a framework should be the depth and complexity of the site's JavaScript needs. For a small site, with JavaScript that's not too elaborate, code you write yourself will likely be better (depending, of course, upon the quality of that code). For a larger site, with a lot of JavaScript that occasionally gets tricky, a framework is a reasonable choice, even if that possibly means a slight degradation of some performance.

From a development perspective, one common issue with frameworks is that they can make debugging more challenging. To combat that problem, see if your framework supports testing and debugging tools (both jQuery and YUI do). Second, be aware that frameworks are designed to implement a broad range of standard functionality with ease. The antithesis is that when you need custom variations on that functionality, you may find that customization to be unbearably difficult to pull off. This depends greatly upon the extensibility of the framework in use, how well it is documented, and what kind of support is available.

To start, you'll use a framework to reliably and quickly do those things covered in:

- Chapter 8, Event Handling
- Chapter 9, JavaScript and the Browser
- Chapter 11, Ajax

These topics, in framework terms, will be the focus for both of the frameworks discussed in this chapter. What you'll see is that, in these areas particularly, the framework will normalize how you go about a task, meaning the same framework code will work across all browsers.

Subsequently, you'll also learn how to use frameworks to implement new concepts, such as dramatic effects or page widgets. These Web features can be tedious to implement without a framework (i.e., to do in what I'll call "straight" JavaScript).

## INTRODUCING **JQUERY**

The jQuery framework (`http://jquery.com`) has caught on over the past few years to a level that very few technologies reach, especially when there is such varied competition. It's difficult to pinpoint exactly why this one framework is so dominant except to say that jQuery just seems to have "it." To many developers, like myself, jQuery feels right. It's a very simple framework to use, once you get past its cryptic syntax, particularly for smaller applications. In fact, a frequent assumption is that many people using jQuery aren't even learning JavaScript in the first place! (This is hopefully an exaggeration, as it's certainly not a good thing.)

For more advanced needs, such as custom functionality and widgets (i.e., date-picking calendars, dynamic tables, photo displays, and the like), there are oodles of jQuery plug-ins available. The documentation for core jQuery is pretty good, although you can spend a fair amount of time finding, and learning how to use, the plug-ins you need.

The official Web site for jQuery is listed above, and for news and more, check out the jQuery Blog (`http://blog.jquery.com`). There's also a support forum at `http://forum.jquery.com` and an alternative presentation of the jQuery documentation at `http://jqapi.com`.

## GETTING STARTED WITH JQUERY

To use jQuery, you must, of course, incorporate the jQuery library into your HTML page. One option is to download the framework, copy it to your Web server, and include it from there:

```
<script src="js/jquery-1.7.1.min.js"></script>
```

An alternative is to use a version hosted on a Content Delivery Network (CDN). A CDN is a series of servers in multiple locations around the world, each able to provide the same content. Through a CDN, users can download content from a server closer to their geographic location, thereby improving how quickly the site loads. Secondarily, if multiple sites use the same CDN for the same content, as would be the case for a JavaScript framework, the user may not need to download the framework at all when he or she visits your site, as a cached version may be on the browser from a previous visit to another site.

For jQuery and many other frameworks, Google provides a copy you can use through its CDN (see http://code.google.com/apis/libraries/ for more):

```
<script src="https://ajax.googleapis.com/ajax/libs/jquery/1.7.1/
    jquery.min.js"></script>
```

After you've incorporated jQuery into your HTML page, you can begin using jQuery within a second script block or external file. All jQuery interactions go through the jQuery() function, which the framework itself shortens to just $().

What you'll commonly do with any framework is interact with the Document Object Model (DOM). To do that, however, you must first be certain that the entire DOM has been loaded. In straight JavaScript, you would normally wait for the window to load, prior to taking any steps:

```
window.onload = function() {
    // Do whatever.
}
```

The jQuery equivalent is:

```
$(document).ready(function() {
    // Do whatever.
}
```

The first part—$(document)—selects the window document. On this selection, the ready() method is called, which has the effect of calling the internal, anonymous function when the "ready" event is triggered. This jQuery approach is actually a slight improvement on waiting for the window to load, as it only waits for the document to be loaded, allowing JavaScript to be executed before images and other non-material content have loaded.

This whole construct is further simplified to just:

```
$(function() {
    // Do whatever.
});
```

This is one of the few difficulties with jQuery: its syntax is cryptic to the point of being daunting, particularly for those not comfortable with JavaScript. But once you understand that the above construct simply waits for the document to be ready before executing the anonymous function, you can start progressing with the framework. To be clear, the code in almost all of the following pages would go within this block (in place of *Do whatever.*) in a live site.

## SELECTING ELEMENTS

The next thing to learn how to do in jQuery is to select page elements. References to page elements are required to add event handlers, manipulate the DOM, fetch form values, etc. In straight JavaScript, this is accomplished using the getElement-ById() and getElementsByTagName() methods of the document object (among other techniques). In jQuery, selections are made through the $() function. In fact, you've already seen how to select the Web document itself: $(document). To select other page elements, use *CSS selectors* in place of document:

- #something selects the element with an id value of *something*

- .something selects every element with a class value of *something*

- something selects every element of *something* type (e.g., p selects every paragraph)

Those three rules are more than enough to get you started, but know that unlike document, each of these gets placed within quotation marks. For example, the code `$('a')` selects every link and `$('#output')` selects the element with an id value of *output*.

These rules can be combined as well:

- `$('img.landscape')` selects every image with a class of *landscape*

- `$('#loginForm input')` selects every input element found within an element that has an id of *loginForm*

jQuery has its own additional, custom selectors, allowing you to select page elements in more sophisticated ways. See the jQuery manual for examples.

Note that `$()` can return one or more elements, depending upon how many met the criterion (or `null`, if no matches were made).

## MANIPULATING ELEMENTS

Once you've selected the element or elements to be manipulated, applying any number of jQuery functions to the selection will change its properties. You can change the attributes of a selection using the `attr()` method. Its first argument is the attribute to be addressed; the second, the new value. For example, the following code will disable a submit button by adding the property `disabled="disabled"`:

```
$('#submitButtonId').attr('disabled', 'disabled');
```

As you can see, jQuery supports and actively promotes *chaining* function calls. The first part finds and returns a selection; the part after the period calls the `attr()` function on the selection. This is just a more direct alternative to using separate lines of code like:

```
var submit = $('#submitButtonId');
submit.attr('disabled', 'disabled');
```

This next chain of calls changes two attributes in one step:

```
$('#submitButtonId').attr('disabled', 'disabled').attr('value',
→ '...Processing...');
```

Another way to manipulate elements is to change the CSS classes that apply to a selection. The `addClass()` function applies a CSS class and `removeClass()` removes one. The following code adds the *emphasis* class to a specific blockquote and removes it from all paragraphs:

```
$('#blockquoteID').addClass('emphasis');
$('p').removeClass('emphasis');
```

The `toggleClass()` function can be used to toggle the application of a class to a selection: adding the class if it isn't applied, removing the class when it is.

You can change individual styles using the `css()` method. Its first argument is the style name and its second is the new value.

The already mentioned functions generally change the *properties* of the page's elements, but you can also change the *contents* of those elements. To get the current contents, such as the text a user entered into a form element, use `val()`. When provided with an argument, `val()` assigns a new value to that form element. For example, in Chapter 8, a textarea was limited as to how many characters the user could enter there. That code in jQuery would be:

```
var comments = $('#comments'); // Get a reference.
var count = comments.val().length;
if (count > 100) { // Update the value:
    comments.val(comments.val().slice(0,100));
}
```

Similar to `val()`, the `html()` function returns the HTML contents of an element and `text()` returns the textual contents. Both functions can also take arguments used to assign new HTML and text, accordingly, similar to using `innerHTML`, `innerText`, and `textContent`.

## DOM MANIPULATION

In straight JavaScript, DOM manipulation is easy but verbose. To add a new paragraph within a DIV but before a form, you would create the new paragraph as an element, get a reference to the DIV, get a reference to the form, and then call the `insertBefore()` method on the DIV. jQuery improves upon this flow in a couple of ways.

First, there are multiple functions for adding content to the DOM (plus variations on these):

- `after()`
- `append()`
- `before()`
- `prepend()`

These methods are nice because they allow you to add content without always obtaining references to two elements. For example, in jQuery, to add a paragraph before a form, you would call the `before()` method on the form:

```
$('#actualFormId').before(/* new paragraph */);
```

No reference to the parent DIV is required.

Similarly, the `remove()` method removes an element (or elements, if multiple were selected) without having to get a reference to the element's parent node:

```
$('#selection').remove();
```

The equivalent in straight JavaScript would be:

```
var elem = document.getElementById('selection');
elem.parentNode.removeChild(elem);
```

A second improvement for DOM manipulation in jQuery is that content to be added can be in multiple formats, including literal HTML. To add a paragraph to a DIV, you don't have to create a new paragraph element; you can just do this:

```
$('#actualFormId').before('<p>This is the paragraph.</p>');
```

Naturally, you can use element references, too, or you can use jQuery selections. The following code moves an element from one location to another by adding a clone, then removing the original:

```
$('#destination').before($('#selection').clone(true));
$('#selection').remove();
```

## HANDLING EVENTS

The next thing to learn is how to associate event handlers with an element in jQuery. You've already seen one example:

```
$(function() {
    // Do whatever.
});
```

That code calls the anonymous function when the "ready" event is triggered by the document object. Following this pattern, in jQuery event listeners are assigned using the syntax *selection.eventType(function.)*

The *selection* part would be like $('.something') or $('a'): whatever element or elements to which the event listener should be applied. The *eventType* value will differ based upon the selection. Common values are *change, focus, mouseover, click, submit,* and *select.* In jQuery, these are all actually the names of functions being called on the selection. These functions take one argument: the function to be called when the event occurs on that selection.

**TIP:** jQuery version 1.7 adds the new on() and off() methods for adding and removing event handlers.

For example, to handle the event of any image being moused over, you would code:

```
$('img').mouseover(function() {
    // Do this!
});
```

As explained in Chapter 7, Creating Functions, on some browsers, the this object can be used within event handlers to refer to the element that triggered the event (as opposed to using the target property of the event object, as required by older versions of Internet Explorer). In jQuery, you can reliably use this, regardless of the browser. The following code adds a change event to an element (theoretically, a select menu) and alerts the selected value:

```
$('#someSelect').change(function() {
    alert(this.val());
});
```

jQuery also defines some methods for associating more complex event handlers with elements. For example, the hover() method takes a mouseover function as its first argument and a mouseout function as its second, letting you create two event handlers with an element in one step. See the jQuery documentation for more.

## CREATING EFFECTS

I haven't discussed effects much up to this point in the book, as the creation of effects in straight JavaScript requires a lot of code. But once you're using a framework, lots of effects become easy to use. For starters, the hide() and show() functions ...um...hide and show the selection. Thus, to hide a form (perhaps after the user has successfully completed it), you would write:

```
$('#actualFormId').hide();
```

The toggle() function, when called, will hide a visible element and show a hidden one (i.e., it toggles between those two states). Note that these functions neither create nor destroy the selection (i.e., the selection will remain part of the DOM, whether it's visible or not).

Similar to show() and hide() are fadeIn() and fadeOut(). These functions also reveal or hide the selection, but do so with a bit of effect added in. More complicated effects can be accomplished using the animate() method or through various plug-ins.

## PERFORMING AJAX

The last use of straight JavaScript that you should know how to perform using jQuery is an Ajax request. There are several ways to perform Ajax requests in jQuery, but I'll explain how to use the $.ajax() method. The ajax() method is not invoked on a selection, as the previous examples were. Also note that you're not *invoking* $, as in $(), but treating it like an object that has a method named *ajax*.

The ajax() method takes one argument, an object of options used to configure the request:

```
$.ajax(options);
```

All of the Ajax request particulars—the resource to be requested, the type of request to make, the data to be sent as part of the request, and how to handle the response—get defined within the options object:

```
var options = {
    url: 'http://www.example.com/somepage.php',
    type: 'get',
    data: /* actual data */,
    dataType: 'text'
};
```

The url property gets assigned the name of the server-side resource to request.

The type property is the type of request being made, with *get* and *post* being the two most common. A GET request is the default, so it does not need to be assigned, but it's normally best to be explicit.

Next, a property named data is assigned the actual data to be passed to the server-side resource (when applicable). The data should be in the format of an object, as in (assuming u and p are variables with values):

```
data: {username: u, userpass: p},
```

With that data object, the server-side resource—the PHP script—will receive the data in $_GET['username'] and $_GET['userpass'], when the GET method is used.

The dataType setting is the data type *expected back* from the server-side request. Allowed values include *text*, *xml*, *html*, and *json*. In the case of JSON, the response data will already be parsed so that it's immediately usable.

The final thing the object has to do is identify the function to be called when the Ajax request successfully completes. This function is assigned to the success property. Note that success means both a readyState value of 4 and a good status code; the function does not need to check for those. The function should take at least one argument, the data that is the server response:

```
success: function(response) {
    // Do something with response.
},
```

**FIGURE 13.1** The jQuery UI date-picker widget.

## JQUERY PLUG-INS

What a framework has, but straight JavaScript does not, is the ability to tap into plug-ins to quickly add complex functionality (the equivalent in straight JavaScript would be libraries, discussed at the end of the chapter). There is an amazing breadth of plug-ins available for jQuery, whether you need an image display tool (e.g., the "lightbox" effect), the ability to handle file uploads via Ajax, or dynamic HTML tables. I would recommend you begin with the jQuery User Interface (jQuery UI, http://jqueryui.com). The jQuery UI defines lots of useful widgets, such as the accordion, the autocomplete, a date picker, and tabs, plus new effects like drag and drop, resizing, and sorting. jQuery UI also has a theme builder tool, which makes it easy to customize the look of a widget to your site's aesthetic. jQuery UI is easy to use, too.

First, after incorporating the jQuery library, bring in jQuery UI:

```
<script src="https://ajax.googleapis.com/ajax/libs/jquery/1.7.1/
→  jquery.min.js"></script>
```

```
<script src="https://ajax.googleapis.com/ajax/libs/jqueryui/1.8.16/
→  jquery-ui.min.js"></script>
```

As you can see, the jQuery UI library is also available through Google's CDN.

Then, for example, to create a date picker, call the datePicker() method on the selection of the element that should trigger the widget (**Figure 13.1**):

```
$('#dateInput').datepicker();
```

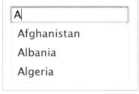

FIGURE 13.2 An Autocomplete widget.

This is how all jQuery plug-ins work: they define new methods that can be called on jQuery selections. Most methods take optional objects to customize the plug-in's behavior. The jQuery UI documentation discusses how to customize the date picker, allowing you to specify the format for the selected date, what default date to use, the earliest or latest date that can be selected, and so on.

In the following pages, you'll look more closely at two plug-ins, but I also want to quickly mention QUnit (http://docs.jquery.com/QUnit), a jQuery-compatible unit-testing tool. See Chapter 12, Error Management, for more on the topic of unit testing.

### THE AUTOCOMPLETE WIDGET

I want to demonstrate, in detail, one widget found in the jQuery UI library: Auto-complete. Autocomplete is the ability of an input, such as a search terms box, to make recommendations as you type. It's a great use of JavaScript, although one that is tricky to implement without using a framework. Autocomplete requires a series of components:

- An event handler that watches for keypress events within the input element

- A searchable data source from which matches can be pulled

- The display of applicable matches

- The ability for the user to navigate and select the matches

The jQuery UI Autocomplete widget can do all of this, using a variety of data sources, including Ajax. As the simplest example, the following uses a hard-coded JavaScript array as its data source:

```
$('#inputId').autocomplete({
    source: ['Afghanistan', 'Albania', 'Algeria']
});
```

The code first selects the target element and then calls the autocomplete() method on it, thereby converting it to an Autocomplete prompt. Just this little bit of code does all the work, creating a list as its output, which is styled using CSS (**Figure 13.2**).

To use an Ajax request as the data source, identify the URL to request as the source:

```
$('#inputId').autocomplete({
    source: 'http://www.example.com/somepage.php'
});
```

The user-entered text will automatically be appended to the source in the format ?term=*X*, where X is the user's input. The corresponding PHP script can use $_GET['term'] to determine what values to return. Let's turn this into a real example in the next series of steps.

The HTML page, country.html, needs a text input:

```
<input type="text" name="country" id="country">
```

The HTML page also needs to include both the jQuery library and jQuery UI. In the next script block, add this:

```
$(function() {
    $('#country').autocomplete({
        source: 'resources/countries.php',
        minLength: 2
    });
});
```

(For the sake of simplicity, in this chapter, the minimal amount of hand-coded JavaScript will just be placed directly in the page.)

First, the functionality will only be added once the document is ready. Then the text input is selected, and the autocomplete() method called on it. The method takes an object as its argument. The object's source property points to the PHP script that will provide the data. It will be written in the subsequent steps. The object's minLength property prevents an Ajax call from being made until at least two characters have been entered.

**To create the PHP script:**

1. Create a new PHP script in your text editor or IDE, to be named countries.php.

```php
<?php // countries.php
```

2. Set the *Content-Type* header:

```php
header('Content-Type: application/json');
```

The PHP script will return JSON data, so it must set this header (see Chapter 11 for details).

3. Create an empty array:

```php
$data = array();
```

The $data variable will store matches.

4. Create a list of countries:

```php
$countries = array( 'Afghanistan', 'Albania', 'Algeria',
→ 'Andorra',...);
```

The script contains the full list. In the real world, a database would probably be the source, which would actually be a bit easier (and should be something the average PHP developer could do).

5. If a term was provided, use it:

```php
if (isset($_GET['term'])) {
```

The jQuery Ajax call will automatically append ?term=X to the URL. The PHP script can access the characters the user typed via $_GET['term'].

6. Loop through the array to find matches:

```php
foreach ($countries as $country) {
    if (stripos($country, $_GET['term']) !== false) $data[] =
    → $country;
} // End of FOREACH.
```

The PHP function `stripos()` quickly finds one string within another, like JavaScript's `indexOf()`. Note that this will find substrings anywhere within the string, not just at the beginning, and is case insensitive.

The function returns the indexed position where the substring was found, or `false` if it was not found. If `false` is not returned by `stripos()`, then the term was found and the particular country will be added to the `$data` array.

7. Complete the `$_GET['term']` if:

   ```
   } // End of IF.
   ```

8. Return the JSON data:

   ```
   echo json_encode($data);
   ```

9. Save the file as `countries.php`, in a `resources` directory, and test `country.html` in your Web browser (**Figure 13.3**).

   Remember that PHP scripts must be run through a URL and so the HTML page must be run through a URL, too.

**FIGURE 13.3** This Autocomplete uses a PHP script for its data source.

## THE DATATABLES PLUG-IN

To wrap up this section on jQuery, I want to discuss a third-party plug-in. HTML was originally conceived as a way to convey information, with tables being a medium for presenting lots of data (not, you know, for controlling layouts). HTML tables are still great for that purpose, although the core functionality of an HTML table, or the lack thereof, leaves a lot to be desired. Adding functionality to an HTML table is an excellent task for JavaScript, and much more easily accomplished using a framework.

There are many table plug-ins for jQuery, but I'll make use of DataTables (`http://datatables.net`). DataTables is open source, easy to use, and has all the features you might need (even though it's free, if you like and use it, you ought to chip in a couple of dollars to the developer).

**FIGURE 13.4** The original HTML table.

**FIGURE 13.5** The enhanced HTML table, now sortable by clicking on the column headings.

**FIGURE 13.4** The original HTML table.

**FIGURE 13.5** The enhanced HTML table, now sortable by clicking on the column headings.

Alphabetical of countries in the world.

| Country | Population | Size (sq. km.) |
|---------|-----------|----------------|
| Afghanistan | 29121286 | 645807 |
| Albania | 2986952 | 28748 |
| Algeria | 34586184 | 2381741 |
| American Somoa | 65628 | 197 |

Show [10] entries

Alphabetical of countries in the world.

| Country | Population | Size (sq. km.) |
|---------|-----------|----------------|
| Afghanistan | 29121286 | 645807 |
| Albania | 2986952 | 28748 |
| Algeria | 34586184 | 2381741 |
| American Somoa | 65628 | 197 |

Showing 1 to 4 of 4 entries

To use DataTables, you must download the library, and then include it in your HTML page, *after* you've included the jQuery library:

```
<script src="https://ajax.googleapis.com/ajax/libs/jquery/1.7.1/
⇥ jquery.min.js"></script>
<script src="js/jquery.dataTables.min.js"></script>
```

Next, make sure you've created a well-formed HTML table, with a proper ID (**Figure 13.4**):

```
<table id="countries">
    <caption>Alphabetical of countries in the world.</caption>
    <thead>
        <tr><th>Country</th><th>Population</th><th>Size (sq. km.)
        ⇥ </th></tr>
    </thead>
    <tbody>
        <tr><td>Afghanistan</td><td>29121286</td><td>645807
        ⇥ </td></tr>
```

Next, in another script block, call the dataTable() method on the selection:

```
$(function() {
    $('#countries').dataTable();
});
```

That's all there is to it (**Figure 13.5**)! To customize the effect of DataTables, provide a configuration object to the dataTable() method call. Naturally, the DataTables documentation lists all the particulars, with plenty of examples.

# INTRODUCING **YUI**

The Yahoo! User Interface (YUI) Library (`http://yuilibrary.com`) was originally created by Yahoo! to be used internally, but was later converted to a public framework. The framework is used by Yahoo!'s own network of sites, meaning that the code is well tested and designed to perform as optimally as possible. The framework excels at complex Rich Internet Applications (RIAs), particularly those that work with a lot of data. If you're already using some of Yahoo!'s own Web services, YUI makes all the more sense. On the other hand, for smaller, simpler needs, jQuery or a similar framework may be more appropriate.

In 2009, Yahoo! released a major overhaul of YUI, version 3, which fixes many of the mistakes that had been made, or eventually developed, in the first two versions of the library. In this chapter, I'll write specifically about version 3, although some of its components are still in beta at the time of this writing. When you encounter YUI-related documentation and tutorials online, be certain to distinguish between YUI 3 and older versions. As you'll see, code in YUI 3 starts with `YUI()`, whereas code in YUI 1 and 2 started with `YAHOO`, although YUI 3 is somewhat backward-compatible.

The official Web site for YUI is listed above, and for news and more, check out the YUI Blog (`http://yuiblog.com`). If you're already familiar with jQuery, you will appreciate the jQuery - YUI 3 Rosetta Stone (`www.jsrosettastone.com`), which does a great job of translating common tasks between the two frameworks.

## GETTING STARTED WITH YUI

To use the YUI framework, you must first incorporate it into your page. You can do so by downloading the framework to your computer, placing it on your Web server, and including it from there. Alternatively, Yahoo! makes the library available on its CDN:

```
<script src="http://yui.yahooapis.com/3.4.1/build/yui/yui-min.js">
  </script>
```

To use YUI, you must create a "sandbox," which is a realm in which YUI will execute. To do that, invoke `YUI().use()`. `YUI()` is the one function that gets placed within the global namespace; all the remaining functionality is performed through it. The `use()` method takes two or more arguments. The first argument(s) will always be the modules you want to load. The final argument will be a function to call:

```
YUI().use('module', function(Y) {

    // Do stuff here.

});

    or

YUI().use('module1', 'module2', function(Y) {

    // Do stuff here.

});
```

The list of modules that are available can be found in the YUI documentation and I'll highlight some of the key ones in this chapter. The two most important are *Node*, for DOM interactions, and *Event*. User-contributed modules can be found in the gallery (http://yuilibrary.com/gallery/). Smartly, YUI will only download modules when they are needed, which minimizes the performance hit of using a framework and multiple modules. Further, YUI will automatically attempt to load all dependent modules. For example, you don't need to formally load the Event module, as it will be loaded automatically by many others.

The function, provided as the last argument, will be called (and its contents executed) once the modules have loaded. This function should be set to accept one argument, which will be a reference to the YUI sandbox instance, Y. Much of what you'll do within the function will use that argument.

To be clear, you can have multiple uses of this construct within the same page, thereby creating multiple sandboxes. One sandbox might establish core functionality; another might create a widget.

Finally, you should know how to wait until the window is ready before interacting with the DOM. To do that in YUI, use:

```
YUI().use('module1', 'module2', function(Y) {

    Y.on('domready', function() {

        // Do DOM stuff here.

    });

});
```

This is roughly equivalent to this in straight JavaScript:

```
window.onload = function() {
    // Do whatever.
}
```

And to this in jQuery:

```
$(function() {
    // Do whatever.
});
```

(Technically, the framework versions will fire the events slightly before `window.onload`, but the point is the same.)

Over the next several pages, I'll talk about a couple of the main modules, with a focus on those the end user will benefit from. If you do begin using YUI, be certain to look into the developer modules: Console, Profiler, and Test. The Console is a debugging tool, Profiler helps you to improve your code's performance, and Test is for creating unit tests (discussed in Chapter 12).

## SELECTING ELEMENTS

Most of what you'll do with YUI requires a reference to one or more page elements. Interacting with the page is done through the Node module, which means it must be loaded:

```
YUI().use('node', function(Y) {
    // Do stuff here.
});
```

Within that function, you can write your specific code. Note that you use the lowercase version of the module name in the `use()` call.

To select a single page element, invoke the `one()` method. To select multiple matching elements, use `all()`. Both are called through the Y argument passed to the function. Both methods will work with the same kinds of CSS selectors used in jQuery:

```
var header = Y.one('#header'); // Element with an id of 'header'.
var links = Y.all('a'); // All link elements.
var errors = Y.all('.error');; // All elements with a class of error.
```

## MANIPULATING ELEMENTS

Once you have a reference to an element (which YUI calls a *node*), you can access its properties using set() and get(). The get() method returns the value of a given property:

```
var email = Y.one('#email');
email.get('value'); // Value entered into the email input.
```

As with jQuery, it makes sense to chain commands together in situations where you won't need to refer to the element later:

```
Y.one('#email').get('value');
```

The set() method takes two arguments: the property to set and its new value. For example, this code disables a submit button:

```
Y.one('#submit').set('disabled', 'disabled');
```

To change an element's text or HTML, instead of one of its properties, use the setContent() method:

```
Y.one('someP').setContent('New text.');
```

This is equivalent to using innerHTML.

There are also several methods for working with an element's styling. The addClass() method adds a new class to an element and removeClass() removes it:

```
Y.one('#emailP').addClass('error');
```

Both methods are safe to use without affecting any other classes that the element might also have. In this way, using addClass() and removeClass() are more powerful and simpler than just assigning values to an element's className attribute, as you would in straight JavaScript. The toggleClass() attribute adds a class if it isn't applied to an element and removes it if the class was already applied.

To retrieve an element's applicable styling, invoke the getStyle() or getComputed Style() method, depending upon whether you're looking for the inline style rules or all applicable styles. Each takes the style you're looking at as its argument:

```
var s = Y.one('#someDiv').getComputedStyle('height');
```

To change an element's inline styling, invoke the setStyle() method, providing the style name and its new value:

```
Y.one('#someDiv').setStyle('font-size', '12em');
```

## DOM MANIPULATION

The create() method of the Node module is used to make new elements. It takes the opening HTML tag as its argument:

```
var p = Y.Node.create('<p>');
```

Note that this is different than using document.createElement(), which just takes the tag name:

```
var p = document.createElement('p');
```

Once you've created an element, use prepend(), append(), or insert() to add it to the page. All are called on the parent element:

```
Y.one('#someDiv').prepend(p);
```

The prepend() method adds the new content as the first child of the parent, pushing any existing content down. The append() method adds the new content as the last child. The insert() method takes a second argument, which is the element before which the new content should be inserted:

```
Y.one('#someDiv').insert(p, Y.one('#someOtherP');
```

Interestingly, these methods can take new nodes (i.e., elements) as the content to be added or they can take raw HTML or just a string:

```
Y.one('#someDiv').prepend('<p>This paragraph of text.</p>');
```

To remove an element from the DOM, call remove() on the element:

```
Y.one('#someElem').remove();
```

Note that you don't need to get a reference to the parent element as you would in straight JavaScript:

```
var elem = document.getElementById('someElem');
elem.parentNode.removeChild(elem);
```

## HANDLING EVENTS

To create event handlers in YUI, invoke the on() method, called on the target element. Its first argument is the type of event; the second is the function to be called when the event occurs:

```
Y.one('#theForm').on('submit', handleForm);
Y.all('a').on('click', handleClick);
```

The full list of events can be found in the YUI documentation, and naturally differ from one type of element to the next.

The handling function will receive the event as its lone argument and will do so across all browsers (i.e., you don't have to check window.event on IE). The event argument is also normalized, meaning its behavior and properties will be consistent and reliable regardless of the browser. For example:

```
Y.all('a').on('click', function(e) {
    // e.target.href is always usable!
});
```

## CREATING EFFECTS

As I explained in the jQuery section on effects, I haven't discussed effects much to this point in the book. With YUI, there are plenty of effects you can implement, starting with the show() and hide() methods. By default, they immediately reveal or hide the element(s) on which they are called:

```
Y.one('#someDiv').show();
Y.one('#someDiv').hide();
```

If you use the value true as the first argument to either of these methods, YUI will fade the element in or out, using the Transition module:

```
Y.one('#someDiv').show(true);
Y.one('#someDiv').hide(true);
```

The documentation for the Transition module shows how to further customize the effect being applied.

## PERFORMING AJAX

To make Ajax requests in YUI, use the IO (Input/Output) utility module. Once the module has been loaded, the io() method performs an Ajax request. Its first argument is the resource to be requested; its second is a configuration object. Through this object you establish all the request particulars, including the type of request to be made, the data to be sent, and what to do when the request finishes.

```
Y.io('somepage.php', {
    method: 'get',
    data: /* actual data */,
    on: {
        success: function(id, response) {
            // Use response.responseText or response.responseHTML.
        }
    }
});
```

The default method is GET, so you can omit the method property unless you're using a different method. (Still best to be overt most times.)

The data property of the configuration object passes data to the server-side resource. The data can be in the format of a string of *name=value* pairs, separated by ampersands, or as a generic object.

The on property takes an object as its value. That object should indicate the functions called for one or more Ajax request events. The most important is *success*, which indicates both a readyState of 4 and the proper status code. When that event occurs, the function will be called. Its first parameter will be a transaction ID, which won't necessarily be meaningful or used. The second parameter will receive the Ajax response, the same as in a straight Ajax request.

## SKINNING **WIDGETS**

A nice feature of YUI is the ability to skin widgets (like jQuery UI's themes). To apply a skin, just add the skin's identifier as a class for the widget container or page:

```
<body class="yui3-skin-sam">
```

That applies the default skin, *Sam*, to the entire page. To use a different skin, you'll change the skin class accordingly, and then link the corresponding CSS. The style sheets are also available through Yahoo!'s CDN. For example, to apply Yahoo!'s *Night* skin to a tab widget, you'd use this:

```
<link rel="stylesheet" type="text/css" href="http://yui.yahooapis.com//build/tabview/assets/skins/
→ night/tabview.css">
```

Or, you can indicate the skin when creating the YUI instance, and YUI will automatically load the needed assets:

```
YUI({skin: 'night'}).use('someModule', function(Y) {});
```

The YUI documentation discusses how to extend the two base skins—Sam and Night—to create your own look or one that matches the rest of your site.

## USING WIDGETS AND UTILITIES

YUI has several predefined widgets for creating HTML content, ranging from date pickers to charts, data tables, overlays (i.e., modal CSS windows), and tabs. I want to demonstrate one of them here: AutoComplete.

### THE AUTOCOMPLETE WIDGET

The autocomplete concept was explained in the jQuery section. In YUI, as the simplest example, the following uses a hard-coded JavaScript array as an Auto-Complete widget's data source:

```
YUI().use('autocomplete', 'autocomplete-filters', function (Y) {
    Y.on('domready', function() {
        Y.one('#country').plug(Y.Plugin.AutoComplete, {
            resultFilters: 'phraseMatch',
            source: ['Afghanistan', 'Albania', 'Algeria']
        });
    });
});
```

To start, the YUI instance loads both the *AutoComplete* module and *AutoComplete Filters*, which defines the available filters to use. Next, the code waits until the DOM has loaded.

Finally, the AutoComplete widget is enabled as a plug-in to the #country element, via the plug() method. This is how most widgets and such are used in YUI: by calling the plug() method on a selection, providing the plug-in as the first argument and a configuration object as the second. In this case, the configuration object sets the type of results to match (using the filter) and the data source.

To use an Ajax request as the data source, just change the source to the URL, appending ?q={query} to it:

```
source: 'http://www.example.com/search.php?term={query}'
```

The user-entered text will be used in lieu of {query} and the corresponding PHP script can use $_GET['term'] to determine what values to return.

To further tweak the widget's behavior, use other object properties, such as maxResults, to restrict how many results are displayed (the default is unlimited), and minQueryLength, which requires a minimum number of characters before autocompletion kicks in (the default is only 1).

**Figure 13.6** shows the AutoComplete widget using the same PHP source script as defined earlier.

As an added bonus, you can have the widget automatically highlight matches within the results using the *AutoCompleteHighlighters* module and the resultHighlighter property (**Figure 13.7**):

```
YUI().use('autocomplete', 'autocomplete-filters',
    'autocomplete-highlighters', function (Y) {
    Y.on('domready', function() {
        Y.one('#country').plug(Y.Plugin.AutoComplete, {
            resultFilters: 'phraseMatch',
            resultHighlighter: 'phraseMatch',
            source: 'resources/countries.php?term={query}'
        });
    });
});
```

**FIGURE 13.6** The Ajax-based AutoComplete widget in YUI.

**FIGURE 13.7** The same AutoComplete widget (and results), with inline highlighting.

**FIGURE 13.8** The YQL Console.

## THE YQL UTILITY

Along with the widgets, YUI has defined several utilities. For example, the ability to sort lists of items is made possible by the Sortable module. There are animation utilities, those for managing the browser's history, ones that create graphics, and tons of utilities for working with data. One in particular that I want to demonstrate is YQL, the Yahoo! Query Language (`http://developer.yahoo.com/yql/`).

YQL is an SQL-like language for querying data over Web services. In other words, instead of retrieving records from a local database using SQL and PHP, you can retrieve records across a network using YQL and JavaScript. (You can also use YQL without YUI, such as directly from a PHP script.)

To start using YQL, you'll want to open the YQL Console in your Web browser. It's available at `http://developer.yahoo.com/yql/console/` (**Figure 13.8**). The console provides an interface where you can practice queries and see the exact results. On the right side of the page you'll find example queries. Just click on any one to see and execute the corresponding SQL statement.

Under the example queries are the available data tables (i.e., sources). At the time of this writing, there are 152 native tables and over 1,000 more community ones. You can search through the tables by keyword or browse through them in the list. Most tables have multiple possible queries. For example, the music source provides the ability to find information about an artist by name, look into a specific album, song, or video, or even find similar artists to a given one.

The weather table is easy to use: click on it in the list, then click on the *weather.forecast* item, and the console will run the query

```
select * from weather.forecast where location=90210
```

Underneath the query, the resulting data is displayed. Click on the tree to easily navigate the results (**Figure 13.9**).

To use YQL with YUI, perform a query using the syntax

```
Y.YQL(query, function(result) {
    // Use result.
});
```

The `result` variable will contain the response you saw in the Console window. With the weather example, `result.query.results.channel.item.description` will contain HTML that can be displayed within the Web browser (**Figure 13.10**). While that may not seem obvious, all you need to do is navigate the tree of results in the Console to confirm this for yourself, where `result.query` is the root of the response. Navigating the tree more, you'd see that `result.query.results.channel.item.forecast[0]` would contain information about today's forecast, and `result.query.results.channel.item.forecast[1]` has information about tomorrow's forecast.

**FIGURE 13.9** The query for grabbing the weather report for a given zip code.

**FIGURE 13.10** Part of the response from the weather request, used to update the page.

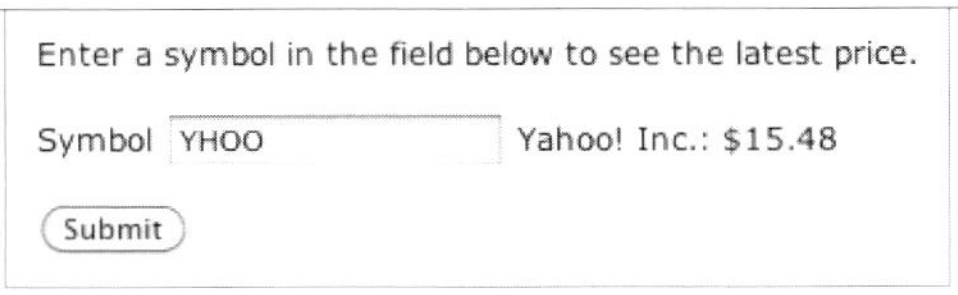

FIGURE 13.11 Yahoo!'s latest
stock price, fetched using YQL.

Enter a symbol in the field below to see the latest price.

Symbol YHOO              Yahoo! Inc.: $15.48

( Submit )

**To reiterate, to use YQL:**

1. Head to the YQL Console.

2. Find the table you need.

3. Create the query you need.

4. Examine the results.

5. Turn to the JavaScript to use those results.

Let's put this into action in the following example, which will take a stock symbol from the user and fetch the latest price (**Figure 13.11**).

The HTML page, to be named stock.html, needs a form for entering the symbol and a place to write the output:

```
<form action="#" method="get" id="theForm">

    <p>Enter a symbol in the field below to see the latest price.</p>

    <p><label for="symbol">Symbol <input type="text" name="symbol"
        id="symbol"></label> <span id="output"></span></p>

    <p><input type="submit" value="Submit"></p>

</form>
```

The HTML page would also include the YUI library, and have another script block where the functionality is defined. That will be written in the following steps.

**To use YQL:**

1. Create a new script block after including the YUI library:

   ```
   <script></script>
   ```

2. Within the script block, create a YUI sandbox:

   ```
   YUI().use('node', 'yql', function(Y) {
   });
   ```

   This JavaScript will explicitly use two YUI modules: Node and YQL.

3. Within the anonymous function just defined, check for the *domready* event:

```
Y.on('domready', function() {
});
```

4. Within the *domready* anonymous function, get the needed document references:

```
var symbol = Y.one('#symbol');
var output = Y.one('#output');
```

The first reference is to the form input where the user will enter the symbol. The second reference is to the span where the output will be written.

5. Still within the *domready* anonymous function, set an event handler on the form's submission:

```
Y.one('#theForm').on('submit', function(e) {
});
```

The rest of the code will go within this anonymous function.

6. Prevent the form's submission:

```
e.preventDefault();
```

7. Assign a message to the output span:

```
output.set('text', '...checking...');
```

This line changes the contents of the span to that string. This is equivalent to assigning a value to the innerText or textContent property. Depending upon how quickly the request is performed and handled, the user may or may not see this message for a brief moment.

8. Perform the request:

```
Y.YQL('SELECT Name, LastTradePriceOnly FROM yahoo.finance.
    quotes WHERE symbol="' + symbol.get('value') +
    '"', function(result) {
    output.set('text', result.query.results.quote.Name +
        ': $' + result.query.results.quote.LastTradePriceOnly);
}); // YQL
```

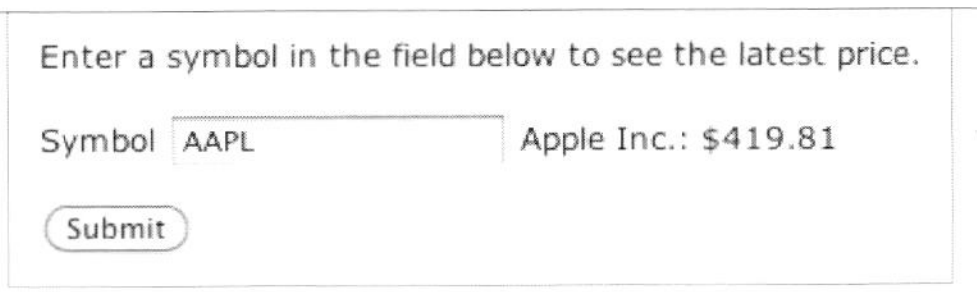

**FIGURE 13.12** Apple's latest stock price.

Enter a symbol in the field below to see the latest price.

Symbol  AAPL          Apple Inc.: $419.81

( Submit )

The request is made using YQL and the command:

```
SELECT Name, LastTradePriceOnly FROM yahoo.finance.quotes
   WHERE symbol="XXX"
```

Within the handling function, the `result` variable will represent the response. Two of its properties are used to set the `span`'s new text: the stock name and its last trade price. Remember that you can verify the result using the YQL Console.

In a real-world script, I'd likely confirm that results were returned, and indicate an error if not.

9.  Save the file and test it in your Web browser (**Figure 13.12**).

## LIBRARIES

Short of using a full-on framework but still an alternative to writing your own code for every problem is to use a library. Libraries aren't as all encompassing as a framework, but sometimes that's an advantage. I want to mention some of the libraries that should be on your radar. For most of these, you should have no problems using them by reading the library's own documentation or one of the many tutorials you can find online.

SWFObject (http://code.google.com/p/swfobject/) has been around for years and years and has historically been one of the most common libraries. This is ironic, because the point of SWFObject is to embed Flash content—using the .swf format—within a Web page. With the advent of HTML5, the need for Flash is undoubtedly diminishing, but there still is a demand.

Modernizr (www.modernizr.com) is a wonderful library that is a must for sites using cutting-edge HTML and CSS. Modernizr makes it safe to use HTML5 and CSS3 in a site, allowing those features to degrade nicely on older browsers.

Head JS (http://headjs.com) is intended to be the only JavaScript file included by your site. It then downloads the other scripts that the site needs. This arrangement, which may seem like simple obfuscation, will improve how quickly the site loads. Head JS also has some of the same HTML5 and CSS3 support features as Modernizr. Similarly, RequireJS (`http://requirejs.org`) acts as a JavaScript library or module loader, with the intent of improving performance and compatibility.

To display video on your site, without using Flash, there are many JavaScript libraries available. Just two are Video JS (`http://videojs.com`) and MediaElement. js (`http://mediaelementjs.com`).

If you plan on doing Web development for mobile devices, there are other libraries and frameworks to consider:

- jQuery Mobile (`http://jquerymobile.com`)

- Sencha Touch (`www.sencha.com/products/touch`)

- Zepto (`http://zeptojs.com`)

While not a framework for use on final Web sites, Blackbird (`www.gscottolson. com/blackbirdjs/`) creates an inline HTML alternative to the console, making debugging easier.

If you're using PHP for your server-side development, there are a few JavaScript libraries intended to bridge that gap, although documentation, viability, and support are inconsistent among them all (from what I've observed).

Although not a library itself, you should check out Microjs (`http://microjs.com`), which lists a slew of microframeworks and microlibraries. These are tools that normally required only 3 KB or less, sometimes less than half a kilobyte. There's a menu at the top of the page to filter the list by a specific need.

## REVIEW AND PURSUE

If you have any problems with these sections, either in answering the questions or pursuing your own endeavors, turn to the book's supporting forum (`www.LarryUllman .com/forums/`).

### REVIEW

- What are the benefits to using a framework? What are some of the negatives?

- What is a CDN? Why is it beneficial?

- How do you confirm that the window is ready for DOM manipulation in jQuery?

- What are some of the ways to select elements in jQuery?

- How do you get, or set, the value of elements using jQuery?

- How do you establish event handlers in jQuery?

- How do you perform an Ajax request using jQuery?

- How do you create a YUI sandbox?

- How do you confirm that the window is ready for DOM manipulation in YUI?

- How do you select one or multiple elements using YUI?

- How do you get, or set, the value of elements using YUI?

- How do you establish event handlers in YUI?

- How do you perform an Ajax request using YUI?

- What is YQL? Where can you go to experiment with YQL?

## PURSUE

- If neither YUI nor jQuery felt right to you, investigate one of the other frameworks mentioned in Chapter 1, (Re-)Introducing JavaScript, or look online for yourself.

- Rewrite any of the examples from the previous chapters (particularly those in Chapters 8, 9, and 11) using a framework.

- Research and experiment with some of the other components in jQuery UI.

- Research and experiment with other third-party jQuery plug-ins.

- Research and experiment with some of the other YUI modules and utilities.

- Research and experiment with some third-party YUI modules.

- Try the YUI AutoComplete example for yourself.

- Try the YUI weather forecasting example for yourself.

- Add validation to the stock-quote-fetching example, both on the user input and on the YQL result.

- For a more advanced application, modify the stock-quote-fetching example to handle multiple stocks. As a hint, you can use an IN clause in the query:

  ```
  SELECT Name, LastTradePriceOnly FROM yahoo.finance.quotes
  WHERE symbol in ('XXX', 'YYY', 'ZZZ')
  ```

  Then you would loop through `result.query.results`.

- Try playing with some of the other YQL tables.

- Research and experiment with some of the libraries mentioned.

## WRAPPING **UP**

Frameworks are an important component of any language, and JavaScript is no exception. Indeed, the creation and evolution of many good JavaScript frameworks have greatly helped developers overcome browser inconsistencies, resulting in more reliable sites. Toward that end, the chapter began with a quick discussion of how one goes about selecting a framework, and how one decides whether using a framework is appropriate or not.

Most of the chapter introduced and demonstrated core concepts in two popular frameworks: jQuery and YUI. jQuery is especially approachable, and can quickly suit lots of needs, but you have to get accustomed to its syntax first. YUI is larger in scope, and does a wonderful job of handling data (particularly that from Web services), but can be daunting to implement in situations where one component depends upon another. Still, you should hopefully have a fair sense of how to use either, from the basics of selecting elements, DOM manipulation, event handling, and making Ajax requests, to creating widgets and using plug-ins.

In the next chapter, you'll return to straight JavaScript, investigating some of its more advanced concepts. Like frameworks, those concepts are crucial to modern JavaScript, but aren't necessary for every project on which you will work.

# 14

# ADVANCED
# JAVASCRIPT

As with any Object-Oriented Programming (OOP) language, working with JavaScript can range from being relatively simple and easily comprehended, to extremely complex and rather obtuse. Since this book is intended for beginners, I've restricted coverage thus far to the most critical yet understandable aspects of the language. However, there are several more advanced concepts with which you should be familiar, and those are the focus in this chapter. Even if you don't immediately begin using these new techniques, they should be in the back of your mind, for retrieval at some future date when the need arises.

# DEFINING **NAMESPACES**

Most OOP languages support *namespaces*: named realms for defining classes, libraries, and modules. Chapter 7, Creating Functions, demonstrated how variables exist in the *global* scope or in the *local* (i.e., function) scope. Namespaces simply create a new local scope that keeps its code out of the global scope. Namespaces are useful once you begin creating libraries of code, as namespaces prevent conflicts. For example, by using namespaces, the error() function you defined in your code won't conflict with the error() function defined in an imported library.

JavaScript doesn't support namespaces in the same way that other OOP languages do, but you can create a namespace by defining an object:

```
var someNamespace = {
    someProperty: 23,
    someMethod: function() {...}
};
```

Once defined, you can access the properties and methods using object notation: someNamespace.someProperty and someNamespace.someMethod(). This, hopefully, looks familiar to you as it was first done in Chapter 8, Event Handling, with the definition of the U library (short for *utilities*). In fact, that's all namespaces are: the creation of a single, globally available object that encapsulates useful code within a local scope.

When defining namespaces, you do need to ensure that the namespace object identifier will be unique. Using your name or initials as part of the name would probably suffice.

If the namespace you're creating represents a library that will be regularly updated and maintained, it would be prudent to add information about the library to its definition:

```
var LARRYULLMAN_UTILITIES = {
    NAME: 'Larry Ullman Utilities Library',
    VERSION: 1.6,
    /* More variables and functions. */
};
```

## CREATING A CONFIGURATION **OBJECT**

Along with namespaces, another common use of an object in distributed code is to act as a configuration tool. To create a configuration object, define a custom object that uses its properties to represent site-specific settings:

```
var CONFIG = {
    host: 'http://www.example.com/',
    errorClass: 'error',
    outputElement: 'output',
    something: 'value'
};
```

Your other JavaScript code could then refer to CONFIG.*x*, such as:

```
elem.className = CONFIG.errorClass;
```

By creating one configuration object, you can more easily use the same body of JavaScript code on multiple projects without needing to hunt through lines and lines of code to edit specific values. Further, when done properly, the rest of the JavaScript library can be upgraded without changing the configuration, and without breaking the site.

Conventionally, information such as this is represented as a constant, which JavaScript does not universally support. Still, the names can still be written in all capital letters (as constants normally are in other languages) to indicate the constant-like intent.

## CREATING CUSTOM **OBJECTS**

JavaScript has defined several objects that serve necessary tasks: Math, String, and so forth. Sometimes you'll want your own custom object type, though, to better represent the kind of data that a particular application will be working with. In a typical OOP language, custom objects are created by defining *classes*, a class being a template. Code then creates instances of those classes, which are objects. Because JavaScript is a *prototypical* OOP language (not a class-based one), a different approach is needed. There are two options: which you choose depends upon whether you need to create a *single custom object* or *multiple instances of the same custom object*.

## CREATING A SINGLE CUSTOM OBJECT

To create a single custom object, just create a new variable of type `Object`:

```
var employee = {
    firstName: 'Joseph',
    lastName: 'Doe',
    department: 'Accounting',
    hireDate: new Date(),
    getName: function() {
        return this.lastName + ', ' + this.firstName;
    } // No comma.
}; // Don't forget the semicolon!
```

That code comes from Chapter 6, Complex Variable Types. This approach is fine in many situations, but you could not create two similar custom objects in this manner (e.g., two separate employees).

## CREATING MULTIPLE INSTANCES OF A CUSTOM OBJECT

The alternative way to create a custom object is to use a function as an object generator. Here is how the employee example would be rewritten:

```
function Employee(firstName, lastName, department) {
    this.firstName = firstName;
    this.lastName = lastName;
    this.department = department;
    this.hireDate = new Date();
    this.getName = function() {
        return this.firstName + ' ' + this.lastName;
    };
}
```

```
>>> var e1 = new Employee('Jane', 'Doe', 'Accounting');
undefined
>>> var e2 = new Employee('John', 'Smith', 'Human Resources');
undefined
>>> e1.firstName;
"Jane"
>>> e2.getName();
"John Smith"
```

**FIGURE 14.1** Two instances of the custom Employee object.

Let's look at what's happening in detail. First, a function to be used as an object generator, called a *constructor* function, is conventionally named with an initial capital letter. Second, within the function, variables are referenced using this. The special this keyword, introduced in Chapter 7, has different meanings in different contexts, but in this situation, this will always refer to the current object. Finally, it's important that the function does not return any values, because the function will be invoked differently than other functions you've created in this book.

With this particular example, the expectation is that the values that differentiate one employee from the next will be passed to the function when it's first called. Those values are then stored in variables. The Employee function itself also defines a function, named getName(), which returns the employee's first and last names, separated by a space.

To have this function create an object, use the new keyword when calling it:

```
var e1 = new Employee('Jane', 'Doe', 'Accounting');
```

That line, with new, creates a copy of the Employee function definition using the specific argument values.

More employees can be created:

```
var e2 = new Employee('John', 'Smith', 'Human Resources');
```

> **NOTE:** Make sure you use the *new* keyword when using a constructor function or strange side effects can occur.

You can now use the object's properties and methods as you would any other object (**Figure 14.1**):

```
e1.firstName; // Jane
e2.getName(); // John Smith
```

**FIGURE 14.2** This example uses two custom objects, with one being passed to the method defined with another.

```
>>> var hr = new Department('Human Resources');
undefined
>>> hr.addEmployee(e2);
undefined
>>> hr.employees[0].lastName;
"Smith"
```

This whole concept is really just the same as how you *can* (but normally don't) create a String, Number, or Object variable:

```
var lang = new String('JavaScript');
```

You can even pass your custom object to functions, as you would any other object. Here is another custom object definition, which then takes an object as an argument to one of its methods (**Figure 14.2**):

```
function Department(name) {
    this.name = name;
    this.employees = [];
    this.addEmployee = function(emp) {
        this.employees.push(emp);
        emp.department = this.name; // To ensure consistency.
    };
}
var hr = new Department('Human Resources'); // Create the object.
hr.addEmployee(e2); // Add an Employee object.
hr.employees[0].lastName; // Smith
```

That last line first grabs a reference to the first employee in the hr department, and then returns the employee's lastName property. As an alternative, you could add a method to the Department object that returns a single employee by indexed position:

```
this.getEmployee(index) {
    return employees[index];
}
```

Then you could do this instead:

```
hr.getEmployee(0).lastName;
```

```
>>> e1.toString();
"Name: Jane Doe
Department: Accounting"
```

```
>> var now = new Date();
>> now.toString();
    "Wed Jan 4 14:34:00 EST 2012"
>> now.valueOf();
    1325705640501
```

**FIGURE 14.3** How the toString() method for an Employee object might represent the object's value.

**FIGURE 14.4** The toString() and valueOf() results for a Date object.

## MORE COMPLETE CUSTOM OBJECTS

To be consistent with the way other objects behave in JavaScript, you could define toString() and valueOf() methods for your custom objects. The toString() method always returns a string representation of the object. With a custom object, it'd be up to you, the developer, to determine what the appropriate representation might be (**Figure 14.3**):

```
function Employee(firstName, lastName, department) {

    // Other stuff.

    this.toString = function() {

        return 'Name: ' + this.firstName + ' ' + this.lastName +
            '\nDepartment: ' + this.department;

    };

}
```

The valueOf() method returns the simplest representation of the object and its value. With many objects, these two methods return the same thing, but with some objects, they don't. For example, the valueOf() a Date object is a number: the time-stamp of that date, as the number of milliseconds since the epoch. The toString() method of a Date object returns the date and time as a string (**Figure 14.4**).

With the Employee object, I'd be inclined to have the valueOf() just return the employee's name, without any labels or additional information. Or, if applicable, the valueOf() method could return something equally unique and meaningful, such as the employee's ID number.

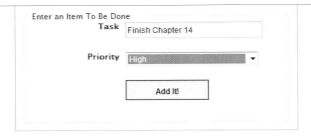

**FIGURE 14.5** The form for adding new tasks.

## PUTTING IT ALL TOGETHER

To practice creating custom objects, let's create another version of the tasks management application, first begun in Chapter 6, and then updated in Chapter 7. In this version, each task will have three properties: its name, its priority, and whether or not it has been completed. The HTML page, to be named tasks.html, will need to have a form that takes two of these three values (**Figure 14.5**):

```
<form action="#" method="post" id="theForm">
    <fieldset><legend>Enter an Item To Be Done</legend>
        <div><label for="task">Task</label><input type="text"
        → name="task" id="task" required></div>
        <div><label for="priority">Priority</label>
        → <select name="priority" id="priority" required>
        <option value="high">High</option>
        <option value="normal" selected>Normal</option>
        <option value="low">Low</option>
        </select></div>
        <input type="submit" value="Add It!" id="submit">
        <div id="output"></div>
    </fieldset>
</form>
```

The form also has a DIV, with an id of *output*, where messages will be displayed. The HTML page includes the tasks.js script, to be written in the following steps.

**To create and use custom objects:**

1. Create a new JavaScript file in your text editor or IDE, to be named `tasks.js`.

2. Begin defining the `Task` function:

```
function Task(name, priority) {
    'use strict';
```

This function will create new `Task` objects. It takes two arguments: the task name and its priority.

3. Assign the parameters to internal variables:

```
this.name = name;
this.priority = priority;
this.completed = false;
```

The two parameters are assigned to variables, and a third variable, `completed`, is given an initial value of `false`.

4. Define a `toString()` function:

```
this.toString = function() {
    return this.name + ' (' + this.priority + ')';
};
```

The `toString()` function returns the task in the format *task (priority)*.

5. Complete the `Task` function:

```
} // End of Task function.
```

6. Begin defining the window's load event-handling function:

```
window.onload = function(){
    'use strict';
```

This anonymous function will be called when the page loads and it will do all the remaining work.

7. Get references to the various elements:

```
var task = document.getElementById('task');
var priority = document.getElementById('priority');
var output = document.getElementById('output');
```

The JavaScript will need access to three page elements: two form elements and the DIV where the output will be written.

8. Declare the tasks variable:

```
var tasks = [];
```

As in the previous versions of this script, this array will store every task.

9. Begin defining a function to handle the form's submission:

```
document.getElementById('theForm').onsubmit = function() {
```

This anonymous function will be called every time the form is submitted. Its role is to create a new Task object and add it to the tasks array.

10. Create a new Task and add it to the array:

```
var t = new Task(task.value, priority.value);
tasks.push(t);
```

To create a new Task object, invoke the Task constructor function, prefacing the call with new. The values for the two arguments will come directly from the form. Next, the task, represented by the variable t, is added to the array using push().

11. Update the output DIV and complete both anonymous functions:

```
        output.innerHTML = 'There are now <b>' +
    ➯  tasks.length + '</b> item(s) in the to-do list.
    ➯  Just added:<br>' + t.toString();
        return false;
    }; // End of onsubmit anonymous function.
}; // End of onload anonymous function.
```

Enter an Item To Be Done

Task  Start Chapter 15

Priority  Normal

Add It!

There are now 2 item(s) in the to-do list. Just added:
Start Chapter 15 (normal)

FIGURE 14.6  Another task has been added!

The output will show the number of tasks currently stored and the information about the task just added.

12. Save the file as tasks.js, in a js directory next to tasks.html, and test it in your Web browser (**Figure 14.6**).

## UNDERSTANDING **PROTOTYPES**

As stated many times over in this book, JavaScript is a different kind of OOP language in that it is *prototypical*. This means that the variables you create are derived from a predefined model, called a *prototype*, not a class definition. This prototypical nature is true whether the prototype is built into JavaScript or defined by you:

```
var lang = 'JavaScript';
var e1 = new Employee('Jane', 'Doe', 'Accounting');
```

In that code, the lang variable is an instance of the String prototype and e1 is an instance of Employee. (One technicality: the value of lang is a literal string, but it will be automatically converted to a String object when it is used like one.)

```
> function Test() {}
  undefined
> var t = new Test();
  undefined
> t.toString();
  "[object Object]"
> t.valueOf();
  ▶ Test
```

**FIGURE 14.7** The empty Test object instance already has some methods defined, inherited from the Object prototype.

## PROTOTYPICAL INHERITANCE

Every JavaScript object inherits the properties and methods defined in its prototype. If you were to inspect a custom object you created, you'd find methods and properties that you did not create (**Figure 14.7**).

And, as you've already seen in the Employee example, objects can also be assigned their own properties and methods, which would not be found in the original prototype. For example, Department has an addEmployee() method, but Object, Department's prototype, does not.

Some variables will have a prototype that in turn has its own prototype. For example, the e1 object is based upon the Employee prototype, which is based upon Object. This is known as the *prototype chain*. When you reference any object property or method, JavaScript looks through the object's prototype chain to find a corresponding attribute. JavaScript will stop looking through the prototype chain when it gets to the root prototype—that from which all other prototypes stem, which is Object. If no corresponding property or method is found in the chain, then undefined is returned.

To differentiate between properties or methods defined within an object or within its prototype chain, you can call the hasOwnProperty() method, providing it with the property in question. This method is defined in Object, and is therefore inherited by all other objects. For example:

```
var test = { thing: 1 };
test.hasOwnProperty('thing'); // true
test.valueOf(); // Object: i.e., there is a valueOf() method
test.hasOwnProperty('valueOf'); // false
```

**NOTE:** The *Math* object is one of the few that you cannot create an instance of (i.e., it cannot be the prototype for any other objects).

```
>>> var e1 = new Employee('Jane', 'Doe', 'Accounting');
undefined
>>> Employee.prototype.getNameBackwards = function() {    return this.lastName + ', ' + this.firstName;}
function()
>>> e1.getNameBackwards();
"Doe, Jane"
```

**FIGURE 14.8** By changing the prototype, any instance of that prototype can make use of the modifications.

## ADDING PROTOTYPE METHODS

In a class-based OOP language, you can change the properties and methods of every instance object by altering the underlying class definition. In JavaScript, which doesn't have classes, you change the prototype's properties and methods by editing the object's prototype property. For example, the Employee object can be altered after its original definition. Here, a new method is added to it:

```
function Employee(firstName, lastName, department) {

    /* Actual code. */

}
Employee.prototype.getNameBackwards = function() {

    return this.lastName + ', ' + this.firstName:

}
```

Now that the new method has been added to the prototype, you can call it on any instance objects: e1.getNameBackwards(). In fact, you can even call this method if the e1 variable was created *prior to* adding the method to the Employee prototype (**Figure 14.8**)!

The ability to retroactively change a prototype even allows you to change the definition of objects built into JavaScript, such as String. This next bit of code adds a trim() method to the String object, if it doesn't already have one:

```
if (typeof String.prototype.trim == 'undefined') {

    String.prototype.trim = function() {

        return this.replace(/^\s+|\s+$/g,'');

    };

}
```

(The ability to actually trim blank space from the beginning and end of a string requires a regular expression.) After executing that code, your JavaScript will have a trim() method for String objects, whether that method was native to the browser (as the method was added in ECMAScript 5) or not.

As another example, you could extend the Date object so that it has a getMonth Name() method, which returns the textual version of the month represented by the date.

Although JavaScript allows for you to modify prototypes, this concept is sometimes called *monkey patching*, and should be used cautiously. Understand that modifying a prototype is a global change that impacts every instance of that prototype. Adding unusual methods and properties to built-in JavaScript objects, such as String, could create bugs in code that expects the prototype to be untainted. The best use of this concept is to create backwards-functional objects, as in the String.prototype.trim() example (i.e., creating a String object that can be used reliably regardless of the browser type or version).

Each method added to a prototype is therefore added to every instance of that prototype, whether it is needed or not. If you only need a function for a specific instance, you can create that function separately and call it while providing the object:

```
function doSomething(obj) {
    // Do something with obj.
}
```

Or you could add the function definition to just the single instance:

```
var obj = {};
obj.doSomething = function() {
    // Do something with this.
}
```

**TIP:** Changing a prototype can also be used to prevent closures from being created, although this is a much more advanced topic.

# WORKING WITH CLOSURES

One of the most important, albeit abstract JavaScript concepts is the *closure*. You'll come across different ways of describing closures, but I think it's easiest to think of a closure as a function call with a memory. In other words, a closure is a function tied to the scope in which it was created. This means that a closure function can make use of the variables that existed (in the same scope) when the function was created.

Loosely speaking, you *might* have a closure situation when:

- One function is defined within another

- The inner function references variables that exist in the outer function (including the outer function's parameters)

- The inner function will be called after the outer function has stopped executing

Let's look at an example to better explain this: The tasks.js script just defined has a closure in it. The key components of the onload anonymous function are:

```
window.onload = function() {
    // Setup variables, including tasks.
    document.getElementById('theForm').onsubmit = function() {
        tasks.push(t);
    };
};
```

The onload function will only be called once: when the page loads. That function defines some variables, including the tasks array. In a normal, non-closure situation, function variables are no longer available once the function execution has completed. This means that without a closure, the tasks array will cease to exist after the onload function has executed all its commands.

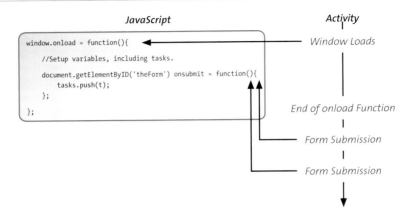

```
window.onload = function(){

    //Setup variables, including tasks.

    document.getElementByID('theForm') onsubmit = function(){
        tasks.push(t);
    };

};
```

*JavaScript*

*Activity*

Window Loads

End of onload Function

Form Submission

Form Submission

The closure is created by defining another function within that outer onload function. All closures require that one function be defined within another. The inner function, which handles the form submission, will be called any number of times, but always after the outer function has finished executing (**Figure 14.9**).

Because the onsubmit function will be called after the onload function has finished executing, and because the onload function has variables with the same scope as the onsubmit function, JavaScript retains those variables after the onload function has completed, creating a closure. Thanks to the closure, the onsubmit function can make use of tasks, because the variable is kept alive. This is the hallmark of a closure: the local variables that were available to the function when the function was defined are still available to that function even when it is called at a later time. The closure creates a persistent but still locally scoped variable.

A variation on this same script created in Chapter 7 also had a closure, this time using an immediately invoked function:

```
(function(){
    var tasks = [];
    function addTask() {
        // Use tasks.
    }
    function init() {
```

```
            document.getElementById('theForm').onsubmit = addTask;
    }
    window.onload = init;
})();
```

The outermost anonymous JavaScript function is executed as soon as JavaScript encounters it. Within that function is a variable, tasks, which exists in the local scope. The addTask() function will be called every time the form is submitted, which will always come after this immediately invoked anonymous function has stopped running. Again a closure is created, with the addTask() function retaining access to the tasks variable.

In a moment I'll walk through another closure example, but I want to highlight one common point of confusion first. As explained, a key feature of closure functions is that they have access to the local variables that existed (in the same scope) when the closure was defined. The trick is that the closure will have access to the value of the variable at the time of the closure function *call*, not its definition. For example, this next onload function is a closure with access to the i variable:

```
(function() {
    var i = 1;
    window.onload = function() {
        alert(i); // 2, not 1
    }
    i = 2;
})();
```

When the inner function is defined, i is initially assigned a value of 1. By the time the inner function is called—in this case, after the outer immediately invoked function has terminated—i will have a value of 2, which is what will be alerted.

This problem most commonly arises when closures are created within a loop. For example, say you want to add a click handler to every link in a page. The click handler will then do something with the link that was clicked. You might think you could do this:

```
function someFunction() {
    var links = document.getElementsByTagName('a');
    for (var i = 0, count = links.length; i < count; i++) {
        links[i].onclick = function() {
            // Use links[i] (but this will not work).
            return false;
        }
    }
}
```

What you would find is that links[i] within the onclick function always returns undefined. To discover why, let's assume there are two links. The for loop would be executed twice, successfully adding a click handler to each link. Then the loop terminates when i becomes 2, which is greater than the length of the links array. When you click on one of the links, because of the closure, the onclick anonymous function will still be able to access i, but its value will be 2, which is the last value that the variable had.

There are more advanced uses of closures, most notably involving situations in which one function returns another function. But the topic itself is difficult enough to grasp that I'm choosing to start with the most accessible uses, specifically related to event handling. For another example of a closure, the following script will use a timer. Timers, by their very nature, have functions that are defined at one time but executed at another (see Chapter 9, JavaScript and the Browser, for more on timers). The following example will use a timer and a closure to create a fader, which changes the opacity of an element from 100 percent to 0 percent to fade it out gradually.

For the HTML page, to be named fader.html, you can create any visible element with an id value of *target*. It doesn't matter whether the element is a paragraph of text or an image. However, you do need to add this CSS to your page, in order for Internet Explorer to recognize changes in this opacity:

```
#target { zoom: 1; }
```

The HTML page should include the fader.js script, to be defined in the following steps.

**To use a closure to create a fader:**

1. Create a new JavaScript file in your text editor or IDE, to be named `fader.js`.

2. Begin defining an onload anonymous function:

```
window.onload = function() {
    'use strict';
    var target = document.getElementById('target');
```

The outer function first gets a reference to the target element.

3. Set the initial opacity:

```
var opacity = 100;
```

The opacity begins at 100 (i.e., percent), and will be decreased within the fader function.

4. Begin defining the `setInterval()` function:

```
var fader = setInterval(function() {
    opacity -= 10;
```

The `setInterval()` function takes a function as its first argument. This function, which will be called repeatedly after the outer, anonymous onload function terminates, will be a closure, with access to the `target` and `opacity` variables.

Within the function, the opacity is reduced by 10, so that each invocation of the function dims the target even more.

5. If the opacity is greater than or equal to 0, change the opacity style:

```
if (opacity >= 0) {
    if (typeof target.style.opacity == 'string') {
        target.style.opacity = (opacity/100);
    } else {
        target.style.filter = 'alpha(opacity=' + opacity + ')';
    }
```

First, the opacity should only be changed if opacity is a positive number. Once the opacity becomes a negative number, the process should stop (in the next step).

To change the opacity, one has to use either the `style.opacity` or the `style.filter` property of the target element, depending upon the browser (see a CSS reference for more details, if needed). For the former, the opacity value needs to be a decimal, so opacity is divided by 100.

Note that although closures have access to the last known value of a variable (the common problem explained earlier), the value of opacity is changed *within* this closure function, meaning its value is retained from function call to function call.

6. If opacity is not greater than or equal to 0, stop the timer:

```
} else {
    clearInterval(fader);
}
```

7. Complete the timer:

```
}, 100);
```

The anonymous function will be called every 100 milliseconds.

8. Complete the onload anonymous function:

```
};
```

9. Save the file as `fader.js`, in a js directory next to `fader.html`, and test it in your Web browser.

There's no point to providing an image for this example, since it's quite hard to demonstrate animation in a book!

# ALTERNATIVE TYPE IDENTIFICATION

In Chapter 5, Using Control Structures, the typeof operator was introduced as a way to identify a variable's type (or any data's type):

```
if (typeof myVar == 'number') {...
```

The typeof operator generally works well enough, and is a reliable way to confirm that something isn't undefined:

```
if (typeof myVar == 'undefined') {...
```

Still, there are situations where the result of using typeof is too vague. For example, the typeof an Object is *object*, but so is the typeof an Array, null, and even a custom object, such as Employee.

An alternative is to confirm an object's prototype, via the instanceof operator:

```
if (myVar instanceof Number) {...
```

This operator was first introduced in Chapter 12, Error Management, as a way of catching specific kinds of exceptions. The instanceof operator looks up the prototype chain to see if the object on the right is a prototype of the value on the left. This means that the instanceof a String would match both String and Object, but instanceof does distinguish between, for example, an Array and an Object. Note that neither of the two operands being compared is quoted, and the object prototype on the right must be capitalized to match its name, unlike with typeof, which uses lowercase (e.g., "number" for Number).

A catch when using instanceof is that the object being tested must have been created new (**Figure 14.10**).

Even more reliable type checking can be accomplished by checking a variable's constructor property. The constructor property reflects the function that would have been called to create the object in the first place:

```
if (myVar.constructor == Number) {...
```

Unlike instanceof, the constructor property represents the prototype whether you create the type literally or using new (**Figure 14.11**):

**FIGURE 14.10** Using instanceof will only work when the object was created with the new keyword.

**FIGURE 14.11** The constructor property has the same value either way the string was generated.

Another way to test a value's type is to use *duck typing*. The name comes from the James Whitcomb Riley line: "When I see a bird that walks like a duck and swims like a duck and quacks like a duck, I call that bird a duck." In programming, the premise is that sometimes it doesn't matter whether a value is technically, say, a String, but whether it can be used as one. You can perform duck typing by checking for the presence of the qualities required by subsequent code: in other words, by using object detection. In object-oriented terms, this means looking for properties and methods required for whatever task about to be attempted. If the necessary property or method exists, treat the object like a duck!

## MINIFYING **CODE**

Once you've written, tested, debugged, optimized, and finalized all of your code, it's time to release it into the wild. This is to say: distribute the code on live sites. There's one more step you could take before doing so: *minify* the code. To minify code is to remove all of its comments and extraneous white space in order to condense the code as much as possible. Minifying a script will significantly reduce its file size, perhaps by as much as 50 percent. This in turn makes the site load faster in the browser, as there will be less data for the user to download.

There are a couple of tools you can use to minify code. A simple solution is Minify JavaScript (www.minifyjavascript.com), a Web-based solution. Just paste your code into the top textarea, click the *Compress JavaScript* button, and the minified version will appear in the second textarea (**Figure 14.12**).

Then, take the minified code and paste it into a new script, named *filename.*min.js (e.g., tasks.min.js). Conventionally, the .min is added to indicate minified code. Be certain not to *replace* the original code or file, as you will lose all of your comments and original formatting during the minification process.

Another Web-based option is Packer (http://dean.edwards.name/packer/), by Dean Edwards. Packer takes minification a step further, also shortening variable names, which condenses the code even more.

More thorough minification can be accomplished using a command-line tool such as:

- JSMin (http://www.crockford.com/javascript/jsmin.html), by Douglas Crockford

- YUI Compressor (http://developer.yahoo.com/yui/compressor/), by Yahoo!

- Closure Compiler (http://code.google.com/closure/compiler/), by Google

Instructions for using these can be found on the corresponding Web sites, or by searching online. (Google's Closure Compiler is also available online at http://closure-compiler.appspot.com/home.)

# REVIEW AND PURSUE

If you have any problems with these sections, either in answering the questions or pursuing your own endeavors, turn to the book's supporting forum (www.LarryUllman.com/forums/).

## REVIEW

- What are *namespaces*? Why are they useful? How do you create and use a namespace in JavaScript?

- What is a *configuration object*? What are its benefits? How would you create and use one?

- What are the two ways can you create custom objects? What is a *constructor function*? How do you invoke a constructor function?

- What does it mean that JavaScript is a prototyped-based OOP language? What is the *prototype chain*?

- What effect will the following code have?

```
Number.prototype.isPositive = function() {
    return (this > 0);
};
```

Secondarily, why isn't that piece of code a good idea?

- What is a *closure*? What conditions generally exist to create a closure?

- What ways of identifying an object's type or prototype have you learned in this book and in this chapter?

- How do you minify your code and why is that beneficial?

## PURSUE

- Return to Chapter 7 and rewrite the employee example to use a constructor function for creating an employee object.

- Think of ways to expand the definitions of the Employee and Department objects to make them more useful.

- Tweak tasks.js so that it clears the form values after the task has been added.

- Expand `tasks.js` so that it displays every task, along with each task's priority.

- For a tougher challenge, have `tasks.js` order the tasks by priority, from highest to lowest.

- For another challenge, add the ability to mark tasks as done.

- Use `Date.prototype` to add a `getMonthName()` method to the `Date` object.

- When you're feeling comfortable enough, read more about closures by searching online.

- Practice using the different kinds of type and prototype identification approaches to see the benefits and challenges of each.

- Experiment with some of the various ways to minimize code.

## WRAPPING **UP**

This is the last chapter in the book where the focus is on teaching new material (in the next chapter, you'll see how to put together an entire project). Here, you encountered a smattering of new ideas, some more complex and advanced than others.

Most of the topics, including *namespaces*, *custom objects*, *prototypes*, and *type identification*, greatly expand the coverage that had previously been given to objects, the most important data type in JavaScript. By now you should be very comfortable with the concept of objects, with OOP in general, and, hopefully, with JavaScript's prototypical design.

A few pages of this chapter focused on *closures*, a key feature of JavaScript. Unfortunately, closures are conceptually hard to grasp, even for the astute and seasoned programmer, so don't be alarmed if the concept did not immediately "click" with you. Closures provide solutions to many problems, and, with time, they'll become more natural for you.

In the next chapter, the last one in the book, you'll take all of the knowledge covered thus far (with emphasis given to that from Part 2: JavaScript Fundamentals), to develop and design a full Web project. That example will use a combination of HTML, CSS, JavaScript, and PHP, with progressive enhancement, Ajax: the works. The best thing about the next chapter is that it will demonstrate how much you now know!

# 15

# **PHP** AND **JAVASCRIPT** TOGETHER

To wrap up the book, this chapter will put the ideas covered in the previous 14 chapters to the test by creating a viable, real-world site. I tried to come up with an example that was a practical, good use of JavaScript, without getting too elaborate. I'll explain the specific example next, and then walk through all of the key parts in the remaining pages.

No new JavaScript will be introduced in this chapter, although you'll encounter new uses of what you've already learned. The example does require server-side technologies, though, for which I've used PHP and MySQL. There is not enough space to explain the PHP code in detail, but I will deliberately walk through the more advanced parts.

# IDENTIFYING THE GOAL

The goal in this chapter is to put forth a practical, real-world example that uses both server-side technologies and JavaScript to create a wonderful user experience. In terms of the JavaScript, I wanted the site to demonstrate the most important concepts:

- Unobtrusive scripting
- Progressive enhancement
- A custom (developer-designed) library
- DOM manipulation
- Ajax
- Closures

Of course, the example would also have to use event handling, custom functions, and so forth. In the end, the project I came up with is the core of an auction site, where items are listed and users can bid on them. Individual auctions will close at a certain time, and each bid must be higher than the last.

For this chapter, I also wanted to demonstrate how to pass values back and forth between JavaScript and PHP. This is a common need, and a common point of confusion, for many Web developers.

Implementing the entire functionality would require half a book, and so this chapter will focus on the hardest components. The trickiest aspect, truly, is managing the closing dates and times in a way that's reliable across multiple time zones. To save space, some features or ideas have been omitted, but those should be easy enough for you to develop on your own.

The core of the auction site is represented by three pages:

- `index.php`, which is the home page and lists the open auctions (**Figure 15.1**)
- `login.php`, which allows users to log in (**Figure 15.2**)
- `view.php`, which shows an individual auction and allows users to bid (**Figure 15.3**)

These pages alone require around 430 lines of JavaScript code. Coupled with the JavaScript are over 550 lines of PHP, plus CSS and HTML. I won't walk through all 1,000+ lines of code in this chapter, but will explain the most important and complex parts. Naturally, you can download the complete code from `www.LarryUllman.com`. If you have any questions or problems, you can post them in my supporting forums at `www.LarryUllman.com/forums/`.

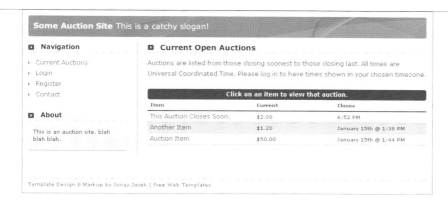

FIGURE 15.1 The home page lists the current, open auctions.

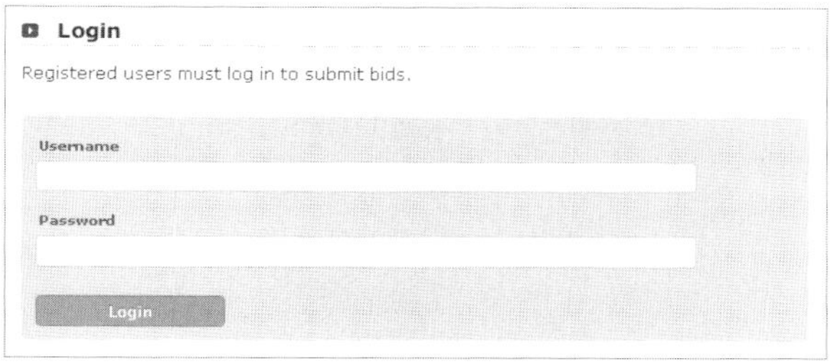

FIGURE 15.2 Users must log in to bid on items.

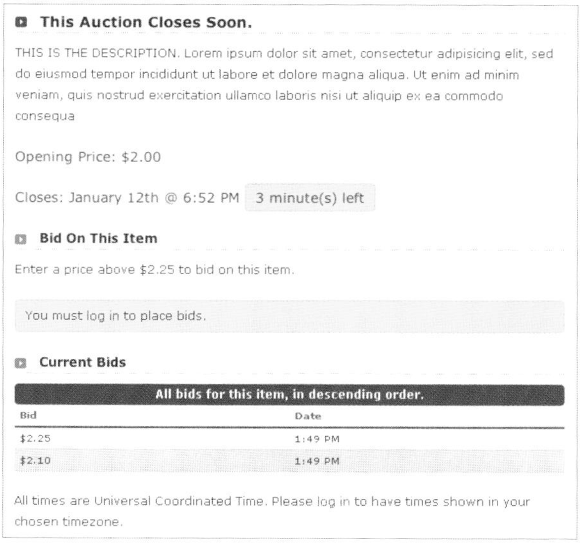

FIGURE 15.3 The view page shows a specific item and is where bids are entered.

# CREATING THE DATABASE

The database required by the example as implemented in this chapter requires three tables: bids, items, and users. The SQL commands to create them (in MySQL) are:

```
CREATE TABLE `bids` (
  `bidId` INT(10) UNSIGNED NOT NULL AUTO_INCREMENT,
  `itemId` INT(10) UNSIGNED NOT NULL,
  `userId` MEDIUMINT(8) UNSIGNED NOT NULL,
  `bid` DECIMAL(7,2) UNSIGNED NOT NULL,
  `dateSubmitted` TIMESTAMP NOT NULL,
  PRIMARY KEY (`bidId`),
  KEY `itemId` (`itemId`),
  KEY `userId` (`userId`)
);
CREATE TABLE `items` (
  `itemId` INT(10) UNSIGNED NOT NULL AUTO_INCREMENT,
  `item` VARCHAR(100) NOT NULL,
  `description` TINYTEXT,
  `openingPrice` DECIMAL(7,2) UNSIGNED NOT NULL,
  `finalPrice` DECIMAL(7,2) DEFAULT NULL,
  `dateOpened` timestamp NOT NULL,
  `dateClosed` datetime NOT NULL,
  PRIMARY KEY (`itemId`)
);
CREATE TABLE `users` (
  `userId` MEDIUMINT(8) UNSIGNED NOT NULL AUTO_INCREMENT,
  `username` VARCHAR(40) NOT NULL,
  `userpass` CHAR(40) NOT NULL,
  `timezone` VARCHAR(100) NOT NULL,
```

```
`dateCreated` TIMESTAMP NOT NULL,
PRIMARY KEY (`userId`),
UNIQUE KEY `username` (`username`),
KEY `login` (`username`,`userpass`)
);
```

Some of the particulars will be explained in conjunction with the applicable code. I will point out here that all dates and times will be represented using Coordinated Universal Time (UTC). Each user will register her or his preferred time zone, allowing for all dates and times to be converted to the user's time. For more information on time zones and MySQL, see my *PHP and MySQL for Dynamic Web Sites: Visual QuickPro Guide (4th Edition)* or, of course, the MySQL manual.

You will need to create these tables, and the database itself, before getting too far along. You'll also need to populate the items and users tables, as there was not space to create scripts for that purpose. The appropriate SQL commands will look like:

```
INSERT INTO `items` (`item`, `description`, `openingPrice`,
→ `dateOpened`, `dateClosed`) VALUES ('This is the item.',
→ 'This is the description.', 1.25, UTC_TIMESTAMP(),
→ '2012-07-05 13:01:00');

INSERT INTO `users` (`username`, `userpass`, `timezone`,
→ `dateCreated`) VALUES ('testing', SHA1('securepass'),
→ 'America/New_York', UTC_TIMESTAMP());
```

The SHA1() function will be used to encrypt passwords. The time zone values come from MySQL's list of time zones, which the MySQL server must have installed (see the MySQL manual). All new records are inserted using the UTC_TIMESTAMP() function, which returns the current moment and time in UTC.

**FIGURE 15.4** The bulk of the site structure.

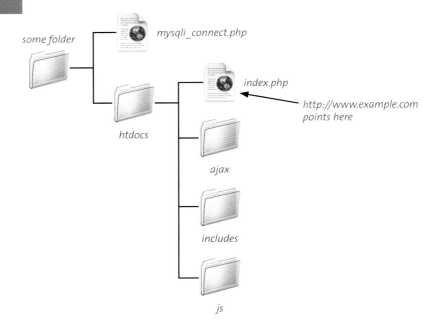

Figure 15.4 shows part of the structure for the site, where htdocs is the Web root directory (i.e., www.example.com points there). I've put the JavaScript in a js folder and the PHP scripts used for Ajax requests in an ajax folder. The includes folder is used for files to be included by PHP scripts:

- config.inc.php, a configuration file
- header.html, which starts the HTML template
- footer.html, which completes the HTML template

Breaking an HTML template into two or more files and then including them is a standard PHP approach. The page-specific content will go within each specific page file: index.php, login.php, and view.php. The header.html page does include one JavaScript file: utilities.js, a library of common code needed by two of the three pages.

The configuration file is well documented, but you will need to change a few values to make the code usable on your server:

```
// Site URL (base for all redirections):
define ('BASE_URL', 'http://www.example.com/');
// Location of the MySQL connection script:
define ('MYSQL', '/path/to/mysqli_connect.php');
```

One more PHP script is required: `mysqli_connect.php`. It establishes the connection to the database. For security purposes, I prefer placing it outside of the Web directory, although it's not horrible if you cannot (in which case, you'd put it within the `includes` folder, and change the reference to it in the configuration file accordingly). Note that you'll need to also edit these lines in the MySQL connection script for your server:

```
DEFINE ('DB_USER', 'username');
DEFINE ('DB_PASSWORD', 'password');
DEFINE ('DB_HOST', 'localhost');
DEFINE ('DB_NAME', 'databaseName');
```

The HTML template for the site was created by Jonas Jacek (`http://jonas.me/`) and is used with his kind permission. In his original template, he used a single letter for some of the directory names, such as `i` for *images* and `s` for *css*. I did not stick with that convention, but doing so would ever so slightly decrease the amount of data each user has to download.

## CODING THE NON-JAVASCRIPT VERSION

The next step in the development process is to create the non-JavaScript version. This should be a fully functional site that will work even if JavaScript is disabled or just not available. The focus here is on the PHP code, then, and JavaScript will be used to progressively enhance this functionality later.

Although PHP is my favorite server-side language, this is not a PHP book, so I won't go through the PHP code in detail. I recommend that you download and examine the PHP scripts for yourself, as they contain sufficient inline comments.

If you're not comfortable with PHP and MySQL, then you can just skim the following pages to get a sense of what's being done (you will probably have difficulty installing this project, however).

The most complicated aspects of the PHP code stem from the need to show all auctions and bids in the user's chosen time zone. You'll see how I handle that in the following pages.

## LISTING AUCTIONS

The home page, index.php, will list the open auctions (see Figure 15.1). For all of the PHP pages that the user will access directly (i.e., for all scripts that aren't included by other scripts or used for Ajax calls), the basic structure is:

```
<?php
require('includes/config.inc.php');
$page_title = 'Some Page Title';
include ('includes/header.html');
require(MYSQL);
/* Page-specific content. */
include ('includes/footer.html');
?>
```

The configuration file sets several parameters, such as the location of the MySQL connection script and whether the site is live or not, so it must always be included early.

Next, the page title is set as a variable that will be used within the header file to customize the browser window title.

The MySQL connection script, mysqli_connect.php, can be included by referencing the MYSQL constant, which is assigned a value in config.inc.php. By assigning this value to a constant, the same line of code can be used for top-level scripts such as this one, as well as for scripts found in subdirectories, such as ajax/getBids.php.

The page-specific content will differ from one page to the next, naturally.

Finally, the footer is included, which completes the template.

The page-specific content on the home page is the display of open auctions within an HTML table (see Figure 15.1). The item name in each row is linked to view.php, passing along the item ID in the URL. The home page's query therefore needs to select four pieces of information: the item ID, the item itself, the item's current price, and the date and/or time when the item's auction closes. The complete query is:

```
SELECT items.itemId, item, COALESCE(MAX(bid), openingPrice),
IF($tz < DATE_ADD(UTC_TIMESTAMP(), INTERVAL 24 HOUR),
→ DATE_FORMAT($tz,'%l:%i %p'), DATE_FORMAT($tz,'%M %D @ %l:%i %p'))
FROM items LEFT JOIN bids USING (itemId)
WHERE dateClosed > UTC_TIMESTAMP()
GROUP BY items.itemId ORDER BY dateClosed ASC
```

This query performs a LEFT JOIN across the items and bids tables. The itemId and item name will be selected from the items table. For those items with bids, the highest bid will be brought in from the bids table.

To select the current price of the item, you have to consider that new items will not have bids. For those new items, the current price is the opening price. For those items *with* bids, the current price is the highest bid price. To select one or the other, utilize the MySQL COALESCE() function, which returns the first non-null value. Hence, COALESCE(MAX(bid), openingPrice) returns the highest bid, if any bids exist, or the openingPrice if not. To use MAX() on the bids, the GROUP BY clause is required, too.

Selecting the date and time is even trickier. For starters, if the user is logged in, the date and time should reflect the user's chosen time zone. If the user is not logged in, the original (UTC) date and time should be used. To accomplish that, I create a PHP variable that represents what should be selected. This will be either the converted date and time or the unmodified version:

```
if (isset($_SESSION['timezone'])) {
    $tz = "CONVERT_TZ(dateClosed, 'UTC', '{$_SESSION['timezone']}')";
} else {
    $tz = 'dateClosed';
}
```

```
+--------+-----------------------------+------------------------------------+------------------------
| itemId | item                        | COALESCE(MAX(bid), openingPrice)   | IF(dateClosed < DATE_ADD
+--------+-----------------------------+------------------------------------+------------------------
|      5 | This Auction Closes Soon.   |                               2.25 | 7:52 PM
|      6 | Another Item                |                               1.20 | January 15th @ 1:38 PM
|      7 | Auction Item                |                              50.00 | January 15th @ 1:44 PM
+--------+-----------------------------+------------------------------------+------------------------
```

That code goes before the query and assigns the right value to $tz. (This code is explained in greater detail in Chapter 17, Example—Message Board, of my *PHP and MySQL for Dynamic Web Sites: Visual QuickPro Guide, 4th Edition,* book.) In theory, the query could now just select a formatted version of the proper date and time using DATE_FORMAT($tz, 'formatting').

Taking the date and time modification a step further, I'd like the page to show just the time portion if the auction closes within the next day. Thus, the fourth value selected by the query changes the closing date formatting based upon how soon the auction closes:

```
IF($tz < DATE_ADD(UTC_TIMESTAMP(), INTERVAL 24 HOUR),
  DATE_FORMAT($tz,'%l:%i %p'), DATE_FORMAT($tz,'%M %D @ %l:%i %p'))
```

If the date and time (represented by $tz, adjusted for the user's time zone, when appropriate) is less than the current UTC timestamp plus 24 hours, the auction closes within the next day and only the hour, minute, and AM/PM indicator is returned. Otherwise, the month, day, hour, minute, and AM/PM indicator is returned.

Whew! A fairly complex query, but as with all advanced sites, complex queries are at the heart of the system. If you have any problems following this query, use the standard PHP-MySQL debugging steps:

- Print out the query being executed using echo $q.

- Run that same query using another interface such as phpMyAdmin or the command-line mysql client.

- Use the results (**Figure 15.5**) or error message to determine what debugging steps to take next.

There are several possible upgrades for this page, starting with pagination of the auctions. Pagination is a simple and common PHP technique. Taken a step further, you could paginate the auctions using JavaScript, too, although I recommend using a framework or plug-in for something as complex as that. You could also add a link to another page that shows expired auctions.

**FIGURE 15.6** The login page upon successfully logging in.

The home page does not use any JavaScript at all as currently written. More complexity and a better user experience can be added by displaying the minutes remaining next to each auction that closes within the hour, and to update the time remaining, and the current price, using Ajax. The view.php script will do both of those, but for a single auction.

## LOGGING IN

The login page is the simplest of the three. Along with the standard structure already explained for the home page, the login page will handle the submission of the login form to validate the user. That's accomplished within this block, which checks for a form submission:

```
if ($_SERVER['REQUEST_METHOD'] == 'POST') {
    /* Form validation. */
}
```

The PHP code performs minimal validation of the username and password fields (see Figure 15.2), and makes the submitted data safe to use in a query. Any errors that occur are added to a PHP array named $errors. If no errors occurred, a database query selects the user's ID, name, and time zone from the database:

```
SELECT userId, username, timezone FROM users WHERE
   (username='$u' AND userpass=SHA1('$p'))
```

These three pieces of information are then stored in a session. Next, a nice message is displayed, the footer is included, and the script is terminated so as not to show the form again (**Figure 15.6**).

FIGURE 15.7 The login page
when one or more errors
occurred.

All errors are shown above the login form, giving the user the chance to try
again (**Figure 15.7**).

The login page will include the login.js script, which will progressively
enhance the login process.

## VIEWING AN AUCTION

The view.php script is by far the most complicated, requiring around 160 lines of
well-documented and spaced code. The script must do several things (see Figure
15.3 for most of these):

- Validate the itemId passed to the page in the URL (from the link in index.
  php).

- Retrieve and display the item's details.

- Provide a form to bid on the item, but only if the viewer is logged in.

- Handle the bid form's submission.

- Show the list of current bids.

I'll walk through these in order.

### VALIDATING THE ITEM ID

Validating the item ID is simply a matter of confirming that it exists and is an integer
greater than or equal to 1. If you're using PHP 5.3 or later, the Filter extension is the
best way to do that. However, this page can be accessed in two ways: by clicking
the link on index.php (which performs a GET request of view.php) or by submitting the bid form back to this same page (i.e., a POST request). To account for both
possibilities, use the following code to validate the item ID:

**FIGURE 15.8** The view page if it does not receive a valid item ID.

```
$itemId = false;
if (isset($_GET['itemId']) && filter_var($_GET['itemId'],
→  FILTER_VALIDATE_INT, array('min_range' => 1))) {
    $itemId = $_GET['itemId'];
} elseif (isset($_POST['itemId']) && filter_var($_POST['itemId'],
→  FILTER_VALIDATE_INT, array('min_range' => 1))) {
    $itemId = $_POST['itemId'];
}
```

For this to work, the item ID will need to be stored in a hidden input in the form, as you'll see shortly.

If, after that code, `$itemId` still has a false value, then an error message will be shown, the footer included, and the page terminated (**Figure 15.8**). You could take this validation another step further and confirm that the item ID successfully points to an item in the database.

## DISPLAYING THE ITEM'S DETAILS

A database query is required to retrieve the item's details: the item name and description, its opening price, its current price, and its closing date and time. That can all be fetched using a query similar to the one on `index.php`, including the factoring in of the user's time zone.

Two more pieces of information will be useful, though: the current auction status (open or closed) and how many minutes are left in the auction. The former can be retrieved via an IF that selects the string *closed* or *open* depending upon whether the closing date and time is in the past:

```
IF(dateClosed < UTC_TIMESTAMP(), 'closed', 'open').
```

FIGURE 15.9 The item details for an auction closing soon.

The number of minutes remaining can be calculated by subtracting the closing date from the current UTC timestamp, and dividing by 60:

```
CEILING((UNIX_TIMESTAMP(dateClosed) - UNIX_TIMESTAMP
    (UTC_TIMESTAMP()))/60)
```

For the math to work out properly, both values need to be timestamps, which is why UNIX_TIMESTAMP() is applied. It may seem unnecessary to apply this function to the UTC_TIMESTAMP() result, but trust me: this is how you guarantee the math works.

The resulting query is this behemoth:

```
SELECT item, description, openingPrice, COALESCE(MAX(bid),
    openingPrice), DATE_FORMAT($closeTz,'%M %D @ %l:%i %p'),
IF(dateClosed < UTC_TIMESTAMP(), 'closed', 'open'),
    CEILING((UNIX_TIMESTAMP(dateClosed) - UNIX_TIMESTAMP
    (UTC_TIMESTAMP()))/60) FROM items LEFT JOIN bids USING (itemId)
    WHERE items.itemId=$itemId GROUP BY bids.itemId
```

The query will return one record, which can be fetched into variables and used to display all the item's details (**Figure 15.9**):

```
list ($item, $description, $openingPrice, $currentPrice,
    $dateClosed, $status, $minutesRemaining) =
    mysqli_fetch_array($r, MYSQLI_NUM);
```

Closes: January 12th @ 2:59 PM

This auction is now closed.

Final Price: $2.25

▶ **Current Bids**

FIGURE 15.10 When the auction has closed, the final price is shown instead of the bid form.

CREATING THE BID FORM

The bid form should only be displayed if the auction is still open:

```
if ($status == 'open') {
```

The form is prefaced by a heading that indicates the required bid, based upon the current value (see Figure 15.9):

```
echo '<h3>Bid On This Item</h3>
<p>Enter a price above $<span id="currentSpan">' .
⇒ $currentPrice . '</span> to bid on this item.</p>';
```

This will always be shown if the auction is open. If the user is also logged in, the form itself is displayed. The form needs to store the item ID and the current price in hidden form inputs:

```
echo '<input type="hidden" name="itemId" id="itemId"
⇒ value="' . $itemId . '">
<input type="hidden" name="currentHidden" id="currentHidden"
⇒ value="' . $currentPrice . '">';
```

These two values will be used when the form is submitted.

(As a reminder, all of the code thus far is meant to work without any JavaScript.)

If the viewer is not logged in, a message is shown indicating that the person must log in to bid:

```
} else { // Not logged in.
    echo '<p class="caution">You must <a href="login.php">log in
    ⇒ </a> to place bids.</p>';
}
```

If the auction is closed, the current price is displayed as the final price (**Figure 15.10**):

```
} else { // Closed!
    echo '<p class="caution">This auction is now closed.</p>
    <h2>Final Price: $' . $currentPrice .'</h2>';
}
```

HANDLING THE BID FORM SUBMISSION

When the bid form is submitted, the data will be posted back to the view.php page. To check for that, use this code:

```
if ($_SERVER['REQUEST_METHOD'] == 'POST') { }
```

Within that code, user ID and bid amount have to be validated (the item ID will have been validated by this point already). I again turn to the Filter extension for both validations:

```
if (isset($_SESSION['userId']) && filter_var($_SESSION['userId'],
→ FILTER_VALIDATE_INT, array('min_range' => 1))) {
    $userId = $_SESSION['userId'];
}
if (isset($_POST['bid']) && filter_var($_POST['bid'],
→ FILTER_VALIDATE_FLOAT) && ($_POST['bid'] >
→ $_POST['currentHidden'])) {
    $bid = $_POST['bid'];
}
```

You'll see that the bid is also checked against the current price, stored in a hidden form element. This structure does allow for the submission of a bid that's lower than the current price, through some hacking. But as the final price will always be based upon the highest bid, there's no gain should a hacker attempts to do that.

If both validation routines are passed, then the bid is entered into the database:

```
INSERT INTO bids (itemId, userId, bid, dateSubmitted)
→ VALUES ($itemId, $userId, $bid, UTC_TIMESTAMP())
```

Messages report upon the success (**Figure 15.11**) or failure (**Figure 15.12**) of the bid.

**FIGURE 15.11** A successful bid has been submitted.

**FIGURE 15.12** The provided bid was not greater than the current price.

### SHOWING THE CURRENT BIDS

The last thing the view page should do is display the list of bids received (see Figure 15.3). Doing that requires a query of just the bids table:

```
SELECT bid, IF($bidTz > DATE_SUB(UTC_TIMESTAMP(), INTERVAL 24 HOUR),
→  DATE_FORMAT($bidTz,'%l:%i %p'), DATE_FORMAT($bidTz,'%M %D @
→  %l:%i %p')) FROM bids WHERE itemId=$itemId ORDER BY bids.bid DESC
```

This query retrieves the bids in descending order of amount: the highest bid is always listed first (which should also be the most recent bid). The date and time of the bid is formatted to the user's time zone, if applicable. As on the home page, bids within the past day are just shown using the bid's time.

## CREATING THE AJAX RESOURCES

With the base functionality in place, you can start progressively enhancing the site. Primarily, this is done via Ajax; hence, the next step I would take would be to create the three PHP scripts that are used as the resources for the Ajax calls. These scripts are:

- login.php
- getBids.php
- bid.php

**FIGURE 15.13** The default response for the login Ajax script.

Let's take a look at each individually. Remember that, as a debugging step, you should always run the Ajax resource scripts directly in your browser to confirm they don't have errors, prior to writing any JavaScript. Even if the script requires data to be sent to it, merely running the script directly can provide peace of mind that there are no PHP errors (while simultaneously showing the results when used inappropriately).

Note that all three scripts will have to start the session themselves, as the scripts will not include the HTML header that otherwise does that.

### THE LOGIN AJAX SCRIPT

Like the login page itself, the login Ajax script will be quite simple. It should receive and validate the username and password, and then query the database for those values. This validation code and the query is the same as in `login.php`. If the provided information was correct, the retrieved data is stored in the session and the script prints only a single word: *VALID*. If the information is not correct, or if those two pieces of information are not posted to the page, the script prints *INVALID* (**Figure 15.13**).

Now, it may be confusing why storing data in a session even works via Ajax. An Ajax script can manipulate the user's session and/or cookies because the Ajax PHP script is being requested by the JavaScript running in the user's browser. Therefore, the request is the same as if the user accessed the page directly and overtly. In this case, this means that the user's session ID is sent to the Ajax script as part of the JavaScript request. When the session data is updated within the script, it is updated for the correct session.

### THE BIDDING AJAX SCRIPT

Another PHP script is used to submit bids via Ajax. The script requires that three pieces of information be sent in the URL: the item ID, the bid, and the current price. Like the bid form handling code in `view.php`, this script will validate those three pieces of information, and also validate the user ID found in the session. The script will then add the bid to the database.

This script will return JSON data with two parts: a status code (*accepted* or *error*) and a message. See Chapter 11, Ajax, for the particulars of returning JSON from a PHP script.

The PHP script assumes that *invalid* bid information was provided, and initially creates a corresponding error message for the response:

**FIGURE 15.14** The response, in JSON format, of successfully bidding via the Ajax script.

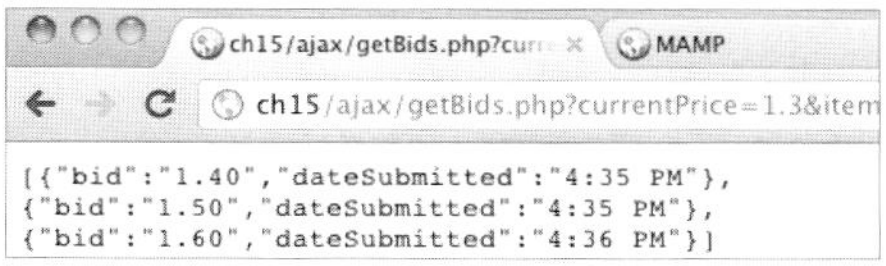

**FIGURE 15.15** The most recent bids for an item are returned as an array of objects, in JSON format.

```
$data = array('status' => 'error', 'message' => 'An invalid bid was
    submitted.');
```

If the data passes the validation and the bid is submitted to the database, this value is overwritten:

```
$data = array('status' => 'accepted', 'message' =>  'Your bid of $'
    . number_format($bid, 2) . ' has been accepted.');
```

At the end of the script, the data is returned as JSON (**Figure 15.14**):

```
echo json_encode($data);
```

## THE GET BIDS AJAX SCRIPT

The third and final PHP script used as an Ajax resource will return all of the bids for an item over a certain amount. With that restriction—a minimum bid amount—this script can provide the view item page with the latest bids, allowing the page to dynamically update the displayed list. When there are no new bids, no bids will be returned by this Ajax script. If there are two new bids, only those two are returned.

The script will also return JSON data (**Figure 15.15**). To do that, an empty array is first created:

```
$data = array();
```

The array is then populated within the loop that fetches the query results:

```
while ($row = mysqli_fetch_array($r, MYSQLI_NUM)) {
    $data[] = $row;
}
```

If you look at the ajax/getBids.php script in the downloadable code, you'll see that the query itself just selects the bid amount and the bid date and time from the bids table:

```
SELECT bid, IF($tz > DATE_SUB(UTC_TIMESTAMP(), INTERVAL 24 HOUR),
    DATE_FORMAT($tz,'%l:%i %p'), DATE_FORMAT($tz,'%M %D @ %l:%i %p'))
    AS dateSubmitted FROM bids WHERE itemId={$_GET['itemId']}
    AND bid>{$_GET['currentPrice']} ORDER BY dateSubmitted ASC
```

As in view.php, the script converts the dates and times to the user's time zone, if applicable, and shows bids within the last 24 hours as just the time. (As you can see in the full getBids.php code, all of the variables will have been validated prior to this point, making them safe to use in a query.)

Finally, the data is converted to JSON and printed:

```
echo json_encode($data);
```

Most of this code was first explained in Chapter 11.


## ADDING THE JAVASCRIPT

With the original functionality in place, and the server-side Ajax scripts written and tested, too, it's time to add the JavaScript layer to the application. Only three JavaScript files are required (although one is quite long):

- utilities.js
- login.js
- view.js

The utilities.js script was first written in Chapter 8, Event Handling. It originally defined the following functions:

- $(), a shortcut to document.getElementById()
- setText()
- addEvent()
- removeEvent()

To this list I've added the getXMLHttpRequestObject() function defined in Chapter 11. I won't otherwise explain the utilities.js script, as it should be familiar to you by now, but see the downloadable code if you have any questions.

The view.php script will also have a small block of JavaScript written directly into the page by PHP itself. I'll explain the hows and whys of that later.

As you read over these next few pages, remember that the goal of JavaScript (in this example, at least) is to *enhance the user's experience*.

## WRITING LOGIN.JS

The JavaScript in login.js has a simple goal: replicate the form submission via Ajax. Let's walk through the whole script in detail.

**To write login.js:**

1. Create a new JavaScript file in your text editor or IDE, to be named login.js.

2. Begin creating an anonymous function that will be invoked immediately:

```
(function() {
    'use strict';
```

To keep the global namespace uncluttered, all of the JavaScript code for this page will go within this anonymous function that will be executed as soon as the browser encounters it. This concept was first explained in Chapter 7, Creating Functions.

3. Define a function for showing error messages:

```
function showErrorMessage(message) {
    var errorDiv = U.$('errorDiv');
    if (errorDiv) { // Already exists; update.
        errorDiv.innerHTML = message;
    } else { // Create and add to the page:
        errorDiv = document.createElement('div');
        errorDiv.id = 'errorDiv';
        errorDiv.innerHTML = message;
```

```
        var loginForm = U.$('loginForm');
        loginForm.parentNode.insertBefore(errorDiv, loginForm);
    } // End of messageDiv IF-ELSE
}
```

The JavaScript may or may not ever have to display any errors to the user. In fact, the large majority of the time, it won't be necessary, which is why I chose not to create the DIV in the HTML in the first place. For the times when errors might be shown—for example, if the user omits a form value or if the submitted values don't match those in the database—this function will be called.

The function begins by looking for the element with an ID of *errorDiv*. It uses the $() shortcut function, defined within the U global object, to do that. If that element exists, then its innerHTML property is updated with the message value received during the function call.

If the DIV does not yet exist, then it will be created and dynamically added to the page, just before the login form. See Chapter 9, JavaScript and the Browser, for the particulars of DOM manipulation (if you're confused by any of this code). The end result will look exactly the same as in Figures 15.6 and 15.7.

In terms of the original functionality, the only additional requirement for this progressive enhancement is that the form and its two elements have ID values.

4. Begin defining the validateForm() function:

```
function validateForm(e) {
    if (typeof e == 'undefined') e = window.event;
    if (e.preventDefault) {
        e.preventDefault();
    } else {
        e.returnValue = false;
    }
```

This function will be called when the form is submitted. It will receive the event as its lone argument. The first bit of code makes sure a valid reference to the event is available (i.e., creating backward compatibility for older IE). Then, the browser's default behavior—the submission of the form to the server—is prevented.

5. Get references to the form elements and validate them:

```
var username = U.$('username').value;
var userpass = U.$('userpass').value;
if ( (username.length > 0) && (userpass.length > 0) ) {
```

The JavaScript will just validate that each form element has a positive length. If there were restrictions on the allowed characters or length of the username and password—set during the registration process—you could use regular expressions here.

6. Get an Ajax object:

```
var ajax = U.getXMLHttpRequestObject();
```

This code is the same as that in Chapter 11, only now the getXMLHttp RequestObject() function is defined within the global U object.

7. Begin defining the onreadystatechange anonymous function:

```
ajax.onreadystatechange = function() {
    if (ajax.readyState == 4) {
        if ( (ajax.status >= 200 && ajax.status < 300)
        || (ajax.status == 304) ) {
```

This anonymous function will be called whenever the Ajax object's readyState property changes. As explained in Chapter 11, the function must first confirm the state value and the status code.

8. If the response was *VALID*, hide the form and the error DIV, and print a message:

```
if (ajax.responseText == 'VALID') {
    U.$('loginForm').style.visibility = 'hidden';
    var errorDiv = U.$('errorDiv');
    if (errorDiv) {
        errorDiv.parentNode.removeChild(errorDiv);
    }
    U.setText('message', 'You are now logged in!');
    U.$('message').className = 'good';
```

The PHP script should only return one of two words: *VALID* or *INVALID*. If the response equals *VALID*, the login form's visibility is set to hidden, to make it disappear. Then the errorDiv element is removed from the page entirely, if it exists. That would be the case if the user provided invalid credentials first, and then provided valid ones.

Finally, the message paragraph, which is part of the PHP script and originally says *Registered users must log in to submit bids.* is assigned a new message and given a class of *good* (which, according to the CSS, highlights the paragraph in green, as in Figure 15.6).

9. If the response was *INVALID*, show an error message:

```
} else { // Bad response, show an error:
    showErrorMessage('<h2>Error!</h2><p class="error">
 →    The submitted values do not match those on file!</p>');
}
```

To display the error message, the showErrorMessage() function is called, providing it with the HTML version of the message.

10. Clear the Ajax object and complete the anonymous function:

```
            ajax = null;
        } else { // Invalid status code, submit the form:
            U.$('loginForm').submit();
        }
```

```
    } // End of readyState IF.
}; // End of onreadystatechange anonymous function.
```

After the Ajax request has completed, the ajax object is assigned a null value.

The else clause applies if the status code was not good, in which case the form will actually be submitted as if the JavaScript wasn't there.

11. Perform the Ajax request:

```
ajax.open('POST', 'ajax/login.php', true);
ajax.setRequestHeader('Content-Type',
 ⟶ 'application/x-www-form-urlencoded');
var data = 'username=' + encodeURIComponent(username) +
 ⟶ '&userpass=' + encodeURIComponent(userpass);
ajax.send(data);
```

The Ajax request uses the POST method, meaning that the *Content-Type* request header has to be set. The data being sent to the page is just the username and the password, encoded for safety.

12. If the user did not complete the form, show an error message:

```
} else { // Didn't complete the form:
    var message = '<h2>Error!</h2><p>The following error(s)
     ⟶ occurred:<ul>';
    if (username.length == 0) {
        message += '<li class="error">You forgot to enter
         ⟶ your username!</li>'
    }
    if (userpass.length == 0) {
        message += '<li class="error">You forgot to enter
         ⟶ your password!</li>'
    }
    message += '</ul></p>';
    showErrorMessage(message);
} // End of validation IF-ELSE.
```

The error message is built up as HTML, then the showErrorMessage() function is called.

13. Complete the validateForm() function:

```
        return false;
    } // End of validateForm() function.
```

14. Attach a submit event handler to the form:

```
    function init() {
        U.addEvent(U.$('loginForm'), 'submit', validateForm);
    } // End of init() function.
    U.addEvent(window, 'load', init);
```

You'll notice that this site only uses the DOM Level 2 event handlers, assigned via the addEvent() method of the U object.

15. Complete the immediately-invoked function:

```
    })(); // End of immediately invoked function.
```

16. Save the file as login.js, in a js directory next to login.php, and test it in your Web browser.

Again, the end result should be the same as in Figures 15.6 and 15.7.

## WRITING JAVASCRIPT WITHIN VIEW.PHP

The view.php script does the bulk of the site's work: displaying an item, showing all of its bids, and allowing users to bid on it. Using progressive enhancement, the view.js file, to be written next, will perform two of these tasks via Ajax: fetching the most recent bids and submitting new bids. In order to do either, the JavaScript in that file will need to know the item ID and the current price. The PHP code that generates the page will have both values represented as variables, but PHP only exists on the server. Somehow this information needs to get to the JavaScript. Transmitting data between PHP and JavaScript is a common point of confusion, and so I wanted to highlight and explain the concept in some detail here.

To start, remember that PHP executes on the server and JavaScript executes within the client (i.e., the browser). PHP cannot reference a JavaScript variable or call a JavaScript function and JavaScript cannot reference a PHP variable or call a PHP function. But there are ways to bridge the gap between the two languages.

The first option is to use cookies. Cookies are one of the very rare overlaps between client-side and server-side technologies. A cookie set by PHP can be read by JavaScript and vice versa. The primary downside to cookies is that they can only be read on subsequent requests after they've been sent. Getting that timing right can be tricky.

The second option is one you've already seen many times over: use Ajax. As in the login.js script, an Ajax request can send any JavaScript variable (well, technically, its value) to a PHP script. An Ajax request can also have the net effect of invoking a PHP function, if need be. And PHP can pass data back to the JavaScript in the Ajax response.

The third way to communicate between PHP and JavaScript is to use HTML as an intermediary. For example, JavaScript could create hidden form elements whose values will be passed to a server-side PHP script when the form is submitted. Or, more commonly, PHP can be used to create HTML that is accessible by client-side JavaScript. More directly, PHP can be used to create the client-side JavaScript itself. I'll explain with an example...

To have JavaScript submit and retrieve bids for the view.php script, the JavaScript code will need access to the item id and its current price. JavaScript *could* read these values from HTML created by PHP, such as the hidden inputs in the bid form that PHP dynamically generates:

```
echo '<input type="hidden" name="itemId" id="itemId"
   value="' . $itemId . '">
<input type="hidden" name="currentHidden" id="currentHidden"
   value="' . $currentPrice . '">';
```

However, since I know JavaScript will need access to this information, why not just create these values as JavaScript variables? To do that, the view.php script will have PHP create actual JavaScript code. This is much easier than you might imagine; just start with the desired goal:

```
<script>
var itemId = 6;
var currentPrice = 1.60;
var minutesRemaining  = 3807;
```

**FIGURE 15.16** This JavaScript code was created by PHP.

```
<script>
    var itemId = 1;
    var currentPrice = 4.25;
</script>
```

Then, have PHP print all or part of this, replacing the values with the PHP variables that represent those values (**Figure 15.16**):

```
echo '<script>
    var itemId = ' . $itemId . ';
    var currentPrice = ' . $currentPrice . ';
    var minutesRemaining  = ' . $minutesLeft . ';
</script>';
```

And that's all there is to it! PHP variables have been passed to client-side Java-Script by simply having PHP create the necessary JavaScript code. As you can see in that example, the PHP in view.php is creating a third variable, which represents the number of minutes left in the auction. This will also be used by view.js.

One thing to be aware of with this approach is that it does result in global variables. Global variables aren't the end of the world, but you should be prudent about creating them. A slightly better solution would be to create one global object that represents the three values:

```
echo '<script>
    var item = {itemId: ' . $itemId . ', currentPrice: ' .
      $currentPrice . ', minutesRemaining: ' . $minutesLeft . '};
</script>';
```

You should also be careful when writing PHP and JavaScript together that you don't generate parse errors within the JavaScript (which is easy enough to do). Also remember to terminate each JavaScript line with a semicolon, which is not to be confused with the semicolon that terminates each PHP line. And remember that JavaScript uses the plus sign for string concatenation while PHP uses the period. Using the wrong one in the wrong code results in a parse error, too.

## WRITING VIEW.JS

The view.js script is included by view.php, but only if the auction is still open (see the PHP code in view.php). The view.js script will do three things:

- Submit bids via Ajax

- Update the list of bids as new bids come in

- Update the display of minutes remaining, closing the auction when time is up

Accomplishing all this requires 240 lines of spaced-out, documented JavaScript code. If it's not the most complex script in the book, then it's certainly the longest. I'll walk through the script in detail in the next sequence of steps, but you'll probably want to download the code from the book's Web site, too.

To get a sense of the script, its general structure is:

```
(function() {
    // Three closure variables.
    function showMessage() {}
    function handleBidAjaxResponse() {}
    function submitBid() {}
    function handleGetBidsAjaxResponse() {}
    function getBids() {}
    function init() {}
    U.addEvent(window, 'load', init);
})();
```

As you can see, the entire script uses an immediately invoked function. Within it, there are six function definitions. Three variables will need to be accessed by the functions, and have a persistent value, so those will be closure variables (see Chapter 14, Advanced JavaScript, for more on closures).

**To write view.js:**

1. Create a new JavaScript file in your text editor or IDE, to be named `view.js`.

2. Begin creating an anonymous function that will be immediately invoked:

   ```
   (function() {
       'use strict';
   ```

3. Declare three variables:

   ```
   var bidAjax = null;
   var getBidsAjax = U.getXMLHttpRequestObject();
   var messageDiv = null;
   ```

   Two Ajax objects are needed by this script. One will handle submission of bids; the other will retrieve new bids. Both variables are declared here, making them available within any of the following functions. This also means that the same Ajax object can be reused time and again (each for its respective purpose). The `bidAjax` object is not initialized here, as some people will view the auction but not bid. It will be initialized when the first bid is submitted.

   The `messageDiv` is where JavaScript will display messages. That variable is declared here, but cannot be assigned a reference to the DIV on the page, as the page has not yet fully loaded at this point.

4. Begin defining a function for showing messages:

   ```
   function showMessage(message, messageClass) {
       if (!messageDiv) {
           messageDiv = U.$('messageDiv');
       }
   ```

This function can be called any number of times. The function takes two arguments: the message itself, which could contain HTML, and the class to apply to the DIV (some messages will be errors; others will not be).

The first time this function is called, the `messageDiv` variable will have a `null` value and the function should get a reference to the DIV on the page.

5. If the DIV still does not exist, create it:

```
if (!messageDiv) {
    messageDiv = document.createElement('div');
    messageDiv.id = 'messageDiv';
    var itemHeading = U.$('itemHeading');
    itemHeading.parentNode.insertBefore(messageDiv,
    ⟶  itemHeading);
} // End of messageDiv IF-ELSE
```

If `messageDiv` still has a FALSE value, that means the DIV doesn't yet exist in the DOM and it must be created.

6. Update the DIV with the class and message, then complete the function:

```
    messageDiv.className = messageClass;
    messageDiv.innerHTML = message;
} // End of showMessage() function.
```

7. Start defining the handleBidAjaxResponse() function:

```
function handleBidAjaxResponse() {
    if (bidAjax.readyState == 4) {
        if ( (bidAjax.status >= 200 && bidAjax.status < 300)
        || (bidAjax.status == 304) ) {
```

This function will be called when the Ajax request that submits a bid returns its result.

**FIGURE 15.17** An accepted bid message, shown within the added DIV.

8. Parse and handle the response:

```
var bidResponse = JSON.parse(bidAjax.responseText);
if (bidResponse.status == 'accepted') {
    showMessage(bidResponse.message, 'good');
    getBids();
} else { // Error!
    showMessage(bidResponse.message, 'error');
}
```

The Ajax response will be in JSON format (see Figure 15.14), which must be parsed. The resulting object will have two properties: status and message. If status equals *accepted*, the bid was accepted. Otherwise an error occurred.

If the bid was accepted, the message, something like *Your bid of $22.40 has been accepted.*, will be shown in the message DIV, using a CSS class of *good* (**Figure 15.17**). If an error occurred, the error message, such as *An invalid bid was submitted.*, will be shown in the message DIV, using a CSS class of *error*.

If the bid was accepted, the getBids() function is also called, in order to immediately update the list of bids to include this new bid.

9. Complete the function:

```
        } else { // Bad status, formally submit the form:
            U.$('bidForm').submit();
        }
    } // End of readyState IF.
} // End of handleBidAjaxResponse() function.
```

If the Ajax request returned a bad status code, then the form will be formally submitted.

**10.** Begin defining the submitBid() function:

```
function submitBid(e) {
    if (typeof e == 'undefined') e = window.event;
    if (e.preventDefault) {
        e.preventDefault();
    } else {
        e.returnValue = false;
    }
}
```

This function will be called with each form submission. It begins by preventing the default behavior, the form's actual submission.

**11.** Validate the bid:

```
var bid = U.$('bid').value;
if (bid > currentPrice) {
```

The bid will only be submitted to the server if it's greater than the current price. The currentPrice variable is global, as it will be created by PHP, as just explained. (As you'll see, the currentPrice variable will be updated for each new bid.)

**12.** Create the Ajax object, if necessary:

```
if (!bidAjax) {
    bidAjax = U.getXMLHttpRequestObject();
    bidAjax.onreadystatechange = handleBidAjaxResponse;
}
```

If bidAjax still has a FALSE value, then it needs to be created as an XMLHttpRequest object and the object's onreadystatechange property needs to be associated with the handleBidAjaxResponse() function.

**FIGURE 15.18** Bids not greater than the current price will result in an error message.

13. Perform the Ajax request:

```
bidAjax.open('GET', 'ajax/bid.php?bid=' + bid + '&itemId=' +
→ itemId + '&currentPrice=' + currentPrice, true);
bidAjax.send(null);
```

The request is of ajax/bid.php, passing to that PHP script the bid amount, the item ID, and the current price.

14. Complete the submitBid() function:

```
    } else {
        showMessage('Your bid must be greater than $' +
        → currentPrice.toFixed(2) + '.', 'error');
    }
    return false;
} // End of submitBid() function.
```

If the submitted bid amount is not greater than the current price, an error message is shown (**Figure 15.18**). The currentPrice is formatted as a number with two decimal places thanks to the toFixed() method.

15. Begin defining the handleGetBidsAjaxResponse() function:

```
function handleGetBidsAjaxResponse() {
    if (getBidsAjax.readyState == 4) {
        if ( (getBidsAjax.status >= 200 && getBidsAjax.status
        → < 300)
        || (getBidsAjax.status == 304) ) {
```

This function will be called when the Ajax request that fetches new bids returns a response. It starts by checking the readyState value and status code.

**16.** Parse the JSON data and check its length:

```
var bids = JSON.parse(getBidsAjax.responseText);
if (bids.length > 0) {
```

The returned response will be in JSON format as an array of objects (see Figure 15.15). If the length of that array is not greater than 0, that means there have been no new bids, and nothing needs to be done.

**17.** Update the current price:

```
currentPrice = parseFloat(bids[bids.length-1].bid).toFixed(2);
U.setText('currentSpan', currentPrice.toString());
U.setText('currentHidden', currentPrice.toString());
```

The bids are always returned in order from oldest to newest. Thus, the very last bid returned will be the current high price. To find that value, refer to one less than the length of the array: `bids[bids.length-1]`. This will be a string, so the construct is converted to a float for internal use, and then fixed to two decimals.

Next, the span that shows the current price is updated with this value, as is the hidden form input. Updating the hidden form input will only be necessary should a subsequent Ajax bid request return a bad status code, in which case the form itself will be submitted.

**18.** Update the bids HTML table with the new bids:

```
var tb = U.$('tableBody');
for (var i = 0, count = bids.length; i < count; i++) {
    var tr = document.createElement('tr');
    var td1 = document.createElement('td');
    var td2 = document.createElement('td');
    td1.appendChild(document.createTextNode('$' + bids[i].bid));
    td2.appendChild(document.createTextNode
       (bids[i].dateSubmitted));
    tr.appendChild(td1);
```

```
        tr.appendChild(td2);
        var trs = document.getElementsByTagName('tr');
        tb.insertBefore(tr, trs[1]);
} // End of FOR loop.
```

Chapter 9, which covered DOM manipulation, did not put forth an HTML table example. There are many ways to dynamically create table rows, but creating actual elements and adding them is the most reliable (an alternative would be to clone a row, update its values, and add the modified clone to the table).

The for loop goes through every new bid returned by the Ajax call. Within the loop, a new table row element is created, along with two new table cells. The table cells are given child text nodes of the bid amount (prefaced by a dollar sign) and the bid date. Then the table cells are appended to the table row and the table row is added to the table.

Older versions of Internet Explorer require that new table rows be added to the table *body* element, not to the table itself, so a reference to the table body is created before the loop. Each new row should be inserted as the top row in the table, after the heading row. The document.getElementsByTag-Name() method will return all table rows; the first non-header row will be indexed at 1. Thus, tb.insertBefore(tr, trs[1]) will add this new row before the second row in the table. Because the list of table row elements is fetched within the loop, this list will always reflect the row just added.

19. Complete the handleGetBidsAjaxResponse() function:

```
            } // End of FOR loop.
          } // End of bids.length IF.
        } // End of status IF.
      } // End of readyState IF.
} // End of handleGetBidsAjaxResponse() function.
```

As an additional check, if the status code was not good, you could add a message to the page indicating an inability to retrieve the latest bids.

**20.** Define the getBids() function:

```
function getBids() {
    getBidsAjax.open('GET', 'ajax/getBids.php?currentPrice=' +
    ⇒ currentPrice + '&itemId=' + itemId, true);
    getBidsAjax.send(null);
}
```

This function performs the Ajax request, sending the item ID and the current price along in the request.

**21.** Begin defining the init() function:

```
function init() {
    U.$('refreshMessage').style.display = 'none';
    U.addEvent(U.$('bidForm'), 'submit', submitBid);
    getBidsAjax.onreadystatechange = handleGetBidsAjaxresponse;
```

Finally, there's the init() function, which establishes all the initial functionality. First, it hides the *Refresh the page to update.* message that the PHP script creates, as JavaScript will now perform the updating.

Second, a submit event handler is added to the bid form.

Third, the getBidsAjax object's onreadystatechange property is associated with the handleGetBidsAjaxResponse() function.

**22.** Create a timer that fetches the new bids every 10 seconds:

```
var getBidsTimer = setInterval(getBids, 10000);
```

This timer will call the getBids() function every 10 seconds (or thereabouts; see Chapter 9 for the particulars of how timers work).

**23.** If there are fewer than 60 minutes remaining in the auction, start defining a timer to update the minutes remaining display:

```
if (minutesRemaining < 60) {
    var span = U.$('minutesRemainingSpan');
    var closingTimer = setInterval(function() {
```

With less than an hour to go in the auction, the PHP code will create a span that shows the minutes remaining (see Figure 15.9). The JavaScript code in this file will automatically update that span using a timer. (As a reminder, minutesRemaining is a global JavaScript variable created by PHP.)

I will admit that this system does not address the possibility that someone opens an auction with 61 minutes to go, and leaves the browser open until the auction closes, therefore never seeing the timer. To address that possibility, you could create another timer that checks the number of minutes remaining (using a new Ajax script) every 30 minutes or so. Or, you could create a timer that reloads the browser every 30 minutes or so, which would have the same net effect (but be more obvious to the user, for better or for worse).

24. Subtract a minute and update the span:

```
minutesRemaining--;

if (minutesRemaining > 0) {

    U.setText('minutesRemainingSpan', minutesRemaining +
    →  ' minute(s) left');
```

25. When the auction is over, perform the necessary cleanup:

```
} else { // Auction is over!

    clearInterval(closingTimer);

    clearInterval(getBidsTimer);

    bidAjax = null;

    getBidsAjax = null;

    U.removeEvent(U.$('bidForm'), 'submit', submitBid);

    var bidForm = U.$('bidForm');

    bidForm.parentNode.removeChild(bidForm);

    span.parentNode.removeChild(span);

    showMessage('The auction is now closed.', 'error');

}
```

Once `minutesRemaining` is no longer greater than 0, the auction is over and several things should happen. First, both timers are removed. Second, both Ajax objects are cleared. Third, the form's submission handler is removed, as is the form itself. Next, the `span` that showed the number of minutes remaining is removed. Finally, a message indicates that the auction is over.

To make the JavaScript result more closely emulate the result when a user views a closed auction (see Figure 15.10), you could have the JavaScript also create a message that clearly indicates the final price.

26. Complete the timer and the `init()` function:

```
        }, 60000);
    } // End of minutesRemaining IF.
} // End of init() function.
```

27. Attach a load handler to the window:

```
U.addEvent(window, 'load', init);
```

28. Complete the immediately-invoked function:

```
})(); // End of immediately invoked function.
```

29. Save the file as `view.js`, in a `js` directory next to `view.php`, and test it in your Web browser.

# COMPLETING THIS EXAMPLE

As I explained at the start of this chapter, the goal for this example was to create a relatively real-world site that made use of PHP and JavaScript together. The example had to strike the balance between being useful while not being too complex for the book or what you should be comfortable with at this point. I hope that I've found that balance, although I expect some of you thought it too complicated and others wish that it had done more.

Some of the functionality required to complete this site depends upon more PHP code, including having a regularly scheduled PHP script—one that executes automatically every minute—that closes auctions. Aside from that, here are some things you would want to do next:

- Create a user registration script, validated with JavaScript.

- Create logout functionality, with or without Ajax.

- Add the ability to create new auctions.

- Minify the JavaScript code.

- Have the PHP code in both versions of view.php only allow bids if the auction hasn't closed (as written, with JavaScript disabled, a person could submit the bid form after the auction has closed, thereby winning the auction).

As for this last suggestion, if you were to write a maintenance script that is run every minute, it would wipe out any bids that occurred after an auction's closing date and time. It would also assign to the items table's finalPrice column the highest (valid) bid received.

Once you've expanded your JavaScript comfort and abilities, you may want to start looking into JavaScript performance. There are tools that help with this area, and certain coding standards make a difference. For example, combining all variable declarations within a function into a single line is recommended:

```
var bidAjax = null, getBidsAjax = U.getXMLHttpRequestObject(),
→  messageDiv = null;
```

I've only avoided this approach in the book in order to promote legibility and discrete steps while learning the language.

# REVIEW AND PURSUE

If you have any problems with these sections, either in answering the questions or pursuing your own endeavors, turn to the book's supporting forum (www.Larry Ullman.com/forums/).

Note that some of the review questions and pursue prompts require that you're comfortable with PHP and MySQL.

## REVIEW

- What are the standard steps for debugging PHP-MySQL problems?

- Why is it important to store all dates and times in UTC?

- After creating a script that will be the target of an Ajax request, what's the next step you should take?

- What are some of the ways that PHP and JavaScript can pass data back and forth?

- How do you create new HTML table rows using JavaScript?

## PURSUE

- As a big and broad suggestion, implement any of the proposed changes or additions found within the chapter.

- Modify header.html so that it shows a *login* link if the user is not logged in and a *logout* link if the user is logged in.

- If you're not comfortable with the subject, look into time zone management in MySQL.

- If you want more precision, have the time remaining on the view page reflect the minutes and seconds. Terminate the auction when its seconds are up.

- If you're still not comfortable with *closures*, read as much as you can on the subject.

- Update view.js to clear the current bid amount when a successful bid goes through.

- Revel in how much you've learned!

## WRAPPING **UP**

Congratulations! You've made it through the book and a somewhat complex example. Hopefully, you were able to follow along well enough and perhaps even foresaw some of the site's shortcomings before they were pointed out. While many details were glossed over or omitted, this project really does represent what you can expect to do as a JavaScript-conversant Web developer. Those steps are:

- Identify the goals of a project

- Create the database

- Set up the site's core structure

- Establish the basic functionality

- Write the scripts to be used as Ajax resources (if applicable)

- Test the Ajax resources (ditto)

- Add the JavaScript layer

- Debug, debug, and debug

Of course, the debugging step wasn't written into the chapter, as I had to do it while writing the code (truly, I did), and you probably had to do some of it while testing the example. Now it's up to you to expand upon and improve this project as you think best.

As the final chapter in the book, this marks the end of the lessons. You can learn the most from here on by *doing*: trying new things, seeing what does work and what doesn't, and debugging the problems that will inevitably occur. I also recommend that you continue researching and reading more on the subject of JavaScript, whether that means what else I have to say or is written by others.

You can find out what other knowledge I have to share through my Web site (www.LarryUllman.com), through my newsletter (to which you can subscribe at the Web site), or by posting questions in my forum.

Thanks for reading this book and good luck with your future JavaScript endeavors!

# INDEX

## SYMBOLS

+ (addition) operator, 100, 102
&& (And) operator, 102, 136, 138
| (alternatives) meta-character, 407
\ (backslash), using with escape
    sequences, 121–122
^ (beginning of string) meta-
    character, 407, 411
?; (conditional) operator, 102
-- (decrement) operator, 102
/ (division) operator, 100, 102
" (double quote), using with strings,
    98–99
] (end of class) meta-character, 407
} (end of quantifier)
    meta-character, 407
$ (end of string) meta-character, 407
) (end of subpattern)
    meta-character, 407
== (equal to) operator, 131
\ (escape) meta-character, 407
( ) (function call) operator, 102
> (greater than) operator, 102, 133
>= (greater than or equal to) operator,
    102, 133
=== (identical to) operator, 131
++ (increment) operator, 102
< (less than) operator, 102, 133
<= (less than or equal to) operator,
    102, 133
! (logical not) operator, 102
|| (logical or) operator, 102, 136, 138
[ ] (member) operator, 102
% (modulus) operator, 100, 102
* (multiplication) operator, 100, 102
! (Not) operator, 136, 138
!= (not equal to) operator, 131
!== (not identical to) operator, 131
.. (periods), using with relative
    paths, 38
% (remainder) operator, 100, 102

; (semicolon), using with
    statements, 95
. (single character)
    meta-character, 407
' (single quote), using with strings, 4,
    98–99
// (slashes), using with comments,
    99, 132
[ (start of class) meta-character, 407
{ (start of quantifier)
    meta-character, 407
( (start of subpattern)
    meta-character, 407
- (subtraction) operator, 100, 102
- (unary negative) operator, 104
+ (unary positive) operator, 102
_ (underscore), using with
    variables, 97

## A

absolute vs. relative paths, 38
accessible pop-up, creating, 323–324,
    338–339
ActionScript, 5–6, 20
addEvent() function, defining,
    275–277
addEventListener() method, 272, 274
addition (+) operator, 100, 102
addTask() function, using with
    arrays, 196
addToSomething() function, 325
Adobe BrowserLab Web site, 75
Adobe Dreamweaver IDE, 67–68
Ajax
    append() method, 438
    asynchronous requests, 430
    client-side JavaScript, 12
    contact form, 456–460
    FormData object, 438
    GET method, 437–438
    GET request, 429

    impact on JavaScript, 7–13
    incorporating, 12
    JSON data, 444–447
    link click handler, 463
    login example, 453–456
    maintaining state, 457
    making requests, 429–431
    onclick anonymous function, 464
    onload anonymous function, 464
    onreadystatechange function,
        435–436
    open() method for requests, 430
    overview, 426
    performing in jQuery framework,
        501–502
    performing in YUI framework, 515
    popularity of, 12
    POST request, 429, 437–438
    preloading data, 461–465
    progressive enhancement, 427
    readyState property, 431–432, 434
    registration form example, 8–9
    result handler, 429
    send() method, 438
    sending data, 436–439
    sending files, 453
    server HTTP codes, 432
    server response, 431–436
    server-side requests, 12–13
    server-side script, 447–450
    statusText property, 433
    stock quotes with timer, 465–469
    synchronous requests, 430
    testing, 434
    URLs (Uniform Resource
        Locators), 430
    XML data, 442–444
    XMLHttpRequest object, 428–429
Ajax debugging, 439–441
    disabling cache, 441
    network monitor, 440
    PHP script, 439

SHA1() function, 557
structure, 558
view.php page, 554–555
autocomplete, implementing, 388–389

## B

Back button, linking text to, 343–344
backslash (\), using with escape sequences, 121–122
BBEdit text editor, 67
Blackbird library, 523
Boolean values, using with variables, 99
boundaries, using, 414
branching statements, 130
break control statement, using, 167
breakpoints, using in Firebug, 88
Brosera Web site, 76
browser events, 284–285
copy, 285
cut, 285
paste, 285
resize, 285
unload, 284–285
browser improvements, 14–15
browser mode, confirming, 30
browser support, 22–23
browser window, moving, 316–317
BrowserCam Web site, 76
BrowserLab Web site, 75
browserling Web site, 76
browsers
Apple Safari, 73–75
Chrome, 15, 69–70, 90
as development tools, 69
elements, 314
Firefox, 15, 69, 71, 90
hash example, 330
history property, 326–328
inner height, 314

Internet Explorer (IE), 15, 69, 72
mobile usage, 69
"modern," 22
object detection, 75
online services for testing, 76
Opera, 69, 72–73, 90
outer height, 314
outer width, 314
print option, 333
redirecting, 329–330
Safari, 15, 69
same origin security, 327
Spoon software, 76
statistics, 69
status bar, 314
testing on, 75–77
toolbar, 314
using virtualization software, 76
window.location property, 330
Browsershots Web site, 75
bugs
caused by assignment operator, 134
occurrence of, 5–6

## C

calculate() function
creating for switch conditional, 147
defining, 104
calculation, performing, 100–101
calculators. See also numbers
creating, 103–107
discounts, 105
event listener, 106–107
init() function, 106
references to form values, 104
returning false, 106
storing order total, 104
with switch conditional, 146–150
tax rates, 105
total calculation, 105
calendar, date-picking, 15

camel-case
use in OOP, 5
using with variables, 97
Cascading Style Sheets (CSS). See CSS (Cascading Style Sheets)
case of characters, changing, 118
catching errors, 474–476
<![CDATA[ ]]> wrapper, using with script, 39
change events, handling, 287
character classes
[] (square brackets), 411
[0-9], 413
[^0-9], 413
[A-Za-z0-9_], 413
[^A-Za-z0-9_], 413
boundaries, 414
[f\r\t\n\v], 413
[^f\r\t\n\v], 413
meta-characters, 411
using, 411–414
characters, referencing in strings, 113. See also meta-characters
charAt() method, using with strings, 113
checkboxes
creating, 396–399
on e-commerce sites, 397
taking action, 397
value property, 396
Chrome browser, 15. See also Google
extensions, 70
features, 70
Firebug extension, 70
JavaScript Tester extension, 70
Pendule extension, 70
Speed Tracer extension, 70
usage statistic, 69
Validity extension, 70
Web Developer extension, 70
Web site, 90
circle, calculating area of, 109–110

passing to functions, 532
tasks management application,
    534–537
toString() method, 533, 535
valueOf() method, 533

## D

data, preloading in Ajax, 461–465
date and time, showing, 178–180
date arithmetic
    calculating intervals, 185, 188
    getX(), 184–185
    setX(), 184–185
    timestamps, 182–184
date methods
    atomic value retrieval, 176
    get*() and to*(), 176–177
    getTime(), 175
    using, 175–180
Date objects, creating, 172, 174, 178,
    180, 187
date-picking calendar, 15
dates
    atomic values, 173
    changing, 181–182
    creating, 172–175
    errors as messages, 189
    event listeners, 189
    process() function, 186
    RFC822/IETF format, 175
    set*() methods, 181–182
    start and end for events, 186–190
    using strings, 174–175
    using timestamps, 174
    validating for events, 187
debugging. See also Firebug
    Ajax, 439–441
    JavaScript, 17
    with text editor vs. IDE, 63
debugging techniques
    alert() method, 85

browser console, 83
browsers, 84
coding, 85
console.trace() function, 86
development browser, 83
external files, 84
IDEs (Integrated Development
    Environments), 83
JavaScript validator, 83
log() method, 85
network monitor, 86
rubber duck, 84
saving and refreshing, 84
text editors, 83
writing messages to console, 85
decrement (--) operator, 102
default behavior, preventing, 297–301
development approaches
    graceful degradation, 39–41
    noscript element, 39–41
    progressive enhancement,
        41–42, 45
    unobtrusive JavaScript, 43, 52
dialog windows. See also windows
    alerts, 310
    confirmations, 311
    customizing, 312
    \n (newline) character, 312
    prompts, 312
    using, 310–312
discount, including in calculator, 105
division (/) operator, 100, 102
do...while loop, using, 166
DOCTYPE
    benefits, 30
    choosing, 28–30
    HTML 4.01, 28
    Transitional option, 28–30
    triggering Quirks mode, 30
    XHTML 1.0, 28
document, requesting from server, 48
document object

using, 333–334
    write() method, 333–334
    writeln() method, 333–334
document.compatMode, 334
document.createElement()
    method, 344
The Dojo Toolkit framework, 16
DOM (Document Object Model), 29
    adding elements to, 345
    changing elements, 342–344
    copying elements, 346
    creating, 48
    creating elements, 344–348
    creating print button, 347–348
    CSS selectors, 341–342
    Level 0 specification, 272
    Level 2 specification, 271, 273
    manipulation, 338–339
    nodes, 336–337
    nodeType property, 337
    overview, 335–337
    removeChild() method, 346
    replacing elements, 345
    shortcuts, 337–338
    tree representation, 335–336
DOM elements, referencing, 48
DOM methods, 340
dot notation, chaining, 5
double quote ("), using with strings,
    98–99
Dreamweaver IDE, 67–68
duck typing, using to test value
    types, 548
dynamically typed language, 6

## E

Eclipse IDE, 68
ECMAScript, 6, 22
EditPlus text editor, 66
Edwards, Dean, 90
Eich, Brendon, 90

else clause, using, 140
Emacs text editor, 67
email address, validating, 414
employee.html page, 212–213
employee.js file
    creating, 213
    opening, 256
    saving, 215, 257
epoch.js file, creating, 280
equal to (==) operator, 131
error causes
    = instead of ==, 82
    angle brackets, 82
    curly braces, 82
    function names, 81
    object names, 81
    object references, 82
    object types, 82
    parentheses, 82
    quotation marks, 82
    reserved words, 82
    variable names, 81
error management
    assertions, 479–481
    unit testing, 481–485
error messages
    adding, 380–383
    creating for forms, 379–383
    removing, 380–383
    span, 381
error types
    logical, 80–81
    run-time, 80–81
    syntactical, 80
errorMessages.js file
    creating, 380
    saving, 383
errors
    catching, 474–476
    finally clause, 476
    in try block, 475

escape (\) meta-character, 407
escape sequences, 121–122
eval() function, using with
        windows, 371
event assigner, creating, 273–274
event handlers
    inline, 269, 272
    naming, 270
event handling
    delegating, 304
    event phases, 302–304
    event properties, 291–295
    finding key pressed, 296–297
    IE (Internet Explorer), 273
    preventing default behavior,
        297–301
    progressive enhancement, 269
    referencing events, 290–291
    traditional, 269–272
    W3C (World Wide Web
        Consortium), 271–273
event listeners
    addEventListener() method, 272
    adding for dates, 189
    adding to calculator, 106–107
    adding to forms, 46–47, 49–50,
        118, 121
    adding to page elements, 274
    adding to random.js file, 165
    creating, 268–274
    using with arrays, 197–198
    using with objects, 215
event phases
    advantages, 304
    bubbling, 302–303
    capturing, 302–303
    relatedTarget property, 304
event types
    browsers, 284–285
    forms, 286–287
    input devices, 278–282
    keyboards, 282–284

event-driven language, explained, 46
event.js file, 186–190
events
    accessibility, 287–288
    associating with functions, 268
    asynchronous, 8
    handling, 46–50
    pairing, 288
    progressive enhancement,
        288–289
    reliability, 287
    reporting on, 292–295
    this variable, 295
events.html page, 292
events.js file, creating, 292
every() array function, 248–249
exceptions, throwing, 475, 477–478
execution context and this variable,
        254–257
expressions .vs statements, 245
Extensible Markup Language (XML).
        See XML (eXtensible Markup
        Language)
ExtJS framework, 16

## F

fader, creating with closure, 545–546
fallthroughs, performing, 144
FALSE
    determining for control structures,
        131, 133
    vs. TRUE conditions, 135
false and true values, 99
file uploads, handling, 401–402
filter() array function, 249
finally clause, adding to try...
        catch, 476
Firebug. See also debugging
    applying to Web pages, 87
    assertions in, 481
    breakpoints, 88–89
    clear() function, 87

conditional breakpoints, 89
Console tab, 87
Continue in Script panel, 88–89
executing lines of JavaScript, 87
inspect() function, 87
opening, 87
Rerun in Script panel, 88–89
Script panel for debugging, 88
Step Into in Script panel, 88–89
Step Out in Script panel, 88–89
Step Over in Script panel, 88–89
using, 86–89
watch expressions, 89–90
Wiki, 89
Firefox browser, 6, 15
Console2 extension, 71
extensions, 71
features, 71
Firebug extension, 71
Greasemonkey extension, 71
JS View extension, 71
Total Validator extension, 71
usage statistic, 69
View Source Chart extension, 71
Web Developer extension, 71
Web site, 90
YSlow! extension, 71
Flash vs. JavaScript, 20
focus, changing, 321
for loop
defining in random.js file, 163
executing, 161–162
program flow, 161
syntax, 161–162
using, 163
using with arrays, 201
for...in loop, using with object
properties, 211
forEach() array function, 248
form data, problems with, 8

form events
blur, 286
change, 286–287
focus, 286
reset, 286
select, 286
form input, assigning values to, 106
form submission
handling, 378
preventing default behavior,
378–379
forms. *See also* contact form;
login form
accessibility, 378
action attribute, 378
autocomplete, 388–389
baseline functionality for, 42
checkboxes, 396–399
client-side validation, 9–10
disabling submit button, 386
error messages, 379–383
file uploads, 401–402
preventing submission of, 106
radio buttons, 400–401
register.js example, 416–420
registration page example, 415–420
select menus, 389–396
server-side validation, 10–11
text inputs, 387–388
textareas, 387–388
tooltips, 383–385
validation, 379
frames, iframe, 328
frameworks, 15–16. *See also* jQuery
framework; YUI framework
arguments against use of, 16
choosing, 16
considering, 493
The Dojo Toolkit, 16
ExtJS framework, 16
jQuery, 16

MooTools, 16
overview, 492, 494
Prototype, 16
script.aculo.us, 16
YUI (Yahoo! User Interface), 16
Fuchs, Thomas, 90
function call (()) operator, 102
function keyword, using, 50
function parameters, 226, 228–229,
241–242
functionality, developing, 44–45
functions. *See also* array functions
anonymous, 257–258, 260–261
applying to variables, 4
as argument values, 246–248
arguments variable, 227
associating events with, 268
context and this variable, 254–257
creating and calling, 232–234,
236–238
defined, 4, 49
defining, 222–223
design theory, 243
immediately invoked, 257–261
lack of default values, 228–229
lack of parameter checking, 228
lack of type checking, 226
local scope, 239
nested, 258–261
as objects, 244–248
passing objects to, 231
passing values, 230–234
passing values to, 223–225
recursion, 261–262
returning objects, 235
returning values from, 234–238
sort() method, 246–248
user-defined, 251–253
variable scope, 238–243
as variable values, 245–246

less than or equal to (<=) operator, 102, 133
libraries
    Blackbird, 523
    Head JS, 522–523
    jQuery Mobile, 523
    MediaElement.js, 523
    Modernizr, 522
    RequireJS, 523
    Sencha Touch, 523
    SWFObject, 522
    VideoJS, 523
    Zepto, 523
LIFO (Last-In, First-Out) data type, 202
literal syntax, using with arrays, 191, 194
literals vs. objects, 94, 124
local scope, explained, 239
log() method, using in debugging, 85
logical operators, 102, 136–138
login form. See also forms
    adding JavaScript layer, 45–46
    base functionality, 44–45
    getElementById() method, 47
    init() function, 49, 52–53
    JavaScript alert, 52
    submission event, 47
    validateForm() function, 52–53
    validating, 50–54
loginForm object, onsubmit property, 49
login.html file, 44
    including ajax.js script in, 453
    readyState change handling function, 454–455
login.js file, 45, 54
    creating Ajax object, 453–454
    saving, 455
    writing for auction site, 573–578
login.php script
    in auction site, 554–555
    creating, 455–456
    submitting login form to, 45

loops
    do...while, 166
    for, 161–165
    for...in, 211
    nesting, 166
    while, 166

## M

MAMP for Mac OS X, 430
map() array function, 249, 252
math, performing with strings, 123
Math object
    abs() method, 110
    ceil() method, 110
    constants, 109
    cos() method, 110
    floor() method, 110
    max() method, 110
    min() method, 110
    pow() method, 110
    predefined methods, 110
    random() method, 110
    round() method, 110
    sin() method, 110
    using, 109–112
MediaElement.js library, 523
member ([]) operator, 102
membership cost calculation, 299
membership.html file, using, 145–150
membership.js file, preventing default behavior, 300–301
meta-characters. See also characters
    | (alternatives), 407
    ^ (beginning of string), 407, 411
    in character classes, 411
    ] (end of class), 407
    } (end of quantifier), 407
    $ (end of string), 407
    ) (end of subpattern), 407
    \ (escape), 407
    . (single character), 407

    [ (start of class), 407
    ( (start of subpattern), 407
    { (start of quantifier), 407
    using with patterns, 406–407
methods. See functions
Microjs Web site, 523
Minify JavaScript Web Site, 548
mobile browsers, usage of, 69
modal windows, creating, 351–356. See also windows
modal.css file, 353–355
modal.html file, 351–353
modal.js file
    closeModal() function, 355
    creating, 355
    openModal() function, 355
    saving, 356
Modernizr library, 522
modulus (%) operator, 100, 102
Mogotest Web site, 76
MooTools framework, 16
mouse and cursor properties, 297
mouseover event, handling, 280–282
Mozilla Firefox. See Firefox browser
multiplication (*)operator, 100, 102

## N

\n (newline) character, using with dialogs, 312
namespace pollution, 243
namespaces, defining, 528–529
NaN value, returning, 102
nested functions, using, 258–261
nesting
    conditionals, 142
    control structures, 142
    loops, 166
NetBeans IDE, 68
network monitor
    for Ajax debugging, 440
    using, 63
    using in debugging, 86

Prototype framework, 16
prototype-based language, 5
prototypes
    changing, 540
    inheritance, 538
    methods, 539–540
    overview, 537
    trim() method, 539
push() method, using with arrays, 200

## Q

quantifiers, 409
Quirks mode, triggering, 30
quotation marks, using with
    variables, 98–99
quote.js file, 466–468
quote.php script, creating, 468

## R

radio buttons
    dynamic effects, 401
    flag variable, 400
    using, 400–401
random numbers
    generating, 164–165
    returning, 237
random.html page, 163–165
random.js file
    creating, 164
    saving, 165
    showNumbers() function, 164
recursion
    .vs iteration, 262
    performing, 261–262
reduce() array function, 249
register.js file, 416–420
registration form example, 8–9,
    415–420
regular expressions
    creating, 404
    defining patterns, 406–408

exec() function, 405–406
    functions, 405–406
    literals, 406
    match() function, 405–406
    meta-characters, 406–407
    overview, 403–404
    performance issues, 412
    RegExp object type, 404
    replace() method, 406
    rules for, 411
    search() function, 405
    split() method, 406
    test() function, 405
relatedTarget property, 304
relative vs. absolute paths, 38
remainder (%) operator, 100, 102
removeEvent() method, defining, 277
reportEvent() function, creating, 292
RequireJS library, 523
Resig, John, 90
resize event, triggering, 285
return statement, using, 167, 236
RFC822/IETF format, using with
    dates, 175
RIAs (Rich Internet Applications), 20
Ruby Web site, 90

## S

Safari browser, 15, 73–75
    Develop menu, 74
    disabling JavaScript, 74
    usage statistic, 69
    Web Inspector, 74
Sauce Labs Web site, 76
screen properties, using with
    windows, 317
script element
    <![CDATA[]]> wrapper, 39
    parsing data in, 39
    using, 37–39
script tags, putting JavaScript
    between, 43

script.aculo.us framework, 16
scripting language, JavaScript as, 6
scripts, organizing, 107
select menus
    creating, 389–390
    dynamic select boxes, 390–396
    linking, 392–396
    validating, 390
Semantic HTML, using, 41–42
semicolon (;), using with
    statements, 95
Sencha Touch library, 523
server-side requests, 12–13
server-side script
    returning JSON, 450
    returning plain text, 447–448
    returning XML, 449–450
server-side validation, 10–11
setHandlers() function, defining, 293
setText() function
    defining, 237, 251
    for utility library, 276
setX(), using with dates, 184–185
Sexton, Alex, 90
SHA1() function, using with
    passwords, 557
Sharp, Remy, 78, 90
shift() method, using with
    arrays, 202
shiftKey property, 297
shopping.html page, creating, 103
shopping.js file, 107–109
single quote ('), using with strings, 4,
    98–99
slashes (//), using with comments,
    99, 132
slice() method
    using with arrays, 203–204
    using with strings, 115–116
some() array function, 248
sort() method, using with functions,
    246–248

sortWords() function
    completing, 253
    defining, 252
span, adding to DOM for errors, 381
sphere, calculating volume of, 111–112
sphere.js file, 110, 138–139
splice() method, using with arrays, 202–203
split() method, using with arrays and strings, 207
Spoon software, using, 76
srcElement event property, 291–292
state, maintaining in Ajax, 457
statements .vs expressions, 245
stock ticker, creating, 466–469
strict mode, invoking, 53
strings
    adding to numbers, 122–123
    beginning and end of, 407
    changing case, 118, 155
    charAt() method, 113
    comparing, 155–159
    comparing to numbers, 156
    concatenating, 118
    converting arrays to, 206
    converting to arrays, 207, 252
    converting to numbers, 123–124
    creating, 112–113
    deconstructing, 113–118
    empty, 99
    escape sequences, 121–122
    example of, 4
    indexes for methods, 113
    indexOf() method, 114, 155, 408
    lastIndexOf() method, 114–115
    length property, 113
    manipulating, 120–121
    matching, 408
    performing math with, 123
    processing contact form, 157–159
    referencing characters, 113
    slice() method, 115–116
    substr() method, 115

substring() method, 115
toLowerCase() function, 118, 155
toUpperCase() function, 118, 155
trim() method, 118
using with dates, 174–175
strongly typed language, 5
style sheets
    addRule() method, 357
    createElement() method, 357
    deleteRule() method, 357
    disabled property, 356
    insertRule() method, 357
    referencing, 356–357
submission event, watching for, 47
submit button, disabling, 386
substr() method, using with strings, 115
substring() method, using with strings, 115
subtraction (-) operator, 100, 102
Subversion version control software, 62
SWFObject library, 522
switch conditionals. *See also* conditionals
    calculator, 146–150
    default case, 144
    expressions, 145
    fallthroughs, 144
    identity matches, 144
    membership.html file, 145–146
    parentheses in, 143
    quotes in, 143
    using, 143–150
syntax highlighting, 60–61

## T

tasks.js file
    closure example, 540
    creating, 196
    custom objects example, 535–537
    saving, 198

tax rate, including in calculator, 105
ternary operator, using, 150–151
testing
    on browsers, 75–77
    JavaScript, 77–79
test.js file, 434–436
tests
    creating for utilities library, 485–488
    defining for unit testing, 482–483
    log() function, 487
    preparing for, 484–485
    running, 487
    running for unit testing, 483–484
    setUp() function, 484–485
tests.js file, 485–488
text, placing in HTML elements, 163. *See also* plain text
text editor vs. IDE (Integrated Development Environment)
    choosing between, 66
    code completion, 61
    code intelligence, 61–62
    common features, 60–64
    comparing, 64–65
    debugging, 63
    file management, 62
    HTML and CSS, 64
    network monitor, 63
    project management, 62
    syntax highlighting, 60–61
    unit testing, 63
    version control software, 62
    vi editor, 64
text editors, 64–65
    BBEdit, 67
    EditPlus, 66
    Emacs, 67
    features, 65
    hardware resources, 64
    Komodo Edit, 66
    Notepad, 66
    price range, 64

URLs (Uniform Resource Locators)
  # part of, 331
  creating, 331–332
  deep linking, 331
  parsing hash in, 331–332
user experience, improving, 24
UTC (Coordinated Universal Time), 180–181
utilities library
  creating, 275–277
  creating unit tests for, 485–488
utilities.js file, 275–277

## V

validateForm() function, using, 47, 50–53
validating
  HTML forms, 46
  HTML pages, 28–29
  JSON, 440
  phone number, 418
  XML, 440
validation, performing, 50–54
validation services, using, 83
validators, W3C Markup Validation Service, 91
value attribute
  using, 105–106
  using with text inputs, 387
  using with textareas, 387
value types
  Booleans, 98
  duck typing, 548
  exponential notation, 98
  Infinity value, 102
  NaN value, 102
  null, 99
  numbers, 98
  quotation marks, 98–99
  strings, 98
  testing, 548–549

true and false, 99
  undefined, 99
values
  assigning to variables, 98
  equal vs. identical, 135
  literals .vs objects, 94
  passing to functions, 223–225
  returning from functions, 234–238
var keyword, using, 95–96
variable scope
  explained, 239
  function parameters, 241–242
variables. *See also* global variables
  applying functions to, 4
  camel-case, 97
  declaring, 94–96, 136
  declaring outside of functions, 96
  global scope, 95–96
  hoisting, 96
  identifiers, 97
  local .vs global, 239–240
  names, 97
  undeclared, 95
  use of underscore (_), 97
  value types, 98–99
  values, 98
version control software, using, 62
vi editor, using, 64
VideoJS library, 523
view.js for auction site. *See also* JavaScript for auction site
  getBids() function, 589
  handleBidAjaxResponse() function, 583
  handleGetBidsAjaxResponse() function, 586, 588
  init() function, 589, 591
  load handler, 591
  structure, 581
  submitBid() function, 585–586
  writing for auction site, 581–591

view.php page
  in auction site, 554–555
  writing for auction site, 578–581
Vim text editor, 67
virtualization software, using, 76

## W

W3C event handling, 271–273
W3C Markup Validation Service, 91
watch expressions, creating in Firebug, 89–90
weakly-typed language, 5, 95
Web browsers. *See* browsers
Web sites
  Adobe BrowserLab, 75
  Adobe Dreamweaver IDE, 67–68
  Ajaxload, 451
  Apple Safari browser, 73
  Aptana Studio IDE, 68
  BBEdit, 67
  Blackbird, 523
  Brosera, 76
  BrowserCam, 76
  browserling, 76
  browsers, 90
  Browsershots, 75
  Chrome, 70
  Cloud Testing, 76
  Crockford, Douglas, 90
  CrossBrowserTesting, 76
  The Dojo Toolkit, 16
  Eclipse IDE, 68
  ECMAScript 5, 22
  EditPlus, 66
  Edwards, Dean, 90
  Eich, Brendon, 90
  Emacs, 67
  ExtJS framework, 16
  Firebug Wiki, 89
  Firefox browser, 6, 71